Florence

INSIGHT ⊙ GUIDES

TUSCANY

www.insightguides.com/Italy

Contents

THE BEST OF TUSCANY: TOP ATTRACTIONS

The enigmatic Etruscans, the wine-loving Tuscans, Italy's loveliest hill towns, the world's finest museum of Renaissance art, the iconic Leaning Tower, countryside that inspired Leonardo da Vinci – Tuscany has it all.

△ **Val d'Orcia landscape.** With its farmhouses, abbeys and conical hills, this pastoral landscape was redrawn in the 14th and 15th centuries to reflect good governance and create an aesthetically pleasing picture that has inspired many artists. See page 214.

△ **San Gimignano, a medieval Manhattan.** As Italy's best-preserved medieval town, Tuscany's time capsule survives, with its bold towers signifying San Gimignano's prestige and prosperity. A beguiling spirit transcends the town's over-popularity. See page 185.

◁ **The Leaning Tower of Pisa.** Finally fully restored, this iconic symbol of Tuscan architectural genius stands alongside the gleaming Duomo and Baptistery on Pisa's aptly named Campo dei Miracoli – the Field of Miracles. See page 153.

△ **Hill towns of Montepulciano and Montalcino.** Montepulciano and Montalcino draw you in with their palaces, seductive lifestyle and cellars of famed wines. Sip Vino Nobile in Cantine Contucci or sample Brunello di Montalcino in the Fortezza. See page 211.

△ **Etruscan Tuscany.** Whether in Volterra's intriguing Etruscan museum or Chiusi's painted tombs, the colour and life of Etruscan art contrasts with the cold perfectionism of the Greeks and Romans. See page 25.

▽ **Florentine churches.** From Brunelleschi's dazzling Duomo to Romanesque San Miniato, Gothic Santa Croce and Michelangelo's Medici tombs in San Lorenzo, Florentine churches are mesmerising repositories of art and history. See page 94.

▷ **Wine-tasting in the Chianti.** Ignore the "Chiantishire" tag and visit a chequered landscape of vineyards, villages and fortified-wine estates that include

the Castello di Brolio, birthplace of the modern Chianti industry. See page 185.

▽ **The Uffizi Gallery in Florence.** The world's greatest collection of Renaissance art includes masterpieces such as Botticelli's *Birth of Venus*, and works by Leonardo da Vinci, Michelangelo, Raphael, Titian and other masters of the High Renaissance. See page 104.

△ **Tuscan spas.** Despite dating back to Etruscan times, Tuscany's new breed of thermal spas combine sophisticated pampering with authentic water cures in incomparable natural settings – as in Fonteverde Terme or Terme di Saturnia. See page 132.

▷ **Siena, the quintessential medieval city.** Siena, the feminine foil to Florentine masculinity, is the city that most lives enfolded in its own private world, from the compelling medieval mood to the pageantry of the Palio horse race. See page 197.

THE BEST OF TUSCANY: EDITOR'S CHOICE

Art, culture, food and history... Here, at a glance, are our recommendations for your visit.

CHURCHES AND MONUMENTS

Brunelleschi's dome. An incredible feat of engineering by the father of Renaissance architecture. See page 94.

Monte Oliveto Maggiore. A secluded 14th-century monastery set among groves of cypress trees. See page 208.

Sant'Antimo. An abbey church built of creamy travertine framed by tree-clad hills. See page 222.

Siena cathedral. A magnificent Gothic structure of banded black and white stone. See page 201.

San Michele in Foro in Lucca. A fine example of the exuberant Tuscan Romanesque style. See page 127.

Santa Maria della Grazia. The domed church just outside the Etruscan walls of Cortona is a hidden gem. See page 242.

San Pellegrino in Alpe. An ancient monastery deep in the Garfagnana mountains, with sweeping, glorious views. See page 143.

Abbazia di Sant'Antimo, southern Siena.

THE BEST TUSCAN HILL TOWNS

Pienza. The ideal Renaissance city is famous for its scenery and its production of tasty pecorino cheese. See page 209.

Monteriggioni. The Sienese hilltown encircled by walls and 14 towers is a truly spectacular sight. See page 185.

Massa Marittima. This town is perched on top of a high hill on the edge of the Colline Metallifere and is the loveliest springboard for exploring the Maremma. See page 180.

Cortona. An enchanting hill town in eastern Tuscany with attractions out of all proportion with its tiny size. See page 244.

Vinci. The genius of Leonardo is proudly celebrated in his birthplace, a tiny hill town situated between the cities of Florence and Pisa. See page 121.

Pitigliano. Once one of the most important settlements in southern Tuscany, this dramatic tufa haunt is found in a forgotten corner of Tuscany. See page 232.

San Miniato. An ancient town straddling three hills in the province of Florence. On a clear day, you can see Volterra and the Apuan Alps from this vantage point. See page 121.

The Pitigliano skyline.

TUSCANY FOR FAMILIES

Florence or Lucca by bike. Or, in the case of Florence, also by rickshaw, Segway or summer boat along the Arno. See page 251. **Giardini di Boboli.** The gardens behind the Pitti Palace are fun for children to clamber around. There is an amphitheatre, strange statues and grottoes, and a handy café. See page 108. **Trips to the Tuscan islands.** Explore the Tuscan archipelago with the ferries and hydrofoils that sail from Porto Santo Stefano to Giglio, and from Piombino to Elba. See page 172.

Giardino dei Tarocchi. A bizarre garden full of colourful fantasy figures. See page 230. **Parco di Pinocchio.** Pinocchio's park at Collodi, near Pisa, has a certain old-fashioned charm. See page 131. **Museo dei Ragazzi.** Dressing up, model-making and other fun activities for kids in the Palazzo Vecchio bring the Renaissance to life. See page 90. **Ice cream.** When all else fails, an ice cream on a town square, most of which are traffic-free, rarely fails to win them over.

Talamone on the Maremma coast.

SEASIDE AND SPAS

Elba. A beautiful island with dramatic scenery and a series of small beaches and coves. Perfect for families. See page 167. **The Maremma.** Backed by a nature reserve, it is one of the most unspoilt stretches of beach on the coast. See page 226. **Forte dei Marmi.** With its villas and chic cafés, this cycle-friendly summer resort is a magnet for the beautiful people. See page 142.

Monte Argentario. A craggy peninsula with several chic fishing ports make it tempting to explore by yacht or by car. See page 228. **Spas.** From the simple but charming (Bagni San Filippo) and the sophisticated and stylish (Grotta Giusti, in a villa) to a cool castle spa (Castello del Nero), Tuscany is Italy's most pampering spa destination. See page 274.

Sunbathing on one of the Tuscan coast's many pleasant beaches.

TOP ETRUSCAN SITES

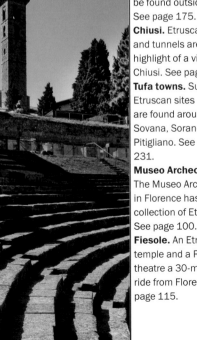

The Teatro Romano in Fiesole.

Volterra. Volterra has some of the best Etruscan funerary art to be found outside Rome. See page 175. **Chiusi.** Etruscan tombs and tunnels are the highlight of a visit to Chiusi. See page 215. **Tufa towns.** Superb Etruscan sites and trails are found around Sovana, Sorano and Pitigliano. See page 231. **Museo Archeologico.** The Museo Archeologico in Florence has a fine collection of Etruscan art. See page 100. **Fiesole.** An Etruscan temple and a Roman theatre a 30-minute bus ride from Florence. See page 115.

A TASTE OF TUSCANY

Wine tasting. As well as in the Chianti (see page 188), Montepulciano (see page 211) and Montalcino (see page 221), visit Bolgheri for the Super-Tuscans and Maremma for Morellino di Scansano (see page 226).

Food festivals. Tuscans are proud of their local produce, which they celebrate with festivals (sagre) – white truffles, chestnuts, Valdichiana beef, wild boar and pecorino cheese all have festivals dedicated to them. See page 268.

Cookery courses. The best include: Cucina Giuseppina in medieval Certaldo (www.cucina giuseppina.com); the Florence Chefs (www.the florencechefs.it); and Badia a Coltibuono (www.colti buono.com), where you can eat, sleep and cook. See page 266.

Mushrooms. In autumn, mushroom-loving Tuscans forage for *funghi*. Wild mushrooms, especially the prized *porcini* and *tartufi* (truffles), are also on the menu. See page 73.

Sweet treats. These include candied fruit cake, *panforte*, almond biscuits, *ricciarelli*, crunchy *cantucci* biscuits, and irresistible *gelati*. See page 204.

RENAISSANCE ART

Masaccio's Florentine frescoes. Found inside the Brancaccio chapel and Santa Maria Novella in Florence, Masaccio's sublime frescoes reflect a range of true Renaisance values: the importance of the human form, human emotion and the use of perspective. See page 98.

The Bargello. A major collection of Renaissance and Mannerist sculpture is housed in this building – a former prison. See page 112.

The Baptistery. Ghiberti's bronze doors are so dazzling, Michelangelo called them the "Gates of Paradise". See page 94.

Lorenzetti's frescoes. Located in Siena's Palazzo Pubblico – a striking allegory of good and bad government, one of the earliest secular paintings. See page 200.

The two Davids. Michelangelo's *David* is Florence's icon, but Donatello's *David* was the first free-standing nude since antiquity. See pages 111 and 113.

Giotto's frescoes, Florence. Santa Croce church displays a significant departure from the flat Byzantine style. See page 100.

Piero della Francesca's frescoes, Arezzo. These are marvels of pastel shades awash with cool light. See page 237.

Walking in the Boboli Gardens, Florence.

VILLAS AND GARDENS

Giardini di Boboli. The regal gardens of the Pitti Palace, now a vast museum. See page 108.

Villa Medicea Poggio a Caiano. The perfect frescoed Medici villa, with beautiful gardens. See page 118.

Villa Demidoff and Parco di Pratolino. The gardens contain extraordinary Mannerist sculpture and grottoes. See page 118.

Lucchesi villas. The area around Lucca is rich in villas, all surrounded by beautiful parks. See page 130.

Villa Medici (Fiesole). A delightful villa and garden with superb views of Florence. See page 118.

Villa Medicea della Petraia. An elegant villa decorated with wonderful frescoes. See page 118.

Villa Medicea di Castello. This villa has beautiful Renaissance gardens. See page 118.

A detail of the magnificent bronze doors of the Baptistery, Florence.

TUSCAN LANDSCAPE

The Crete Senesi. The dramatic landscape of rounded hills, stately cypresses and isolated farms, this the Tuscany of postcards and posters. See page 208.

Parco Regionale della Maremma. Beautiful, unspoilt beaches backed by steep cliffs, parasol pines and wild Mediterranean scrubland. See page 227.

Chianti Country. Gentle hills cloaked in vineyards and dotted with medieval castle estates where wine-tasting is on offer. See page 185.

Parco dell'Orecchiella. A wild mountainous area, rich in wildlife, the region's most spectacular park. See page 68.

Apuan Alps. Behind the well-groomed beaches of the Versilia is a rugged hinterland of marble quarries, mountain ridges and narrow gorges. See page 144.

The Casentino. Ancient forests of the upper Arno valley. See page 239.

Monte Amiata. The site of an extinct volcano with a profusion of thermal springs and quaint hamlets. See page 232.

A typical landscape in southern Siena.

FESTIVALS AND EVENTS

Carnival fun in Viareggio.

Il Palio. Siena's traditional horse race is a heart-racing and passionate affair, involving all of the town's *contrade*. See page 206.

Lucca Summer Music Festival. This takes place in July and attracts some big celebrity names. See page 266.

Puccini Festival. This celebration of Puccini's musical genius is held at the composer's villa on Lake Massaciuccoli. See page 266.

Luminaria di San Ranieri. A lovely Pisan festival when thousands of candles light up the River Arno and celebrations are brought to a close with a boat race. See page 268.

Carnevale. Viareggio's riotous carnival is a memorable experience and one of the best carnivals in all of Italy. See page 269.

Estate Fiesolana. This enjoyable music and arts festival held in Fiesole in the province of Florence is well worth catching. See page 266.

The beautiful Val d'Orcia landscape.

The Duomo in Florence, built with different-coloured marble and topped by Brunelleschi's famous dome.

THE TUSCAN MIRACLE

Birthplace of the Renaissance, a strong tradition of village life, picturesque countryside: these factors and more contribute to the enigma that is Tuscany.

Bean crostini.

From the top of a village tower, the Tuscan landscape lies below: the most civilised rural scene on Earth. Yet driving through southern Tuscany at night, there is little sense of civilisation, still less of domesticity – even farm animals are kept indoors. In the distance, a succession of small lights trails across the black countryside: tenuous links with separate inward-looking communities. The spaces in between are remote, uncivilised. The blackness and emptiness of the countryside go back to medieval times and beyond; the "Tuscan Miracle" only illuminates the cities, leaving the gaps unfilled.

In giving birth to the Renaissance, Tuscany designed the modern world. In his paintings, Giotto projected Tuscany into space. Brunelleschi crowned space with his Florentine dome, the greatest feat of Renaissance engineering. In the Carmine frescoes, Masaccio peopled space with recognisably human figures. His *Expulsion from Paradise* reveals Adam and Eve in all their naked beauty. Gone is the medieval coyness; present is the palpable suffering of a couple who have lost everything.

The Tuscan miracle, however, is not a frozen Renaissance portrait but a living procession of Tuscans completely at ease with their artistic setting and identity.

Etruscan sarcophagus, Chiusi.

Tuscans do possess an innate aesthetic sense but the Tuscan tapestry is a rich weave that has been created by many different threads. Literary Tuscany is a strand that can be clearly traced through Boccaccio, Petrarch and Dante. Republican Tuscany is best glimpsed through its fortified town halls, while humanist Tuscany is enshrined in poetry, sculpture and art, the fruits of patronage and craftsmanship. Aristocratic Tuscany still lingers in Medici palaces, villas and sculptured gardens, as well as the ancestral homes of the Rucellai, Corsini and Frescobaldi. Bourgeois Tuscany parades along Florence's Via Tornabuoni, patronises the arts and restores family farms. Peasant Tuscany traditionally takes a little of everything from the land: game, beans, chestnut flour, unsalted bread, olive oil and, of course, the grapes needed to make Chianti and Brunello. Tuscan cuisine combines proportion and variety to produce delicious, hearty fare. Like the Tuscans themselves, it is of good peasant stock.

TUSCANY TODAY

Despite the region's resounding popularity, Tuscany is not succumbing to "Disneyfication" – and a new environmental awareness means that the lifestyle is more seductive than ever.

It's a travesty to equate Tuscany to "Chianti-shire", a parody of an English country-house party transposed to Italy. It is also misleading to reduce the region to Renaissance art, Florentine architecture and Chianti vineyards. The Tuscan landscape is as beautiful as the art. The soothing scenery, dotted with hill towns, inspired the Renaissance masters and nurtured a lifestyle with timeless appeal. This rose-tinted Tuscan lifestyle is arguably now the greatest lure, with villa-living or farm-stays the ideal way of living the dream. The Tuscans seem to have found a perfect balance between country and city living. And, as bedazzled fans, we come in search of the secret, as if it lay in the princely countryside, the pasta feasts and the pampering hot springs.

Pienza is perfect Tuscany. This tower-capped outpost overlooking sun-baked valleys is all an Italophile could wish for – so much so that this town of 2,100 has around 100,000 visitors a year. In the rush to enjoy the rural idyll, we risk turning high-season Pienza into an elbow-to-elbow mêlée. And this is Tuscany's dilemma. Her beauty is in danger of becoming her beast. While Rome does government and Milan does commerce, La Toscana does cypress-lined rolling hills and the Renaissance. The region's wealth is her landscape and heritage, and the question for the future is how to preserve this while finding room for some 10 million visitors a year.

The price of paradise

As Italy's most popular region, Tuscany's long-standing relationship with tourism is finely balanced. Pisa is grappling with the quick-fire habits of the tourist in search of little more than a snapshot of himself, arms askew, mimicking the Leaning Tower behind him. Florence is reeling. The city that caused Stendhal

Dining alfresco in the Piazza Cisterna, in the popular medieval hilltop town of San Gimignano.

Syndrome – the dizzying disorientation some visitors experience when they overdose on Florentine Renaissance masterpieces – is in danger of sending tourists' heads spinning in front of the Uffizi Gallery.

While ostensibly true, this snapshot is still misleading and restricted to tourism "hotspots" such as the Leaning Tower, the great Florentine galleries and San Gimignano. Beyond these beautiful bottlenecks, Tuscany is as spacious yet enveloping as ever it was. Many evocative hamlets on Monte Amiata see far too few visitors, as do Maremma's Etruscan sites, wild Garfagnana and cities of the stature of Massa Marittima. But even just beyond San Gimignano's walls, you can still lose yourself on walks through epic countryside that has been cultivated since time immemorial.

Environmental factors and "Slow Travel"

Tuscany has also woken up to environmental issues, with classic hill towns, such as Montepulciano, closed to traffic, or partly pedestrianised, as is Siena. Florence is dabbling with trams to the suburbs and electric buses in the historic centre, with a futuristic Norman Foster-designed rail hub due to hopefully open

The secret of Tuscan identity lies in each town's sense of completeness. Tuscan towns go against the grain, shunning spurious modernity if it simply means homogeneity. Instead, without being fossilised, Florence is becoming more Florentine and Siena more Sienese. For a Tuscan, city life feels narrow but it is also invitingly deep. The watchwords are tradition, civility, good taste and a sense of ease with the past.

The heritage scene

Temperamentally left-wing, Tuscans can be deeply conservative when it comes to herit-

Cycling through southern Siena – a fantastic way to see the stunning countryside.

in 2015. And Tuscans, not just tourists, have taken to cycling, especially in Pisa, Lucca, the Chianti and the Versilia coast. Pisa currently boasts more pedestrians than cars, and more bicycles than motorcycles and mopeds. Despite traffic restrictions, cities such as Siena, Lucca and Massa Marittima are more liveable than ever, big enough to take tourism in their stride, but small enough for civic pride to define who they are. Equally harmonious are Volterra, the Val d'Orcia villages, Montepulciano, Pietrasanta, and the "tufa towns" (a type of local stone) around Pitigliano.

Such places embody the essence of "Slow Travel" – confident enough to be revitalised by tourism, careful not to be denatured by it.

age – and with good reason. Apart from being the cradle of the Renaissance, Tuscany boasts no less than seven Unesco World Heritage Sites: from Florence, Siena, San Gimignano, Pisa and Pienza to the landscape and lifestyle of the Val d'Orcia via the Medici villas and gardens. The Pisan Unesco site was expanded to embrace the cluster of sacred buildings on the Campo dei Miracoli beyond the legendary Leaning Tower.

Safe in its historical time capsule, Florence has often struggled to break free from its self-serving reputation as a museum-city, marooned in its glorious past. In recent times, its sleepy attitude to culture post-Michelangelo has been shaken up by the success of the

Palazzo Strozzi, which has put the city on the contemporary art map. The duality of the Tuscan temperament when it comes to heritage – conservatism with a dash of radicalism – is reflected in the Renaissance Palazzo Strozzi, and its contemporary-arts space, La Strozzina. The Establishment space can stage art blockbusters, leaving its cutting-edge sister to play with new trends and talents. As its director James Bradburne says: "Florence has a deep connection to its Renaissance past, but citizens have a right to have a place that feels like a city of today."

Young boys wearing the colours of their contrada, drinking from a fountain during the Palio, Siena.

Reconciling the cultural past and present

Encouraged by its former mayor, the young and charismatic and now prime minister Matteo Renzi, Florence has been experiencing a cultural revival. The Palazzo Vecchio stays open until midnight in the summer season, and there is pressure on the more staid State-owned museums to follow suit. The greatest, the Uffizi Gallery, has opened new rooms and the city also has a new opera house and auditorium. In addition, former convents, a fortress, a station and even a prison have been converted into cultural centres, concert halls, libraries, galleries and venues for fashion shows, exhibitions and eclectic events. This new dynamism is not restricted to Florence. Prato's Pecci museum of contemporary art is thriving, and an elite group of Tuscan arts festivals are gaining international recognition, from Florence's Maggio Fiorentino to Cortona's Tuscan Sun festival and Lucca's celebrity-studded summer music festival.

But there's no escaping the constraints of the 16th-century straitjacket. If the glory of Florence is that it contains the world's greatest concentration of Renaissance art and architecture, the price is responsibility to future generations, and perpetual restoration. Critic Mary McCarthy put the dilemma forcefully: "Historic Florence is an incubus on its present population. It is like a vast piece of family property whose upkeep is too much for the heirs, who nevertheless find themselves criticised by strangers for letting the old place go to rack and ruin."

THE NEW MEDICI OF WINE

Many Tuscan wine estates are still the preserve of aristocrats who trace their lineage back to Medici Florence or beyond. The noble names include the Antinori (the largest family-run wine business in Italy), Frescobaldi and Ricasoli. But now the rock stars are moving in as the new Medici of wine.

In Tenuta degli Dei, flamboyant Florentine designer Roberto Cavalli creates Tuscan Merlots at his wine estate and stud farm in the heart of Chianti country (www.deglidei.it). Tuscan opera legend Andrea Bocelli also dabbles in wine-making, his greatest passion after music and horses. Sienese rock star Gianna Nannini crafts Sangiovese-style reds in a former monastery near

Siena (www.certosadibelriguardo.com). In gentleman-farmer mode, superstar Sting sells his wine, organic oil and honey on his Tenuta il Palagio retreat in Chiantishire. Bob Dylan quaffs his own Visions of J Montepulciano, named after an old Dylan hit. His wine maker, Antonio Terni, compares the Montepulciano grape to "a block of marble waiting to be turned into a statue".

Tuscan actors and artists are equally keen to till the soil. Actress Stefania Sandrelli produces genuine Chianti on her estate, and artist Sandro Chia makes award-winning Brunello. Castello Romitorio, Chia's 12th-century estate, is dotted with arresting artworks that would have caught the Medici eye. (www.castelloromitorio.com).

Renovation and protection

Yet there is much to celebrate in the capital and in Tuscany as a whole. In Siena, the glorious pilgrims' hospital of Santa Maria della Scala has become a magnificent medieval museum. In Pisa, the (slightly straighter) Leaning Tower was finally unveiled in 2011. In the Maremma, Sovana's monumental Etruscan trails have recently been restored. A welcome trend in conservation is the return of artworks to the churches for which they were created. In Florence, Michelangelo's wooden Crucifix returned to Santo Spirito, as did Masaccio's fresco of the Trinity to Santa Maria Novella. More recently, a once-neglected Crucifix has been restored, declared a genuine Giotto, and returned in glory to its home in the Ognissanti church.

Even so, restoration is never-ending in Tuscany, with each project accompanied by public scrutiny from some of the most artistically aware citizens in Europe. In Piero della Francesca's superb fresco cycle in Arezzo, for instance, the restorers were accused of repainting rather than simply restoring. As for major sculpture, the threat of pollution means that "cloning" carries the day, with restored statues replaced by copies.

Florentine belle.

Reading a daily newspaper in Florence.

TUSCANY IN THE CINEMA

Tuscany is cinematic by nature, with its rolling hills and quaint villages perfect for expat dramas, from *Room with a View* (1985) to *Under the Tuscan Sun* (2003). Bernardo Bertolucci's *Stealing Beauty* (1996) plumped for Chiantishire, while Jane Campion's stylish *Portrait of a Lady* (1996) preferred the Lucca countryside. Franco Zeffirelli's semi-autobiographical *Tea with Mussolini* (1999) is set in wartime Florence, a period also perfectly evoked by Anthony Minghella's *The English Patient* (1996). In the last film, Piero della Francesca's frescoes in Arezzo's Basilica di San Francesco are revealed by flares to the enchanted Hanna (Juliette Binoche).

Tuscan film sets transcend period drama. Ridley Scott made his epic, *Gladiator* (2000), in lush Val d'Orcia, while *Hannibal* (2001) saw the charismatic psychopath lap up Florence, from the Ponte Vecchio to the Porcellino. More recently, Carrara's marble quarries saw action in *Quantum of Solace* (2008), with the film thundering to a climax during Siena's Palio horse race.

Artier films include Zeffirelli's Oscar-winning *Romeo and Juliet* (1968) and Tarkovsky's *Nostalgia* (1983), set in the mysterious spa pool at Bagno Vignone. And just when many feared that Tuscany had fallen out of favour with directors, along came a vampire story, *Twilight: New Moon* (2009) and a romantic drama, *Letters to Juliet* (2010).

In a sense, the pattern was set by the removal of Michelangelo's *David* to the Accademia. The cloning issue divides critics, with realists opting for copies and romantics preferring the works to grow old gracefully, or disgracefully, in the place for which they were created. But given Florence's new environmental initiatives, more sculptures may well remain *in situ*.

Tuscans and their landscape

The counterpoint to the compact urban artistic heritage is the endless countryside. Etruscans cultivated it, Tuscans civilised it, and foreigners

of jobs. Villages that had been the hub of rural life for thousands of years became ghost towns. Although the medieval *mezzadria* system of sharecropping (in which a landowner allows a tenant use of the land in return for a share of the crop produced) was banned in 1978, old traditions die hard. Apart from large wheat and cattle farms in the Val d'Arno and Val di Chiana, farming is mostly labour-intensive, under-mechanised and organic. Partly through poverty and tradition, Tuscany has gained a reputation as a leading region for small-scale sustainable farming.

Enjoying the sun in Castiglione della Pescaia on the Maremma coast.

romanticised it. Tuscans still prefer living in large villages or small towns, echoing the Etruscan ideal, which was confirmed by the rural perils of medieval Europe. These deeply urban people cultivate a close relationship with the land, but it is a wary bond that doesn't imply mastery. Even so, rural traditions have deep roots. Lucca's olive trees date back to Roman times, while the region's ancient vineyards are terraced on slopes that have been cultivated for centuries.

World War II shattered rural life in Tuscany – ending the feudal *mezzadria* system of land being governed by the wealthy nobility. With the ancient paternalistic social structure gone, thousands of farmers and villagers abandoned their homes and headed for the cities in search

CHIANTISHIRE COMMUTERS

Peasant farmers could not believe their luck when crumbling, empty farmhouses began to be seen, in the 1960s, as an opportunity to create a rural idyll. A British presence in this revival gave birth to the nickname Chiantishire. Tuscans often protest that the Chiantishire commuters have priced locals out of their native villages, but foreigners argue that they saved places such as Sovicille near Siena, or Bugnano near Lucca from total abandonment. *Agriturismo* (farm-stays) helps to generate funds for further restoration. What's more, many foreign residents are now well integrated, as in the marble-carving town of Pietrasanta.

The countryside revival

Even so, beyond the sought-after wine and oil estates, the countryside has been suffering from depopulation. The influx of the olive-nibbling classes has helped to reverse the trend, with tumbledown farmhouses being snapped up by the Chiantishire set. Villas, castles and fortified estates have been turned into sleek spa resorts. Semi-abandoned villages are being reborn as boutique retreats, as in the case of Il Borro, a resort restored by the Ferragamo family. Castelfalfi is the most ambitious rural resort, with a hotel, villas, farmhouses and a golf course devel-

its wild pine groves a reminder that Tuscany is blessed with more forest than any other region in Italy. These remote swathes are the riposte to those who decry Tuscan "Disneyfication". The same is true of the beaches, such as Marina di Pisa, Castiglione della Pescaia and the silver coast of Monte Argentario, which win Tuscany awards as one of the cleanest coastlines in Italy.

In Tuscany, quality of life is cultivated like an olive grove: few would jeopardise this heritage by turning to heavy industry. The industries Tuscans speak of with pride, such as Siena's *panforte*, Carrara's marble, Volterra's alabaster

Alabaster craftsman working in Volterra.

oped by TUI, the huge German tour operator. Critics mutter about "the German conquest", but the lovely village, with views towards Volterra, was previously abandoned. Other slumbering villages are being saved by novel local schemes. Pari, a depopulated village between Monte Amiata and Petriolo, is running a "reopen the shutters" project to win back young families, offering to pay their rent for three years. Proof, indeed, that tourism is not the only answer.

In fact, beyond the Florence–Siena axis, the effects of tourism fade away. Here another Tuscany emerges, in the Apuan Alps and Garfagnana, with their rugged mountains, plunging valleys and marble mines. And to the west, the Maremma is still imbued with a sense of mystery,

and Arezzo gold, date back to medieval times. In keeping with tradition, true Tuscans are provincial, conservative and independent; civic culture and rural pride are their touchstones. For all its Dantesque grandiloquence and Renaissance finery, Tuscany's heart is rural. Its largest city is home to less than half a million people, and the nickname for Tuscans is "*Mangiafagioli*" (bean eaters). So it is perhaps not surprising that the province's best-loved son comes from the Arezzo countryside. Italy's tragicomic clown-prince – Oscar-winning actor Roberto Benigni – speaks lovingly of his homeland as "a region of hunters and hares, of large peasant women and wild and poetic beauty". And who would argue with Tuscany's "*grande Roberto*"?

DECISIVE DATES

Etruscans and Romans

800–500 BC

Etruscan civilisation flourishes. Etruria Propria, a confederation of 12 states, includes Arezzo, Chiusi, Fiesole and Volterra.

480–290 BC

Romans annexe Etruria and found colonies at Ansedonia, Roselle, Volterra, Luni and Lucca.

Lorenzo de' Medici.

80 BC

Faesulae (Fiesole) becomes a Roman military colony.

59 BC

Colony of Roman veterans founds Florentia (Florence) on the banks of the Arno.

AD 200–600

Region invaded by Lombards, Goths and Franks.

AD 306

Constantinople capital of Roman Empire; the Byzantine period follows.

AD 476

The Fall of Rome.

Medieval Tuscany

1000–1300

Germans conquer Italy; warring between Guelfs (supporters of papacy) and Ghibellines (supporters of Holy Roman Empire).

1062

Pisa triumphs over Saracens in battle off Palermo.

1115

Florence becomes an independent city governed by a mercantile-class council.

1118

Pisa Cathedral consecrated.

1125

Florence begins expansion with takeover of Fiesole.

1173

Bonnano Pisano begins Pisa's Leaning Tower.

1246–50

Work on Florence's Santa Maria Novella begins and Bargello built.

1260

Sienese defeat the Florentines in battle of Montaperti.

1294

Arnolfo di Cambio begins Florence's Santa Croce.

1296

Di Cambio begins Florence's Duomo.

1310

Siena's Palazzo Pubblico is completed.

1314

Dante Alighieri begins *The Divine Comedy*.

1334

Giotto begins Florence's Campanile.

c.1345

Florence's Ponte Vecchio is erected by Taddeo Gaddi.

1348

Black Death hits Florence, killing a third of the population.

1390

John Hawkwood becomes Captain General of Florence; inter-city wars.

The Renaissance

1406

Pisa is defeated, becoming part of Florentine state.

1420

Papacy returns to Rome.

1434–64

Cosimo de' Medici rules Florence.

1436

Brunelleschi completes dome for Florence's Duomo.

1452

Alberti's *Ten Books on Architecture* is published.

1469–92

Lorenzo de' Medici rules Florence.

1478
Sandro Botticelli paints *La Primavera*.

1498
"Mad monk" Savonarola hanged for heresy in Florence's Piazza della Signoria.

1504
Michelangelo completes *David*.

1513
Niccolò Machiavelli writes *The Prince*.

1527
The Sack of Rome.

1530
Republic of Florence ends as armies of Pope Clement VII and Emperor Charles V besiege the city.

1550
Giorgio Vasari's *Lives of the Artists* first published.

1554
Siena is defeated, becoming part of Florentine state.

1564–1642
Galileo Galilei discovers the principles of dynamics.

The aftermath of the 1966 flood.

Grand Duchy Tuscany

1716
Grand Duke establishes Chianti wine laws.

1737
Gian Gastone, the last male Medici, dies.

1796
Napoleon's first Italian campaign.

1815
Grand Duchy absorbed into the Austrian Empire.

Modern Tuscany

1848
The War of Independence.

1861
Kingdom of Italy proclaimed.

1865–71
Florence capital of Italy.

1915
Italy enters World War I on the Allies' side.

1922
Benito Mussolini elected.

1940
Italy enters World War II against Allies.

1945
Mussolini executed.

1946
Italy becomes a republic.

1957
The Treaty of Rome; Italy a founder member of EEC (now EU).

1966
Massive flooding in Florence – artworks damaged.

1993
Mafia bomb kills five and damages Uffizi, Florence.

1994
Right-wing government ushers in Second Republic. Silvio Berlusconi elected premier (re-elected in 2001 and 2008).

2004
Val d'Orcia declared Unesco World Heritage Site.

2005
Pope John Paul II dies, succeeded by Benedict XVI.

2011
Restoration on Pisa's Leaning Tower ends after 20 years of work. Oldest-ever Etruscan necropolis found near Livorno.

2013
Medici villas and gardens designated Unesco World Heritage Site.

2014
Former mayor of Florence and Democratic Party leader Matteo Renzi becomes Italy's prime minister. Florentines elect the young Dario Nardella from the same party as their new mayor.

THE ETRUSCANS

Long before the Romans left their mark on the landscape, the Etruscan people established their own sense of regional identity, humanistic values and peaceful society in Tuscany.

The story of Tuscany begins with the Etruscans, its earliest known inhabitants, whose origins are shrouded in myth and mystery. The Romantics and latter-day writers believed that the Etruscans sailed from Asia Minor. However, Dionysius, writing as the Etruscan civilisation neared its end, held that the Etruscans were natives with an indigenous culture too deeply ingrained to be oriental. Most modern scholars believe that the Etruscans migrated from Eastern Europe over the Alps and represent the flowering of the early Italic tribes. What is clear is that between the 8th and 4th centuries BC "Etruria Propria" flourished as a confederation of 12 city-states in central Italy.

Etruscan seafarers and merchants first settled on the coast and began smelting iron ore from Elba and importing oriental ceramics, glass and silverware. Greek naval supremacy meant an opening to Hellenistic culture: ships sailed to Corinth with honey, gold and bronze figurines, and returned to Vetulonia and Pop-

Part of the fortification wall at Chiusi, one of Tuscany's major Etruscan sites.

> *Northern Etruria, roughly equivalent to modern Tuscany, included Arezzo, Chiusi, Cortona, Populonia, Vetulonia and Volterra.*

ulonia with perfume and painted wine jars. The inland cities such as Chiusi and Volterra thrived on hunting, farming and trade. Over the next two centuries, the Etruscans allied themselves to the developing Roman power, and by the 1st century BC, all Etruscan territory was annexed. Although Etruscan and Latin co-existed, Etruscan culture was crushed; its role degenerated into the provision of soothsayers, musicians, dancers and fighters for Rome.

Etruscan society

The original confederation had a complex urban and social structure: each city was originally run by a king, later by local aristocrats, and finally by a priestly oligarchy. The lords owned large land-holdings or navies and were served by serfs and slaves. Whereas the serfs were rewarded with agricultural plots, the slaves danced and sang for their supper. With urbanisation, an independent class of artisans and merchants began to emerge. The granting of the same Roman citizenship to the middle classes as to the aristocratic priests and magistrates was a severe blow to the Etruscan princely tradition.

The Etruscans were expert builders. Their cities followed the contours of the land and sited the necropolis below the city walls and the living city above. If cities of the dead predominate today, it is by accident and not by design. Public buildings, constructed of wood and clay, did not survive. From what remains of the cities, there was enough to impress Roman and Renaissance architects. Volterra's Porta all'Arco, a deep gateway inspired by

Mesopotamian architecture; the huge drystone walls at Saturnia, rebuilt to defend the city against Roman incursions; the neat town plans of Pitigliano and Sovana – all these scattered remains are evidence of the vitality and ingenuity of Etruscan builders.

New discoveries of Etruscan artefacts continue to be made around the region. Recently, east of Livorno, archaeologists unearthed a 3,000-year-old necropolis, dating from the end of the Bronze Age, and the oldest Etruscan site ever found. To trump that, a Palaeolithic man, Tuscany's oldest *Homo sapiens*,

The town of Pitigliano, inhabited during Etruscan times.

BEST ETRUSCAN SITES

Scrape the surface of the most enigmatic Tuscan towns and an Etruscan spirit lies beneath, with temple walls recycled into Roman buildings, or ancient epigraphs encrusted within Renaissance palaces.

In Volterra, the Porta all'Arco Etrusco reveals a Roman arched vault, incorporating three Etruscan basalt heads, on massive Etruscan bases. The superb Etruscan Museum displays *The Shadow of the Evening* sculpture. Although over 2,000 years old, this bronze figure seems modern in both message and design. Florence's Archaeological Museum boasts the reconstructed Inghirammi Tomb, a semicircular Etruscan tomb from Volterra. Finer still is the muse-

um's bronze *Chimera* from Arezzo.

Chiusi has one of the best museums, stuffed with *bucchero* ware and Canopic urns, cinerary urns with an idealised effigy of the deceased on the lid. The only painted tombs in Tuscany are here, along with underground galleries and a mysterious labyrinth that reputedly conceals the sarcophagus of Lars Porsenna, mythical king of the Etruscans.

In the Maremma area, Sovana is riddled with deep, ravine-like Etruscan roads and "pigeonhole" tombs, niches cut into the rock. In Vetulonia, the remote, rural setting contrasts with tangible proof that this was once one of the richest cities in Etruria.

was found in Monteriggioni in 2011. In Sesto Fiorentino, outside Florence, the Etruscan Tomb of La Montagnola has recently been opened, with its impressive secret vaulted corridor and noble burial chamber. In 2011 at Poggio Colla two Etruscan depictions of a woman in childbirth were discovered.

Etruscan art

Fascinating tombs, in every shape and form, can be seen in the Etruscan necropolises: "temple" tombs at Saturnia; melon-shaped tombs at Cortona; oriental "trench" tombs at Vetulo-

lovers, absorbed wrestlers, erotic dancers or grieving warriors reflect the fullness and variety of Etruscan life.

Noblewomen enjoyed freedom, influence and social status. They are frequently depicted attending banquets without the company of their husbands, riding covered wagons to their land-holdings and playing flutes or lyres at funerals. The men are rarely still: they charge through games, boar-hunts, processions, journeys, dances, banquets and diving competitions. The "ordinary" Etruscan is only glimpsed in passing: a prized blonde

Sarcophagus dating from the 2nd century BC, Tarquinia.

nia. It is the tombs that remain as a cultural testimony to the power, wealth and beliefs of their owners. Death reflected life: the poor were often buried in shallow graves or their ashes put in small urns; the rich were buried in chamber tombs and stone sarcophagi decorated with pottery.

Since there is no extant Etruscan literature, our knowledge of the living Etruscans is oddly dependent on a reading of this funerary art for clues. We know them as they would like to be known, these idealised aristocrats elevated by Greek myths. The women were depicted as pale, while the men were uniformly reddish-brown, either suntanned or ritually painted. Friezes of serene married couples, tender

courtesan flits past dancing slaves; a serf mourns his dead master.

The Roman legacy

Rome annexed Etruria in 351 BC, and, from the 3rd until the 2nd century BC, as part of the massive road-building programme that was to transform the entire country, four great Roman roads were built across the territory: the Via Aurelia, which ran up the western seaboard to Pisae and the naval base at Genua in Liguria; the Via Clodia, which stopped at Saturnia; the Via Cassia, built in 154 BC to connect Rome with Florentia; and the Via Flaminia, built in 220 BC to connect Rome to Umbria and the Adriatic Sea.

Etruscan roads were all designed to connect the interior with the coast, whereas Roman roads all led to Rome, thus the axis was turned 90 degrees, from east–west to north–south. The more impressive new Roman roads purposely avoided the great Etruscan cities, which slowly fell into decline, whereas the new Roman cities such as Pistoriae (Pistoia), now better connected, grew steadily in importance.

New colonies were founded at Ansedonia, Fiesole, Roselle, Populonia, Volterra, Luni and Lucca. The cultural identity of the Etrus-

humanistic and regional values that far outlived the Roman Empire itself. But by creating the roads and major cities of Tuscany, the Romans also left a permanent imprint on this part of the Italian landscape.

A millennium later, the ruins of their great bridges, amphitheatres and city walls were the inspiration for the next great blossoming of Italian culture: Tuscany's coming of age, the Renaissance. The art critic John Ruskin even saw an unbroken line of tradition from the tomb paintings of the Etruscans to Giotto and Fra Angelico.

The remains of the Roman theatre in Volterra.

cans was gradually absorbed into that of the Romans, a process that was accelerated in 91 BC when Roman citizenship was extended to the Etruscans.

The Romans learnt many things from the Etruscans – principally, the Tuscan arch, which they developed as a key element in their extraordinary aqueducts, bridges and buildings, relegating the classical columns of Greece to a more decorative role in their architecture.

Certainly, the Etruscan influence on the Romans was considerable. Apart from introducing to Rome the purple toga, an abundance of gods and competent soothsayers, the Etruscans also added a set of religious,

MYSTERY LANGUAGE

The Etruscan language may be as mysterious as the people's origins, but its unintelligibility is still part of a glamorous myth. Although the alphabet is borrowed from Greek, the language, read from left to right, belongs to no known linguistic group. True, there are no external keys such as dictionaries or bilingual texts, but the core grammatical and phonetic structure is known, and most of the 10,000 shorter texts can be read accurately. These texts are mostly funerary inscriptions and religious dedications. The one known book, a priest's manual discovered wrapped around an Egyptian mummy, has only been partially deciphered.

Roman Tuscany

Apart from the roads, the Romans' greatest legacy is their template for the classic town plan, with the forum – evolving into the piazza – the focal point.

It's hard to imagine the impact that Roman roads, giant engineering projects, must have had on the colonised Etruscans, as regimented teams spanned rivers with elegant stone bridges, built drains to prevent their new roads from flooding, and at times even cut through the hills themselves.

Florentia

Detective work is necessary to unearth Roman Florence, Florentia; the Roman gridiron street plan is clearly visible on maps, with the Piazza della Repubblica following the outline of the old *castrum*.

Faesulae

Nearby, Fiesole, which possibly dates from the 8th century BC, was an Etruscan settlement but, as Faesulae, became a Roman military colony from 80 BC and later became the capital of Roman Etruria. The Piazza Mino da Fiesole occupies the site of the Roman forum. The archaeological site, on a hillside near the Duomo, features a remarkably well-preserved Roman theatre, still used for performances. Beyond are Roman baths, and on the far side, the ruins of a Roman temple, both 1st century BC, as well as a 3rd century BC Etruscan temple, set against the Etruscan city walls.

Lucca

In Lucca, the original street plan is also still evident. Lucca began as a military colony in 178 BC and featured a 10,000-seat amphitheatre, outside the walls. In time, it was largely dismantled, and most of its remains are below street level. During the Middle Ages, however, houses were built using the remaining walls of the amphitheatre, thus fossilising its outline and four main entrances. Fragments of it are still visible from the surrounding lanes, incorporated in the outer walls of the houses. Volterra, which became an important Roman municipality in the 4th century BC, also recycled its history, as well as retaining the ruins of the 1st century BC Roman theatre beyond the city walls.

Luna

Luni, called Luna by the Romans, was founded in 177 BC and was the springboard for the conquest of the Ligurian tribes. The Roman city, its forum, a number of houses and its amphitheatre have been excavated.

Rusellae

Another extensively excavated site is at Roselle, the Roman Rusellae, one of the most important Etruscan cities of northern Etruria. Originally an island, the Etruscan city was taken by Rome early in the 3rd century BC. The ruins are satisfyingly

View from the Teatro Romano, Fiesole.

complete, with Romano-Etruscan walls, a Roman forum, paved streets, basilicas, villas, amphitheatre, workshops and baths.

Cosa

Ansedonia, the Roman Cosa, was founded as a Roman colony in 273 BC. The ancient hilltop city has been excavated, and the site contains the ruins of a main street, forum, walled acropolis and the *capitolium* – a tripartite sanctuary for the triad of Jupiter, Juno and Minerva. The city's 1.5km (1-mile) wall is virtually intact, as are many of its 18 guard towers and forum. The site is slightly overgrown, and many of the ruins are covered in brambles, creating a beguilingly elegiac mood, but it has fabulous views out to sea and is worth a visit.

THE RENAISSANCE AND THE MEDICI

From feuding factionalism to the rise of the Medici, the aspirations of small city-states to remain independent were often dashed – but wealth, power and patronage still fostered an artistic flowering.

Between the ending of the Roman Empire in the 5th century AD and the beginning of the foreign invasions in the 16th century, the story of Italy is a catalogue of conflict between its cities, each of which was a sovereign state. In Tuscany, a three-way battle was conducted between Florence, Pisa and Siena.

The *condottieri*

In the early stages, the battles between the city-states were conducted by the citizens themselves, but when Florence crushed Arezzo in 1289 at Campaldino, the bloodshed was so great that thereafter the cities began to fight out their differences with mercenaries, the *condottieri*.

Throughout the 14th century, the *condottieri* held the balance of power. Commanding companies numbering thousands of men, they sold their services to the highest bidder. The city that could afford them – and control them – dominated its neighbours. Few could control them, however, and that is why the *condottieri* system failed. The *condottieri* had a vested interest in conflict: from being paid to fight on behalf of a city, it was a short step to blackmailing that same city into paying you not to attack them.

Some *condottieri* were bought off – Sir John Hawkwood, the piratical leader of the much-feared White Company, was given a palatial villa and a substantial estate as his reward for retiring gracefully from the fray. Hawkwood craved immortality and wanted an equestrian statue to be erected in Florence – instead, the miserly Florentines opted for the less expensive solution of an illusionistic fresco, painted by Paolo Uccello to look like a statue, in Florence Cathedral.

Detail from Ambrogio Lorenzetti's Effects of Good and Bad Government (1338).

The burden of paying the *condottieri* fell to the merchant class. They were caught on the horns of a dilemma, desiring domination over their trade rivals, and yet aware of the high cost of war, in terms of both taxes and economic instability. When they waged war on neighbouring cities, they often did so in the name of "Guelf" or "Ghibelline" partisanship. The Guelfs were broadly made up of the rising merchant class, bankers and members of the trades guilds, who nominally supported the papacy in its long battle against the Holy Roman Emperor, and who wanted a greater role in city government. Conversely, the Ghibellines, the old feudal aristocracy, supported the emperor, because he seemed the best guarantor of their virtual autocracy. Since the emperor was often German or Spanish and an absentee ruler, paying nominal allegiance to such a distant figurehead was far preferable to the threat of the pope exercising real and temporal power much closer to home.

Outside Tuscany, many city-states fell under the dominion of a single ruler – some of them former *condottieri* who ended up rulers of the cities they once protected, founding dynasties. The Tuscan city-states and republics maintained their independence far longer, but eventually even they fell to a dynastic power, as the Medici transformed themselves from private citizens to grand dukes.

The rise of the Medici

Ruefully reflecting on the mistakes that had led him to be imprisoned and tortured before being cast from office, Niccolò Machiavelli, former Chancellor of Florence, wrote his masterpiece *The Prince*, in which he admiringly recounted the ruthless methods used by the Medici to claw their way to absolute power in Tuscany. Even more remarkable is the way that

The map known as the Carta della Catena showing Florence around 1470.

DANTE'S FLORENCE

In the medieval heart of Florence, an unassuming tower-house is reputedly the birthplace of Dante Alighieri (1265–1321), Italy's most revered poet. His epic poem, *The Divine Comedy*, set the Tuscan dialect as the model for Italian literature. The Casa di Dante is an evocation of Dante's Florence rather than an attempt to explore the poet's genius. As a citizen of Florence, Dante's horizons embraced the Bargello, the Baptistery and the Badia Fiorentina. The museum presents the Guelf-Ghibelline political struggles, including family crests and battle maps. Unjustly cast into exile after disputes within the Guelf faction, Dante declared himself "a Florentine by birth but not by character". The poet died in exile in Ravenna, but his native city belatedly redeemed itself with a Dante memorial in Santa Croce.

On display in the poet's home is a copy of Henry Holliday's Pre-Raphaelite painting, *The Meeting of Dante and Beatrice*, alluding to the doomed infatuation that inspired much of the poet's work. The earliest-known portrait of Dante was recently discovered in the medieval meeting hall of the Magistrates Guild. Now both a moody museum and restaurant, Alle Murate reveals portraits of other Florentine legends, including Petrarch and Boccaccio. (Alle Murate: 6 Via del Proconsolo, Florence; www.allemurate.it. Casa di Dante: Via Santa Margerita, Florence; www.casadidante.it).

the dynasty threw up gifted individuals, generation after generation. The Medici were masters of realpolitik and military strategy but also patronised the arts, helping to make Florence and Tuscany the engine of cultural regeneration that we know as the Renaissance.

The man who laid the foundations for the family's meteoric rise was Giovanni de' Medici (1360–1429), founder of the Medici bank. This was just one of 100 or so financial institutions in 15th-century Florence, but Giovanni's masterstroke was to develop a special relationship with the Church, eventually securing a monop-

> *"Whoever desires to found a state and give it laws must start with assuming that all men are bad and ever ready to display their vicious nature whenever they may find occasion for it." (Niccolò Machiavelli)*

oly over the collection of the papal revenues.

Giovanni's son, Cosimo, developed this relationship still further: one of his great coups was to attract the prestigious General Council of the Greek Orthodox and the Roman Catholic churches to Florence. These two great Christian churches had been at loggerheads for six centuries. Their assemblies in Florence were intended to find ways of burying their differences and creating a unified Christian church. This they failed to do, but the meetings had a lasting impact on Florence. Not only did they create a stimulating climate of theological and intellectual debate, out of which the Renaissance was to grow, but also they fuelled artistic debate. The pomp and pageantry of the papal entourage, and the flamboyance of its Greek counterparts, provided artists with an array of exotica.

Cosimo himself eschewed such riches. He took pride in simplicity, ordering Brunelleschi, the temperamental genius behind the dome of Florence Cathedral, to modify his designs for the Medici palace, as they were too ostentatious. More to his taste was Michelozzo, who designed the marvellously airy library in San Marco, Florence, as a repository for the Medici book collection, the world's first-ever public library. Such generosity was typical of Cosimo, who spent a fortune endowing Florence with public buildings. Among his friends he counted humanists

who shared his thirst for classical knowledge, for this was an era in which the lost classics of Greece and Rome, including works by Plato and Cicero, were being rediscovered.

Though a devout Christian who regularly retreated to his private cell at San Marco, Cosimo believed strongly that God's grace was best leavened by human reason. This made him an effective and humane ruler – even if, following his father's advice to "keep out of the public eye", Cosimo never sought public office. Instead, he wielded immense influence behind the scenes.

A portrait of Lorenzo de' Medici.

GOOD AND BAD GOVERNMENT

In Siena's Palazzo Pubblico, Lorenzetti's great frescoes, *The Effects of Good and Bad Government*, served as a lesson to the city's medieval rulers. *Bad Government* depicts a countryside ravaged by bandits, with fields left uncultivated, churches in ruin, and women raped in broad daylight. By contrast, *Good Government* depicts a city-state populated by peaceable citizens, attentive students and prosperous merchants. The adjoining room is dominated by a portrait of Guidoriccio da Fogliano in ceremonial battledress. As the city's *condottiero*, he was responsible for delivering the peace that underpinned the Sienese social order.

Lorenzo de' Medici inherited his father's love of the classical philosophers, and his gift for diplomacy. An outstanding poet in his own right, he promoted the study of Dante in Tuscan universities, elevating the Tuscan dialect to equal status with Latin. His greatest gift was peace. By using his diplomatic gifts to hold the great rival powers of the papacy and the Holy Roman Empire apart, Tuscany enjoyed a period of relative prosperity, in which merchants thrived and great fortunes were made. With the countryside no longer ravaged by war or held to ransom by lawless mercenaries, wealthy

hero standing up to the bullying giant Goliath, as a symbol of the city's desire to rid itself of the Medici. He also fashioned new defences for the city, but when the combined forces of the Medici and the Holy Roman Emperor held the city to siege in 1530, he took himself off to hide – irony of ironies – in the Medici mortuary chapel, attached to San Lorenzo. Vasari attributes his cowardice to the artistic temperament, and while he was in hiding he worked the masterly reclining figures of *Dawn, Evening, Day* and *Night*, which now adorn the Medici tombs.

Painting depicting Cosimo I planning the conquest of Siena in 1555.

individuals began to build the villas that are still such a characteristic feature of the Tuscan countryside. Lorenzo himself led the way, staying regularly to his rural retreats at Fiesole and Poggio a Caiano.

The Medici lose support

Prophetically, Pope Innocent VIII declared that "the peace of Italy is at an end" on learning of Lorenzo's death in 1492. A period of turmoil ensued when Lorenzo's successors, who lacked the political acumen of their forebears, were expelled from the city and Savonarola, a firebrand preacher, took centre stage.

But the Medici swiftly returned in 1512. Michelangelo had carved his *David*, the boy

BONFIRE OF THE VANITIES

From 1494, Girolamo Savonarola, a Dominican preacher, filled the Florentines with anti-Medici zeal. He argued that their fondness for pagan philosophers and the artistic depiction of heathen gods would bring God's wrath on the city. In 1497, erotic sculptures, fine clothes, secular poetry, mirrors and paintings were burnt in what Savonarola termed "the bonfire of the vanities". Even Botticelli supported the movement, renouncing his past attachment to humanist ideals, and turned to painting Christian allegories, such as *Nativity*. But the Florentines tired of their firebrand friar, and burnt him at the stake in Piazza della Signoria.

Alessandro de' Medici, who led the victorious siege, rubbed salt into the wounds of his fellow citizens by having himself crowned Duke of Florence, claiming absolute power where his predecessors had been content with influence. When he was murdered in 1537 by his own cousin, with whom he had been having a homosexual affair, the city sought a successor. Cosimo, descended from Giovanni de' Medici via the female line, emerged victorious, partly by convincing his fellow citizens of his probity.

Once in power, Cosimo revealed his true colours, as he systematically set about destroying based in the Uffizi (literally, the "Offices") in Florence. This proved effective right up to the point when Tuscany joined the United Kingdom of Italy in 1861. So effective was this civil service that Tuscany continued to be ruled effectively even when Cosimo's successors proved to be corrupt, incompetent, self-indulgent or mad. Few made a major mark on the city, though Cosimo II did the world a great favour by patronising Galileo, making him court mathematician to the Medici and providing him with a home after his trial and excommunication by the Inquisition.

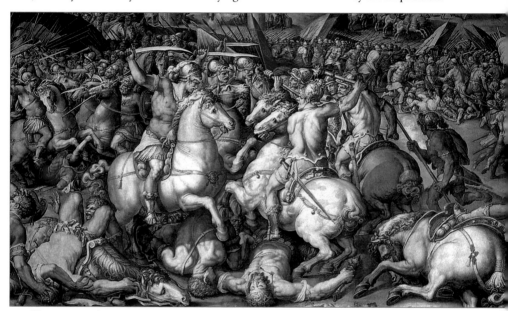

Detail from a painting by Vasari portraying Florence's victories over Pisa and Siena.

all opposition. Not only was he unrelenting in his pursuit of the republican leaders who had opposed his election, tracking them down in their exile and bringing them back to be tried and executed in Florence, he also set about conquering old enemies – Pisa, Siena, Massa Marittima, Montepulciano – with a ruthlessness and brutality that is still remembered and resented to this day. The whole story is told on the ceiling of the Palazzo Vecchio council chamber in a series of bloody frescoes painted by Vasari to honour Cosimo I in 1563–5.

To his credit, Cosimo not only forced Tuscany into political unity and established security in the region, he also set up an effective civil service to administer the dukedom,

The Medici art collection

The dynasty also amassed a truly astonishing art collection, which Princess Anna Maria Lodovica, the last of the Medici line, bequeathed to the city of Florence upon her death in 1743, along with all the extraordinary Medici palaces and gardens, thereby ensuring that a large number of the greatest works of the Renaissance were not sold off or dispersed, but would remain in the city that gave them birth. Today, these priceless works of art form the backbone of Florence's three main galleries: the Uffizi, the Pitti and the Bargello.

For more about Renaissance art and architecture, see page 47.

VIA
S. AGATA

MODERN TUSCANY

After the Renaissance, Tuscany became an economic backwater. Italian Unification, international conflict and political corruption have all had an impact on modern Tuscany, and the "Tuscan model" is now often seen as a wise balance between prosperity and a peaceful pace of life.

Since the glories of Rome and the Renaissance, Italy has written little history. The head of Italy's Bureau of Statistics likens modern Italian history to a muddle, "a happy antheap where everyone is running about and no one is in control". The alternative is the "strong man" view of recent history, as expressed in the Florentine saying, "Whose bread and cheese I eat, to his tune I dance". But, while Rome danced to martial music, Tuscany sometimes starved or burned.

Tuscany has been buffeted rather than enriched by its recent past. Well-kept war memorials in shabby towns attest to the loss of two generations, one abroad and one at home. Look at Asciano, a village dwarfed by its *carabinieri* stronghold, built by Benito Mussolini and still used to this day to maintain law and order. Visit Montisi where, for the price of a drink, locals will describe the German bombing of the village tower, a story complete with sound effects, gestures and genuine sorrow. Ask proud Florentines why the medieval houses on the south side of the Arno are lost for ever.

Illustration of 1860 depicting the event of Tuscany becoming part of a newly unified Italy.

The effect of Italian Unification

In 1865, Florence briefly became the capital of the newly united Italy. Although its exalted role would only last five years before Rome was then made the permanent capital, Florence underwent profound and rapid change during this time. An ambitious plan of expansion and modernisation sadly led to the demolition of, among other things, the old city walls, and their replacement with a wide ring of avenues punctuated with large piazzas in keeping with the French urban taste of the times. Quarters for the middle classes and the Piazzale Michelangelo were built. Later, old areas of the centre, including

the Ghetto, were declared to be in dangerous condition and unwholesome, and were razed; the soulless Piazza della Repubblica was created partly in their place. The square remains a bold flourish of nationhood, but when the capital was transferred to Rome, Tuscan allegiance unquestionably remained in Tuscany. Unification, under the leadership of Count Camillo Benso Cavour, a French-speaking Piedmontese, was seen as a foreign threat to the *de facto* sovereignty of Florence and the smaller city-states. Defenders of the Risorgimento, the movement for Italian unification, appealed to nascent patriotism. Critics of unification cited Dante's pleas to Tuscan liberty, before both sides settled down to start subverting the power of the new rulers. The merging of Tuscans into Italians started promisingly enough, but the end result is still only to be seen abroad or at international football matches.

World War I

Unification represented a missed chance for Italy. By failing to help shape a national identity, Tuscans also fell victim to the clearer vision of a "strong man". Even before World War I, Mussolini was making inflammatory speeches while a weak parliament practised the art of "timely resignation", a ploy used ever since to stage-manage a new coalition.

Although the pre-war Tuscan economy thrived under weak government, it was no match for growing social pressures and a deepening gulf between society and state. With few real policies, one of the last liberal governments blundered into World War I. Italy's unpopular late entry into the conflict cost Tuscan lives and support. The pyrrhic victory was exacerbated by a power vacuum, economic problems and a revolutionary working class. Benito Mussolini, from neighbouring Emilia, wasted no opportunity in

Montecatini in the early 1900s.

THE GROWTH OF THE GRAND TOUR

The most anglophone city in Italy, Florence has been a magnet for foreign visitors since the 17th century, when daring adventurers explored this strange land. By the 1700s, rich aristocrats were attracted to the region's alien psyche, perfect climate, low cost of living and undervalued art. Florence became an essential stop on any European tour and, in the 18th century, the middle classes joined the aristocratic *dilettanti* and *literati* on the road to Tuscany. Art was on the agenda, with foreign visitors flocking to see the Uffizi sculptures and Botticelli's *Birth of Venus*. By the 1850s, visitors from Victorian England had made Florence *"une ville anglaise"*. "They toil not, neither do they spin" was the cool judgement on his contemporaries by Irish novelist Charles Lever. Lever's biographer, William Fitzpatrick, damns the expatriate circle as "the society of diplomats and demireps, swells and snobs, princes and pretenders, wits and worthies, snarlers and social men".

By the 20th century, the Anglo-Florentine community was well established, though World War I chased many away. The Grand Tour resumed in the 1920s, mainly for society figures and intellectuals. The tradition continues today, with sons and daughters of the Establishment coming to learn Italian and attend art courses on the Renaissance — occasionally enjoying the designer labels rather than the artistic treasures.

claiming, "Governing Italy is not only impossible, it is useless", before proceeding to govern it impossibly but fairly usefully for 20 years.

By 1922, the corporate state was literally under construction. The economic benefits lasted until 1929, but the aesthetic effects linger on in functionally "improved" cities all over Tuscany. Florence railway station was the first Functionalist station in Italy.

World War II

At the outbreak of World War II, most Tuscans were cautiously neutral. Mussolini, despite

loyalties emerged: while the director of the British Institute was a known Fascist sympathiser, the German consul risked his life to protect Florentines who had been denounced. After the liberation he was granted the freedom of the city.

Florence was liberated in August 1943, but Mussolini and the German forces survived the winter behind the so-called "Gothic Line" in the Apennines. Apart from Florence, the partisans were very active in the Monte Amiata area, as well as in the Val d'Orcia, where the writer Iris Origo, an Englishwoman married to an Ital-

Santa Maria Novella railway station in Florence, one of the key architectural works of Italian Modernism.

having signed the Pact of Steel with Germany, only entered the war in 1940, after the fall of France. By 1943, the north was under German control, but the Allies were progressing northwards from Sicily. Allied bombing, German entrenchment and an emerging Tuscan Resistance transformed Tuscany into a battleground.

Anti-Fascist cells had been secretly set up by the Communists and Catholics in key towns under German and neo-Fascist control. Florence was split: while it was the intellectual centre of the Resistance, it also harboured strong Fascist sympathisers. Even after the city was captured by the Allies, individual Fascists held out, firing from the rooftops. Surprising

ian *marchese*, sheltered many refugees and prisoners of war in her villa, La Foce.

Writing about it at the time, she observed: "In the last few days I have seen Radicofani and Cortignano destroyed, the countryside and farms studded with shell holes, girls raped, and human beings and cattle killed. Otherwise the events of the last week have had little effect upon either side; it is the civilians who have suffered."

Nor were the Allies completely blameless. The modernity of Grosseto, Livorno and Pisa today owes much to Allied bombing in 1943. The British War Office reports naturally exonerated the Allies: "No damage of any significance is attributable to Allied action [in Florence]."

Foreign Writers in Tuscany

Generations of enraptured writers have penned paeans to Tuscany, which often say more about themselves, and their romantic projections, than they do about Tuscany.

Virginia Woolf saw "loneliness" in the landscape.

Shelley pronounced Tuscany a "paradise of exiles" tempted by art, adventure and escape from persecution. But the exiles' motives were as varied as their prose styles. The Scottish writer Tobias Smollett (1721–71) failed to appreciate the entrepreneurial nature of the Tuscan aristocracy, finding it undignified for "a noble to sell a pound of figs or to take money for a glass of sour wine". The Romantics were more enthusiastic. Lord Byron was "dazzled, drunk with Beauty" in Santa Croce. Shelley adored Pisan landscapes and Livornese seascapes, tragically drowning near La Spezia less than a month before his 30th birthday. Tuscany soon became a place of pilgrimage for the later Romantic poets, such as Tennyson and Wordsworth.

Stendhal Syndrome

Although officially a diplomat in Florence, the French novelist Stendhal spent most of his time absorbing Renaissance frescoes and planning his novel, *Le Rouge et le Noir* (1830). As with Byron, the Santa Croce Effect sent Stendhal reeling: "I walked in constant fear of falling to the ground." This aesthetic sickness is now known as Stendhal Syndrome.

Henry James was one of the few foreign writers able to see through Tuscany's literary and artistic veil, taking a more pragmatic approach. His *Portrait of Places* gives an opinionated but sensitive picture of the region in the 1870s.

The Brownings

The most romantic Victorian couple was undoubtedly the poets Elizabeth Barrett Browning and Robert Browning. Robert brought his wife to Florence because of her poor health. There he used Chianti to wean Elizabeth off her addiction to laudanum. Their 15th-century *palazzo*, redecorated in Victorian style, is now a museum.

A Room with a View

The 20th century brought E.M. Forster, with his ironic analysis of the resident English community at play. Forster's *A Room with a View* portrays the heroine's encounter with an alien culture and alien passions. Virginia Woolf saw her own image reflected in the landscape, "infinite emptiness, loneliness, silence", while D.H. Lawrence, living in his "grave old Tuscan villa", imagined that he was communing with the original Etruscans.

World War II prevented further literary flowering, but in *War in Val d'Orcia*, Iris Origo, an Anglo-Florentine, painted a dramatic picture of the Tuscan battlefield. Soon after the war, the Welsh poet Dylan Thomas came to Tuscany and was entranced: "The pine hills are endless, the cypresses at the hilltop tell one all about the length of death, the woods are deep as love and full of goats." He apparently enjoyed a hedonistic lifestyle, vegetating in the sun and devouring strawberries and wine.

An enduring love

Tuscany still draws literary pilgrims. Frances Mayes' bestseller, *Under the Tuscan Sun* (1996), brought a fresh wave of American tourists in search of the Tuscan dream. This book and her ensuing memoirs, *Bella Tuscany* (1999) followed by *Every Day in Tuscany* (2010), are only the latest in a long line of tributes penned by besotted foreigners.

Commendable feats of Allied bravery included the penetration of enemy lines via the Vasari Corridor, a secret route used by the Medici in similar crises.

The Allies issued their troops with booklets listing various buildings to be protected, including the tricky prospect of safeguarding the "living museum" of Florence: "The whole city of Florence must rank as a work of art of the first importance." According to one report, "the

"Red belt" Tuscany

Tuscans may be conservative by nature, but they are also fiercely independent. Since World War II, they have tended to vote for right-wing governments nationally, but for left-wing councils locally. Until 1994, this meant Christian Democracy at national level and Communism at regional level. On the surface, this appeared a rather curious recipe for success.

Given the level of national opposition to Communists, the Communist Party evolved an aggressively pro-regionalist stance. The reward was the "red belt" across central Italy, run by

Hitler and Mussolini salute at Florence's Tomb of the Fascist Martyrs.

great monuments, nearly all of which lie north of the river, escaped practically undamaged because, though the enemy held the northern bank against an advance, our troops deliberately refrained from firing upon them".

Despite Allied concern and care, Florence nevertheless lost innumerable bridges, streets, libraries, churches, *palazzi*, paintings and Tuscan lives. But, in contrast to the "mutilated victory" of 1919, Italy lost the war but won the peace.

Massimo Salvatore, a supporter of the partisans in Florence, saw the war as a character-building exercise: "Without it [we] would surely have sunk into a morass of low politics and intrigues." That was still to come.

left-wing coalitions since the first regional elections in 1970. Red Tuscany formed the central strand between Emilia Romagna's model economy and rural Umbria. Despite the transformations in the "new Italy", left-leaning Tuscany survives as one of the most efficient of regional governments.

The Tuscan left believes in a broad but increasingly secular Church. Civic culture, regional pride and fierce individualism form the real faith. The power of the left is as much a reflection of regional hostility to Roman centralisation as an espousal of social democratic principles. Even in "red belt" Tuscany, the region's most popular newspaper is the right-wing but regional *La Nazione*, not the left-wing but national *La Repubblica*. How could a Roman product possibly compete with a Florentine/Sienese masterpiece?

At a national level, however, by the early 1990s, more than 50 post-war "swing door" governments had come and gone. To many observers, the source of this crisis lay in Italy's administration and dubious morality. Senior party leaders tended to die in office, governments suffered from opportunism, not lack of opportunity. *Partitocrazia* (party influence) supplanted democracy, extending from government to public corporations, infiltrating bank-

Party, which had dominated Italian politics since the war, collapsed under the weight of its own corruption. Two former prime ministers – the socialist Bettino Craxi and the Christian Democrat veteran and seven-times former prime minister Giulio Andreotti – were investigated.

Craxi died in self-imposed exile in Tunisia in 2000, while Andreotti, charged with Mafia ties, was eventually acquitted. The appeal judges found Andreotti to have enjoyed "friendly" and direct relations with the Mafia "up until 1980", but not later – so "Beelzebub" escaped prosecution thanks to the statute of limitations.

Paintings from the Uffizi laid out for restoration after the 1966 flood.

ing, the judiciary and media, and the public tacitly condoned this "old boys' network".

Corruption and terror

The early 1990s saw a series of political scandals involving bribes, and the result was the *Mani Pulite* ("Clean Hands") campaign under the fiery leadership of Antonio di Pietro, a former magistrate who became Italy's most popular moral crusader. A vast network was uncovered, in which public contracts were awarded by politicians to businesses in return for bribes. Italian public life was convulsed by the scandal, dubbed *Tangentopoli* – literally, "Bribesville". Dozens of MPs and businessmen were arrested, with others committing suicide. The Christian Democrat

THE FLOODING OF FLORENCE

When the Arno broke its banks in 1966, the havoc caused to the city's heritage was immediate: Santa Croce was soon under water; the Duomo lost sections of its marble facade; panels from the Baptistery doors were swept away; over a million historic books and illuminated manuscripts were destroyed; and countless artworks were damaged. Although most works have been restored to their original state, Cimabue's *Crucifix* in Santa Croce was controversially left semi-restored. Instead of recreating the missing sections of the work, restorers simply painted in the spaces with patches of neutral colour to symbolise the city's "wound".

In the midst of the political upheaval, in May 1993, Florence suffered a devastating blow when a bomb planted by the Mafia behind the Uffizi gallery rocked the city. Five people were killed, priceless paintings and sculptures damaged and a handful destroyed. The Uffizi's buildings were damaged, and several medieval buildings around the corner were virtually destroyed.

The Mafia's aim was to use the attack, and others in Milan and Rome, to force the Italian state into submission, and to agree to a deal of mutual convenience with the Mob, as had been enjoyed with the Christian Democrats. The jailed Sicilian Godfather, Salvatore "Toto" Riina, was sentenced to life for the Uffizi bombing in 1998. Meanwhile, while no area of Italy appeared to have been left untouched by corruption, including Florence, in the end few, if any, *Tangentopoli* politicians served much real time in jail.

In a frank interview in July 2005, the film director Bernardo Bertolucci told the *Corriere della Sera*: "Italy lost a great opportunity after *Tangentopoli*. It should have had a real examination of conscience, in order to understand how on earth it could be that there were so many corrupt figures populating our landscape, accomplices of a system which goes from small tips in return for small favours, to large *tangenti* (bribes) for big contracts. And instead we have wound up with an illegal prime minister, who was elected amid conditions of almost complete control of the media." He was referring to Silvio Berlusconi, the media tycoon-turned-prime minister.

Silvio Berlusconi

Berlusconi, the populist, perma-tanned tycoon, was first elected premier in 1994, on an anti-corruption ticket, and has led two further administrations. Ironically, Berlusconi's career has been dogged by charges of everything from conflict of interests to embezzlement and false accounting. His classic response is that such allegations have been politically motivated by rivals and a biased judiciary.

Clowning, corruption and "bunga bunga" sex scandals aside, Berlusconi has dominated Italian life, as much by his oversize personality as by his

Bettino Craxi, former Prime Minister of Italy.

ECCENTRIC EXPATRIATE COLLECTORS

Anna Maria Gastone, the last of the Medici, left centuries of art treasures and palaces to Florence in perpetuity. In her wake came a succession of patrons who left treasures that can still be seen *in situ* today. Among connoisseurs, the 19th-century race for progress produced an artistic backlash, a desire for escapism coupled with nostalgia for an idealised past. In response, the Florentine foreign collectors pursued a private Arcadia. Often the reaction took the form of a romanticisation of the Gothic era, a period perceived as a heady amalgam of medieval chivalry and costumed romp. Other collectors were inspired by the Florentine heyday, conjuring up a Renaissance stage set.

The art historian Herbert Percy Horne (1864–1916) left his idealised Florentine Renaissance *palazzo* to posterity. Frederick Stibbert (1838–1906) was the classic case of a collector who succumbed to *fin de siècle* aestheticism, leaving behind his museum of armour in a villa steeped in decadent Gothic gloom. Charles Loeser, heir to Macy's store, bequeathed his collection of Old Masters to the Palazzo Vecchio in 1928. The art historian Bernard Berenson (1865–1959) pioneered Renaissance studies and his villa, I Tatti, is now Harvard's Centre for Renaissance Studies. The Anglo-Florentine aesthete Sir Harold Acton (1904–94) left Villa La Pietra, his home and art collection, to New York University.

vast wealth. Some see Berlusconi as a product of Italian culture, tapping into the traditions of patronage and family. The billionaire's business empire spans the media, entertainment, insurance, construction and sport (the tycoon owns AC Milan football club). Berlusconi's fans felt that only a successful businessman could transform a recalcitrant country into a model business. His critics cite conflict of interests, including the media mogul's ownership of three television channels, and undue influence over the public-broadcasting networks. They believe that Berlusconi entered politics to protect his

empire and evade legal charges. The right may wear the trousers in Rome but, almost as a matter of regional pride, far fewer Tuscans voted for Berlusconi than in other regions.

Berlusconi's second term, from 2001–6, made him the only post-war prime minister to govern for a full five-year term. Despite bringing a semblance of stability, the empire-builder narrowly lost out to Romano Prodi in 2006, ceding to a fragile left-wing coalition whose eventual collapse prompted fresh elections. Disillusionment with a lack of leadership from the left led to the right regaining power in 2008, masterminded

Aftermath of the Uffizi bombing.

A TUSCAN HALL OF FAME

There's a saying that Tuscany is "equally blessed by the genius of man and nature". And history has proved the proverb, with the greatest Tuscans achieving worldwide fame. Unsurprisingly, many are from the world of art: Giotto, Leonardo da Vinci, Michelangelo, Donatello, Masaccio and Cellini were all born in or around Florence, as was the architect Brunelleschi. The painter and art historian Giorgio Vasari is famed for his *Lives of the Artists*.

Literary celebrities include the triumvirate of Dante, Petrarch and Boccaccio (born in Paris, but raised in Florence). In the music field, the composer Puccini hailed from Lucca, and opera itself was born

in Florence in the late 1500s. Tuscany was also home to the astronomer Galileo, mathematician Leonardo Fibonacci, political theorist Machiavelli, and merchant-turned-explorer Amerigo Vespucci. Alas, in the banking field, the great Florentines are anonymous, including the creators of the florin *(fiorino)* in 1189, and the inventors of double-entry book-keeping.

Many famous modern-day Tuscans are linked to the fashion world: the late Emilio Pucci, Guccio Gucci and Salvatore Ferragamo (a transplanted Neapolitan), plus Roberto Cavalli. Showbiz representatives include the singer Andrea Bocelli, film-maker Franco Zeffirelli, and comedian Roberto Benigni.

by Berlusconi's People of Freedom party. The flamboyant billionaire businessman was elected on a platform of reducing public spending, lowering taxes, reforming the judiciary, and modernising the infrastructure.

The consensus is that Berlusconi, bogged down by personal scandals and pursuing his own interests, failed to deliver on all fronts. By mid-2011, the country was in a perilous position amid fears that it would fall victim to the eurozone debt crisis. Despite being its third-largest economy, Italy has not embarked on reforms or tackled public debt. After faring badly in local elections in 2011, Berlusconi's chances of surviving until the general elections in 2013 looked slim. He was also involved in four trials, with charges ranging from illegal sex with an underage prostitute to corruption and perverting the course of justice.

After dominating the political scene for 17 years, Berlusconi, the country's longest-serving post-war prime minister stepped down in 2011. Overwhelmed by the scale of Italy's debt crisis, the consummate survivor finally made way for respected economist Mario Monti, who formed a government of technocrats to steer the country through uncharted waters. Monti's time in power was short-lived: his centrist coalition Civic Choice lost the 2013 general elections and he was replaced by Democratic Party's Enrico Letta, whose time in the limelight was even shorter as he resigned in early 2014. A new government was formed by Matteo Renzi, also from the Democratic Party. Renzi was the first ever Italian politician to become prime minister while holding the post of city mayor (2009–14).

Florentine revival

When he was elected Florence's mayor in 2009, Matteo Renzi was the youngest mayor in Italy. He rejuvenated the Tuscan political stage, declaring that Berlusconi's sleazy generation of politicians should stand aside. Apart from introducing merit as the main criterion for council jobs in Florence, Renzi appointed women to half of the posts. Meritocracy has been a bold new concept in such a closed, clubby and recalcitrant political culture. Elected on a platform of making the city cleaner, more liveable and more accountable, the mayor's first public act was to pedestrianise Piazza del Duomo, since extended to other areas, notably Piazza Santa Maria Novella and chic Via de Tornabuoni.

Returning visitors can now savour the Duomo without the din of traffic, apart from the clatter of hooves from the horse-drawn carriages. You can even take in the stripy Gothic facade of Santa Maria Novella without fear of being hit by careering cabs shooting out of the station.

The changes have gone beyond pollution-cutting measures and spruced-up squares. Culturally, the revitalisation was extended to revamped galleries and museums, more cosmopolitan nightlife, and a fresh perception of Florence as a creative, contemporary city, not mired in the past. Bicycles have been made more

Matteo Renzi, former mayor of Florence and now Italy's Prime Minister.

readily available, inspired by schemes in Paris and London, while Segway tours and rickshaw rides have also been encouraged. Museums have become more user-friendly, with longer opening hours and better ticketing. Major galleries have been taking invisible masterpieces out of the store-rooms and put them into the public domain. A "Firenze Card" has finally been introduced, a simple, convenient three-day pass that combines public transport and the top museums. When Renzi was elected prime minister in 2014, he was replaced as Florence's mayor by Dario Nardella, another young and dynamic Democratic Party politician, who has worthily continued his predecessor's work.

RENAISSANCE ART

Art historians divide the Renaissance into three waves: the trecento (1300s) was the era of the workshop and fresco; the quattrocento (1400s) welcomed a new realism featuring perspective and emotion; the cinquecento (1500s), or High Renaissance, was the apogee followed by a sharp decline, as political and economic decay eventually took its toll.

One of the great myths of history provides a kind of Hollywood scenario for the "birth of the Renaissance", linking it to the fall of Constantinople in 1453, when scholars were supposed to have escaped, clutching their precious Greek manuscripts, to Italy. There, these manuscripts became a kind of magical seed, taking root, growing and bearing fruit almost immediately as "the Renaissance".

Of course, this is nonsense; like any other human phenomenon, the Renaissance had roots deep in history. It was the political fragmentation of Italy that created the Renaissance, each little city-state contributing something unique to the whole. But the process certainly started in Florence, and the city dominated the cultural scene until the early 16th century. Again and again over the centuries, attempts have been made to analyse the causes of the Florentine flowering, with reasons ranging from the poverty of the soil to the quality of the light. But it is no more possible to "explain" this than it is any other mystery of the human spirit.

Detail from the Dying Slave (c. 1513), one of four "unfinished" Slaves by Michelangelo (Accademia), intended for the tomb of Pope Julius II.

Defining the Renaissance

The very word "renaissance" is a Florentine invention. In his book *Lives of the Most Excellent Architects, Painters and Sculptors*, first published in 1550, Vasari, first of the art historians, remarks that the reader "will now be able to recognise more easily the progress of [art's] rebirth *(il progresso della sua rinascita)*".

But what, exactly, did Vasari mean by *rinascita*? What was being "reborn"? Vasari was referring to a rebirth of the art and architecture of classical times, that is, before Emperor Constantine transferred the seat of empire to Constantinople at the beginning of the 4th century AD, causing it to become the centre of art and culture. A distinctive architecture, based on Roman models, using bricks and featuring domes and cupolas, was developed. Byzantine art was hierarchical in style, using flattened forms and no perspective.

Architects drew and measured the ruins of the Roman cities, rediscovering their building techniques and their rules of proportion, the "classical orders". Vitruvius's *Ten Books on Architecture*, the only surviving manual from classical times, was studied anew and became the basis, in the 15th century, for Alberti's treatise of the same name.

Painting, which of all the arts is preeminently *the* art of the Renaissance, owed little to antiquity, partly because no Roman examples survived to be used as models. Renaissance artists broke new ground, discovering perspective and observing the natural world that surrounded them. The 14th-century Florentine artist Cennino Cennini gave good advice to his fellow artists. "If you wish to draw mountains well, so that they appear natural," he wrote, "procure some large stones, rocky, not polished, and draw from these." The idea of a handful of stones standing in for the Alps or the Apennines

Detail from the Coronation of the Virgin (c.1330) altarpiece by Giotto (Santa Croce, Florence).

BYZANTINE ART

Byzantine artists covered interiors with mosaics, a Roman decorative device that became a sumptuous art form, with myriad glazed-stone fragments catching the light in a way no fresco ever could. Inspired by cupolas in Constantinople, the best Byzantine art in Italy is in Ravenna, dating from the 5th century. But the style prevailed in 11th-century Venice, and even influenced 13th-century Florence. But to its Florentine critics, notably Vasari, Byzantine art was static and stiffly formalised. It was this aspect that Vasari decried as "a certain residue of the Greeks" – and that was completely overthrown by the Renaissance artists.

might seem ludicrous, but it was a pointer to the new road the artist was taking, the road to reality in nature.

The classical world provided the inspiration for the artist to rise above the narrow medieval world, with its emphasis on theological studies. But, once he had started, he went his own way. What was reborn was an artistic sensibility but not a recycled past.

The trecento

Until the quattrocento (15th century), the term "artist" had no particular significance, being virtually interchangeable with "artisan" or "craftsman". All were members of guilds, or *arti:* there was an *arte* for the shoemaker, no more and no less valid than the *arte* for the goldsmith, itself a subdivision of the immensely powerful Silk Guild. Everything was linked to the power of the guilds and the emergence of artistic workshops.

The growing popularity of the process known as *buon fresco* also demanded a cooperative approach. The medium of fresco painting had been introduced about a century earlier, and time had shown that it was the most permanent of all forms of mural art to date, since the colouring became an intrinsic part of the plaster itself.

In addition to large commissions, the workshop (or *bottega*) would produce a variety of smaller articles for sale, ranging from painted scabbards to holy pictures and statues. There was widespread demand for religious art, which provided the bread and butter for hundreds of small *botteghe*. A peasant might have scraped together enough for a tiny picture; a parish priest might have a large sum at his disposal to commission a mural or even an altarpiece; or a wealthy merchant might be anxious to propitiate fate and show an appropriate level of piety.

The potential client had little interest in the identity of the craftsmen producing his order. But, if expensive colours were used (gold, silver, or blue made from the semi-precious lapis lazuli), then the fact was clearly stated in the contract, along with the date of delivery of the finished piece. Commissioned work was almost invariably recorded in a contract that, in addition, usually specified how many figures were to appear in the finished painting, as well as their activities and attributes. Sacred art touched on the delicate area of religious orthodoxy, and the wise craftsman ensured that his client stated exactly what he wanted.

The identity of most of the workers in the *botteghe* is unknown. They were conscientious and skilled, rather than brilliant, but they formed the subsoil from which the genius of the quattrocento could flourish. The actual working pattern of the *bottega*, whereby a group of lesser craftsmen would paint the main body of a picture, leaving it to the identified master to put the finishing touches to it, would continue into the High Renaissance, the cinquecento. This made it difficult, at times impossible, for the most skilled art critic to say that such a painting was, beyond a doubt, the work of a particular famous artist.

Early Renaissance art

Comparing trecento (or Gothic) paintings in any Tuscan art gallery with the work of quattrocento (or early Renaissance) artists reveals a compelling difference: whereas Gothic paintings are iconographic, revelling in the use of celestial gold and presenting a spiritual Madonna and Child for worship and contemplation, the same subject in the hands of Renaissance painters becomes a study in living flesh, the figures of mother and child endowed with attitudes, character, emotions and psychological motivation. Scholars argue endlessly about why this great change occurred, but there is near-universal agreement on who started it: Giotto di Bondone (1267–1337), who, according to Vasari, "restored art to the better path followed in modern times".

But Giotto was not entirely alone in injecting life, and naturalism, into art. Nicola (1223–84) and Giovanni (1245–1314) Pisano the father-and-son team, were achieving similar advances in sculpture at the same time as Giotto was breaking new ground in art.

When the Pisani were living and working in Pisa, it was the fashion for Pisan merchants to ship home Roman sarcophagi from the Holy Land or North Africa for eventual reuse as their own tombs. Scores of them still line the cloister surrounding Pisa's Campo Santo cemetery. Inspired by the realistic battle scenes carved on these antique marble tombs, the Pisani created their own versions: great pulpits sculpted with dramatic scenes from the life of Christ,

which can be seen in Pisa's cathedral, and in Sant'Andrea church in Pistoia.

In architecture, the classical inspiration that helped to define the Renaissance had never disappeared to quite the same degree as it had in art. The very term Romanesque – meaning derived from or in the Roman style – indicates the essential continuity between the architecture of Rome and that of Tuscany in the 1300s. Churches were still built to the same basilican plan as those of the late Roman period, and, though the facades of many Tuscan churches look quite unclassical,

Scene from the Life of St Nicholas (c.1327–30) by Lorenzetti (Uffizi).

THE GUILDS

The guilds extended their control over the decorative as well as the practical arts. Sculptors and architects were enrolled with the masons, and painters formed a subdivision of the apothecaries, as they needed a grasp of chemistry to prepare their colours. Far from resenting the obligation to join associations, painters and sculptors formed their own groups, or *compagnie*, within larger guilds. This meant members could help one another, sharing profits and losses. Increased teamwork also meant that several men might be engaged at successive stages in the shaping of a pillar, from rough hewing to final carving, conveyor-belt style.

they are still based on the geometry of the Roman hemispherical arch, as distinct from the four-centred arches of Venice or the pointed arches of French Gothic. What distinguishes Tuscan Romanesque from Lombardic or Piedmontese is the exuberant use of polychrome marble to create complex geometrical patterns. Pisa was the seminal influence here – trade links with Spain and North Africa led to the adoption of Arabic numerals in place of Roman, and to the fondness for surface patterning in architecture, copying Moorish tilework and textiles. From Pisa the oriental influence spread to Lucca, Prato, Pistoia, and even to Florence, where it was to pave the way for the great polychrome Campanile designed by Giotto.

The quattrocento

A great breakthrough took place in Florence at the beginning of the 15th century, a moment so important that it can be dated to within a few years, and a new philosophy of life flowed through the city. Until the 1470s, Florence was a dynamo, providing light and energy for the entire peninsula. The city retained its dominance in art for barely a lifespan, however, because it exported so much of its native talent – which ensured the spread of Renaissance values but, with them, ensured Florence's own relative eclipse.

The breakthrough began when the Florentine *Signoria*, or government, decided to refurbish the ceremonial centre of Florence: the group of buildings consisting of the cathedral, the Campanile – begun by Giotto in 1334 and finished after his death but to his design in 1359 – and the octagonal Baptistery. This little black-and-white building had a special place in Florentine affections, and when, in 1401, it was decided to offer a thanksgiving for the city's escape from plague, the Baptistery was chosen to benefit. The wealthy Wool Guild announced that it would finance the design and casting of a second set of bronze doors that would be even grander than those of Pisano. The design for them was thrown open to competition.

Out of the many entrants, seven were chosen, each to execute a panel on the same

Adoration of the Magi (1423) by Gentile da Fabriano (Uffizi).

GIOTTO DI BONDONE

Tradition has it that Giotto (1267–1337) was working as a shepherd boy until Cimabue, himself a pioneer of greater naturalism in art, discovered that Giotto could draw a perfect circle freehand, and offered to train him as an artist. Pupil soon surpassed master, and Giotto went on to create the great *St Francis* fresco cycle in the Upper Basilica in Assisi and the *Life of Christ* fresco series in the Scrovegni Chapel in Padua. In Florence, his main masterpiece adorns the Franciscan church of Santa Croce, where his work covers the walls of the two chapels to the right of the choir. To measure the breadth of the Giotto revolution, it is enough to compare his frescoes with the static 13th-century altarpiece nearby.

Despite Giotto's supposedly rural background, in his work nature is formalised and subservient to humanity. It is the figures who occupy the foreground, vibrantly *alive*. Giotto was ahead of his time in introducing character and individuality to his art. Straddling two ages, Giotto has been claimed both as a Gothic artist and as the pioneer of the Renaissance. Perhaps if war and the Black Death had not ravaged Europe from the 1340s, the Renaissance might well have blossomed sooner than it did. As it was, another 60 years were to pass before the naturalism pioneered by Giotto was to re-emerge, this time as a mass artistic movement.

subject: the sacrifice of Isaac. Two of the entrants, the 21-year-old Brunelleschi, later credited as the creator of the "Renaissance style" in architecture, and the 20-year-old Lorenzo Ghiberti, produced work that caused considerable difficulty to the judges. Both the panels exist today, one preserved in the Museo dell'Opera del Duomo, the other in the Bargello museum. Comparing the two, posterity finds it impossible to say which is "better". The *Syndics*, at a loss to choose, came up with a compromise, suggesting that the artists should share the work. Brunelleschi

Learning from the ancients

Meanwhile, in Rome with his friend Donatello, Brunelleschi was discovering how the ancients had built their enormous structures. In an entirely new approach to the past, he examined originals rather than copies of copies. One of his findings – or, possibly, inventions – was the *ulivella*. Intrigued and puzzled by the existence of regular-shaped holes in the huge stone blocks of the ancient buildings, he assumed that they had been made to allow the block to be gripped by some device, and designed a kind of grappling iron to fit. Whether or not

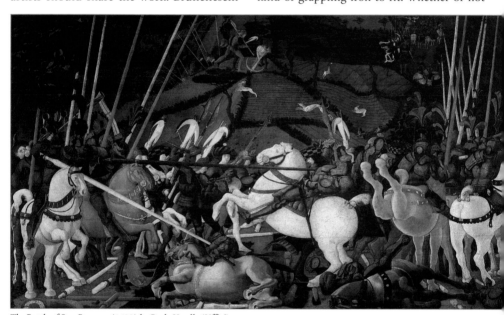

The Battle of San Romano (1432) by Paolo Uccello (Uffizi).

declined and set out for Rome, while Ghiberti began work on the doors, completing them 22 years later.

He was offered the commission to produce a second pair: these took him 27 years. During the almost half-century that he worked on the project, it is possible to see in his contracts the changing status of the artist. In the first contract he is treated essentially as an artisan, expected to put in a full day's work "like any journeyman".

In later contracts for his employment, he is treated far more as a free agent, permitted to undertake commissions for other work. Ghiberti, too, made explicit this change by boldly including his own self-portrait among the reliefs on the door.

the Romans had actually used such a device, it was very useful – and a demonstration of the benefits to be gained by studying the past.

Brunelleschi returned to Florence at about the time that the *Syndics* of the Wool Guild, who also had the responsibility for the cathedral, were puzzling over the problem of completing it. Arnolfo di Cambio had begun it in 1296, and it had been completed, all except for the dome, by 1369. Nobody knew how to bridge this immense gap, which, for half a century, had been covered by a temporary roof.

In 1417, a special meeting was called to debate the problem and consider suggestions, and Brunelleschi put forward his solution. He was mocked for it because it dispensed with the wooden centring over which architects traditionally built their arches and vaults, supporting their weight until the keystone was in place. But, in desperation, the *Syndics* offered him the job. Brunelleschi solved the problem by building a dome that was pointed in sections, supported by ribs with the lightest possible in-filling between them. He built two shells, an outer skin and an inner one: one way in which the crushing weight of the dome, the problem that had prevented its construction, was considerably reduced.

The work took 16 years, and was completed on 31 August 1436. This was the first Renais-

Trinity (c.1425) by Masaccio, the pioneer of perspective (both in Santa Maria Novella, Florence)

sance dome in Italy, the largest unsupported dome in Europe, bigger than the Pantheon in Rome, which Brunelleschi had studied, bigger even than the great dome that Michelangelo raised a century later over St Peter's in Rome.

It was Brunelleschi's successor, the scholar Alberti, who first applied the classical orders to domestic architecture and created what we now think of as the Renaissance palazzo. Whereas Brunelleschi introduced the columns, pediments and cornices he copied from Roman ruins into his churches, there were no surviving examples of Roman domestic architecture for the 15th-century Florentines to copy. When Rucellai, a wealthy Florentine merchant, asked

Alberti to design a palace for him, Alberti took as a model the Colosseum in Rome and applied its tiers of arches to the facade of a three-storey palazzo. Although it was the only palazzo he built, and though Brunelleschi's design for the Medici Palace never got beyond the model stage, these two architects developed a new type of building, a system of proportion and an elegance of line that is still in use today.

Brunelleschi's other major breakthrough was his use of perspective. Alberti described its effect to a generation for whom it appeared almost a magical technique: "I describe a rectangle of whatever size I wish, which I imagine to be an open window through which I view whatever is to be depicted there." Donatello (1386–1466) eagerly used the technique in his bas-relief of *Salome Offering John's Head to Herod*. The observer is looking at a banquet where the diners are recoiling in horror from the offering. Beyond the banqueting rooms can be seen a succession of two more rooms, giving a remarkable and, for contemporaries, almost eerie sense of depth.

A new perspective

Like the difference between Giotto's mobile, dramatic figures and their static, formal predecessors, perspective gave a new vista to civilisation. Its most dramatic form was that employed by the young Masaccio. His great painting of the *Trinity*, in the church of Santa Maria Novella, is an intellectual exercise in the use of perspective that is also infused with religious awe. Beneath a trompe l'oeil classical arch stands the immense figure of God the Father, half-supporting a cross on which there is an equally immense figure of Christ; below them are various saints and donors and a memento mori of a skeleton in a sarcophagus revealing an ancient warning: "I am what you are, and what I am, you shall be."

The huge figures stand out from the background and appear to loom over the observer. As a young man, Michelangelo used to stand before these, copying them again and again to fix the style in his mind. Eventually, therefore, some essence of this experimental period of the Renaissance found its way into the Sistine Chapel, that shrine of the High Renaissance dominated by Michelangelo's work.

The classical arch in Masaccio's painting is a pointer to a curious development that took place during the quattrocento – the clothing of biblical figures in a totally anachronistic way, either in classical Roman attire or in contemporary Florentine dress. The frescoes that Ghirlandaio (1449–94) painted in the Sasseti Chapel within the church of Santa Trinità supposedly concern the prophecies of Christ's birth, and the location should be Augustan Rome. But it is a Rome that bears a remarkably close resemblance to 15th-century Florence, and the people waiting for the awesome news are all citizens of Florence in normal dress. Lorenzo de' Medici is there, as is his mother, his children, friends and various colleagues.

Early Renaissance painters were preoccupied with technique. Their subject matter remained largely unchanged: religion was still the most important concern. But in the second half of the quattrocento a new, exciting and somewhat disturbing element began to appear: the mythological and the allegorical. The supreme practitioner in this field was Sandro Botticelli, who worked with Leonardo da Vinci in Verrocchio's workshop but developed in a totally different direction.

La Primavera (1478) by Botticelli (Uffizi).

BOTTICELLI'S SPRING

La Primavera (1478) is Sandro Botticelli's most famous painting – and certainly the most mysterious of the Early Renaissance. Hung in the Uffizi, it depicts nine supernatural creatures placed in an exquisite natural setting. On the left, a young man is pointing at something. Next to him a group of grave-faced women are performing a solemn ritual dance. On the right is the only figure who seems to be aware of the observer: Botticelli's stunningly beautiful "mystery" woman with a provocative half-smile. Beside her what appears to be an act of violence adds a discordant note: a bluish figure is leaning out of the trees and clutching at a startled girl.

In the background, but dominating the whole, is the most enigmatic figure: a pale woman whose expression has been variously described as frowning, smiling and melancholy; whose stance has also been described in conflicting ways, as dancing, as that of a consumptive, as pregnant and as offering a blessing. The figure is claimed to be both Venus and the Virgin Mary. Botticelli was trying to restate classical mythology in Christian terms while remaining true to the original – and to his own quirky self. However, he was later influenced by the gloomy, savage friar Savonarola and, almost overnight, ceased his joyous mythological paintings, concentrating instead on orthodox religious subjects.

The High Renaissance

Even to the untutored eye, there is a profound difference between the work produced before and after the 1520s in Tuscany and elsewhere, most noticeably in Florence. Partly this was the result of an immense political crisis. Italy had become a battleground, invaded again and again by warring foreigners. In 1527 a savage army, composed partly of mercenaries, sacked Rome and held the pope to ransom. Italy was never to recover from that experience, which was the curtain-raiser for a period of foreign domination that would not come to an end until the 1800s.

From the middle of the 16th century, Florentine artists tended to be court artists, dancing attendance on the Medici dukes. Among them was the artist-turned-art historian Giorgio Vasari (1511–74).

Until recently, Vasari's work as an artist was dismissed almost as contemptuously as his work as an art historian was received enthusiastically. However, posterity owes him a debt of gratitude, both as an architect and as a painter. In 2011, worldwide celebrations to mark the fifth centenary of his birth provoked a re-evaluation of his artistry. Not only did he

Birth of John the Baptist (1485) by Ghirlandaio.

The apogee of the Renaissance – in Florence, at least – was ushered in with Leonardo da Vinci and Michelangelo. But the decline swiftly followed, particularly when Michelangelo and Raphael left for Rome, to work for Pope Julius II. Other artists followed suit: the major Florentine families – other than the Medici – could no longer afford to make commissions, so the art scene moved on.

Shortly after the sack of Rome, the Medici Pope Clement VII clamped down on his native city of Florence, ending republicanism and preparing the way for the first dukedom. Meanwhile, in the world of art, the glory was departing from Florence, as the impetus of the Renaissance shifted to Rome and Venice.

build the Uffizi for Duke Cosimo I, and the Vasari Corridor, but he frescoed the interior of Brunelleschi's dome. Vasari also remodelled the Palazzo Vecchio and decorated its parliamentary chamber, the great Salone dei Cinquecento, with outstanding contemporary representations of the city and its surrounding countryside.

Leonardo da Vinci

Although the glory was departing from Florence, the sunset was stupendous. It could scarcely be otherwise with two such giants as Michelangelo and Leonardo still on the scene. Leonardo, born in 1452, trained in Verrocchio's *bottega*, thus carrying the medieval systems on into the new era. One of Vasari's anecdotes claims that Verrocchio, on seeing his young apprentice's work, laid down his brush and never painted again. Unlikely though the incident is, the anecdote shows that Leonardo was recognised as being almost a freakish genius in his own lifetime.

Leonardo left Florence for Milan at the age of 30. He returned in 1502 when commissioned by the *Signoria* to create the great mural, the *Battle of Anghiari* in the Council Chamber, and eventually crossed the Alps to become court painter to François I of France. His contribution to the history of ideas is incalculable, but his legacy in Tuscany is restricted to several Madonnas and the unfinished paintings of the *Battle of Anghiari* and the *Adoration of the Kings*, all in the Uffizi. The two best-known masterpieces, the *Mona Lisa*, set against an exquisite Tuscan background, and the *Virgin of the Rocks*, are in Paris and London respectively. However, there is at least a museum of his fantastical creations in Florence, which displays working models of his flying machines, armoured tanks and swing bridges, all before his time (see page 92).

Michelangelo is another story, however. His greatest work, the Sistine Chapel, is also situated outside Florence, but he did leave an enduring imprint upon his home city, in the form of the walls that gird it and the sculptures that grace it.

Michelangelo

Michelangelo was nearly a generation younger than Leonardo, born in 1475 when the

Renaissance was approaching its apogee. His father was a poor but proud country gentleman who disapproved of the idea of his son becoming an artisan or artist; in his mind, there was no clear distinction. Indeed, Michelangelo was apt to be touchy on the subject. Although he served his apprenticeship in a *bottega*, he later rejected the idea that he touted for trade: "I was never a painter or a sculptor like those who set up shop for the purpose."

Michelangelo was just 18 when Lorenzo de' Medici died in 1492. Florence was plunged into chaos, because Lorenzo's son, Piero, was

A sketch in charcoal by Leonardo (Uffizi).

MICHELANGELO IN FLORENCE

A Vasari anecdote describes how a 13-year-old Michelangelo Buonarroti (1475–1564) made a drawing of the tools in the workshop. His master, Ghirlandaio, was so impressed that he told Lorenzo de' Medici, who invited Michelangelo to enter his princely household and study with his own children.

Michelangelo also worked for the next 40 years on a thankless task: the great tomb for his patron, Pope Julius II. The unfinished statues for this tomb, the famous *Slaves*, are now in Florence's Accademia gallery. Five centuries later, the sculptor's technique is still clearly visible; shallow depressions surrounding the figure, made by the rounded head of a chisel, seem to

be "freeing" the figures.

Florence boasts many statues by Michelangelo; although often unfinished, they always reveal the chisel strokes of a master. They include the iconic *David*, and the statues of *Dawn, Evening, Day* and *Night* in the Medici Chapel. Florence's Casa Buonarroti (Via Ghibellina), once owned by Michelangelo, showcases the sculptor's working drawings and a few early works. The quintessential Renaissance man is not fully represented here, either in spirit or in sculpture. Still, thanks to his descendants, the palace conveys the atmosphere of a family home and remains a touching tribute to the great sculptor, painter, architect and poet.

extravagant and unpopular, and the Florentines chased the tyrant out of the city. The artist's links with the Medici were no longer so advantageous, and so he took the road to Rome, where the Sistine Chapel awaited. Although Michelangelo is remembered as a painter and sculptor, he was also a gifted engineer and a poet of a good deal of sensitivity and insight.

Cellini

Michelangelo was just 25 when Benvenuto Cellini was born in 1500. Like so many of

decadence that his best-known work would be the elaborate golden salt cellar crafted for François I of France.

Raphael

Raphael (Raffaello) was a gentle, handsome young man who seemed to have no enemies. Born in Umbria in 1483, he received his basic training in the workshop of Perugino, working on frescoes in Perugia. In 1500, at the impressionable age of 17, he came to Florence, where he absorbed the works of Michelangelo and Leonardo da Vinci (who returned to the city

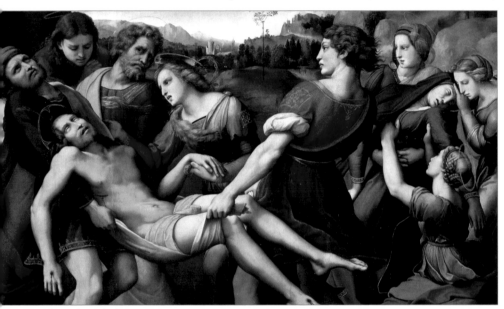

Entombment by Raphael.

the artists of his time, Cellini was a jack of all trades – including, improbably enough, a gunner. He played a role in the tragic sack of Rome which, in effect, brought the Renaissance to an end. Acting as gunner in defence of the Vatican, he assured his supporters that the pope promised him absolution "for all the murders that I should commit".

In Florence, his most famous work is that beautiful but curiously heartless statue of *Perseus Slaying Medusa*, commissioned by Cosimo I for the statue-filled Loggia dei Lanzi on the Piazza della Signoria – a message to anyone in Florence who dared to resist the might of the Medici. But it is indicative both of Cellini and of the enveloping atmosphere of artistic

from 1500 to 1506). Raphael eventually left Florence in 1508, attracted to Rome by the fiery new Pope Julius II, who was planning a series of architectural embellishments to the Vatican. There the young Raphael made a mark by painting the series of rooms known as the Stanze della Segnatura, generally regarded as his greatest masterpiece. Under Julius II's successor, the Medici Pope Leo X, he was placed in charge of archaeological excavations in Rome itself.

Thus, the last true artist of the Renaissance introduced into the mother city of Europe that passionate search for the past that had triggered the Renaissance in Florence nearly two centuries earlier.

Literary Classics

"Florentine firsts" are not restricted to the art world – Dante, Italy's finest poet, and Machiavelli, the first political theorist, are just two names to conjure with.

In a crowded field, three towering figures provide some orientation to Tuscan literature. Dante, Petrarch and Machiavelli follow each other chronologically and, as each caused, as well as recorded, great changes, it is possible to plot the course of the region's history through them.

Dante

Born in 1265, Dante was an exact contemporary of Giotto, whose work he admired. But where Giotto kept out of politics, Dante involved himself wholeheartedly and was exiled for his pains. *The Divine Comedy*, which deals with the great mysteries of religion, had a profound effect on Italian thought.

Petrarch

Francesco Petrarch, though a Florentine, was born in Arezzo, where his parents had been exiled during the same feuds that caused Dante's expulsion. Petrarch was one of the first to retrieve the lost classical literature that helped to usher in the Renaissance. He travelled widely, had an enormous circle of friends and it was often through his letters that the "new learning" was disseminated. In poetry, he devised the sonnet form that took his name – Petrarchan – which was greatly to influence the poets of Elizabethan England.

Machiavelli

Niccolò Machiavelli was born in 1469. Viewed from almost any angle, his life appears a failure. As a career diplomat, he never wielded real authority. As a republican, he was obliged to curry favour with the openly despotic Medici. In his political writings, the tone is ice-cold, logical, in total command. In real life, he was lecherous and adulterous. But he was, nonetheless, a realist who exposed the immorality of leaders. *The Prince* is still treated as a political manual today. Classic advice includes: "When neither their property nor their honour is touched, the majority

of men live content"; "It is better to be feared than loved, if you cannot be both" and "A prudent man should always follow in the path trodden by great men and imitate those who are most excellent."

Other luminaries

Although innovations in literature were less spectacular than in art and architecture, there are a number of outstanding "firsts". Francesco Guicciardini wrote the first true *History of Italy*, and Giovanni Boccaccio (1313–75) produced Europe's first novel, *The Decameron*, a collection of tales

Dante and the Divine Comedy in Florence's Duomo.

told by 10 young aristocrats who retreat from the plague that struck Florence in 1348. Staying in a country house, they spend the time telling erotic stories and reciting poems, and poking fun at the clergy. All the stories demonstrate Boccaccio's well-honed skills as a storyteller.

Finally, there were the true "Renaissance men" who mastered both art and literature – as exemplified by Michelangelo's poetry and Cellini's swashbuckling *Autobiography*. Cellini, a brilliant sculptor and soldier, was also a superb writer and wrote an account of the casting of the exquisite bronze sculpture *Perseus* for the Loggia dei Lanzi. At a crucial moment, he ran out of metal and had to throw in the family pewter in order to complete the statue.

ARCHITECTURAL TREASURES

Tuscany combines a rich urban heritage
with a delightful rural legacy, to create
a unique architectural tableau.

C uriously, Tuscan architecture is characterised as much by diversity as it is by
harmony: harmony in its aesthetic sweet-
ness; diversity in its range of buildings, from
Romanesque cathedrals to Renaissance palaces,
town halls to tower-houses.

Tuscan town halls

Civic architecture is particularly rich. The Tuscan town hall, with accompanying bell tower,
encapsulates a civic ideal. In the past, it promised a degree of democracy to the merchant
guilds, the nobility and the people. The Palazzo
del Comune, known by different names, has
been the seat of local government since medieval times. This imposing, fortified building
dominates the square today, as surely as it has
always dominated the lives of local citizens. The
best known is the fortress-like Palazzo Vecchio
in Florence, its austerity belying its palatial interior. However, even the smallest commune has a
grand town hall. In the Mugello, Palazzo Vicari
in Scarperia resembles Palazzo Vecchio, with its
impressive 14th-century merlons and corbels.
Such public palazzi are often studded with
stemmata, stone-carved coats of arms belonging
to prominent citizens or noble clans.

In numerous cities, including San Gimignano,
there is also an adjoining balcony known as the
arengo, from which politicians would harangue
the crowd. Nearby is usually a loggia, providing
shelter from the sun or rain, as well as a meeting
place, today often used as a small market. Thus,
Tuscany's grandest buildings serve much the
same purpose today as they have always done.

Urbanisation

Visually, urban Tuscany is the product of medieval and Renaissance builders, even if Roman

The Abbazia di Monte Oliveto Maggiore.

and Etruscan stones were recycled. Dismissing
the Middle Ages as a period of decadence and
decay does an injustice to the region's prosperity and architectural heritage. In Tuscany, the
period represented a marked social rebirth, with
the flowering of independent city-states in the
11th century. By 1200, most towns had become
burgeoning centres with distinctive identities
and a civic pride evident in the grandiose town
halls and tower-houses. The medieval cathedrals
and civic buildings were a testament to the citizens' refined taste, just as the ordered country
estates later became a Renaissance symbol of
peace and prosperity.

The medieval "skyscrapers" of San Gimignano signified the civilising effect of urban

living, with the *signori* (feudal lords) encouraged to relinquish their castles for city life. The *borgo*, or fortified city, was also home to landowners and merchants, particularly with the rise of the *popolo grasso*, the wealthy middle class in the 14th century. The medieval city became a symbol of safety during the city-state conflicts.

Tuscan Romanesque

This style is less solemn, less philosophical than French, English or German Romanesque. Its hallmarks are surface decoration and space

world. As a result, the severe colonnaded galleries owe much to Norman models, while Sicily inspires the seductive decoration, including exuberant arabesques. A hallmark of the style was its talent for selecting a theatrical space: in Pisa the main buildings present a unified whole, placed on the lawn like prisms on a baize cloth.

Medieval cityscape

Given the rich Roman heritage that was available to them, Tuscans did not take to Gothic gables and sheer verticality, but preferred

Pisa's glorious "Square of Miracles" at night.

rather than sobriety and solidity, with simple bricks transformed by a marble veneer. The style, centred on Florence, favours contrasting patterns of dark and light marble as well as striking geometric designs. The form was first realised in the city baptistery, with its round-headed arches, classical proportions and a striving for weightlessness. The Florentine model retains a certain simplicity of form, contrasting the austerity of Romanesque with the traditional Tuscan love of polychrome marble patterns.

Pisan Romanesque is more eclectic, as befits its cosmopolitan heritage. The maritime republic of Pisa was an 11th-century power, trading with northern Europe and the Muslim

MARBLE CATHEDRALS

The cathedrals of Siena, Pistoia, Florence, Prato and Lucca use stripes and an interplay of light and shade. The geometry of multicoloured marble is quintessentially Tuscan, striking visitors as bold or brash, spellbinding or superfluous. The palette contrasts white marble from Carrara, rosy pink from Maremma and dark green from Prato. The predominant Pisan style combines a Tuscan taste for marble with an austere Norman Romanesque form, inspired by a Moorish Sicilian aesthetic. The Pisan Duomo was the prototype, with its contrasting bands of colour, blind arcading, colonnaded gallery and, of course, the geometry of inlaid marble.

symmetry instead, balancing height with breadth. In great churches such as Santa Croce in Florence, naves and aisles are not vaulted, but use the open trusses favoured by Romanesque architecture.

Not that Gothic gables are a guide to a medieval atmosphere, of course. Many Tuscan towns are authentically medieval, as is the case with Cortona, Lucca, San Gimignano and Volterra. As the largest medieval city in Europe, Siena is arguably the most authentic of them all, with strict building regulations in place since the 13th century. Certainly, its Gothic spirit is intact,

the massive *fortezza* in Siena and Montalcino, both of which have now been converted into wine-tasting centres.

Tower-houses were castle residences serving as both warehouses and fortresses, self-sufficient enclaves symbolising the wealth and influence of the feudal nobles or prosperous merchants and their scorn for civil authority. Key features of these grand buildings included a well for a constant water supply, an inner courtyard to provide light and ventilation, and an external staircase to the *piano nobile*, the grand residential first floor.

Piazza Salimbeni, Siena.

The Basilica of Santa Croce in Florence.

from red-brick palaces to herringbone alleys, all moulded to a mystical Sienese sensibility.

Tuscan fortifications

Fortifications played an important role in medieval Tuscany. Walled towns, often known as *borghi* and built on hilltops, so that advancing enemies would be easily spotted, are emblematic of the Tuscan cityscape. Anghiari, Buonconvento, Monteriggioni and Montepulciano all provide proof that walls help preserve a distinct identity. The region abounds in ruined or restored examples, including castles at Poppi and Prato, and the pair of fortresses in Florence. Siena province alone boasts San Gimignano's *rocca* and watchtowers, as well as

PERFECT PIENZA

Florence may be the most innovative Renaissance city, but Pienza is the best preserved. Built by Pius II as a papal city, Pienza brought both an echo of imperial patronage and a humanist memorial to his papacy. In 1462, the architect Rossellino grafted a monumental Renaissance core on to medieval grandiosity. All civic life revolves around one tiny square which, using a wellhead as the lynchpin, embraces an episcopal palace, a town hall with an airy loggia, and culminates with a bold tower embodying Tuscan pride. In his private palace here, the pope delighted in hanging gardens, delicate loggias and rooms for every season.

In medieval Tuscan architecture, a castello was a fortified village or a castle, a rocca was a defended garrison post, and a fortezza was a fortress of strategic importance.

Medieval domestic architecture

As the great Tuscan families grew wealthy on banking and the cloth trade, their homes became more palatial and domesticated. In time, decorative details were added, notably graceful courtyards complete with sculpted

the new humanist spirit, architects designed gracious private palaces as proof of their revivalist skills, not simply as symbols of patrician pride. Foremost amongst the trailblazers was Michelozzi (1396–1472), who pursued the architectural principles of Alberti and Brunelleschi. Michelozzo designed the Florentine Palazzo Medici-Riccardi, the Medici home and banking headquarters, a massive mansion with an arcaded inner courtyard. He also designed Palazzo Pitti (1444), the prototype of a patrician palace, boasting strict classical proportions and a rusticated facade.

The fortified town of Monteriggioni.

wells, coats of arms, ornate arches and a loggia above. The Florentine Palazzo Davanzati preserves much of its medieval atmosphere, from its iron-bolted doors and formidable facade to an internal courtyard boasting a well with a pulley system designed to supply water to each floor. The interior presents a charming portrait of domestic life, from 15th-century frescoes and tapestries to the *cassoni*, Tuscan wedding chests, and even a privileged child's bathroom.

Renaissance palaces

The Florentine palazzo was a direct descendant of the tower-house, but without an outmoded defensive function. In keeping with

Yet there are lingering traces of feudal times in the Gothic windows and heavy cornices. Built for Cosimo de' Medici, Palazzo Pitti clearly symbolises the power and prestige of the owner.

However, some nobles simply modernised their feudal seats. Palazzo Spini-Ferroni, a crenellated three-tiered fortress close to the Arno, was a 13th-century watchtower before becoming a palatial home. Just around the corner looms the grandiose Palazzo Strozzi, a rusticated stone cube of mammoth proportions built for the greatest banking dynasty. Rustication was intended to underline the Strozzi's power. Whereas Palazzo Strozzi emphasises strength and stability, homes such as Palazzo Rucellai were more harmonious, embellished with elegant loggias, classical motifs and decorative friezes.

Renaissance architects

As the cradle of the Renaissance, Tuscany is where the profession of architect first came into its own. Imbued with a new humanist spirit, architects of the stature of Brunelleschi, Alberti, Michelozzo, Rossellino and Sangallo made their mark on churches, palaces and villas. Florence, which saw itself as the inheritor of Roman grandeur, is the Tuscan city with the greatest concentration of Renaissance monuments. Strongly influenced by Tuscan Romanesque, the buildings were models of visual restraint, dedicated to proportion, perspective and classical motifs. Brunelleschi (1377–1446), the father of Renaissance architecture, left his masterpiece on the Duomo in Florence. His spectacular dome was the fulfilment of the Renaissance ideal, an astounding feat of Florentine engineering.

Alberti (1404–72) rivalled Brunelleschi in his gift for geometry and desire to revive "the immutable laws of architecture", yet also

Arezzo's stately main square.

SACRED SIGHTS

Religious architecture is one of the highlights of Tuscany. Any tour would certainly take in the cathedrals of Florence, Lucca, Pisa and Siena. Lesser-known gems include Barga's Romanesque cathedral, Montepulciano's Renaissance San Biagio and the Romanesque San Miniato al Monte in the Florentine hills. Given city rivalries, Tuscan Romanesque delights in distinctive regional variations, as in the differentiated stripes and arcading in Lucca. In San Michele the chiselled style of the delicate colonnades emphasises the height and exuberance of the facade. In many cases, architecture is inextricably bound up with artistic wealth on the walls, as in Santa Maria Novella in Florence or Arezzo's San Francesco.

However, exteriors can be austere or unfinished, a sign that patrons argued or ran out of funds.

Setting is also significant, with cathedrals usually constructed on spots hallowed since Roman or Etruscan times. Mendicant churches were often built outside city walls, with surrounding squares becoming major city markets. Abbeys and monasteries, often as large as medieval towns, were built on new sites, and blended civic and Christian concerns. Some good examples are the Romanesque abbey of Sant'Antimo the Baroque Certosa di Pisa, the Carthusian foundation of Camaldoli; and the Benedictine Monte Oliveto Maggiore, in the woods south of Siena.

respected the Tuscan taste for decoration. As an architectural historian, he revived Vitruvius's theories and put them into practice in Florence. The laws of proportion, perspective and the use of the classical orders all came into play in the Duomo and in the Florentine Palazzo Rucellai (1446). This landmark palace was inspired by the Colosseum and classical Rome. The Roman influence is present in the porches and panelled doors, as well as in the frieze. The magnificent Rucellai loggia was the last to be built in 15th-century Florence, such was the profligacy it engendered. Weddings and festivities in the loggia may be no more, but the family remains ensconced in the palace.

Rural retreats

Tuscany's rich urban heritage risks overshadowing the delightful rural legacy of sunny villas and picturesque hilltop farmhouses. In medieval Tuscany, the traditional battlemented manor or fortified seat evolved into the gracious villa residence of Renaissance times. In the 13th century, there were two forms of rural retreat, the feudal domain – the grand preserve of the landed nobility – and the *casa da signore*, the hub of a country estate. This was a crenellated property with a watchtower, surrounded by farm buildings and cottages, and owned by the gentry or bourgeoisie.

The villa as a country retreat was a Renaissance concept, reflecting the gracious rural lifestyle cultivated by the Tuscan nobility, even today. The villas were mostly elegant but unostentatious, reflecting the cultural conservatism of the Florentine nobility. However, the grandest Medici villas, such as Cafaggiolo, designed by Michelozzo, were sumptuous princely estates. Poggio a Caiano is the model Renaissance villa, with its harmonious design and colonnaded loggia harking back to the grandeur of classical times. The rural design reflected a desire for symmetry and a rationalisation of form and function. Embellished by

porticoes, the villa was built on a square plan around an inner courtyard, with a loggia on the first floor. Set in ornamental gardens and encircled by walls, the villa enjoyed superb views, often from a hilltop.

At a time when peace reigned in the Tuscan countryside, the gardens were regarded as a bucolic retreat, featuring a *giardino segreto*, a geometrical walled garden, with formal parterres and topiary, kitchen and herb gardens, lined by stately avenues of cypresses or lemon trees. The design, enlivened by water gardens, was set in the 16th century, when the Man-

Villa Medici La Petraia, originally bought by the Brunelleschi family.

nerist style acquired colonnades and statuary, grottoes and follies.

By the 17th century, the crisp geometry of the gardens was matched by formal terraces, virtuoso waterworks and sculptures of sea monsters cavorting with mythological figures. In their ease and openness, the gardens demonstrated a harmony with the house and with the patrician owner.

As the Renaissance architect Alberti declared, "Only the house of a tyrant can look like a fortress: an ideal home should be open to the world outside, beautifully adorned, delicate and finely proportioned rather than proud and stately".

Foce Carpinelli, between Lunigiana and Garfagnana.

WILD TUSCANY

Nature-lovers sated with the art treasures of the region will find plenty of wild refuges in which to rest or roam.

Classic Tuscany is a civilised scene of silvery olive groves, vine-cloaked hills, sunflowers shimmering in the heat and dark silhouettes of cypresses, arranged in double file along timeless avenues. The Welsh poet Dylan Thomas, who was no stranger to life on the wild side, praised the Florentine countryside – "The pine hills are endless, the cypresses at the hilltop tell one all about the length of death, the woods are deep as love and full of goats" – a seductive rural image that has attracted so many visitors to this lush region in search of their version of earthly paradise.

Given the civilisation of the landscape, "wild Tuscany" might seem a misnomer. Yet, beyond the classic chessboard of vineyards, a rugged wilderness awaits keen explorers. Tuscany is Italy's most thickly wooded region. Mountains soar, and in the northwest there are woods as thick as rainforests, while on the west coast the Maremma marshlands

Under the pines.

remain the emptiest and most ecologically pure stretch of coastline in the country. The south, meanwhile, has the unexpected primeval emptiness of the Sienese moonscape.

> *The Apuan Alps are named after the Apuani Ligures tribe who lived in this region in ancient times.*

The Apuan Alps, Lunigiana and Garfagnana

This mountain chain, with its awe-inspiring landscape, runs parallel to the coastline and the Apennine ridge. Behind the well-groomed beaches of Versilia, on the western side of the chain, lurks a rugged hinterland of marble quarries and mountain ridges, narrow gorges, deep caves and thermal springs.

Mountainous Lunigiana, north of Carrara (famous for its marble), is wedged between Emilia and Liguria. The region is crisscrossed by streams, with canoeing popular in the clear waters of the river Magra. From Aulla, a convenient base, there are organised tours of glacial moraines, karst gorges, caves and botanical gardens.

Garfagnana lies on the borders of Emilia Romagna and northern Tuscany, between the Apuan Alps and the Apennines. Parco dell'Orecchiella is the region's most spectacular park. While closely resembling the Apuan Alps, it is higher and wilder, with a mixture of woodland and pasture, picturesque clearings and mountain streams.

The Apennines

While the Apuan Alps are more varied, the Apennine range of mountains has not been ravaged by quarrying. They include the range on the Emilian border, the loftiest in the northern Apennines, as well as those in the Casentino and Mugello.

The Casentino, north of Arezzo, forms a series of razor-like crests and deep woods that straddle Emilia and northeast Tuscany. Centred on Bibbiena in the Upper Arno, these ancient forests are the region's finest. While the Emilian side is characterised by steep bluffs and stratified outcrops, the Tuscan side presents a softer atmosphere and range of scenery, with picturesque waterfalls and streams.

The Mugello, the hilly region north of Florence, resembles a landscape painted by Giotto,

Hiking to San Gimignano.

HIKING FOR TUSCANY

Tuscany is beguiling walking country, with a typical hike from Volterra to San Gimignano encompassing an old Etruscan trail and the Via Francigena, the route that led medieval pilgrims from Canterbury to Rome. The dusty trail, mostly along typical Tuscan *strade bianche*, follows these unpaved roads past vineyards, sunflowers and honey-coloured hamlets. Naturally, you wind into a sleepy hilltop hamlet, such as Casole d'Elsa, in time for lunch in an arty *trattoria*, with olive-oil coated *crostini* and *panzanella* salad washed down with a crisp Vernaccia di San Gimignano. After fording a few streams and passing abandoned farmhouses, you can fall into a farm-stay for a *Fiorentina* steak and bed.

But without the right planning, the reality can shock you out of any reverie. The region is often let down by poor maps, haphazard signposting and the lack of passing help. Contrary to popular belief, Tuscany is not Chiantishire: far from being assailed by linen-clad compatriots, you may not meet a soul *en route*, apart from languid-eyed Chianina cattle. For "soft hiking", opt for a walking holiday through a specialist operator. You can still do the trails independently, but following a wonderfully detailed route-map without nasty surprises – no getting lost in the forest, or arriving at the sole *trattoria* on closing day. The walking itinerary described is available through Headwater (www.headwater.com).

> The Apennines are divided into three sections: northern (Appennino settentrionale), central (Appennino centrale) and southern (Appennino meridionale).

whose homeland this was. The Mugello can be explored on horseback, by following the old bridle paths between the cities of Bologna and Florence. The valleys along the Sieve, the main tributary of the Arno, are dotted with villages, olive groves and vineyards. The transition from valley to mountains means that olive groves give way to chestnut and oak forests before culminating in beech woods and waterfalls. Upper Mugello is a harsh, wild landscape of mountain peaks and passes, with ridges and ravines carved out by flowing rivers over the years.

Classic Chianti

While the Florentine Chianti is devoted to wine, the Sienese side is wilder, with vineyards gradually giving way to slopes covered in holm oaks, chestnuts and juniper. A 15km (9 mile) hilly hike from Greve in Chianti to Panzano covers the Via Chiantigiana and its offshoots, passing farms, cypresses and chestnut groves along the way.

In subtle Siena province, much of the landscape is classic Tuscany, with olive groves, gently rolling hills and dark cypresses standing sentinel. However, stretching from Siena to Montepulciano is a singular moonscape known as Le Crete Senesi, the strange hillocks marking the Sienese badlands. Barren or virtually treeless, this is beguiling territory nonetheless, with solitary farmhouses marooned on the crests of hills. This seemingly empty terrain is in fact home to a range of wildlife including foxes, badgers and wild boar.

Monte Amiata, the site of an extinct volcano further south, presents the province's wilder face, with a profusion of thermal springs bubbling amid the beech and chestnut groves. With its mossy banks and majestic grandeur, the mountainous setting is suitable for hiking, horse riding and skiing.

Marshy Maremma

Maremma, the southern coastal strip, is a composite of natural Tuscany. The Parco della Maremma, with its soft whalebacked hills parallel to the coast, is dotted with Spanish watchtowers, parasol pines and coastal dunes.

On La Spergolaia ranch, the legendary *butteri*, the last of the Maremman cowboys, break in sturdy wild horses. The park can be explored on horseback or on foot from Alberese, where waymarked paths connect the shoreline and steep cliffs.

For more information on hiking in Tuscany, see page 269, and consult the Italian parks website, www.parks.it.

The wooded regions of Tuscany should not be overlooked.

ANIMAL MAGIC

Italian hunters' fondness for the chase means that the wildlife has taken flight. The power of the hunting lobby has depleted numbers, with the exception of wild boar. Outside designated reserves, wildlife-spotters fare less well than botanists. Hawks and golden eagles still enjoy the majesty of the mountains, but life is no idyll for deer, ravaged by hunting. But, against the odds, Apennine wolves have made a comeback in the mountains, encouraged by the profusion of their favourite dish, short-fleeced mouflons. Even so, sightings of the short-fleeced sheep or wild boar are more frequent than glimpses of the eagle owl, weasel or wildcat.

A Walk in the Park

Tuscany's parks and wild places are increasingly becoming centres for rural pursuits, whether a stroll in the park with the family or a major mountain trek.

Away from the cultural crowds, nature-lovers and adrenalin junkies can indulge in hiking, skiing, horse riding, mountain biking, climbing, caving, gliding, paragliding, sailing and surfing.

Riding is very popular in Tuscan parks, with more riding stables and well-trodden mule tracks than anywhere else in Italy.

This is also a rambler's paradise. The trails are marginally better mapped than in most Italian regions, and run from relaxed to rigorous. Serious hikers can follow the long-distance trails organised by the Italian Alpine Club (CAI) (see www.cai.it for more details).

Parco Appennino Tosco-Emiliano

The Apennine ridges that span the border between northern Tuscany and Emilia Romagna offer diverse landscapes, from moorlands and lakes to craggy summits and waterfalls. The wildlife includes golden eagles, wolves and roe deer.

The new visitor centre is at Fivizzano (tel: 0585-947 200; www.parcoappennino.it).

In the Parco dell'Alto Appennino, Abetone, commanding the mountain pass separating Tuscany and Emilia, is the region's most important wintersports resort. Fortunately, the mountain air also makes Abetone invigorating during a stifling Tuscan summer, when the cable car takes walkers up to the leafy heights.

Despite the ravages of hunting, the forest is home to roe deer, mouflons and marmots, with golden eagles swooping over the crags. One of the most rewarding stretches of the rugged long-distance path (GEA) lies between here and Cisa.

Yet Abetone is also suitable for less energetic walkers – well-marked trails in the woods are available for those who prefer to stroll.

Parco delle Foreste Casentinesi

Home to the secluded monasteries of Camáldoli and La Verna, this corner of the Casentino lies along the ridge that divides eastern Tuscany and Emilia Romagna. Deer, golden eagles and wolves inhabit these ancient beech and chestnut woods.

The park headquarters are to be found in Prato Vecchio (Via Brocchi 7; tel: 0575-50301; www.parks.it/parco.nazionale.for.casentinesi), with information offices at Camáldoli (tel: 0575-556 130) and Campigna "La Villetta" (tel: 346-603 1097).

Parco Alpi Apuane

The park extends for over 20,000 hectares (49,000 acres) between the coastal plain and the rivers Magra, Aulella and Serchio. The Apuan Alps are different from the Apennines and feature deep valleys, steep slopes and mountains of glistening white marble. Forests of chestnut and beech give cover to some 300 species of bird, while marmots can be spotted on the higher slopes.

Lago di Vaglia, in the heart of the mountains, is a reservoir containing a submerged medieval village that can be seen periodically. The underground landscape is equally inspiring, with caves often as deep as the mountains are high, and notoriously long and labyrinthine.

In Fornovolasco, east of Forte dei Marmi, the Grotta del Vento boasts the region's most fascinating network of caverns, riddled with steep gorges and secret passages, slowly revealing stalagmites and stalactites, fossils and alabaster formations, as well as crystal pools and echoing chambers.

The visitor centre in Castelnuovo di Garfagnana (Piazza Erbe 1; tel: 0583-644 242; www.parks.it) provides help on hiking, climbing, cycling and horse riding. Park guides are available for hikes or visits to caves.

Parco dell'Orecchiella

The mountains of the Orecchiella park in the Garfagnana region are higher than the neighbouring Apuan Alps, but the landscape is more tame and subtle, and crisscrossed by hiking trails.

The area is centred on the high broad plain of Pania di Corfino, overlooked by a dramatic limestone peak that dominates the Serchio valley. The wildlife includes deer, wild boar, mouflons, badgers, otters, weasels and wolves. San Pellegrino monastery offers fabulous views and houses a folk museum.

San Romano in Garfagnana visitor centre (tel: 0583-619 098; www.ingarfagnana.it) makes a good base for exploring.

Parco di Migliarino, San Rossore, Massaciuccoli

This park covers the coastal hinterland behind the beach resorts between Viareggio and Livorno, and includes the forest of San Rossore and Lake Massaciuccoli.

Huge holm oaks and maritime pines grow right up to the beach and provide shelter to a variety of animals including wild boar, fallow deer and countless species of native and migratory birds. The San Rossore archaeological site, where a fleet of Roman ships was unearthed, can be visited (by appointment only).

coves. There are no human settlements, and just one access road links Alberese, the park entrance, to Marina Alberese, a virgin seaside stretch that attracts migratory birds on their journey to Africa. The dense vegetation here provides the perfect habitat for wild boar, the symbol of the Maremma, while herds of Maremman cattle and horses of the *butteri* (local cowherds) roam on its plains.

The Alberese visitor centre (Via Bersagliere 7; tel: 0564-407 098; www.parco-maremma.it) works with Naturalmente Toscana, which offers walking, riding and canoeing trips – as well as

Poppies brighten the fields of Tuscany in springtime.

There is a visitor centre at Coltano (Villa Medicea, Via Palazzi 21; tel: 050-989 084), while the Tenuta San Rossore organises walking and cycling tours (tel: 050-530 101; www.parcosanrossore.org). Boat tours of Lake Massaciuccoli depart from Torre del Lago.

Parco della Maremma

This beautiful, unspoilt wilderness, covering over 100 sq km (40 sq miles), stretches along the Tyrrhenian coast from Principina a Mare to Talamone. It is centred on the Monti dell'Uccellina, which rise up from the sea.

The rugged landscape is a mixture of marshland, mountains and coast backed by umbrella pines, interspersed with rocky outcrops and

free food and wine tastings onsite (tel: 0564-407 269; www.naturalmentetoscana.it).

Parco dell'Arcipelago Toscano

This is Europe's largest marine reserve and is popular with diving enthusiasts. It covers the seven islands of the Tuscan Archipelago: Elba, Capraia, Gorgona, Pianosa, Montecristo, Giglio and Giannutri. The coastline and sea bed vary enormously from island to island, hence the variety of flora and fauna on show to curious visitors. Sea birds such as shearwaters and black-headed gulls proliferate, while dolphins, sperm whales and even the rare monk seal may also be sighted.

The marine park is based in Elba (tel: 0565-919 411; www.parks.it/parco.nazionale.arcip.toscan).

A Sienese celebratory feast during the Palio.

A TASTE OF TUSCANY

Traditional Tuscan cuisine is *cucina povera*, robust "peasant food" – but this deceptive simplicity is now valued as tasty authenticity, served straight from the land.

Tuscany has everything to offer the foodie, with dishes designed to bring out the richness of the wine. From T-bone steaks to peasant soups, wild-boar stews, truffle sauces, hearty cheeses and divine cakes, this is as far from faddish "creative" cuisine as you can get.

What is immediately striking about Tuscan food is that it is rustic, simple but robust, nourishing the soul and the spirit as much as the body. The Tuscan monks who cultivated wine and oil estates knew what they were doing and, in some cases, are still doing. The cooking is never elaborate or excessive; there are no fussy finishing touches, complex reductions of sauces or subtly blended flavours. But there is a basic earthiness about the dishes that has made them popular the world over.

Tuscany produces its own inimitable versions of Italian staples: pasta dishes with gamey wild-boar sauce; *pici* pasta with fresh ceps; and *fagioli all'Uccelletto*, beans in tomato sauce. But along with a traditional attitude to food, the region also offers distinctive delicacies and seasonal dishes, such as truffles and wild mushrooms.

Bean-eaters rule

The Tuscans are known as *Toscani Mangiafagioli* – bean-eaters, because the pulse enriches so many dishes. Legumes are a mainstay in Tuscany, where *cannellini*, white kidney beans, add a smooth texture. Served in terracotta pots, thick soups and hearty bean stews are often enhanced by a trickle of olive oil added at the table. Many chefs rate Tuscan oil the world's finest but rarely agree on which area, let alone which estate, produces the very best. As the locals are never impartial, foodie visitors are left to compare the virtues of oil from Lucca, the Chianti, the Maremma and Siena.

Preparing bistecca alla Fiorentina.

Soups are made of the ubiquitous beans, and include *acquacotta*, a vegetable soup with an egg added before serving, and *pappa al pomodoro*, a thick soup of bread and tomatoes. Even more typical is the Florentine winter speciality, *ribollita* ("reboiled"), which improves the flavour of the soup.

Elsewhere, the rugged Garfagnana region favours tasty spelt soups, enriched by oil, onions and *borlotti* beans.

Coastal Livorno produces delicious *cacciucco*, a filling shellfish-and-fish soup that supposedly inspired the French *bouillabaisse*. The story goes that the soup originated in the port after a tremendous storm that left a widowed fisherman's wife desperately trying to feed her hungry brood. The children came home with handfuls of mussels, shrimps, half a fish and some fish heads – which the wily mother tossed into a pot with herbs and tomatoes to create the glorious *cacciucco*. While *zuppa di pesce* (fish soup) can be eaten all over Italy, *cacciucco* can be eaten only around Livorno, ladled over toasted, garlicky croutons.

Bread and cheese

Tuscan bread is made without salt, supposedly because salt was once reserved for "precious" foods such as salami. Dante wrote of Flor-

Picking olives, as depicted by a 15th-century artist.

entine bread, comparing it favourably with the salty bread he was forced to eat in exile. The importance of bread is revealed in local expressions, such as "Bread cannot be made with flour alone", or "Better stale bread at home than a roast at someone else's house". In fact, stale bread finds its way into *panzanella*, a typical peasant dish made with tomatoes, onions, cucumber and basil, drenched in olive oil. You will also sample bread in the form of *bruschetta* or *crostini*, coated with olive oil or liver-based spreads.

Tuscan cheeses are varied and plentiful. There is a delightful overspill of cheeses from neighbouring Emilia Romagna, including Parmesan, *parmigiano reggiano*, which complements Tuscany's marvellous pasta dishes and soups. Other stalwarts include pecorino, a hard, healthy ewe's-milk cheese, produced since Roman times. Although ideally suited to grating, pecorino matures well and can also be used in pasta fillings. Lesser-known cheeses include *marzolino*, a ewe's-milk cheese made in March, when milk is most plentiful in the Chianti valley; *mucchino*, cow's-milk cheese made in and around Lucca by the same procedure as pecorino; and all the local rustic *cacciotte* and ricotta made with cow's, goat's and ewe's milk. Pienza is a key centre for artisan cheeses, especially *cacio pecorino*.

Hearty stews and barbecues

Tuscan cooks favour rustic, outdoor cooking – a grill over an open wood fire is not uncommon behind a chic Florentine restaurant or in the garden of a rural *trattoria*. Fresh sage, rosemary and basil are used, as they grow in abundance.

The Tuscan meat dish *par excellence* is the *bistecca alla Fiorentina*, a vast, tender, succulent T-bone steak – preferably from cattle raised in Val di Chiana. With expressive eyes and long-limbed grace, the beautiful white Chianina breed was used in Roman triumphal marches, or sacrificed to the gods in Etruscan times. The meat is brushed with the purest virgin olive oil and grilled over a scented wood fire of oak or olive branches, then seasoned with salt and pepper. In good Florentine restaurants, you will be able to see the meat raw before you order.

Another famous Tuscan meat dish is *arista alla Fiorentina*, pork loin highly seasoned with rosemary and ground pepper. The dish dates

EXTRA VIRGIN

Tuscans are passionate about olive oil, and cook with oil rather than butter. Tuscan olive oil has long been famous for its quality, flavour and texture, and is accorded DOC status, an equivalent to the French *appellation contrôlée* system for wine. Quality is measured by acid content, with *Extra vergine* the top quality, with less than 1 percent acid content. Excellent delicate, fruity oils include Extravergine di Scansano, Extravergine del Chianti, and Extravergine Badia á Coltibuono. The Badia dí Coltibuono is Tuscan perfection: a tranquil, medieval oil and wine estate set in landscape that has been cultivated since time immemorial.

back to the 15th century, when the Greek bishops were served it at a Florentine banquet and pronounced it *"aristos"*, meaning "very good" in Greek. The name stuck, and it has become a feature of Tuscan cuisine ever since.

In the Sienese countryside, the white-striped Cinta Senese breed has been producing the region's finest pork and charcuterie since Etruscan times. The odd-looking pig is even depicted in Lorenzetti's famous 14th-century fresco of *Good Government* in Siena's Town Hall.

Hunting is a popular sport, resulting in plentiful offerings of *cinghiale* (wild boar), which comes in many guises. Despite conservationists' pleas, small birds, from sparrows to quail, are also still considered fair game.

Autumn harvest

The "fruits of the forest" are particularly prized in Tuscany, especially chestnuts, mushrooms and truffles. Chestnuts are a staple, particularly in mountainous regions, where they are made into flour, pancakes, soups and sweet cakes such as *castagnaccio*, flavoured with rosemary and pine nuts. The season peaks around mid-October, when chestnut lovers can travel on

The Fruit Vendor, a 16th-century painting by Vincenzo Campi, celebrates the region's harvest.

TRUFFLE TROVE

"Truffles taste and smell of people and sweat," says chef Giorgio Locatelli. Pungent and pricey, the white truffle is a paradox; a princely treat harvested by peasants since Roman times.

Dubbed "the white diamond", it is actually a dirty yellow-brown in colour. Emperor Nero called truffles "the food of the gods", while excitable food critics wax lyrical about truffles as "the sex of the gods". Truffles are underground fungi, developing close to the roots of oaks, poplars and hazelnut trees. But the exact location of a "truffle trove" is a well-guarded secret, with trufflehunters regarding their talented dogs, who unearth the tuber, as important members of their families.

Although the most prized white truffles come from Piedmont, Tuscany also has its share, centred on San Miniato, which hosts a truffle festival in November. The precious white truffle is available from September to December, while variants of black truffle are available all year. Connoisseurs favour simplicity in use, with shavings of white truffle grated over pasta, fried egg, salad or risotto. Black truffles suit more complex dishes, but are equally delicious grated over a *crostini* (grilled bread) coated with *stracchino* cheese.

Set in a castle in San Giovanni d'Asso, the Truffle Museum provides information on truffle fairs, tours and inns (http://museotartufo.museisenesi.org, www.assotartufi.it).

a restored 1920s steam train from Florence to Marradi's *Sagra delle Castagne*, or chestnut festival, to join the celebrations.

In the autumn, when the rains fall, the hills are awash with family outings. Long lines of cars park along the side of the mountain roads – particularly in the Maremma, Garfagnana and Mugello areas, where locals arm themselves with baskets and hooked knives, in search of *funghi*. The wild-mushroom season is eagerly awaited but if you want to join in, go with a local, since many types of mushroom are poisonous. Or simply purchase *funghi* from a road-

mushrooms, it is the *tartufo*, or truffle – particularly the white variety.

Saffron is another autumn harvest, cultivated around San Gimignano for over 800 years. The valuable spice was even used as a currency, given its prestige and transportability. In 1200, the Bishop of Volterra used saffron to bribe the counsellors to the Roman Curia. Saffron only flowers for a fortnight between October and November, and must be gathered at dawn when the purplish flower is closed. Over 500 hours of work are required to produce a kilo, since the rust-coloured filaments are picked by

It is claimed that Italy's famous gelato was invented in Florence.

Fresh funghi.

side market during the August–October season. The varieties of wild mushrooms depend upon the type of tree nearby – but the most sought after are the perfect *porcini (Boletus edulis)*, ceps that grow to enormous size and thickness.

Fresh wild mushrooms are best grilled in the Tuscan way, like a steak: rub each with a slice of lemon, season with slivers of garlic and sprigs of thyme – or, even simpler, just brush with olive oil and salt. Dried *porcini* are even tastier, as the dehydration concentrates the flavour. When regenerated by soaking in lukewarm water, they are ideal for use in risotto or pasta sauces. Mushrooms can also be used to flavour *pici*, the typical Tuscan spaghetti. But if there is one food that provokes more excitement than wild

hand, then dried and "toasted", before finding their way into risotto and sauces.

Sienese sweetmeats

Siena is the most sweet-toothed city, famous for its pastries, biscuits and cakes. *Panforte*, a Sienese Christmas speciality, is unmistakable in its brightly coloured octagonal box. It is a rich, sweet cake of candied fruit, nuts, spices, honey and sugar, sandwiched between sheets of rice paper. *Ricciarelli* are delightful, diamond-shaped almond cakes, also saved for Christmas, along with the rich, golden rice cake called *torta di riso*. Instead, *cavallucci* are hard biscuits served at the end of a meal and dipped in Vin Santo dessert wine. The local *pasticcerie* are filled with delectable varieties.

Siena faces stiff competition from the cake shops of Lucca, Pistoia, Prato and the Garfagnana. Lucca favours a plain, ring-shaped cake known as *buccellato*, and a sweet tart of spinach and chard with pine nuts. Pistoia produces the pretty *corona di San Bartolomeo* for the feast of St Bartholomew on 24 August, when mothers lead their children to church wearing this cake "necklace" to receive a blessing from the saint. *Cantuccini* are typical Tuscan biscuits: Prato's version, *biscottini di Prato*, are made from almonds, eggs, flour and sugar, and are delicious dipped in Vin Santo. Castelnuovo

Tuscany is truly a food-lover's paradise, riddled with wine and food trails that invariably run through a patchwork of vineyards and olive groves or cornfields edged with sunflowers. The Chianti route is a chance to enjoy a T-bone steak and Chianti Classico wines. In the Tuscan capital, if you can stomach it, there is a trail that includes tripe, a Florentine delicacy. In the Garfagnana, book a Slow Food tour with Sapori & Saperi to savour, or even harvest, chestnuts, salami, wild mushrooms and bread baked in a wood-fired oven (www. sapori-e-saperi.com).

A meal with a view in Florence.

della Garfagnana specialises in a simple chestnut cake called *torta garfagnina*, while closer to the Emilia Romagna borders, look out for a baked-apple cake, the *torta di mele*.

No visit to Florence would be complete without ice cream – the Florentines claim to have invented *gelato*. Always look for the sign *Produzione Propria* (home-made). The city produces *zuccotto*, a sponge-cake mould with a filling of almonds, hazelnuts, chocolate and cream. Once eaten, it is never forgotten. Literally translated as "small pumpkin", this dome-shaped Florentine speciality either alludes to the cathedral (Duomo) or to the clergy: in Tuscan dialect, a cardinal's skullcap is also called a *zuccotto*.

EATING ITALIAN-STYLE

Tuscans love their food. But there are "rules" to be followed if you want to "eat as the Italians do". Cappuccino in the afternoon? You'll be branded a tourist. Usually, breakfast consists of just an espresso or cappuccino, drunk on the hoof in a local bar if not at home. Traditionally, a full-blown meal begins with an *antipasto* – salami or some roasted peppers, for example. Then follows the first course, *il primo*, usually a pasta or soup. *Il secondo* is next, consisting of meat or fish and vegetables. Salad follows, cleansing the palate for *i formaggi* (cheese) and *i dolci* (dessert), often followed by an espresso. *Buon appetito!*

Watching the crowds go by in Cortona.

Monteriggioni in the Chianti region.

INTRODUCTION

A detailed guide to the region, with the
principal sites clearly cross-referenced
by number to the maps.

Pisa's famous Leaning Tower.

For many visitors, Tuscany is the true Italy – as conjured up by clichéd Merchant-Ivory film adaptations of E.M. Forster novels – a land of swaying cypress trees, olive groves and vineyards, scattered with medieval castles and Medici villas. Tuscans are more nuanced about their rural idyll. To them, Tuscany evokes the wild as well as the tamed, stretching from the Carrara-marble quarries to the Maremma wilderness, embracing the rugged coastline, rolling Chianti vineyards and the wooded slopes of Monte Amiata. Despite a deep relationship with the land, the heirs to the Etruscans recognise the tough realities of rural life. Tuscans are also innately sociable and will always prefer living in large villages or small towns to an isolated farmhouse, however idyllic.

The appeal of Tuscan towns is their timelessness, civility and sense of ease with their past. Florence, the cradle of the Renaissance, retains a huge number of the artworks created in its honour. Gazing at the skyline from Piazzale Michelangelo reveals how little the cityscape has changed since its artistic heyday. Variety underpins Tuscan townscapes: from medieval hilltop eyries to Etruscan outposts; from *fin-de-siècle* spa towns to sophisticated beach resorts; from the splendour of a Renaissance palazzo to a stark Romanesque church. Medieval Siena and Renaissance Florence may be unmissable, but spare some time for Etruscan Volterra, genuine Massa Marittima or cyclist-friendly Lucca. Tuscan towns are built on a human scale. As for scenery, lap up the Unesco-protected Val d'Orcia countryside, mountainous Garfagnana, and wild, coastal Maremma.

A cypress-surrounded villa.

For all Tuscany's artistic and architectural riches, however, most visitors would agree that as much pleasure can be derived from lunch on the shady terrace of a rustic trattoria and banter with its owner, as an encounter with Michelangelo's David and Botticelli's Venus. As Forster observed: "The traveller who has gone to Italy to study the tactile values of Giotto, or the corruption of the papacy, may return remembering nothing but the blue sky and the men and women who live under it."

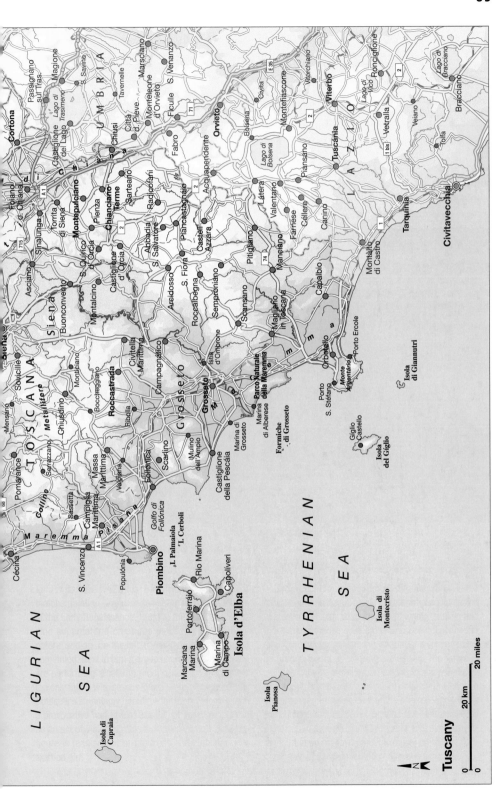

Tuscany

N

0   20 km
0   20 miles

LIGURIAN SEA

TYRRHENIAN SEA

Isola di Capraia

Isola Pianosa

Isola di Montecristo

Isola del Giglio

Isola di Giannutri

Isola d'Elba

TOSCANA

SIENA

GROSSETO

UMBRIA

LAZIO

Cortona
Passignano sul Tras.
Magione
Lago di Trasimeno
Castiglione del Lago
S. Savino
Tavernelle
Marsciano
Montelèone d'Orvieto
Città d. Pieve
Ficulle
S. Venanzo
Marsciano
Foiano d. Chiana
Chiusi
Chianciano Terme
Sarteano
Radicofani
Fabro
Acquapendente
Orvieto
Bolsena
Civita
Montefiàscone
Vitorchiano
Viterbo
Roncigliōne
Lago di Bracciano
Bracciano
Veiano
Tolfa
Tarquinia
Civitavecchia
Montalto di Castro
Tuscània
Vetralla
Canino
Farnese
Pitigliano
Manciano
Capàlbio
Magliano in Toscana
Orbetello
Monte Argentario
Porto Ercole
Porto S. Stéfano
Giglio Castello
Isola del Giglio
Scansano
Sorano
Semproniano
Roccalbegna
S. Fiora
Santa Fiora
Arcidosso
Castel. Azzara
Castelnuovo
Abbadia S. Salvatore
Piancastagnaio
Pienza
Montepulciano
Torrita di Siena
Sinalunga
Asciano
S. Quirico d'Orcia
Castiglione d'Orcia
Montalcino
Buonconvento
Sovicille
Siena
Montisi
Ribolla
Civitella Marittima
Roccastrada
Campagnàtico
Istia d'Ombrone
Grosseto
Marina di Grosseto
Marina di Alberese
Parco Naturale della Maremma
Formiche di Grosseto
Boccheggiano
Chiusdino
Monterotondo
Massa Marittima
Montieri
Serrazzano
Pomarance
Mensano
Cécina
Sassetta
Campiglia Marittima
Suvereto
Valpiana
Scarlino
Follónica
Golfo di Follónica
Mulino dell'Ampio
Castiglione della Pescaia
Marina di Grosseto
Ponteàccio
Ponsano
S. Vincenzo
Populónia
Piombino
J. Palmaiola
'I. Cerboli
Rio Marina
Capoliveri
Portoferràjo
Marciana Marina
Marina di Campo
Maremma
Collline Metallifere
Pisana
Latera
Valentano
Gradoli
Gèllere
Piansano
Lago di Bolsena

The snow-capped dome of
Florence's famous Duomo.

THE CITY OF FLORENCE

One of the world's architectural masterpieces, packed with palaces and art galleries, a revitalised Florence is an essential stop on any modern-day Grand Tour.

Firenze

More than any other Italian city, Florence is defined by its artistic heritage. The city is both blessed and burdened by a civic identity bound up with the Renaissance, and basks in its reflected glory. As the birthplace of the Renaissance, the city witnessed the Florentine miracle, a flowering of the human spirit that has left a lasting artistic imprint. The churches, palaces and galleries are studded with the world's greatest concentration of Renaissance art and sculpture. In 1743, Anna Maria Lodovica, the last of the Medici line, bequeathed her property to Florence, ensuring that the Medici collections remained intact forever. As a result, Florence is still awash with many of the treasures that Vasari, the first art historian, mentions in his *Lives of the Artists* (1550).

Although artistic treasures predominate, Florence is experiencing a revival that makes it far more than a Renaissance theme park. Upon becoming the city's mayor in 2009 Matteo Renzi, now Italy's prime minister, uttered these words: "Florence was on everyone's must-see list, and we got lazy. The sites were run for the benefit of bureaucrats. It is my duty to change this." True to his word, he pedestrianised swathes of the city, improved public transport, tackled pollution, sanctioned bicycle-friendly routes, extended museum opening

times, and introduced a combined museum and transport pass.

Fortuitously, Florence is also experiencing a cultural resurgence, linked to the proliferation of new arts centres, theatre-dining clubs, cool bars, contemporary-art galleries and music venues, including the new opera, ballet and classical music complex **Opera di Firenze** on Viale Fratelli Rosselli.

To make the most of your stay, and to avoid the lengthy queues, either buy the three-day Firenze Card or pre-book the "blockbuster" museums,

Main Attractions

Piazza della Signoria
Galleria degli Uffizi
Bargello
Duomo and Battistero
Museo dell'Opera del Duomo
Cappelle Medicee
Galleria dell'Accademia
Santa Croce
Ponte Vecchio
Palazzo Pitti

A view of the River Arno running through the centre of Florence.

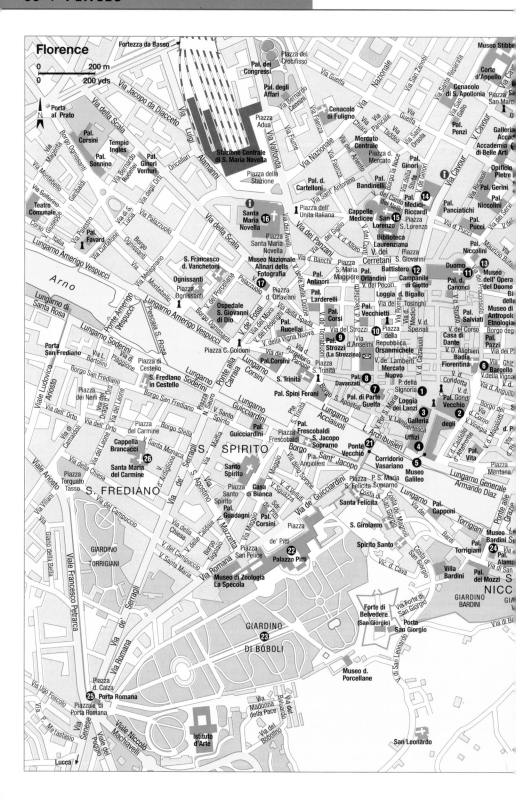

Florence

0 — 200 m
0 — 200 yds

Fortezza da Basso

Museo Stibbe

Porta al Prato

Via Jacopo da Diacceto

Via della Scala

Pal. Corsini
Tempio Ingles
Pal. Sonnino
Pal. Ginori Venturi

Via Luigi Alamanni

Via Valfonda

Stazione Centrale di S. Maria Novella

Piazza della Stazione

Piazza Adua

Pal. dei Congressi
Pal. degli Affari

Piazza del Crocifisso

Via Guelfa

Via Faenza
Chiara

Cenacolo di Fuligno

Via Nazionale

Mercato Centrale
Piazza d. Mercato

Via Santa Reparata

Via San Zanobi

Corte d'Appello

Cenacolo di S. Apollonia

Piazza San Marc

Pal. Penzi

Galleria Accad
Accademia di Belle Arti

Pal. Ginori

Opificio Pietre

Pal. Gerini

Via Cavour

Teatro Comunale

Pal. Favard

Corso Italia

Lungarno Amerigo Vespucci

Arno

Lungarno di Santa Rosa

Porta San Frediano

Piazza dei Nerli

Borgo San Frediano

S. FREDIANO

GIARDINO TORRIGIANI

Viale Francesco Petrarca

Santa Maria Novella

S. Francesco d. Vanchetoni

Ognissanti
Piazza Ognissanti

Museo Nazionale Alinari della Fotografia

Ospedale S. Giovanni di Dio

Piazza C. Goldoni

Pal. Corsini

Ponte alla Carraia

S. Frediano in Cestello

S. SPIRITO

Cappella Brancacci
Santa Maria del Carmine

Pal. Antinori

Pal. d'Ottaviani

Pal. Larderelli

Pal. Rucellai

Pal. Corsi

S. Trinità

Pal. Spini Feroni

Pal. Guicciardini

Piazza Frescobaldi

Borgo

Casa di Bianca

Pal. Guadagni
Pal. Corsini

Piazza San Felice

Palazzo Pitti

Museo di Zoologia La Specola

Piazza d. Calza

Porta Romana

Piazzale di Porta Romana

Istituto d'Arte

Lucca

GIARDINO DI BOBOLI

Museo d. Porcellane

Via del Bobolino

Via Madonna della Pace

Forte di Belvedere (San Giorgio)

Porta San Giorgio

San Leonardo

Santa Felicita

S. Girolamo

Spirito Santo

Villa Bardini

Pal. dei Mozzi

GIARDINO BARDINI

Museo Bardini

Pal. Torrigiani

Lungarno Torrigiani

Ponte Vecchio

Corridoio Vasariano

Museo Galileo

Piazza P. S. Maria Soprarno

Duomo

Battistero
Campanile di Giotto

Museo dell' Opera del Duomo

Museo di Antropol. Etnologia

Casa di Dante

Badia Fiorentina

Orsanmichele

Pal. Davanzati

Mercato Nuovo

P. della Signoria

Loggia dei Lanzi

Pal. Vecchio

Galleria degli Uffizi

Pal. Medici-Riccardi

San Lorenzo
S. Lorenzo

Cappelle Medicee

Biblioteca Laurenziana

Pal. Niccolini
Pal. Pucci
Pal. Panciatichi

Pal. Strozzi (La Strozzina)

such as the Uffizi Gallery (tel: 055-294 883; www.firenzemusei.it or tel: 055-238 8651/652; www.uffizi.com).

Viewed from the surrounding hills, Florence seems to be floating in a bowl that, at dusk, is tinged violet. The honey-coloured walls and rose-coloured roofs combine to make a unity that is dominated by a single, vast building, the Cathedral, or Duomo. It is by far the biggest building for miles around, with its roof and dome in the same subtle colour-range as the surrounding smaller buildings, above which it also seems to float like a great liner among tugs.

There are few towers or spires to be seen in Florence. Giotto's multicoloured Campanile next to the Duomo, plain in outline but intricate in detail, and the thrusting tower of the Palazzo Vecchio, elegant and sombre, soar above a low-slung skyline. The overall impression is not that of a city, but of one single, vast building, a majestic palace.

Close contact with the city can be initially disconcerting, even disappointing and claustrophobic. The streets are narrow, hemmed in by towering, plain buildings. There is no delicate filigree, as in Venice, or cheerful Baroque, as in Rome, to tempt the eye. Indeed, some of the city's buildings resemble 19th-century warehouses – grim structures that were erected at a time of social unrest, their primary function being that of fortresses. As for palaces, Florentine architectural taste runs to the monumental, macho and unembellished.

Here, the city has been grouped into four sections, starting with the area around Piazza della Signoria and the Palazzo Vecchio, followed by the Duomo area, and then by three important religious foundations (which, though physically scattered around the city, have been grouped together in this chapter). The final section is the River Arno and beyond. Many of the sights are within easy walking distance of each other – despite Florence's size, its historic centre is reasonably compact.

Piazza della Signoria: the civic centre

Florence is dauntingly monumental, nowhere more so than the **Piazza della Signoria ❶**, which is an open-air museum

Palazzo Vecchio at night.

of sculpture, starring *David*, a copy of Michelangelo's famed heroic boy. More than any other square in Italy, the Piazza della Signoria evokes the ancient world and the overweening pride of the Renaissance city. Even so, of all the great city squares, Florence's is the most perversely irregular. There is nothing in the Piazza della Signoria to compete with the grace of Siena's curved Campo, or the simple majesty of Rome's Capitol. Tucked on one side is the **Palazzo Vecchio** ❷ (tel: 055-276 8325; www.museicivicifiorentini.comune. fi.it; Fri–Wed 9am–7pm, Thur until 2pm), the seat of government for the past six centuries.

The Medici administration was based in the Palazzo Vecchio, which remains the town hall, and which was redesigned during the reign of Cosimo I. The palace, under different guises, has been the emblem of Florentine power since the 14th century. With its bold swallowtail crenellations and asymmetrical bell tower, the Palazzo is the most evocative of city symbols.

The courtyard, with its copy of an enchanting fountain by Verrocchio, is a delight. Vasari's monumental staircase leads to the frescoed **Salone dei Cinquecento**, the Hall of the Five Hundred, where members of the Great Council met. Cosimo I set his stamp on the chamber by commissioning a series of vast frescoes, painted by Vasari, which glorified his military triumphs.

Beyond the art and the style, the palace reveals everyday Medici court life. It also houses the new "Traces of Florence" permanent exhibition presenting the history of Florence, centred around the collections from the former historical-topographical museum Firenze Com'Era ("Florence as it was") which closed in 2010.

It is also one of the few museums in conservative Florence to have moved into the 21st century in terms of presentation. The use of multimedia, "secret itineraries", and a children's perspective on great artworks has proved a resounding success. The **Museo dei Ragazzi** (Children's Museum) organises workshops with actors who bring the history to life.

The huge fountain in the centre of the piazza is the subject of affectionate mockery by Florentines themselves, and no two buildings in the piazza seem to have the same facade. With a despot's love of order, Cosimo I tried to impose an artificial unity on the square, but his schemes came to nothing, leaving the piazza as a perfect illustration of Florentine "unity in diversity".

The square has changed little over the centuries. The **Marzocco**, the lion symbol of the city that prisoners were forced to kiss, can be found here, as well as a copy of Michelangelo's immense statue of *David* (the original is in the Accademia), commissioned in 1501 to mark an important change in the constitution. Nearby is a statue of the first Medici duke, Cosimo I.

Next to the Palazzo Vecchio stands the elegant **Loggia dei Lanzi** ❸, crammed with statues. The loggia (named after the mercenaries employed by Cosimo) has an impressive statue of a triumphant Perseus holding the severed head of Medusa, which Cosimo commissioned from Cellini. Most stunning among the other statues in the loggia is Giambologna's *Rape of the Sabine Women* on the opposite side.

Galleria degli Uffizi

Adjoining the piazza are the immense galleries of the **Uffizi** ❹ (tel: 055-238 8651/652; www.uffizi.com, www.virtual uffizi.com; Tue–Sun 8.15am–6.50pm, Fri late opening till 10pm; free on first Sunday of each month). Pre-booking is advisable, and you can do this through the Firenze Card, which covers all museums and transport, www.firenzecard.it, or through www.uffizi.com and www.virtualuffizi.com.

Now Tuscany's foremost gallery, t.he Uffizi was the administrative nerve centre of the grand duchy, reinforcing the chain of command between the Palazzo Vecchio, the Medici power base, and the court at the Pitti Palace. Founded by the Medici, this is now the greatest art gallery in Italy. Francesco de' Medici (1541–87) decided to transform the second floor of the Uffizi into a museum, coincidentally paying tribute to the Medici's dynastic glory. For the introverted ruler, the gallery was essentially his private playground "for walking, with paintings, statues and other precious things".

On display are paintings by masters from Giotto to Botticelli, Piero della Francesca, Michelangelo, Leonardo da Vinci, Raphael, Titian and Caravaggio. Although Tuscan art reigns supreme, the panoply of Italian art is also well represented, particularly painters from Umbria, Urbino, Emilia and the Veneto. Since most visitors come to see the Early Renaissance works, the High Renaissance rooms are far more peaceful and, by the time Titian and Veronese finally make way for Caravaggio and Tiepolo, Rubens and Rembrandt, the crowds have faded away as miraculously as a Tiepolo trompe\l'oeil. By the same token, the wonderful

Strolling among the artworks for sale.

The courtyard of Palazzo Vecchio.

classical and cinquecento statuary in the gallery corridors is often overlooked in the lemming stampede to see specific Renaissance paintings.

So rich is the Uffizi's collection that proposals for major expansion have been hotly debated for decades. The controversial new loggia entrance plan designed by cutting-edge architect Arata Isozaki has stalled. The focus is currently on remodelling the second floor now that new ground floor rooms have opened, see page 104 for more information on the Uffizi.

Just behind the Uffizi is the **Museo Galileo ❺** (www.museogalileo.it; daily 9.30am–6pm), formerly called the Museum of the History of Science. The revamped museum, housed in the 14th-century Palazzo Castellani, makes a refreshing change after an overindulgence in the arts. The collection of scientific instruments shows that Renaissance Florence was pre-eminent as a centre of scientific research. Amid the museum's prized collection of Galileo's instruments, the mathematician's middle finger of his right hand is displayed like the relic of a Christian saint.

Other rooms are devoted to astronomy, navigation, the science of warfare, and to the Medici who founded this scientific treasure trove.

The Bargello

Chronologically, the Palazzo Vecchio is the second city hall of Florence. Its predecessor, the **Bargello ❻** (tel: 055-294883; www.uffizi.org; daily Oct–mid-Mar 8.15am–1.50pm, mid-Mar–Sept until 4.50pm, all Fri until 9pm; free on the first Sun of the month), was built 50 years earlier in 1250 as the seat of the chief magistrate, the *Podestà*. The Bargello was, in effect, the police headquarters, and its courtyard witnessed public executions. The building is now a wonderful museum of sculpture, with a rich collection of works by artists such as Michelangelo, Cellini, Donatello – and is not nearly as bewildering as the Uffizi. The Bargello's tantalising calling card is Donatello's coquettish *David*, a rival to Michelangelo's more virile version in the Accademia.

Palaces and piazzas

Just west of the Piazza della Signoria is a loosely linked cluster of buildings that span four centuries of Florentine history, from the embattled Middle Ages to the era of ducal control. The **Palazzo di Parte Guelfa** ❼ (just off Via delle Terme) was the headquarters of the all-powerful Guelf Party, which, after the defeat and expulsion of the rival Ghibellines, ruled the city.

For light relief, drop into the engagingly touristic **Mercato Nuovo** – the 16th-century covered market. Remember to stroke the *Porcellino*, the bronze boar whose snout is polished to gleaming gold: touching it supposedly guarantees your return to the city.

Also referred to as the Museo dell'Antica Casa Fiorentina, the **Palazzo Davanzati** ❽ (daily 8.15am–1.50pm) is the best-preserved example of a patrician home and provides an insight into life in medieval Florence.

Built in about 1330, its painted Trecento walls serve to soften and brighten the interior, turning the fortress into a home. The great Gothic halls on the upper floors are frescoed to give the semblance of fabrics and drapery. Other striking aspects include the vaulted entrance hall and the staircase supported by flying buttresses. In style and decor, the lofty, galleried palace bridges the medieval and Renaissance eras, making Palazzo Davanzati the most illuminating example of a patrician dwelling from the period.

From Palazzo Davanzati, Via de' Sassetti leads you to the grandiose **Palazzo Strozzi** ❾ (tel: 055-264 5155; www.palazzostrozzi.org; daily 10am–8pm, Thur until 11pm), an important cultural hub and the setting for blockbuster art exhibitions. This bombastic building is also a testament to the overweening pride of the powerful merchant banker, Filippo Strozzi, who dared to build a bigger palace than the Medici's. The monumental nature of the rusticated facade is echoed by the bold inner courtyard. As the quintessential 15th-century Florentine

princely palace, Palazzo Strozzi was a model for centuries to come.

Situated in the restored cellars of the Palazzo Strozzi, **La Strozzina** (www.strozzina.org; Tue–Sun 10am–8pm) is a challenging exhibition space – which is exactly what it was until the "great flood" of 1966, when the River Arno inundated these cellars.

Worth a visit while you're in the vicinity is the Romanesque church of **Santa Trinita** (Mon–Sat 8am–noon, 4–6pm, Sun 4–6pm; free), which features a fresco cycle of the life of St Francis painted in 1483 by Domenico Ghirlandaio.

East of Palazzo Strozzi, **Piazza della Repubblica** ❿ was laid out over the medieval market quarter and Ghetto, which were demolished in the 19th century. The plan to develop central Florence was conceived between 1865 and 1871, when the city was briefly the capital of Italy. The ancient and "squalid" buildings were to be swept away and replaced by broad avenues, symbolic of the new age of the United Kingdom of Italy. Thankfully, the scheme was abandoned. The self-important square, with

Milan may be the fashion capital, but Florence has its fair share of home-grown designers of international repute. Nearly all have their outlets at the southern end of Via de' Tornabuoni, including the shoemaker, Ferragamo.

The Museo Galileo.

Florence by bike: there are numerous cycle-rental points dotted throughout the city: the main ones are at the main railway station, on Piazza Santa Croce and Piazza Annigoni by Sant'Ambrogio market. Also contact Alinari (Via San Zanobi 38R; tel: 055-280 500; www.alinari rental.com). Or try a bicycle rickshaw with Tre Rote (tel: +39 338-638 9245; www.pedicab firenze.it)

Piazza della Repubblica.

its old-fashioned cafés, remains rather soulless, a modern intrusion into the heart of the city.

The Duomo: the religious centre

The street that links the two great monuments of the Palazzo Vecchio and the Duomo is still known as the Street of the Hosiers – Via dei Calzaiuoli – after the stocking-knitters who plied their trade here. The guilds were gathered in this area, hence the guild church of **Orsanmichele** (church Tue–Sun 10am–5pm; museum Mon 10am–5pm; free). It is, in effect, an open-air sculpture gallery, with an array of statues displayed in individual niches in the walls.

Holding up to 20,000 people, the enormous **Duomo** ⓫ (www.museum florence.com; daily 10am–5pm, winter until 4.30pm, Sun pm only; free) only serves to emphasise the smallness of the surrounding square, and the narrowness of the adjoining streets. At no point can one take in the whole. But now fully pedestrianised, the square is yours to wander freely, possibly even

in a horse-drawn carriage, which can be picked up in the piazza.

The Baptistery

Despite the Duomo's dominating presence, the **Battistero** ⓬ (Mon–Fri 11.15am–6.30pm, Sun and first Sat of the month 8.30am–1.30pm) easily holds its own. The oldest building in the city, it was built on, or reconstructed from, a 7th-century building sometime between 1060 and 1120 and served as the cathedral of Florence until 1228. Dante was among the eminent Florentines baptised there, and the wealthy Wool Guild *(Calimala)* lavished vast sums on the superb Venetian mosaics decorating the cupola.

The *Calimala* then turned its attention to the three great doors, first commissioning Andrea Pisano to create bronze doors for the south entrance, then initiating a competition for the other doors, which was won by Lorenzo Ghiberti. There is no mistaking the second pair (the east doors, facing the Duomo) – which took Ghiberti 27 years to create, and which Michelangelo described as the "Gates

of Paradise". But the present panels are copies. The original panels are in the **Museo dell'Opera del Duomo** ⑬ on the east side of the Piazza del Duomo (the museum was closed for refurbishment at the time of writing, check www.museumflorence.com for new opening times), while the competition panels are in the Bargello.

The two doors are divided into 10 panels, each representing a scene from the Old Testament. Round the panels are heads of the Sibyls and the Prophets. Seek out Ghiberti's self-portrait, halfway down on the right-hand side of the left-hand door: although minuscule, it is a perfect portrait – a small, balding man peering knowingly out.

It took the Florentines over 400 years to decide on the kind of facade they wanted for the west front of the Duomo, with the present, controversial facade designed in 1887.

Inside the Duomo

After the multicoloured splendour of the freshly restored exterior, the interior of **Santa Maria del Fiore** (the Duomo's official name) is muted, coming to life only at the time of religious festivals, when immense crimson banners adorn the walls. But the eye falls on two large murals high on the wall to the left of the entrance. The right-hand one is of an Englishman, John Hawkwood, a mercenary soldier (*condottiero*) who first attacked Florence for his paymasters and then became the city's Captain-General in 1375.

Further along the aisle is the painting of *Dante Declaiming The Divine Comedy by Michelino*. On Dante's right, Hell and Purgatory are depicted, contrasted with a contemporary view of the city's major monuments.

The Duomo's greatest treasure is Michelangelo's unfinished *Pietà*, sculpted for his own tomb in 1550, and now in the museum collection. It is entirely different from his earlier, more famous *Pietà* in St Peter's, in Rome; where that is all calm, resigned acceptance, this is simply the utter defeat of death.

The dome and bell tower

It is still Brunelleschi's dome that defines Florence, over 500 years after

The south doors of the Baptistery were the work of Andrea Pisano (c.1270–1348) – goldsmith, sculptor and architect rolled into one.

The cupola mosaics of the Battistero.

TIP

The quiet cloister in the north of San Lorenzo, with its box-lined lawns and pomegranate bushes, leads to the Biblioteca Laurenziana (open for exhibitions or scholars only, hours variable; tel: 055-2930 7911). Designed by Michelangelo between 1524 and 1534, the Laurentian Library houses more than 10,000 manuscripts (including the famous 5th-century Virgil codex) from the Medici collection.

The interior of Brunelleschi's dome.

it was built. Filippo Brunelleschi created the purest Renaissance architecture, buildings striking in their simplicity and pared-down loveliness. The cupola of the Duomo, which uses rigorous geometry based on classical forms, is the perfect expression of a rational use of space. His stroke of genius was to devise a cunning system of an inner shell and outer dome to distribute the weight of the cupola, with thick walls negating the need for further buttressing. Out of respect for Brunelleschi's achievement, the city forbade the construction of any building taller than the Duomo – to this day, the massive dome dominates the red rooftops, rising almost higher than the surrounding hills.

If you have a head for heights, ascend to the gallery of the dome (Mon–Fri 8.30am–6.20pm, Sat 8.30am–5pm). It is not for vertigo sufferers: the gallery is narrow and the balustrade low, but only here can Brunelleschi's stupendous achievement be fully appreciated. The interior of the dome is covered in Vasari's bold allegorical frescoes, although the original plan was to cover the space with mosaics, which would have emphasised its soaring majesty. But its majesty is not in doubt.

Scarcely less tall, at 85 metres (278ft), is the **Campanile** (daily 8.30am–6.50pm) alongside, begun by Giotto shortly after he was appointed chief architect in 1331, and finished off after his death in 1337 by Andrea Pisano and then Talenti. Work was eventually completed in 1359. The climb to the top is worth the effort for intimate views of the Cathedral's upper levels and the panoramic city views.

Memories of the Medici

A few streets northwest of the Duomo is the heartland of Medicean Florence: the **Medici Palace** and the church of **San Lorenzo**, which is surrounded by a boisterous market. The palace – now known as the **Palazzo Medici-Riccardi** ⓮ (Thur–Tue 8.30am–7pm) – is dignified but not ostentatious. It still has the look of a fortress about it, particularly in the rusticated facade with its massive blocks of masonry. The Medici lived here from its completion in 1452 until 1540, when they

moved into the politically symbolic Palazzo Vecchio. While much of the palace is swathed in institutional gloom, the courtyard and loggia are striking, and the Cappella dei Magi revels in the most uplifting fresco cycle in Florence.

The museum contains various mementoes of the family, including the poignant death-mask of Lorenzo, but it is the chapel that displays the brightest jewels in the Medici crown, including the *Journey of the Magi* by Benozzo Gozzoli (*c*.1460). This painting breathes the spirit of the Florentine Renaissance in its mixture of real figures of identifiable people, historical recreation and delight in colour. The immense procession, winding its way through a vividly improbable landscape, is led by a handsome, richly dressed youth on horseback – the young Lorenzo. Behind him comes his grandfather, Cosimo, soberly dressed, attended by a black servant, but look out for the painter himself, with his name inscribed on his hat. In the distance is the Medici retreat, Villa Cafaggiolo – and a couple of camels to remind the observer that the picture is set in the Middle East.

San Lorenzo

The church of **San Lorenzo** ⑮ (Mon–Sat 10am–5.30pm, summer also Sun 1.30–5.30pm) is one of the earliest and most harmonious of all Renaissance churches, representing a break with French Gothic and a return to an older, classical style. The facade is rough and unfinished, though the Mayor has mooted a plan to complete it according to Michelangelo's designs.

The interior is outstanding, a gracious composition of the grey stone *pietra serena* and white walls. Giovanni, father of Cosimo de' Medici, commissioned Brunelleschi to design San Lorenzo in 1419, but neither lived to see it completed. Thereafter, successive members of the Medici family continued to embellish it, commissioning the greatest artists of their age to add frescoes, paintings and – ultimately – their mausoleum. Of particular note in the basilica are Donatello's pulpits with bronze reliefs of the Passion, and the Old Sacristy adorned with sculptures, also by Donatello.

The Mercato Centrale, Florence's main food market.

The church of San Lorenzo, with its unfinished facade.

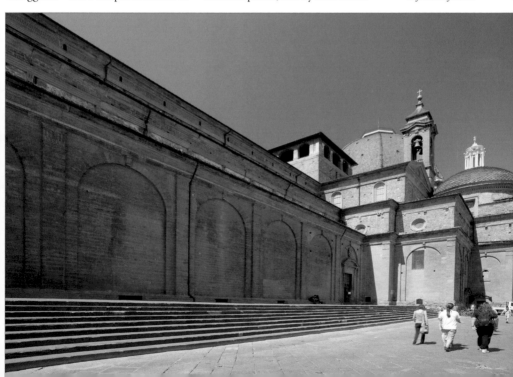

The Medici chapels

The entrance to the **Cappelle Medicee** (Oct–mid-Mar daily 8.15am–1.50pm, mid-Mar–Sept until 4.50pm, Fri until 9pm all year-round) is outside the church, in the Piazza della Madonna degli Aldobrandini. You go in via the crypt, where a floor slab commemorates Anna Maria Ludovica (died 1743), the last in the Medici line. Stairs lead to the opulent **Cappella dei Principi** (the mausoleum of the Medici grand dukes) and the **New Sacristy** (the Medici tombs), the latter Michelangelo's first architectural commission, and a chilly cocoon. The two New Sacristy tombs of Giuliano (son of Lorenzo the Magnificent) and Lorenzo (his grandson) are graced with the reclining figures of *Dawn, Evening, Day* and *Night*, conveying an unforgettable feeling of uneasiness, sadness and loss.

Santa Maria Novella, San Marco and Santa Croce: three influential churches

The three great buildings of Santa Maria Novella, San Marco and Santa Croce are some distance apart – the first near the Stazione Centrale, the second in the north, and the last on the far eastern side of the city. They are grouped together here because they illustrate a truth about Florence, that religion was a driving force – probably even stronger than commerce or the desire for self-aggrandisement – a force that nearly drove the city to destruction.

Santa Maria Novella

The church of **Santa Maria Novella** ⑯ (Mon–Thur 9am–5.30pm, Fri 11–5.30pm, Sat 9am–5pm, Sun Oct–June 1–5pm and July–Sept noon–5pm) was designed by Dominican monks in 1246. Though dignified and indeed majestic, it reflects their gloomy preoccupations: striped like a tiger, the family chapels are sombre and overwhelming, their murals little more than illustrations of sermons. The **Spanish Chapel** carries this to extremes, with its murals dedicated to the 13th-century theologian, Thomas Aquinas, who was, of course, a Dominican. The chapel now lies within the **Cloister Museum** (same hours and

St Thomas Aquinas, depicted on one of the stained-glass windows of Santa Maria Novella.

Giotto's Crucifix in Santa Maria Novella.

TO BE COMPLETED...

The "finishing" of landmark buildings has always been controversial, particularly with regard to facades. Florentines will vote whether the facade of San Lorenzo should be finished according to Michelangelo's 500-year-old plans – his models and drawings still exist. Even in their heyday, the Florentines were notorious for not completing buildings, and 19th-century benefactors were happy to help. The foreign intelligentsia, in the grip of the Gothic Revival, set about dressing key city churches in evocative neo-Gothic facades, beginning with the Duomo and Santa Croce. The result is more atmospheric than authentic; critics describe the stripy green, white and pink marble facade as "a cathedral wearing pyjamas".

ticket as the church) adjoining the church, as do Uccello's frescoes. In the church itself is Masaccio's *Trinity*, and the chapel is frescoed by Fra Filippino Lippi and Ghirlandaio. Although Brunelleschi's decorative touches lighten the spirit, the church feels oppressive.

At the southern end of Piazza Santa Maria Novella, the **Museo Nazionale Alinari della Fotografia** has one of the best photographic collections in Europe. Founded in 1852, the Alinari brothers' photographic studio supplied 19th-century Grand Tourists with prints, postcards and art books. (The museum is closed indefinitely at the time of writing; please check www.alinarifondazione.it for information.)

Long neglected, and once a gathering place for vagrants, **Piazza Santa Maria Novella** has returned to its former glory, prompted by renovation of the Dominican complex, with the finest façade in Florence, and by the pedestrianisation of the square. Helping to raise the tone are a cluster of chic boutique hotels, from JK Place to Palazzo dal Borgo, which overlooks the historic perfumery of the **Officina di Santa Maria Novella** (Via della Scala), where monks have been concocting precious potions since the 13th century.

San Marco

The convent of **San Marco** was almost entirely rebuilt with money provided by Cosimo de' Medici; the irony lies in the fact that San Marco became the headquarters of the friar Girolamo Savonarola, who was the greatest enemy of Cosimo's grandson, Lorenzo. Cosimo engaged his own favourite architect, Michelozzo, who had designed the Palazzo Medici, to build San Marco, and endowed it with a magnificent library.

Savonarola was Prior of San Marco from 1491 until his execution in 1498. During those years he dominated Florence, nearly succeeded in overthrowing the Medici and even presented a challenge to the papacy. The vivid portrait of him by Fra Bartolomeo, which

can be seen here, shows a man with a forceful but ugly face, a great beaked nose and burning eyes.

San Marco is now a **museum** (Mon–Fri 8.15am–1.50pm, Sat–Sun until 4.50pm, closed alternate Sun/Mon). The prize exhibits are the murals of Fra Angelico, himself a Dominican, but one who brought a delicacy to his work quite at variance with the austere tenets of that order. Each of the friars' cells is graced by one of his murals, and at the head of the stairs is Fra Angelico's masterpiece, the *Annunciation*. Savonarola's cell is laid out as he knew it, complete with desk and severe-looking chair.

Just south of San Marco is the legendary **Galleria dell'Accademia** (entrance at No. 60; tel: 055-294883; www.accademia.org; Tue–Sun 8.15am–6.50pm; Fri until 9pm), often identified by the enormous queues outside. Its star attraction – and the museum's raison d'être – is the colossal statue of *David*, which was carved between 1501 and 1504 from a single piece of marble, and established Michelangelo as the foremost sculptor of his time

San Marco nuns and priest.

TIP

Beyond the remnants of the city wall is a reminder, though a rapidly fading one, that Florence is a country town: a brisk walk along Via di San Leonardo will take you from the very heart of the city out into vineyards, olive groves and maize fields.

before the age of 30. The statue now standing in front of the Palazzo Vecchio is an impressive copy.

Near to the Accademia, on the Via Alfani, is the **Opificio delle Pietre Dure** (Mon–Sat 8.15am–2pm), where restoration of artistic treasures takes place. Exhibits include inlaid semi-precious stones used in *pietra dura*, as well as workbenches and instruments once used by the craftsmen.

Nearby, the **Museo Archeologico** (Tue–Fri 8.30am–7pm, Mon, Sat–Sun 8.30am–2pm) in Piazza d. S.S. Annunziata features an important collection of Greek, Egyptian, Etruscan and Roman art. The highlights include the recreation of an Etruscan tomb and bronzes of Etruscan mythological beasts.

Santa Croce

The great **Piazza Santa Croce** was a favoured place for processions, horse races and tournaments. *Calcio Storico*, an historic football match, is still staged here every June. The square, dominated by a statue of Dante, is also home to the fascinating Santa Croce Leather School, a testament to Florentine craftsmanship.

Although the facade of **Santa Croce** ⓴ (Mon–Sat 9.30am–5.30pm, Sun from 2pm) dates from the mid-19th century, Arnolfo di Cambio began work on the church in 1294. With the lightness and elegance associated with Franciscan churches, it is the Pantheon of Florence – and, indeed, of Italy, since this is where so many of the country's illustrious dead were laid to rest, from Galileo to Ghiberti.

The tomb of Michelangelo, designed by Vasari, invariably has a little bunch of flowers laid upon it, unlike the grave of Machiavelli, who died in 1527. Crowning the whole are the frescoes painted by Giotto and his school.

The cloisters, designed by Brunelleschi, lead to the recently restored **Cappella de'Pazzi**, which contains 12 terracotta roundels of the Apostles by Luca della Robbia.

The **Museo dell'Opera di Santa Croce** (Mon–Sat 9.30am–5.30pm, Sun opens at 2pm) houses the beguiling *Tree of the Cross* by Taddeo Gaddi and Cimabue's iconic 13th-century *Crucifix*, which was badly damaged in

THE CONTEMPORARY CITY

If sleepy Florence has finally woken up, much credit is due to three Prince Charmings. Canadian James Bradburne put the city on the contemporary art map with Palazzo Strozzi and its inclusive yet international approach to culture. Not that he takes credit for it: "Florence has the highest concentration of intellectual, creative and business firepower that I have ever seen. It punches way above its weight. Here everyone from art historians to plumbers is able to carry on extraordinary conversations about art and literature. The question is, why doesn't Florence do more with this firepower?"

Mayors Matteo Renzi, between 2009 and 2014, and Dario Nardella, since 2014, have followed suit, supporting a host of creative projects, including the Nuovo Teatro del Maggio, the city's new opera house and concert hall. New festivals, art galleries and *aperitivi* bars have sprung up, along with vibrant theatre-dining clubs, such as the Teatro del Sale. Disused stations, convents and fortesses have been turned into multimedia libraries and events centres. Le Murate, a former nunnery

and prison on Via Ghibellina, now offers live music, arty bars and an outdoor cinema. The Universale, once a run-down cinema, has been reborn as a designer-chic club with cinematic screens. Stazione Leopolda, a reconverted neoclassical station, now stages fashion shows, concerts and exhibitions. Symbolically, Norman Foster's avant-garde railway hub, with a view to opening in 2015, will strengthen the city's international links. Only the controversial Uffizi expansion project is on hold, considered too cutting edge for traditionalists, particularly the loggia entrance proposed by architect Arata Isozaki. Inside however, the museum's second floor rooms are being wonderfully revamped and remodelled, and numerous new ones have opened on the ground floor. Franco Zeffirelli, the Florentine-born film director, decries it as a form of "being blackmailed by progressivist culture". And many agree. But most other "grand projects" command popular support. Damien Hirst's diamond-encrusted skull has even been displayed in the Palazzo Vecchio. Bizarre, but Florence can finally claim to be about more than Renaissance art.

Map on page 88

the 1966 flood. It has only been partially restored since then as a poignant reminder of the city in peril.

Oltrarno: across the river

The Florentines regard their river with mixed feelings. It has brought both wealth and disaster in its unpredictable wake. The Arno becomes a raging brown torrent in winter, although it can shrink to a trickle along a dried-up bed during summer. Recently, sun-worshippers have become fond of its enjoyable urban beach.

The **Ponte Vecchio** ㉑ was erected by Taddeo Gaddi sometime after 1345 and has become a symbol of Florence itself. Fortunately, the Germans spared it when they blew up every other Florentine bridge during World War II. It bears the same appearance that it has borne for six centuries. Even the goldsmiths and jewellers who throng it today were established there in the mid-16th century. Before the goldsmiths, the shops on the bridge were occupied by butchers and tanners, who used the river as a dumping ground until they were evicted in 1593.

It was for Ferdinando's father, Cosimo I, that Vasari built the extraordinary **Vasari Corridor** in 1565. Running from the Uffizi to the Pitti across the Ponte Vecchio, the private raised walkway made a physical as well as symbolic link between the two centres of Medicean power. In his film *Paisà*, Roberto Rossellini shot an unforgettable sequence of the fighting that took place along this gallery during the German retreat. The corridor, renovated in 2013, holds over 1,000 paintings and self-portraits by renowned artists. It is now open to visitors but advance booking is essential; guided tours can be booked through www.uffizi.com or agencies such as Live Your Tuscany (tel: 055-407 998; www.liveyourtuscany.com).

The Pitti Palace

The part of Florence south of the river, the **Oltrarno**, has a bohemian character all of its own, with its charm enhanced by the gradual pedestrianisation of this area. Yet in the 15th century, this area was the centre of opposition to the Medici, spearheaded by the Pitti family. It was they who

Charming Ponte Vecchio.

built the **Palazzo Pitti** ㉒ (The Palazzo Pitti museum ticketing deals are confusing but pre-booking is advisable, tel: 055-294 883; www.firenzemusei.it; or through the Firenze Card, www.firenze card.it.), the most grandiose of all Florentine residences, which, by the irony of history, eventually became the seat of government for the Medici dukes themselves. Today it is home to Medici museums and art galleries, notably the **Galleria Palatina** (Tue–Sun 8.15am–6.50pm, closed Jan), adorned by masterpieces by artists such as Raphael, Rubens, Van Dyck and Titian.

Adjoining the gallery are the **Appartamenti Monumentali or Reali** (State Apartments, same times as the gallery), lavishly decorated with impressive works of art. The palace also contains the **Galleria d'Arte Moderna** (Modern Art Museum; Tue–Sun 8.15am–6.50pm), the **Galleria del Costume** (Costume Museum; Nov–Feb daily 8.15am–4.30pm, Mar until 5.30pm, Apr, May, Sept, Oct until 6.30pm, June–Aug until 7.30pm, closed 1st and last Mon of the month) and the **Museo degli Argenti**.

An excellent antidote to the overwhelming splendours of the Pitti are the beautiful adjoining Boboli Gardens, the **Giardino di Boboli** ㉓ (daily 8.15am–sunset; closed 1st and last Mon of the month). For more details see page 108.

Also included in the Boboli ticket is the **Giardino Bardini**, accessible from Via dei Bardi 1r or Costa San Giorgio 2 (tel: 055-263 8599; www.bardinipeyron. it; 8.15am–sunset). The park offers stunning vistas, a café and quiet spots for meditation, as well as access to the **Villa Bardini** (contact as above; Tue–Sun 10am–7pm).

Once owned by antiquarian Stefano Bardini, the villa is now home to a fine restaurant and small museums dedicated to the modern artist Annigoni and fashion maestro Roberto Capucci. But Bardini's heart belonged to his Renaissance art collection down the hill in **Museo Bardini** ㉔ (Via dei Renai 37; tel: 055-234 2427; Fri–Mon 11am–5pm). The newly reopened collection mixes works by Donatello with eclectic finds, such as the original Porcellino, the wild-boar bronze created for the Mercato Nuovo.

Alternatively, from Villa Bardini, continue up Costa San Giorgio to the **Forte di Belvedere** (currently closed to the public; open for exhibitions only), a 16th-century fortification designed by Buontalenti for the Grand Duke Ferdinando I de' Medici. The fort, which commands breathtaking views over Florence, hosts modern-art and photography exhibitions.

The Porta Romana

The **Via Romana**, which begins just past the Palazzo Pitti in Piazza San Felice, goes to the **Porta Romana** ㉕, stretching from the city centre, via the Ponte Vecchio, to the outside world. The larger gates of Florence were, like the 14th-century Porta Romana, both a garrison and a customs post, collecting dues on all the goods that came into the city. You can now walk a section of the ramparts near Porta Romana.

The facade of San Miniato al Monte.

Oltrarno churches

Several churches of note lie on this south side of the city. The first, not far from the Ponte Santa Trinità, is **Santo Spirito** (Mon–Sat 9.30am–12.30pm and 4–5.30pm, Sun 11.30am–12.30pm and 4–5.30pm; free), its modest 18th-century facade masking the harmonious interior designed by Filippo Brunelleschi.

Just west is **Santa Maria del Carmine** ㉖, which contains one of the greatest treasures of Italian painting – the **Cappella Brancacci** frescoes (tel: 055-276 8224; www.museicivicifiorentini. comune.fi.it; Mon, Wed–Sat 10am–5pm, Sun 1–5pm; reservation required). Considered by many to rival even Michelangelo's Sistine Chapel in Rome, the work of Masolino (including *The Temptation of Adam and Eve*), Masaccio (*The Expulsion from Paradise* and *The Tribute Money*) and Filippino Lippi is truly magnificent. Unfortunately, due to the popularity of the frescoes, visitors are only allowed 15 minutes to see them.

Further east, dominating a hilltop, awaits **San Miniato al Monte** ㉗

(daily 8am–1pm, 3.30–7pm, free). A building stood on this site as early as the 4th century, but the present complex dates from 1018 and is a fine example of Florentine Romanesque. Inside, seek out the **Cappella del Crocifisso**, a tiny vaulted temple, and the 11th-century crypt, which houses the relics of St Minias. You can hear the monks chanting here each afternoon at 5.30pm.

San Miniato towers above the **Piazzale Michelangelo**, reached from the Porta Romana along the enchanting Viale dei Colli, or else by climbing up from the river, past the Porta San Niccolò, taking the winding paths through the gardens to the piazzale.

Adorned with bronze copies of Michelangelo's various works of sculpture, this touristic terrace is a Florentine pilgrimage destination that entwined lovers feel obliged to visit. Even if the views are far lovelier from **Bellosguardo**, above Porta Romana, Piazzale Michelangelo is picture-postcard Florence – from the sheepish couples and nude *David* souvenirs to the city at sunset decked out below.

The Expulsion from Paradise by Masaccio (c.1427) in the Cappella Brancacci. They are among the most powerfully emotive figures ever painted in Western art.

View of the city from Piazzale Michelangelo.

THE UFFIZI

The greatest collection of Renaissance art to be found anywhere in the world.

THE EASTERN CORRIDOR

The two corridors from which the 45 rooms on the second floor lead off are filled with sculptures, while the strip connecting the sides allows magnificent views down the river and towards the Ponte Vecchio. Rooms 2–4 are dedicated to works from Siena and Florence during the duecento and trecento (13th and 14th centuries), exhibiting the decorative and iconographic pre-Renaissance style. Notable works are the interpretations of the Madonna by Giotto and Duccio, as well as that of Cimabue, Giotto's master.

Room 7 is dedicated to the early Renaissance period and its founders and leading exponents, who include Masaccio and Uccello and, later, Fra Angelico. The Filippo Lippi Room (8) holds the Franciscan monk's lovely *Madonna with Angels*, as well as a number of other celebrated works, and is worth visiting to see Piero della Francesca's portraits of the Duke and Duchess of Urbino I. Room 9 holds works by the Pollaiuolo brothers, whose paintings display no distinctive style as such but are nonetheless decorative.

After a room of sculpture, the Tribuna (Room 18) is an octagonal room lit from above, with a beautiful mother-of-pearl-encrusted ceiling designed by Buontalenti. This room's structure and decor was designed to allude to the four elements and previously exhibited the objects that were most highly prized by the Medici. It holds a collection of portraits and sculpture, as well as Rosso Fiorentino's ubiquitous *Putto che Suona*, or *Musical Angel*. The circular route visitors must take around the room unfortunately renders it somewhat difficult to either appreciate the art from a good distance or to linger in front of the portraits.

The Botticelli Rooms (10–14) are the most popular in the Uff containing the world's best collection of work by the artist. He are the famous mythological paintings, which fused ideas of th spiritual and the secular: the Birth of Venus, painted around 1485, and La Primavera (Spring), painted some five years earlier. The meaning of the latter work remains a subject of fervent discussion, while Venus has overtones of the Virgin Ma

Room 15 exhibits Leonardo da Vinci's early works – includi the Annunciation (1475) and the unfinished Adoration of t Magi (1481) – and also paintings by Perugino and Signorel

Musical Angel, by Giovan Battista di Jacopo (aka Rosso Fiorentino), c. 1522.

The High Renaissance continues in Room 19, with Perugino and Signorelli's work. These Umbrian artists worked during the 15th and 16th centuries, and the latter's tondo (circular painting) Holy Family is reputed to have inspired Michelangelo's version. Room 20 is a break from Italian art, with work by Dürer, including his Madonna and the Pear, and Cranach. The last few rooms on the eastern corridor hold works from the 15th and 16th centuries: the Venetian school in Room 21, followed by Holbein and other Flemish and German Realists (22) and more Italian work by Mantegna and Correggio in Room 23. Room 24 contains a collection of miniatures.

THE WESTERN CORRIDOR

Most rooms in this corridor, including 26–34, 41 and 43–44, are currently closed for restoration. Only the Michelangelo (25) and the Florentines room (35), the Niobe room (42) and the room devoted to the 15th century Venetian, Umbrian and Northern European painters (45) remain open.

THE GROUND FLOOR

On the ground floor are 31 new rooms, as well as the Verone sull'Arno – the bottom of the U-shaped corridor that looks over the Arno and the Piazza degli Uffizi the other side.

The Blue Rooms focus on 17th–18th century Dutch and Flemish masters; 11 Red Rooms feature among others Rosso Fiorentino and Raphael; six "Modern Manner" Rooms house *inter alia* works by Correggio and Giorgione, and there are four Caravaggesque Rooms as well as the Sala del Caravaggio (90), which holds three paintings by the troubled artist whose style is characterised by his realism and use of light. More new rooms are being worked on and there is also restoration work in progress on the old ones.

The Vasari Corridor, the picture-lined overhead passageway connecting the Uffizi to the Palazzo Pitti via the Ponte Vecchio, is now open to the public but you have to book your tour in advance (www.uffizi.com).

Rooms 5–6 form the International Gothic Rooms, whose paintings exhibit a more conservative and less lavish approach, in keeping with the medieval mindset. Lorenzo Monaco's Crowning of Mary provides a good example of this by one of the main practitioners of the era.

The Duke and Duchess of Urbino I, in the Eastern Corridor.

PALAZZO PITTI

The gigantic Palazzo Pitti and the Boboli Gardens were once the royal residence.

Set in a massive Renaissance palace that dominates the Oltrarno, the Pitti houses seven museums, and provides access to the splendid Boboli Gardens that became a model for Italian landscaping. To appreciate the sumptuous Medici art collection and the lifestyles of the Grand Dukes, the Royal Apartments and Palatine Gallery (Galleria Palatina) are the obvious choices. The Silver Museum (Museo degli Argenti) comes a close second, more for the magnificently decorated rooms than for the contents. In terms of art history, the Modern Art Museum (Galleria d'Arte Moderna) takes up the story where the Uffizi leaves off, and gives a sense of the lavish but somewhat dubious decorative tastes of the last residents, the rulers of the houses of Lorraine and Savoy. By comparison, the Porcelain Museum and the Costume Museum are more for connoisseurs.

On the ground floor, the Museo degli Argenti (Silver Museum) contains much more than silver, ranging from antique vases much loved by Lorenzo the Magnificent to baubles encrusted with semi-precious stones and jewellery. The frescoed rooms alone make a visit worthwhile – in particular the Sala di San Giovanni, which formed part of the summer apartments. The frescoes by the artist after whom the room is named depict the reign of Lorenzo de' Medici, portrayed as a great patron of the arts.

The **Galleria Palatina** (Palatine Gallery) on the first floor houses an extraordinary range of paintings collected by the Medici family. In the west wing of the building are the rooms comprising the **Royal Apartments**. They are garish and ostentatious, decked out in heavy carpets, wallpapers, fabrics and furnishings, and overstuffed with treasures. Several of the rooms are named after the colour in which they are themed, and contain paintings and portraits fitting with the mood, followed by the Queen's Apartments, the King's Apartments and a ceremonial room, all filled with ponderous period furniture.

The lavish Galleria Palatina.

The most important rooms, named after the planets, are frescoed by Pietro da Cortona to allegorise the stages of Prince Ferdinando's education: Sala di Saturno, Sala di Giove, Sala di Marte and Sala di Venere. These contain works such as Rubens' The Consequences of War (Sala di Marte), Raphael's Portrait of a Lady (Sala di Giove). Other important paintings such as Raphael's The Pregnant Lady (Sala dell'Iliade), Lippi tondo of The Madonna and Child (see below; Sala di Prometeo) and Sleeping Cupid by Caravaggio (Sala dell'Educazione di Giove) are found in the smaller rooms.

Sala di Giove ceiling detail.

The ornate Prometheus Room in the Galleria Palatina.

MODERN ART

The Galleria d'Arte Moderna contains mainly Italian works from the neoclassical and Romantic movements, dating from the 18th century to the period after World War I, including *Portrait of Alaide Banti* by Michele Gordigiani. The most notable feature of the second-floor collection is its holding of paintings by the Macchiaioli, 19th-century Italian Post-Impressionists. Also situated on the second floor is the Galleria del Costume, which is an intriguing display of Italian costume and fashion, especially from the Medici to the modern period, including creations by designers such as Capucci.

Portrait of Alaide Banti by Gordigiani, in the Galleria d'Arte Moderna.

...ne of the finest rooms is the Sala di Apollo, in which hang ...portant works by Andrea del Sarto (including his Lamentation ...Christ, 1522–3). The Sala di Venere includes works by another ...aster of the High Renaissance, Titian; notably his The ...terrupted Concert and Portrait of a Man (above).

GIARDINO DI BOBOLI

The gardens' landscaping, following the slope of the hill, provides the perfect complement to Palazzo Pitti, with longer walks leading to Forte Belvedere and the Bardini Gardens.

The gardens were commissioned by Cosimo I and created by a range of prolific figures of the day, from Vasari and Ammannati to Buontalenti. One of the most compelling characteristics of the Boboli is the shadowy dark-green colour of the cypress and box hedges that serve to highlight the statues of amorous nymphs, satyrs and statuesque deities, as well as the grottoes and fountains. The steps lead up to the terrace behind the palace and in front of Susini's fountain of 1641. The amphitheatre surrounding the fountain occupies the site of a quarry used to obtain much of the stone for the palace, and contains an Egyptian obelisk. A series of terraces leads up the hill to the Neptune Fountain, round to the Rococo Kaffeehaus and up to the statue of *Abundance*. At the summit lies the Giardino del Cavaliere, or Knight's Garden. This delightful garden – with its low hedges, rose bushes and little cherub fountain – gives open views of San Miniato to the left and the village of Arcetri to the right, rising above the valley.

The cypress-statue-lined avenue known as Il Viottolone leads to the Vasca dell'Isola (Island Pool) with its Oceanus Fountain by Giambologna, murky green water, ducks, fish, strange mythical creatures and circular hedge. The route from here to the exit leads past the Grotta di Buontalenti, named after the sculptor who created this cavern in 1583–8. Copies of Michelangelo's *Slaves* (the originals are in the Accademia) are set in the four corners. Finally, on the right as one exits and nestling below the wall of the corridor, is the naked, pot-bellied statue of Pietro Barbino, Cosimo I's court dwarf, seated on a turtle. In 2013 the Boboli Gardens became a Unesco World Heritage site.

The gardens are dotted with classical and Renaissance statues.

The Pitti Palace and Boboli Gardens, painted in 1599-1602. Because of the massive size of the palace, the enterprise ruined the Pitti family; however, the Medici completed the project according to Brunelleschi's plans, with the façade enlarged to its mammoth proportions in 1620.

The Bacino di Nettuno is named after the slimy statue of Neptune who brandishes his trident at threatening sea-monster.

The Porcelain Museum displays pottery as well as objets d'art.

PORCELAIN MUSEUM

The Museo delle Porcellane (Porcelain Museum; daily 8.15am–sunset; closed 1st and last Mon of the month), which displays porcelain as well as objets d'art, is the only one of the Pitti museums to be situated in the Boboli Gardens, more specifically in the exquisite Giardino del Cavaliere.

Igor Mitoraj's Tyndareus Cracked (1998) is the only contemporary sculpture in the Gardens.

At the end of the Medici reign in 1737, the palazzo became the home of the Lorraines, and its elongated cubic form was further extended by the wings that curve round to frame the paved square at its front. Work on the outside was paralleled by alteration to the interior decor, which exhibits the ostentatious tastes of the period of the Lorraines and the Savoys, the next to take up occupancy within its walls. The history of the palazzo includes brief tenure by the Bourbons and the Emperor Napoleon before the last ruling monarch, Vittorio Emmanuele III, transferred the house to the public.

...e Grotta di Buontalenti houses replicas of Michelangelo's ...ves; the originals were moved to the Accademia in 1908. ...pervised by Vasari in the 1550s, the folly was completed by ...mmannati and Buontalenti.

THE ACCADEMIA

Originally the world's first school of art, the gallery is now home to Michelangelo's most famous work, *David*.

Michelangelo's *David* is the main attraction of the Galleria dell'Accademia. Most visitors dutifully come to gasp over the famous statue and then call it a day, scarcely realising that this is one of the city's finest galleries, despite its stifling intensity. The collection dates back to a school of fine arts founded by Cosimo I de' Medici in 1563. Although many treasures have moved to the Uffizi and San Marco, the remaining array of Florentine Byzantine and Gothic art justifies a visit, without the added inducement of a certain Michelangelo. The foremost sculptor of his age, or arguably of all time, is well represented by the authentic *David*, and by his magnificently unfinished *Four Slaves*. *David*, the city's most deified statue, was produced in a heroic age of sculpture. It was, in public-minded Florentine fashion, placed in front of the Palazzo Vecchio as a civic lesson. In keeping with the rulers' dissimulation of power, ostentation and self-aggrandisement were publicly frowned upon in Florence, as was the glorification of the individual. Yet the statue became both the symbol of liberty and a symbol of the artistic aspirations of the city.

David may be the centrepiece, but the so-called *Nonfiniti* (unfinished) *Slaves* illustrate the magnitude of Michelangelo's talent and ambition. In the brooding intensity of his figures one can sense the laying bare of the innate idea, the eternal truth that his art strove to attain. More clearly than in other masterpieces, these works reveal Michelangelo's philosophy: the genesis of a sculpture is not the classic shaping of art out of chaos but the struggle to free a creature that already exists. Even if his paintings have a rare sculptural quality, only the sculpted naked body can express Michelangelo's most sublime concepts.

Botticelli's delightful Madonna and Child is in the Sale del Quattrocento Fiorentino.

Pacino di Bonaguida's Tree of Life, dating from the 14th century

Lorenzo Monaco's Anunciation Triptych, of which only two panels are shown here, is also in the gallery.

DAVID

As the most famous sculpture in Western art, *David* has immediate appeal, both thanks to the sculpture's recognition factor and to its accessibility. When criticising the gigantism of the work, it has to be remembered that the statue was intended for a large civic space, not designed to be cooped up in a corner of an airless museum. Michelangelo's statue was installed, with much pomp, in a specially created Tribune here, in the Accademia, in 1873.

To most modern visitors, *David* is a celebration of the nude, stripped of his original cultural and political significance. It is therefore remarkable that, even without any artistic background, the average high-school student is still awed enough to be drawn into an appreciation of Renaissance art through Michelangelo's boyish ambassador. Giorgio Vasari, Michelangelo's reluctantly admiring contemporary, concurred, praising its grace, serenity, proportion and harmony: "This figure has overshadowed every other statue, ancient or modern, Greek or Roman."

But this timeless icon of virility is under threat and may yet be on the move again. After the discovery of cracks in the 500-year-old marble, the statue has been declared at risk of toppling over. The cracks in the statue's ankles are believed to have developed after *David* spent over a century leaning forward dangerously from his proud perch on Piazza della Signoria. The weight of the marble, bearing down on *David's* left ankle, is also partly to blame, as are the vibrations from the traffic and roadworks outside the gallery and the seismic tremors the region experiences episodically. Fortunately, the experts have declared that Florence's most famous statue is not in danger of imminent collapse, but as a precaution, it will soon be getting an anti-seismic plinth. There is also perennial talk of transferring the symbolic statue to a purpose-built site on the outskirts of the city.

David, the most famous sculpture in Western art.

…ong the most notable pieces is Filippino Lippi's striking …osition from the Cross, which was finished by Perugino on …former's death. Other highlights are Christ as a Man of …rows – a poignant fresco by Andrea del Sarto – and Fra …tolomeo's Prophets.

THE BARGELLO

The Bargello holds Florence's most important collection of sculpture from the Medici and private collections.

Unlike the Accademia, the Bargello would be a major site even without its art treasure trove. As the oldest surviving seat of government in Florence, the Bargello preceded the Palazzo Vecchio. The collection clearly shows the transition from statuary that was flaunted as public symbols to sculpture that was appreciated as private treasures.

The Bargello is also the best place in which to gain a sense of the interconnectedness of Florentine Renaissance sculpture. It provides a clear overview, with works of art by the greatest masters. Moreover, despite the virtuosity of Michelangelo, the Bargello is more of a shrine to his predecessor, Donatello, the only sculptor to lay claim to equal gifts. Unlike Michelangelo's work, Donatello's sculpture betrays little sign of creative torment and virtuosity for virtuosity's sake, which accounts, at least in part, for Donatello's less glittering reputation. However, in the Bargello at least, Donatello is the undoubted star. Those single-mindedly in pursuit of Renaissance sculpture would do well to head straight for the Donatello gallery, followed by the Verrocchio and della Robbia rooms, set on the floor above. To fully appreciate the sculpture, avoid being waylaid by the distracting displays of unrelated decorative arts.

The Bargello museum is situated in an impressive Gothic palazzo constructed in the mid-13th-century on Via del Proconsolo, in the heart of the ancient city. The building has previously been used as a barracks and a prison.

The Bargello contains works by Andrea della Robbia, a Renaissance sculptor specialising in glazed terracotta, including Bust of a Woman.

The sacrifice of Isaac, by Lorenzo Ghiberti (1401). The bronze tile was made for the competition for the portal of the Baptistery.

THE DONATELLO AND BRONZE GALLERIES

The Salone del Consiglio Generale is often nicknamed the Donatello Gallery. Apart from *David*, other works by Donatello in the room are *Saint George*, designed for the Orsanmichele church, and *Cupid*. You can also see the bronze panels submitted by Ghiberti and Brunelleschi for the Baptistery doors here. The walls of the room feature several glazed terracotta works by Luca della Robbia, while the first floor chapel (Cappella Maddalena) features frescoes depicting Hell: look out for the figure on the right dressed in maroon thought to be a depiction of Dante. Also on the first floor is a corridor displaying an eclectic group of 5th- to 17th-century objets d'art, including ivories and Islamic treasures.

Upstairs the Verrocchio Room displays Tuscan sculpture from the late 15th century, including portrait busts of notable Florentines and an interpretation of *David* by the artist who lends his name to the room, Andrea del Verrocchio. The adjoining rooms are filled with work by members of the della Robbia family – predominantly Andrea and Giovanni – dominated by the often overbearing large reliefs coloured in yellow, green and blue.

The last major room in the museum is the Bronze Gallery. This has one of the most rewarding displays in the Bargello. The sculptures generally depict mythological tales or Greek history, in the form of both models and more functional articles such as candelabra. The model for Giambologna's *Rape of the Sabines* (on display in the Loggia dei Lanzi) stands out, as do two others of his statues: *Kneeling Nymph* and *Hercules and Antaeus*.

Completing the second floor is a collection of medals.

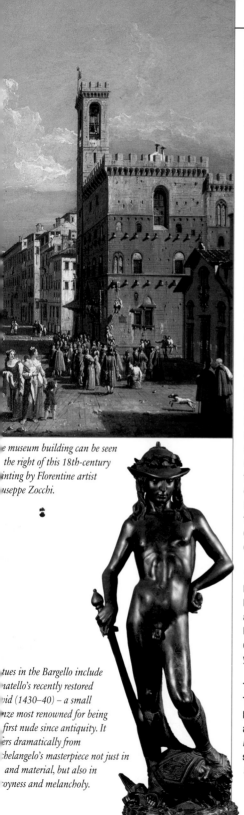

...e museum building can be seen ...the right of this 18th-century ...inting by Florentine artist ...useppe Zocchi.

...tues in the Bargello include ...atello's recently restored ...id (1430–40) – a small ...ze most renowned for being ...first nude since antiquity. It ...ers dramatically from ...helangelo's masterpiece not just in ...and material, but also in ...oyness and melancholy.

Attractive villas cling to the hillsides above the city.

AROUND FLORENCE

Along with vineyards, the Unesco-listed Medici villas are one of the glories of the Florentine countryside, even if the encroaching nature of the suburbs sometimes tarnishes their allure.

U nder the Medici, villa building became a form of self-exaltation and self-indulgence, allied to bucolic pleasures and property speculation. Perched on a scenic hill, the patrician villa became not just a rural estate and glorified hunting lodge, but also a place for feasting and festivities, and an escape from the summer heat. The picture of rural harmony extends to hamlets perched on steep, cypress-covered hills and to vineyards that have been producing famous wines since the Renaissance. Chianti country is close by, while, north of Florence, lies the Mugello, the fertile Apennine region bordering Tuscany and Emilia Romagna. Indulge in a little wine tasting before exploring the harsher Mugello, the Medici homeland.

Hilltop retreat

The best view of the mountains is a seat in the Roman theatre of **Fiesole ❶**, a delightful hill town 8km (5 miles) northeast of Florence. Fiesole was first settled by Etruscans probably in the 8th century BC. The Romans later named the place Faesulum – praising it for its freshwater springs and strategic location. During the 15th century Fiesole became a city suburb where wealthy Florentines built their villas. Today, a villa on the slopes of Fiesole's verdant

hill is one of the most sought-after addresses.

The main route from the centre of Florence is the Via San Domenico (the No. 7 bus goes from Piazza Stazione or Piazza San Marco), which climbs up to Fiesole's centre. The views on the way up reveal a landscape of extraordinary beauty, dotted with Renaissance villas perched on the slope of the hill.

Everything you will want to see in Fiesole lies a short distance from the Piazza Mino da Fiesole, the main square. A lane leads north to the

Main Attractions
Fiesole
Mugello Valley
Castello del Trebbio
Medici Villas
Prato
San Miniato

View from Sant Alessandro, Fiesole.

The Teatro Romano, with its numbered seats, could originally accommodate an audience of up to 2,000 people. It is in a remarkable state of repair, and is still used for dances and shows during the summer festival season.

Teatro Romano, where you can buy tickets for Fiesole's **Zona Archeologica** (daily Apr and Oct 10am–6pm, Nov–Mar 9.30am–5pm, May–Sept until 7pm, closed Tue Nov–Feb), entered from the ticket office and comprising the city's 1st-century BC Roman theatre, public baths of the same era, and an Etruscan temple, built in the 4th century BC and dedicated to Minerva, goddess of wisdom and healing. Also within the complex, the **Museo Archeologico**, built in the style of a Roman temple, is packed with finds from excavations in Fiesole. Included in the ticket is entry to the **Museo Bandini**, behind the cathedral on Via Duprè – a small art gallery with a fairly wide and representative selection of paintings from the early and middle Renaissance.

On the square, the huge **Cattedrale di San Romolo** (daily) is almost completely unadorned except for four frescoes, including a serene portrait of St Sebastian by Perugino (early 16th century). The Cathedral's jewel is the marble funerary monument to Bishop Leonardo Salutati, by Mino da Fiesole (1429–84), with a realistic bust of the smiling bishop.

From the southwest corner of the square, Via Vecchia Fiesolana leads to the **Villa Medici** (entrance along Via Beato Angelico), a Unesco World Heritage Site since 2013, together with 11 other Tuscan villas and two gardens. Any of the downhill paths from this point can be taken to reach the hamlet of **San Domenico**, about a 15-minute walk. The church of San Domenico (1406) contains a restored *Madonna with Angels and Saints* (1430), an early work of Fra Angelico who began his monastic life here before transferring to San Marco.

Opposite, the Via della Badia dei Roccettini descends to the **Badia Fiesolana** (Mon–Fri 9am–5pm, Sat 9am–noon; free), once a monastery and now home to the European University Institute. The unfinished brick facade of the huge church (dull inside, so don't worry if it is closed) incorporates the lovely green-and-white Romanesque facade of an earlier and smaller church. The No. 7 bus can be caught in San Domenico for the return journey to Florence.

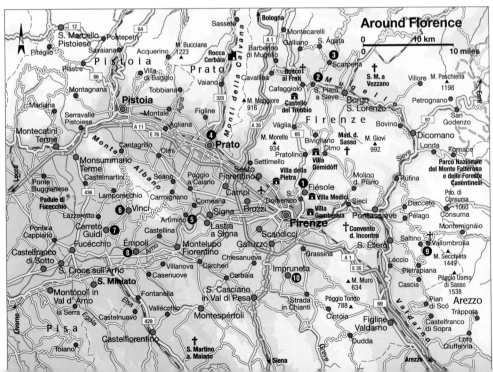

The Mugello valley

Just a few kilometres north of Florence, the Apennine foothills and Sieve river basin form the Mugello region. Like the Chianti, only less well trodden, it is characterised by bluish-green hills, brooding oak and chestnut woods, silvery olive groves and well-tended vineyards. The landscape is at its most picturesque in the western Sieve valley.

The Mugello has great associations with the Medici, who originated from here and lavished a lot of attention on the region. In 1451, Cosimo il Vecchio had Michelozzo alter the old fortress of Cafaggiolo just west of **San Piero a Sieve ❷** to create a country retreat, where Lorenzo il Magnifico spent part of his childhood, and writers and artists were lavishly entertained. The palace was modified by the Borghese family, who acquired it in the 19th century. Although recently restored, this original Medici seat, known as the **Castello Mediceo di Cafaggiolo** (tel: 055-847 9396) is privately owned and closed to the public for the foreseeable future but

used for weddings, events and a cookery school.

A little further south, **Castello del Trebbio** (tel: 055-830 4900; www.vino-turismo.it; guided visits Tue and Thur 10.30am and other times; booking essential) received similar treatment at the hands of Michelozzo, and, more than any other 15th-century Tuscan villa, retains the feudal atmosphere of a Medici villa. Deservedly popular for Chianti wine tastings, welcoming cookery classes and gourmet feasts in the vaulted cellars, this castle-like retreat is a place that celebrates all these activities in one day.

Overlooking San Piero a Sieve, high on a thickly wooded outcrop, is the **San Martino** fortress built in 1569 by Lanci and Buontalenti to enable Cosimo I to defend the Florentine state. This massive pentagonal castle is privately owned and currently being restored, although you can walk along its walls.

Just north of San Piero a Sieve is the town of **Scarperia ❸**. **Palazzo de Vicari**, in the main street, is one of the finest examples of 13th-century

Badia Fiesolana, former monastery and now home to the European University Institute. From the terrace in front of the church there are views down the Mugnone River valley back to Florence.

Fiesole in autumn.

Villa Country

The Medici villas reflect Florentine fine taste during the Renaissance, when these retreats were a haven for philosophers, artists – and the Medici rulers themselves.

The idea of a country retreat, so popular in Tuscany today, originated with the Romans. The villas were either working farms or were planned purely for pleasure. In the 15th century, the idea of the country villa was revived by the Medici family, who commissioned magnificent residences and elaborate gardens, modelled on classical principles. In 1452, Leon Battista Alberti decreed that a truly well-appointed country retreat had to be on a slope, full of light and air, with rooms grouped round an inner hall.

Many of the villas are now privately owned or have been transformed into American university campuses, thereby restricting what can be viewed and rendering the opening hours erratic. The villas and gardens described here are all easily accessible from Florence, but it's wise to call ahead.

Cypress avenue leading to Villa la Pietra.

The **Villa Medici** (Via Beato Angelico; tel: 055-239 8994; www.villamedicifiesole.it; Mon–Fri 9am–1pm; gardens appointment only) at Fiesole, described as "the first true Renaissance villa", was designed by Michelozzo for Cosimo il Vecchio between 1458 and 1461. It commands a superb view of Florence and the Renaissance gardens are of great interest.

On the outskirts of Florence, the 15th-century **Villa la Pietra** (tel: 055-500 7210; www.nyu.edu/lapietra; villa and garden guided tours Fri pm, garden tours Tue mornings; advance booking necessary) was the home of the writer Sir Harold Acton. He bequeathed the villa and his Renaissance art collection to New York University.

Another American-owned villa in the Florentine hills is the historic **Villa i Tatti** (tel: 055-603 251; www.itatti.harvard.edu; Tue and Wed afternoons, advance booking only; free), beside the pretty village of Settignano. Formerly the home of art collector Bernard Berenson (1865–1959), who restored the villa to house his Renaissance art collection, it is now the Harvard University Center for Renaissance Studies.

Nearby, the **Villa Gamberaia** (tel: 055-697 205; www.villagamberaia.com; gardens Mon–Sat 9am–6pm, Sun 9am–5pm; villa by group tours and reservation only) is another fine Renaissance villa whose original garden survives.

The **Villa Medicea Poggio a Caiano** is often dubbed the perfect villa. The facade was modelled by Sangallo on a Greek temple to satisfy the tastes of Lorenzo the Magnificent. In the 19th century, the gardens were converted according to the fashionable English style, with romantic temples, fountains, an aviary and a mock-Gothic ruin.

Set on a steep hill, the **Villa Medicea della Petraia** (Via della Petraia; tel: 055-452 691; daily 8.15am–sunset; villa by guided tour only on the hour from 8.30am; free) was designed by Buontalenti for Ferdinando de' Medici as an elegant villa for sumptuous entertaining. The interior is marred by the pretentious taste of the house of Savoy, but the Italianate gardens are a delight.

Only the gardens of the **Villa Medicea di Castello** (Via di Castello; tel: 055-452 691; daily 8.15am–sunset; free) can be viewed. Grottoes and statuary abound.

Another villa with attractive surroundings is the **Villa Demidoff** and **Parco di Pratolino** (tel: 055-408 0734; May–Oct Sat–Sun 10am–10pm; free), whose Mannerist gardens were remodelled in the English romantic style.

civil architecture in Tuscany, similar in style to Florence's Palazzo Vecchio. The outer facade, decorated with the coats of arms of local notables, carved in stone or worked in della Robbia terracotta, faces the **Oratorio della Madonna della Piazza** in the small square, which features a *Madonna and Child* by Taddeo Gaddi. At the bottom of the main street, near the entrance to the town, is the **Oratorio della Madonna dei Terremoti**, dedicated to Our Lady of Earthquakes, which contains another fresco of the *Madonna and Child*, said to be by Filippo Lippi.

Scarperia is famous as a centre of knife-making. In local workshops traditional methods are still used to fashion knives by hand. There is even a museum dedicated to the craft, the **Museo dei Ferri Taglienti** (Museum of Cutting Tools) in the Palazzo dei Vicari (Nov–May Wed–Fri 10am–1pm, Sat–Sun 10am–1pm and 2.30–6pm, June–Oct 10am–1pm and 3–7pm), and in September the town hosts an international knife exhibition.

Scarperia is also known for the race-track on its outskirts. The scenic "Mugello" circuit is used as a Ferrari F1 test centre and hosts the Italian motorbike grand prix in June.

A turning on the left of the southern approach to Scarperia wends its way through dense woodlands to the remote **Bosco ai Frati** Franciscan convent (tel: 055-848 111; Mon–Sat 10am–noon and 6–7pm, Sun 9–10am and 11.30am–noon and 6–7pm; free). This retreat retains the peace and solitude of the Franciscan ideal that places such as Assisi lack; no touring hordes, no postcard-sellers, only the peace and quiet offered by a church and its convent in a clearing in the woods. The monastic buildings were remodelled by Michelozzo around 1440 for Cosimo il Vecchio. They house a little-known, large wooden *Crucifix*, attributed to Donatello, one of the greatest masters of the Italian Renaissance.

Prato

Prato ❹, to the northwest of Florence, is the third-largest city in Tuscany, and long-time rival of Florence. Refreshingly, Prato doesn't depend on tourism but on trade, and revels in its confident, mercantile personality. The city is renowned for its textile-manufacturing industries, with numerous factory outlets selling fine fabrics, cashmere and designer clothes. Although the trade has made contemporary Prato a rich city, it was already a leading textile town in the 12th century and its magnificent monuments are evidence of its former wealth. Amid the industrial estates, and factories dominated by Chinese immigrants, lies a compact *centro storico*, contained within medieval walls. But Prato is also a cosmopolitan city, drawn to contemporary art, as witnessed by the Henry Moore sculpture that greets most visitors.

The city possesses an extraordinary relic: in the delightful green-and-white **Duomo** (Mon–Fri 7.30am–7pm, Sun 7.30am–noon and 1–7pm; free) is what is believed to be the girdle of the Virgin Mary. The legends

GLORIOUS GARDENS

The centrepiece of any Medici villa was the garden, which provided a harmonious link with the wild countryside beyond the walls. The enclosed medieval garden, the *giardino segreto*, survived at first, with vegetable and herb gardens planted nearby. However, Renaissance landscape gardeners embellished the concept of enclosure and, in keeping with humanistic ideals, it became a symbol of tamed nature.

The villa and garden were considered an organic whole, linked by loggias, porticoes and new perspectives. Emphasis was placed on geometrical rigour and the laws of perspective were used to create terraced gardens with straight avenues lined by cypresses or lemon trees in tubs. Semicircular ponds, adorned with sculpture, closed the line of vision.

The Mannerist era witnessed a profusion of allegorical fountains and grotesque sculpture, much of which remains. The main players were Buontalenti, who brought architectural rigour to garden design, and Il Tribolo, a pupil of Michelangelo who was responsible for the Boboli Gardens. Four of the best gardens are at: Villa Gamberaia; Villa Demidoff; Villa Medicea della Petraia; and Villa Medicea di Castello. The Pratolino gardens at Villa Demidoff became a Unesco World Heritage site in 2013.

The Pulpit of the Holy Girdle on Prato's Duomo.

The impressive Castello dell'Imperatore.

surrounding this relic have been celebrated by Agnolo Gaddi, whose frescoes cover the walls of the Chapel of the Holy Girdle. Above the high altar are fresco cycles of *The Life of St Stephen* and *The Martyrdom of St John the Baptist* by Filippo Lippi. Outside the Duomo is the Pulpit of the Holy Girdle, decorated with dancing cherubs by Donatello, where, on Christmas Day and several other holy days in the year, the girdle is displayed. The **Museo dell' Opera del Duomo** (Mon, Wed–Thur 9am–1pm, Fri–Sat 10am–1pm and 3–6pm, Sun 10am–1pm) in the cloister contains paintings, sculptures and reliefs by Donatello, Fra Lippi and others.

Other notable monuments include the church of **Santa Maria delle Carceri** (daily 7am–noon and 4–7pm; free), built by Giuliano Sangallo in typical no-frills Brunelleschian style. In front of the church is the **Castello dell'Imperatore** (Wed–Mon 10am–4pm; free), built by Frederick II Hohenstaufen in the first half of the 13th century, and unique in Tuscany, taking as its model the Norman castles of Puglia. A walk along its ramparts offers a good view of Prato.

In Via Rinaldesca is the 14th-century frescoed **Palazzo Datini** (daily 10am–1pm and 3–6pm), former home of Francesco Datini (1330–1410), better known as the Merchant of Prato. Datini, a successful wool merchant, died one of the richest men in Europe, leaving his money to city charities, and is commemorated in statues around the town.

For a break from Renaissance art, the **Centro per l'Arte Contemporanea Luigi Pecci** (tel: 0574-5317; www.centropecci.it) lies on the edge of town. The museum's attitude and energy were once more important than the collection of contemporary works on display – this could be about to change as the museum is undergoing massive structural change to double its exhibition space.

Outside the historic centre is the more engaging **Museo del Tessuto** (Via Santa Chiara 24; www.museodeltessuto.it; Tue–Fri 9am–3pm, Sat 10am–7pm, Sun 3–7pm), dedicated to the fine textiles that made Prato's fortune. Gorgeous masterpieces of antique cloth are on display, and the skills that led to their production are not lost, as the section on contemporary textiles clearly demonstrates.

Leonardo country

A gentle meander into the countryside due west of Florence takes in some lovely views, a few small towns and Leonardo's alleged birthplace of Vinci. Head west out of Florence on the SP66 (in the direction of Pistoia), and turn south at **Poggio a Caiano**, site of Lorenzo the Magnificent's favourite retreat, built by Sangallo (1480–85). It is one of the most magnificent and best preserved of Florentine rural retreats (garden daily 8.15am–sunset, free; villa by guided tour only, closed 2nd and 3rd Mon of the month).

The walled village of **Artimino ❺**, about 11km (7 miles) from Poggio a Caiano, is a classic case of a *borgo*

reborn as a villa, wine estate and medieval residential complex. It is also the setting for another huge Medicean villa (tel: 055-875 1426; www.artimino. com; open by appointment only), this one built by Bernardo Buontalenti as a hunting lodge for Ferdinando I in 1594 and curious for the number of tall chimneys on the roof. It has been beautifully restored, and converted into a distinguished hotel, complete with a restaurant specialising in dishes with Medici origins. Part of the villa is open to visitors, including a small Etruscan museum. After wandering round Artimino *borgo*, consider dining in the Biagio Pignatta (see page 255) in the villa stables, or in the rustic Cantina del Redi (tel: 055-875 1408) overlooking the villa.

A tortuous road leads through olive groves and vines from Artimino to **Vinci** ❻, alleged birthplace of Leonardo. Here, the 13th-century castle in the centre of town is home to the **Museo Leonardiano** (tel: 0571-933 285; www.museoleonardiano. it; daily Mar–Oct 9.30am–7pm, Nov–Feb 9.30am–6pm), which has a vast selection of mechanical models built to the exact measurements of Leonardo's drawings. In neighbouring **Anchiano**, Leonardo's birthplace museum reopened in 2012 after major restoration, and now showcases the latest multimedia technology (tel: 0571-933 285; www.museoleonardiano.it).

Five kilometres (3 miles) southwest of Vinci is the hill town of **Cerreto Guidi** ❼. Once owned by the Guidi counts, it now produces a good Chianti Putto wine and boasts yet another Medici villa, the austere **Villa di Cerreto Guidi** (Mon–Sat Oct–Mar 10am–6pm; Apr–Sept 9am–6pm, Sun 10am–7pm; closed 2nd and 3rd Mon of the month; free), built in 1564 for Cosimo I as a hunting lodge. It contains some fine portraits of the Medici family. Isabella, daughter of Cosimo I, is said to have been murdered here by her husband for her infidelities.

West of Florence

West of Florence, the first major stop along the superstrada is **Empoli** ❽, a prosperous, modern market town with a small *centro storico* and a superb

Ancient San Miniato.

SAN MINIATO

The ancient town of San Miniato, whose origins go back to Etruscan times, is set on the top of three hills, equidistant from the important historical cities of Pisa, Florence, Lucca, Pistoia, Siena and Volterra. On the proverbial fine day you can gaze as far as Volterra and the Apuan Alps. High on the hillside are the two towers of the **Rocca** (Tue–Sun 11am–6pm), rebuilt in the 12th century by Frederick II. The older tower, the **Torre di Matilde** (Sat 10am–1pm and 2–5pm, Sun 2–5pm), was converted into a bell tower when the **Duomo** (Mon–Sat 9.30am–7pm, Sun 8.15–7pm, summer until 8pm) was added, with its Romanesque brick facade. The **Museo Diocesano d'Arte Sacra** (Oct–Mar Fri 10am–5pm, Sat–Sun 10am–1pm, Apr–Sept Mon–Thur 10am–4pm, Fri 10am–5pm, Sat-Sun 10am–6pm; closed for lunch daily 1–2pm), in the old sacristy of the Duomo, displays art and sculpture, including works by Lippi, Verrocchio and Tiepolo. Built by the Lombards in the 8th century, the magnificent church of San Francesco (daily 8am–12.30pm and 3–7pm) is the oldest building in San Miniato.

But to most Italians, San Miniato means one thing only: white truffles. The town produces a quarter of Tuscany's crop, which are best tasted during the November truffle fair. The Association of Trufflers of the San Miniato Hills issues a map showing where to find the aromatic fungus, which is dug out of the ground with a pole called a *vangheggia*.

TIP

The 72-euro 72-hour Firenze Card (www.firenze card.it) also provides access to some sites outside Florence, including the Zona Archeologica and Museo Bandini in Fiesole and the Villa Medicea Poggio a Caiano.

Romanesque church, the **Collegiata Sant'Andrea**. The green-and-white-striped facade is reminiscent of Florence's San Miniato, and the small **museum** (Tue–Sun 9am–noon, 4–7pm) contains a surprising amount of precious Florentine art.

A few kilometres west of Empoli is **Fucecchio**, noted for the **Padule di Fucecchio**, to the north of town. Now Italy's biggest inland marsh, covering 1,460 hectares (3,600 acres), this was a Medicean fishing ground in the 16th century, and Cosimo I had a bridge and weirs built to facilitate the sport. It is now home to rare birds and a variety of flora. The land is privately owned, but the wetland centre in **Castelmartini di Larciano** (tel: 0573-84 540) organises guided tours.

Valdarno

East of Florence, off the SS70, a narrow pass climbs up the western slope of the Pratomagno hills to the monastery of **Vallombrosa ❾**, founded in the 11th century, but remodelled over the centuries, and its **Museo d'Arte Sacra** (tel: 055-862 251; daily 10am–noon and

3–6pm). The reward for making the journey is not so much the monastery itself as the splendid beech wood that surrounds it. Romanesque churches worth visiting in the vicinity include **San Pietro in Cascia** and **Sant'Agata in Arfoli**. Nearby, the tiny village of **Saltino** is handy in the winter for the ski runs of **Monte Secchieta**.

Towards Chianti

Not far south of Florence, towards Chianti, is the town of **Impruneta ❿**, an important sanctuary in the early medieval period when a shrine was erected here to house an image of the Virgin Mary, thought to have been the work of St Luke and believed to be capable of performing miracles. This shrine, the **Basilica di Santa Maria** (Mon–Sat 7.30–11.30am and 4.30–6.30pm, Sun 7.30–noon and 4.30–7pm), with its terracotta tabernacle by Luca della Robbia in Michelozzo's Chapel of the Cross, underwent alterations over the centuries, and was bomb-damaged in World War II.

Subsequent restoration and repair to this and to other pre-17th century buildings has meant that Impruneta has retained a great deal of its early character, though without the patina of age. Brunelleschi insisted that the tiles for the roof of the Duomo in Florence be supplied by Impruneta, which is still an important centre for terracotta production. Call into the **Tesoro**, the cathedral treasury, too (tel: 055-203 6408; Apr–Oct Sat–Sun 9am–1pm and 4–7pm, Nov–Mar Sat–Sun 9am–1pm and 3–6pm; free).

West of Impruneta, **San Casciano in Val di Pesa** is a quiet old Chianti town, enlivened every February by carnival. The town's reputation today rests solely on the art displayed in the Collegiata church, the convent, the church of St Francis and the church of the Misericordia, including paintings by Simone Martini, Ugolino di Neri, Taddeo Gaddi and Fra Bartolomeo.

We are now in the Chianti region covered on page 185.

Impruneta, just south of Florence, is an important centre of terracotta production.

LUCCA AND PISTOIA

Take some mountains and spas, add a scattering of grand villas, blend in two underrated cities full of character, and you begin to paint a picture of Lucca and Pistoia provinces – where you can swim, ski, shop or soak in the spas to your heart's content.

Perfectly proportioned Lucca, and its harmonious, villa-studded countryside, occupy the alluring heart of this region. Lucca, like Siena, is a city built on a human scale, designed to be savoured slowly, and on foot. To the west of the walled city is the Tuscan Riviera, known as Versilia, a broad strip of land between the sea and the Apennines – and, to the north, are the steeply mountainous Garfagnana and Lunigiana regions.

Despite its charms, neighbouring Pistoia always feels marooned in a historical backwater. Pistoia province, sandwiched between Lucca and Florence, and fought over for centuries by both, has yet to make its mark. Its lower profile is partly due to its bewildering diversity. Part-fertile plain and part-mountains, the province is bordered, in the north, by the Apennines, where Abetone is Tuscany's premier ski resort. Further south, spa country rules, with Montecatini Terme playing the dowager to Grotta Giusti's laid-back younger sister.

Miniature cultural capital

Often bypassed by fans intent on ticking off the Leaning Tower of Pisa, **Lucca ❶** is Tuscany's self-deprecating star. In spite of this, it is the only Tuscan city to see tourism expand exponentially in recent years. Its perfectly preserved walled heart, quiet sophistication and peaceful pace of life are all credited with winning over visitors. And that's before talking about its pinky-gold palaces, pedestrian-friendly bastions, crowd-pleasing concerts, enchanting churches, and its renowned olive oil and wine estates. To jaded urbanites, Lucca represents life as it should be led.

Sitting on a marshy plain between the Apennines and Monte Pisano, Lucca has been inhabited since

Main Attractions
Lucca
Casa Museo Puccini
Villa Reale
Montecatini Terme
Monsummano Terme
Cattedrale di San Zeno, Pistoia
Abetone

Cycling in the sunshine in Lucca's Piazza Anfiteatro.

A jewellery shop in Lucca.

ancient times. Little remains of Etruscan Luk, but Roman Luca survives in the grid design of streets, and in the elliptical Piazza Anfiteatro, around which houses were subsequently built. As an independent city-state, 11th-century Lucca spent the next 400 years defending itself against an ever more belligerent Florence. Even though the Florentines won the title of capital of the region, Lucca never ceded its political and economic autonomy. It remained an independent republic, apart from a brief period of Pisan rule, until the Napoleonic invasion of 1796.

This graceful and prosperous provincial capital, 77km (48 miles) west of Florence on the A11, is a city of many charms, not least the walls encircling the city. They were built after 1500 to keep Lucca's enemies at bay. In 1817, the massive ramparts were planted with a double row of plane trees, which shade the broad avenue running along the top of the walls, now used by Lucca's citizens as a playground, promenade, jogging trail and cycle route.

The Cathedral square

A path from the walls leads directly to the **Duomo di San Martino** Ⓐ (mid-Mar–Oct Mon–Fri 9.30am–6pm, Sat until 6.45pm, Sun 9–10am and 11.45am–6pm, Nov–mid-Mar Mon–Fri 9.30am–5pm, Sat until 6.45pm, Sun 11.45am–5pm). The Cathedral's striking facade is decorated with a sculpture of St Martin dividing his cloak (the original sculpture is now just inside the church). The inlaid marble designs typify Tuscan Romanesque style: hunting scenes figure large, with dogs, boars, and huntsmen on horseback. Flanking the central portal are scenes of the *Labours of the Months* and the *Miracles of St Martin*.

Inside is the octagonal *tempietto* that contains a larger-than-life *Crucifixion* in carved and painted wood. Known as the *Volto Santo* (Holy Face), the Romanesque carving was once believed to be a true portrait of Christ, carved by Nicodemus, who witnessed the Crucifixion (in fact, the highly stylised figure is probably a 13th-century copy of an

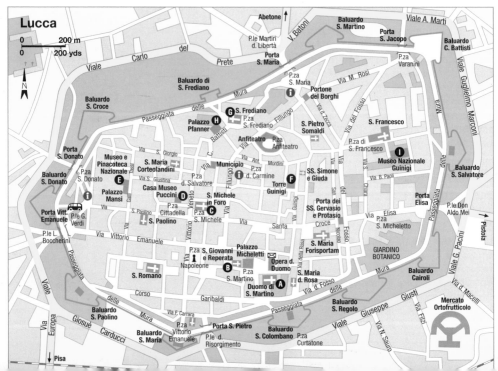

11th-century copy of an 8th-century original). Each year, on 13 September, this revered relic is paraded through the streets at dusk. Off the south aisle is the **Sacristy** (mid-Mar–Oct Mon–Fri 9.30am–5.45pm, Sat 9.30am–6.45 pm, Sun 9–10.45am, and 11.30am–6pm, Nov–mid-Mar Mon–Fri 9.30am–4.45pm; Sat 9.30am–6.45 pm, Sun 9.30–10.45am and noon–5pm). This contains the greatest treasure: Jacopo della Quercia's tomb of Ilaria del Carretto, who died in 1405. It's a tender effigy, depicting a faithful dog at her feet, waiting for his mistress to awake. As the wife of Paolo Guinigi, Lord of Lucca, Ilaria died at the age of 24, following the birth of their second child.

Across the square is the church of **Santi Giovanni e Reperata** Ⓑ (mid-Mar–2 Nov daily 10am–6pm, 3 Nov–mid-Mar Sat–Sun only 10am–5pm). Originally Lucca's cathedral, the church has been excavated to reveal a wealth of Roman and Romanesque features. The earliest is a 1st-century BC mosaic floor, superseded by a 2nd-century Roman bathhouse, which itself gave way to a 5th-century baptistery, later joined by a series of churches, culminating in the present 12th-century building. Highlights include the Roman font, Romanesque pavements and the coffered ceiling.

Via del Duomo leads west of the Cathedral to Piazza del Giglio, home to the theatre and opera house. Adjoining the square is Piazza Napoleone, shaded by tall plane trees and lined by restaurant terraces.

Pisan Romanesque to Puccini

Heading north out of the square takes you to Piazza San Michele, ringed by Renaissance arcades. At the centre of the square, the church of **San Michele in Foro** Ⓒ (daily 7.30am–noon and 3–6pm; free), built on the site of the Roman forum, has one of the most spectacular Pisan Romanesque facades in Italy. Flanked by Lucca's loveliest bell tower, the tiered arcades are decorated with delicate motifs and allegories; hunting scenes carved in green and white

TIP

The Bar San Michele on Piazza San Michele is a great place to stop for a drink and admire San Michele in Foro. Alternatively, head for Piazza Anfiteatro for an exquisite artisan ice cream or crêpe at Gelateria Anfiteatro. Several caffès serve the local speciality, *buccellato* – a sweet bread with raisins and aniseed – either with a coffee or sweet Vin Santo wine.

Buskers in Piazza San Michele.

marble, with creatures both exotic (bears, dragons and elephants) and domestic (a rabbit, a duck and a crow eating grapes). The church is topped by a huge gilded statue of Archangel Michael slaying the dragon, flanked by two angels.

Turning your back on the facade, take Via di Poggio, which leads to the **Casa Museo Puccini ⓓ** (Apr daily 10am–6pm, Mar–Oct daily 10am–7pm, Nov–Mar Mon, Wed–Thur 10am–1pm, Fri 10am–4pm, Sat–Sun 10am–6pm), the birthplace of Lucca's celebrated composer, Giacomo Puccini.

Heading west, feel your way through Lucca's maze of medieval alleys to Palazzo Mansi, in Via Galli Tassi, which houses the **Museo e Pinacoteca Nazionale ⓔ** (Tue–Sat 9am–7pm, Sun 9am–2pm). Deities and allegorical figures romp across the ceilings of the splendidly furnished 17th-century home of Cardinal Spada (1659–1724). Upstairs, at the end of a sequence of rooms decorated around the theme of the Four Elements is a sumptuous

bedchamber dedicated to Fire. This fire is not a destructive one, but the flame that burns when Eros strikes with his arrow. The room features a gorgeous double bed, its lovely hangings decorated with birds and flowers.

Remnants of medieval wealth

The wealth of Lucca, like that of Florence, was based on banking and its silk industry. As early as the 12th century, bankers were plying the Mediterranean or travelling north to Bruges, Antwerp and London, buying and selling silk and woollen cloth. Successful bankers, such as the Guinigi family, built ostentatious tower-houses, although only one of these remains, the 14th-century **Torre Guinigi ⓕ** (daily Jan–Feb Nov–Dec 9.30am–4.30pm, Mar and Oct until 5.30pm, Apr–May until 6.30pm, Jun–Sept until 7.30pm). As in San Gimignano (see page 185), such fortified homes were both medieval status symbols and retreats in times of trouble. Climb the tower to admire rural views, and

GIACOMO PUCCINI

Both a giant of 19th-20th-century opera and a crowd-pleasing showman, Giacomo Puccini (1858–1924) was a musical master of erotic passion, pathos and despair. His lush operas are characterised by soft harmony, gentle orchestration and an emotional sensitivity that is very modern. Ever the populist, Puccini was the composer with the most in common with musical theatre, and conceived of opera as drama set to music.

Puccini was born into a musical family in **Lucca**, where his newly restored home is now a museum in his honour. The young Puccini womanised at **Torre del Lago**, where his villa, set between the sea and reedy **Lake Massaciuccoli**, welcomed bohemian painters, beautiful women, gamblers and hunters as keen as himself. As Puccini boasted, "I am a mighty hunter of wildfowl, beautiful women and good libretti." He was deeply attached to the lake where he went poaching as a boy and would even compose at the piano, dressed in breeches and riding boots, with a loaded gun and hunting dogs ready by his side. Here, in this villa overlooking the Luccan hills, Puccini's jealous wife would

lace her husband's wine with an aphrodisiac antidote if she felt any female guests were too alluring. The raffish playboy was reckless with women, fast cars and yachts called *Mimi*, naturally named after the heroine of *La bohème*.

Puccini's music is of more lasting allure, despite his scandalous private life. "Nessun Dorma" from *Turandot* even became the theme music for the 1990 Football World Cup. Although Stravinsky dismissed *Madama Butterfly* as "treacly violin music", director Jonathan Miller disagrees: "I'm made to cry by Puccini and I never am by Verdi."

Lucca's international Puccini festival, **Puccini e la sua Lucca** (www.puccinielasualucca.com), is the only permanent festival in the world, with musical events taking place every Friday and Saturday at 7pm. Recitals, opera performances and other special concerts by renowned singers and pianists are all staged at the lovely San Giovanni Basilica right in the centre of town. And all this in honour of the greatest Luccanese of all time, much loved by his compatriots.

to make out the outline of Lucca's Roman Amphitheatre (Anfiteatro), perfectly preserved in the buildings that were constructed against it in the Middle Ages.

For a closer look at the resulting egg-shaped piazza, turn right out of the tower, and first right in Via delle Chiavi d'Oro. Passing the Art Deco baths (now a cultural centre), keep going until you reach the curving wall of the **Anfiteatro**. Ringed by pavement cafés, restaurants and souvenir shops, the Amphitheatre is an atmospheric place in which to enjoy an ice cream or linger until the evening for dinner.

Leave through the opposite archway, following the curve of the Amphitheatre to Via Fillungo, Lucca's main shopping street and **San Frediano Ⓖ** (Mon–Sat 8.30am–noon and 3–5pm, Sun 10.30am–5pm; free), with its huge gold-and-blue facade mosaic of *Christ in Majesty*. The treasure of this church is its Romanesque font carved with scenes showing Moses and his entourage of camels, leading his people (dressed in medieval armour) through the divided Red Sea.

To the rear and left of the church is the **Palazzo Pfanner ⒽⒾ** (www. palazzopfanner.it; daily Apr–Nov 10am–6pm), a delightful 17th-century residence. Without paying, you can catch a glimpse of the wonderful garden and external staircase at the rear by climbing on to the city walls behind San Frediano church and walking left for a short distance. Highlights inside include swathes of 17th-century Lucchese silk in the bedrooms and beer-making equipment in the cellar – the palace was used as a brewery until 1929.

The Guinigi were not the only ones to flaunt their wealth by creating towers. A picture hanging in the **Museo Nazionale Guinigi Ⓘ** (Tue–Sat 8.30am–7.30pm) shows that the city was once, like San Gimignano, a forest of towers, and illustrates just how wealthy medieval Lucca was. Among the artistic treasures here is a *Madonna and Child* in bas-relief by Matteo Civitalli, a contemporary of Donatello, and Lucca's most renowned sculptor.

A variety of delicious biscotti on sale.

Bird's-eye view of Lucca and the Apuan Alps beyond.

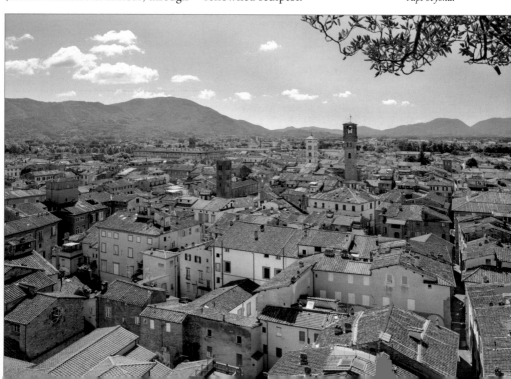

Ornate staircases at Villa Garzoni.

Lucchesi villas

The area surrounding Lucca is rich in villas: the patrician Villa Torrigiani, the Baroque Villa Mansi and the Villa Reale at Marlia are all surrounded by beautiful parks. Most of these villas are still in appreciative private hands, but often the gardens can be visited even if the house is not open to the public. Wandering through fragrant shrubbery and cool grottoes, past whimsical statuary and fountains, is a delightful diversion on a hot summer's afternoon.

Leave Lucca on the SS12 in the direction of the Garfagnana, and after passing through Marlia, turn off at **Villa Reale** ❷ (www.parcovillareale.it; gardens open to the public Mar–Oct daily 10am–6pm, Nov–Feb Sat–Sun 10am–4pm, weekdays by advance booking only). It was built in the 17th century by the noble Orsetti family, and substantially remodelled by Elisa Bacciocchi, Napoleon's sister. There is a lush park with a lake, which surrounds the formal Italian gardens. Most wonderful of its many fine features is the *teatro verde*, an outdoor theatre surrounded by clipped yew hedges, a key setting for concerts during Lucca's summer festival.

Continue on through a fairly built-up area to Segromigno in Monte and the charming **Villa Mansi** (tel: 0583-920 234; Apr–Oct Mon–Fri 9am–4pm, Sat–Sun 2–6pm, Nov–Mar Mon–Fri 10am–1pm, Sat–Sun 2–5pm), with beautifully landscaped gardens. Just 2km (1.2 miles) away in Camigliano, **Villa Torrigiani** (Mar–2nd Sun in Nov daily 10am–1pm and 3–6.30pm) is a fine example of Baroque architecture. Also consider **Villa Bernardini** in Vicopelago just outside Lucca (tel: 0583-164 6057; www.villabernardini.it; visits by request).

Equally splendid is the **Villa Garzoni** (villa closed for renovation; gardens: Mar–Oct daily 8.30am–sunset, Nov–Feb 10am–sunset, other days open for groups by request) in the town of **Collodi** ❸, with a glorious Baroque garden full of mythical monsters modelled in terracotta, fountains and topiaried animals. The steep terraces of the 17th-century garden lead to some memorable viewing points.

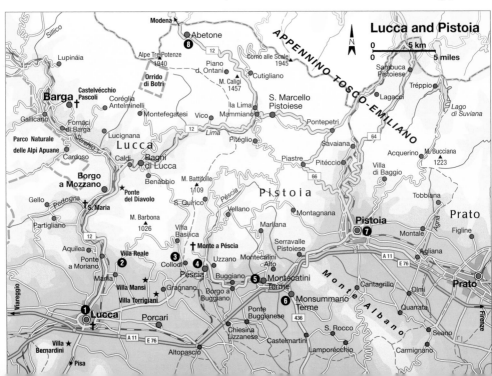

If you were entranced as a child by the adventures of a wooden puppet with a remarkable nose, you may recognise the name of this town as being that of the author of *The Adventures of Pinocchio* (1881). Carlo Lorenzini adopted Collodi as his pen-name because he had fond memories of staying here as a child. The town now has **Parco di Pinocchio** (tel: 0572-429 342; www.pinocchio.it; same hours as Villa Garzoni gardens) devoted to Pinocchio, consisting of mosaics, mazes and statues based on scenes from the story. Contemporary children, accustomed to virtual reality and adrenalin-fuelled theme parks, may find it rather tame, but there are plans to enhance the attractions at the nearby Villa Garzoni.

En route to the spa resorts

Where Lucca's villa country ends, Pistoia Province begins, as does the route east to the thermal-spa resorts of Montecatini Terme and Monsummano Terme. Just south of Collodi is **Pescia** ❹, cradled in the plain of the Valdinievole. Pescia is famous for its flower production and has the largest flower market outside the Netherlands. Prosperous Pescia is surrounded by nurseries, greenhouses, olive groves and hills dotted with gracious villas. Divided by a river, the medieval town boasts several fine churches, including the cathedral and Sant'Antonio, as well as a crenellated town hall. In the hills above town is the Convento di Colleviti, a Renaissance monastery, accessible by footpath from Pescia.

Just south of Pescia are two appealing villages, notably the shabbily scenic **Uzzano**, which has a curious church on the crest of the hill, and well-tended **Buggiano**, with an interesting church and lovingly restored palazzo.

Further east awaits **Montecatini Terme** ❺, once famed throughout Europe for its elegance and luxury. It was remodelled by Grand Duke Leopold of Tuscany in the 18th century and became a destination spa resort before the term was invented. Belle Epoque nostalgia is still the order

In the spring, the peach blossoms of Pescia are outstanding; every September in even-numbered years, Pescia hosts the colourful Biennale del Fiore – Festival of Flowers.

The grand Villa Torrigiani.

The Spa Renaissance

The new breed of thermal spas marks a return to Roman roots: these are both pampering and restorative spas that bathe body, mind and spirit.

An age-old ritual

Taking the waters has become fashionable once more. Water cures, popular since Etruscan and Roman times, have always been part of local culture. In the 1st century AD, Emperor Augustus's physician issued a prescription to the poet Horace to visit the Tuscan spas, one of the first medical prescriptions on record. The Romans saw spas as both curative and civilising, distinguishing their citizens from the Barbarians, who didn't know how to combine warm water with warm company and well-being.

Thermal spas were also recreational in the days of the Tuscan Grand-Dukes, when resorts such as Bagni di Pisa welcomed the crowned heads of Europe to wallow in the waters, gamble in the casino and dance in the ballrooms. But somewhere

The Grand Duke hammam at Saturnia Terme.

along the line, the spas languished, and lost out to "liver-boosting water cures" in echoing marble halls.

The best spas

However, the scary white-coat brigade has been banished from the best Tuscan spas, such as Chianciano's **Terme Sensoriali** (www.termesensoriali.it), one of the most approachable yet seductive day spas.

Neighbouring **Fonteverde** (www.fonteverdespa.com), floating on a sea of hills in Val d'Orcia, is a terraced spa resort clustered around a late Renaissance villa. The stylishly simple estate is dotted with thermal pools but, as a destination spa, also delivers oriental massage, skin consultations, dietary advice, yoga and spiritual healing – all presented clearly, without pushiness or psychobabble.

While not throwing the baby out with the bathwater, spas such as **Grotta Giusti** (www.grottagiustispa.com), in Monsummano Terme, manage to combine gracious 19th-century living with superb massage, thermal pools, sprawling grounds, and steamy grottoes dubbed "the eighth wonder of the world" by the composer Giuseppe Verdi. Health-seekers don bizarre boiler suits to follow the Dantesque route into "Inferno", where grottoes named Purgatory, Paradise and Hell induce a surreal detox. After sweating in Hell, there's floating under the thermal jets in the giant pool, Ayurvedic massage or sneaky golf sessions.

Set at the foot of low-slung mountains, **Bagni di Pisa** (www.bagnidipisa.com) is a delightful retreat with a view of the Leaning Tower. This romantic 18th-century resort is charmingly nostalgic, with vaulted bedrooms, a winter garden, frescoed halls, and a folly Byron was fond of. The hammam is a steamy, couples-only cavern and stone-clad pool with a 38-degree temperature conducive to chilling out, detoxing and lowering the blood pressure.

In the Maremma, **Saturnia Terme** (www.termedisaturnia.it) is a sophisticated affair, as befits a spot that has provided rest and recreation to Romans, ancient and modern. Fed by historic springs, a beguiling thermal pool is matched by an indoor recreation of Ancient Roman baths, outdoor cascades and timeless views of the Etruscan countryside.

For a full list of spas offering health and beauty treatments, see page 274.

of the day, even if many foreign spa-goers feel more comfortable in the purely pampering spas. Avenues of neoclassical spa pavilions dispense health-giving waters to drink and offer treatments ranging from inhalation to mudbaths. With its fountains and Art Nouveau flourishes, Tettuccio is the grandest and most languid. Cast aside your wariness and dip a toe in the waters: whether sipping them in marble pavilions, strolling through the magnificent parks, or committing yourself to a complete cure.

Montecatini Alto is the original medieval fortified town above the thermal springs, and can be reached by funicular or by road. Although over-popular in high season, it is still a restful place to visit, with a shady chestnut-tree walk along the lower terrace, and panoramic views over Valdinievole, "valley of the mists". Drink something stronger than water in the main square, Piazza Giusti, and cast your eye over the ruined fortress and equally ruined Romanesque church, unfortunately marred by an ill-judged restoration.

Montecatini represents a cross-roads, from where you can continue east to Pistoia, make a brief foray north, or collapse in a superb spa just south. Driving north of Montecatini along the N633, you arrive at **Marliana** via a scenic mountain road, and can meditate over views from Marliana's castle and campanile. A little further on, medieval **Vellano** makes a good lunch stop, with rustic inns overlooking the valley slopes and olive terraces. Alternatively, south of Montecatini, **Monsummano Terme** ❻ is home to an extraordinary spa, Grotta Giusti Spa Resort, where you can bathe in thermal pools or sweat it out in a bizarre steamy grotto, best savoured on an overnight stay.

Cycling in Lucca

Lucca is full of lanes too narrow for cars, so the locals often get about by bicycle. This, combined with Lucca's reputation for culture and intellectual pursuits, has earned the city the nickname of the "Cambridge of Tuscany".

The old walls are equally popular with walkers and joggers. Every now

Bikes for rent in Lucca.

Cheeky decorative tiles at Tettuccio Terme, Montecatini.

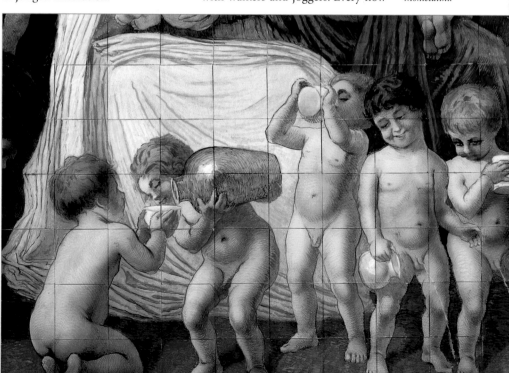

Detail from the entrance to the Cattedrale di San Zeno.

and again, you can take the sloped exit down into the town and cycle around the key sites, locking the bike up to a gate when entering a museum or walking around a piazza.

You can hire a bike at Rent Bike Lucca on the square in front of the railway station (www.touristcenterlucca. com; current bike hire for a day costs from €12 per person) or at Barbetti, Via Anfiteatro 23, and Cicli Bizzarri, Piazza S. Maria 32. Cycling is also a healthy alternative to a day on the beach. Near Lucca, one leisurely coastal route runs from the Viareggio seafront to Lido di Camaiore, Marina di Pietrasanta and Forte dei Marmi. Another 20km (12.4-mile) trail links Viareggio with Torre del Lago Puccini. To book a short bike trip, or a bigger cycling holiday in Tuscany, contact Gusto Tours (www.gustocycling. com) or consult Love Italy (www.love italy.co.uk).

Unsung Pistoia

The path most travelled from Montecatini leads east to **Pistoia** ➐. The provincial capital tends to be overshadowed by its glittering neighbour, Florence, only 37km (22 miles) distant, and is rather unfairly neglected as a result. Its historic heart is delightful, and it has a profusion of elegant shops, inns and hotels tucked away in the medieval streets. What's more, the citizens of Pistoia take great pride in their monuments and churches, and when dusk falls, the shadowy, lamp-lit streets have an authentic atmosphere. Church bells peal, Franciscan monks stride along in their unmistakable brown habits and rope belts, and the stone slabs outside the shops are laid out with goods for sale just as they might in the Middle Ages.

Pistoia was originally a Roman town, founded as a staging post on the Via Cassia. It flourished as a banking centre during its medieval heyday, but was constantly buffeted between Florence and Lucca, eventually falling under the dominion of Florence. The impressive trapezoid walls that encompass the city are part of the bastion built by the Medici during the 15th century. Much of the area around

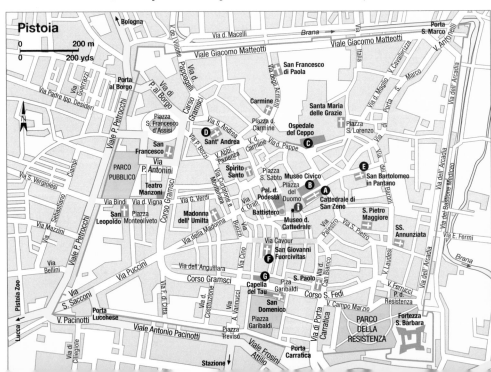

the **Piazza del Duomo** has been pedestrianised, and, when not full of market stalls (Sat and Wed), the piazza is a peaceful place for taking stock of Pistoia's riches.

The **Cattedrale di San Zeno** Ⓐ (daily 8am–12.30pm, 4–7pm; free) originated in the 5th century, but was rebuilt in Romanesque style with a splendid Pisan-style facade of green and white marble stripes. A marble porch was added later and decorated with an exquisite blue-and-white Andrea della Robbia bas-relief.

Inside are many medieval frescoes, an impressive Crucifix (1274), Renaissance paintings and – most glorious of all – the massive, ornate silver altar in the **Chapel of Saint James** (contact the sacristan), decorated with bas-reliefs and statues over a period of two centuries by many different artists, including Brunelleschi. Next door in the Palazzo dei Vescovi (Bishops' Palace), above the helpful tourist office (tel: 0573-21622), is the **Museo della Cattedrale** (Tue, Thur and Fri; guided tours only 10am–1pm, 3–5pm).

Beside the Duomo is the soaring **Campanile**, originally a watchtower, naturally adorned with three tiers of green-and-white Pisan arches, echoing the Duomo facade. You can climb the bell tower for magnificent views over the town (by reservation at one of the tourist offices). Opposite is the 14th-century octagonal **Battistero** of San Giovanni in Corte, designed by Andrea Pisano (daily 10am–1pm and 3–6pm).

The piazza is lined with Renaissance palaces, including the **Palazzo del Podestà**, still the city's law courts, with a finely decorated inner courtyard. Opposite is the **Palazzo del Comune** (Town Hall), with a harmonious facade of arches and delicately pointed windows, decorated with the ubiquitous Medici crest and a grim black-marble head. Inside is a courtyard and sweeping stairway, and sculptures by local artist Marino Marini (1901–80), many of them based on his favourite theme of riders and horses. Upstairs in the first- and second-floor rooms is the impressive art collection of the **Museo**

Della Robbia's majolica frieze above the Ospedale del Ceppo loggia.

Pistoia's market is set up on the pretty Piazza della Sala.

Civico **B** (Thur–Sun 10am–6pm), which includes a rare 13th-century painting of St Francis.

To the north of the Duomo, in Piazza Giovanni XII, is the **Ospedale del Ceppo ⊙**. It was founded in 1287 and still functions as a hospital. Above the loggia is a brilliantly coloured majolica frieze by Giovanni della Robbia that depicts the *Seven Works of Mercy*: worthy citizens handing out food to the poor, comforting prisoners and washing the feet of dusty travellers. The figures are realistic, often humorous, despite the gravity of their occupations.

A congregation of churches

Pistoia's striped churches encircle the historic centre like zebras – with the Pisano pulpits the great pride of the town. **Sant' Andrea ⊙** (8am–6pm), in the Via Sant'Andrea, has an arcaded facade and reliefs above the central door. Inside is a richly painted wooden ceiling and narrow nave, well lit from the upper clerestory. Here is Giovanni Pisano's

hexagonal pulpit (1297), modelled on the Nicola Pisano pulpit in the Pisa Duomo. The sharply carved marble reliefs border on the melodramatic in their depiction of *The Life of Jesus* and *The Last Judgement*.

San Bartolomeo in Pantano ⊙ (St Bartholomew in the Swamp; 8am–7pm), in the Piazza San Bartolomeo, is one of Pistoia's oldest churches, built in the 12th century with a five-bay facade. Inside there is a pulpit by Guido da Como (1250) depicting *Christ's Nativity*, with the edifice resting on the backs of men and lions carved out of marble.

In the pedestrianised *Via Cavour* is the 12th-century church of **San Giovanni Fuorcivitas ⊙** (7.30am–noon and 5–6.30pm) adorned with an almost psychedelic green-and-white striped marble facade in Pisan style. The treasures inside include a pulpit created in 1270 by Fra Guglielmo da Pisa, a pupil of Nicola Pisano, a water stoup by Giovanni Pisano, and a touchingly beautiful white-glazed terracotta of *The Visitation* by Luca della Robbia.

In Piazza Garibaldi, the monastery of **San Domenico** (Mon–Sat 8–11.50am, 4.30–6pm, Sun 8am–12.30pm, 4.30–7pm) was insensitively restored after damage in World War II, but seek out the Renaissance tombs, cloisters and the colourful Benozzo Gozzoli fresco.

Opposite San Domenico is **Cappella del Tau** Ⓖ (Mon–Sat 8.15am–1.30pm). This former chapel is now an artistic monument, with darkly dramatic Gothic frescoes and vaulted ceilings, including a fine fresco of *The Fall*. The Palazzo del Tau is now home to the **Museo Marino Marini** (www.fondazionemarinomarini.it; Oct–Mar Mon–Sat 10am–5pm, Apr–Sept until 6pm), named after Pistoia's most famous 20th-century son. Marino Marini (1901–80) made his native city an important bequest of his sculptures, etchings, prints and drawings based on the recurring theme of horses and riders.

Recover from an overdose of art and churches in a café on the Piazza della Sala, where the fruit-and-vegetable market is set out around an old well. At night the piazza is home to a number of lively bars. If still in need of light relief, browse the shops for embroidery, shoes, leather and jewellery on Via Cavour, Via Cino, Via Ateo Vannucci and Via d. Orafi. Ever earnest, Pistoia can even turn shopping into a dutiful museum experience.

The city is famous for its embroidery, fine examples of which can be admired in the **Museo del Ricamo**, housed in the Palazzo Rospigliosi (via Ripa del Sale 3; Tue–Thur 10am–1pm, Fri–Sat 10am–1pm and 3–6pm).

Alternatively, consider visiting **Pistoia Zoo**, which is set in a pine forest in Via Pieve a Celle about 5km (3 miles) outside town (tel: 0573-911 219; www.zoodipistoia.it; daily 9.30am–5pm).

From Pistoia, clear your head in the mountains, going via **San Marcello Pistoiese**, the main town, traditional **Cutigliano**, and the lofty, all-year-round resort of **Abetone** ❽, which is only 90 minutes' drive from Pistoia (see box).

Pistoia's Cattedrale di San Zeno and campanile, built in the 12th century.

MOUNTAIN PURSUITS

The drive into the mountains north of Pistoia is stunningly beautiful, especially in autumn. But winter-sports enthusiasts will prefer it with a good covering of crisp snow.

The main town is **San Marcello Pistoiese**, traditionally known for the **Mongolfiera**, or hot-air balloon, launched on 8 September to mark the end of summer. Near San Marcello, at Mammiano, is a spectacular suspension footbridge, 220 metres (720ft) long, connecting to the road across the River Lima. **Cutigliano**, situated further down the valley, is surrounded by fir trees, but has limited skiing on its 13km (8 miles) of pistes, so serious skiers will prefer to head to Abetone.

Abetone, set 1,400 metres (4,660ft) above sea level, is the most popular ski resort in the Apennines. It offers a wide range of pistes served by 25 ski lifts; has three ski schools and some fine new hotels, designed in "Swissified" mountain style. In the absence of good snow, the snow machines can cover 40km (25 miles) of slopes. In summer, Abetone makes an invigorating centre for climbing and walking expeditions in the surrounding pine and chestnut woods. *Rifugi*, or mountain shelters, are dotted around the area, often combining basic accommodation with an inn serving rustic fare.

The dizzying Ponte della Maddalena spanning the River Serchio.

VERSILIA, GARFAGNANA AND LUNIGIANA

Tuscany's northern corner is one of its wildest, loveliest, yet least explored areas – from the Versilia coast to a dramatic landscape of pine-covered mountains, craggy ravines, remote castellated villages and marble peaks. And all this with the famous beach resorts of Forte dei Marmi and Viareggio attached.

Versilia is renowned for its sociable beach resorts, which range from sophisticated Forte dei Marmi to laid-back Viareggio. But beyond the seaside bustle lies an elemental landscape that challenges popular perceptions of Chiantishire. The coastal lowlands of the Versilia give way to a dramatic hinterland of snowcapped mountains, terraced hillsides, deep gorges and mountain streams, populated by deer, wild boar, badgers, stone martens and wolves, not to mention walkers, rock climbers, cavers and canoeists. Tuscany's northernmost tip is an untamed rocky region known as the Lunigiana, bordered by the Apuan Alps in the south, Liguria in the west and Emilia to the east. Bordering it to the south is the Garfagnana, cut through by the Serchio River, which flows between the Apuan Alps and the Apennines. Together they make up one of the wildest, most beautiful, yet least explored parts of Tuscany.

Versilia

This coastal region lies west of Lucca, squeezed between the Apuan Alps in the east, and Lago di Massaciuccoli in the south. Michelangelo built a road from the marble quarries to transport the marble to waiting ships – and inadvertently created a summer playground. Once pine-covered,

the coast has succumbed to rampant development, but in the place of rustic charm it offers fine seafood restaurants, a sense of fun, and beach entertainment, Italian-style – all against the backdrop of the Apuan Alps. Whereas Forte dei Marmi is the resort for socialising and being seen, Viareggio is for everyone.

Viareggio ❶ is the oldest resort in the Versilia, and famous for its Carnival as well as for its beaches and boat-building tradition. The pre-Lent Carnival, one of the biggest and

Main Attractions

Viareggio
Torre del Lago Puccini
Pietrasanta
Forte dei Marmi
Castelnuovo di Garfagnana
Parco dell'Orecchiella
Barga
Carrara Marble Quarries
Pontrémoli

Fishing at Torre del Lago Puccini.

TIP

In Viareggio, a carnival museum, the **Museo della Cittadella** (Via Santa Maria Gorretti 16; tel: 0584-530 48; June–mid-Sept Fri–Sun 8.30–11am, mid-Sept–May 4–7pm; free), on the site where the floats are made, tells the story of the origins and characters of the famous Carnival.

boldest in Italy, sees thematic floats spiced up with political satire. The resort enjoyed its heyday at the beginning of the 20th century, as testified by a handful of seafront cafés, beach clubs and historic hotels, such as the Plaza de Russie, originally built for the pre-Revolution Russian aristocracy. Today's Russian tycoons much prefer Forte dei Marmi, where their opulent villas nestle between the beaches and the Alps. Instead, unpretentious Viareggio offers pockets of genteel charm, seafood restaurants and leisurely cycle rides. The seafront boulevard, the **Passeggiata Margherita**, is at the heart of the action, especially since cycling has taken off on this stretch of the coast. For a stylish meal, seek out the Art Nouveau **Gran**

Caffè Margherita (Viale Margherita 30) – Puccini's favourite.

On the downside, the beach clubs have a regimented feel: the sea can be reached only if you pay an entrance fee and wish to lie on a sunbed among rows of others, on sand carefully raked and flattened.

Lakeside retreats

An operatic pilgrimage just south of Viareggio takes you to **Torre del Lago Puccini ❷**, best reached through the deep Macchia Lucchese pine groves. Here, on **Lago di Massaciuccoli** is Giacomo Puccini's villa, where all his operas save *Turandot* were composed. This pleasant but over-popularised retreat was a peaceful backwater in Puccini's day. **Puccini's villa** (daily

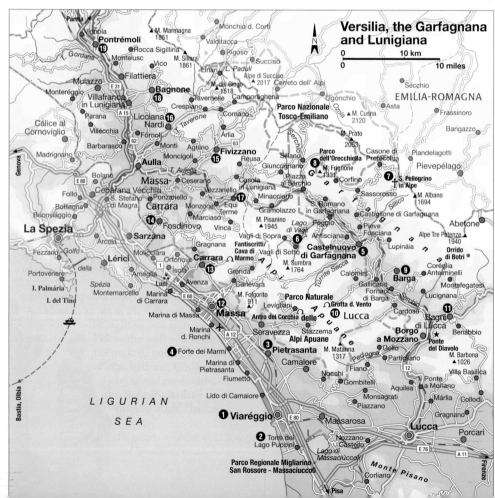

Apr–May 10am–12.30pm, 3–6pm, June–Oct 10am–12.30pm and 3–6.30pm, Dec–Mar 10am–12.30pm and 2.30–5.30pm, closed Mon morning; guided tours) displays his musical instruments – as well as his guns. Puccini is buried in the nearby chapel. In August, a summer opera festival takes over the atmospheric lakeside stage beside Puccini's villa – the maestro would have approved.

The lake and neighbouring wetlands form a nature reserve and haven for birdlife – the **Parco Regionale di Migliarino-San Rossore-Massaciuccoli** (tel: 050-525 500) is best explored on a boat trip around the lagoon.

Seaside resorts

Continuing north from Viareggio, the resorts fall into line in quick succession. **Lido di Camaiore** is slightly downmarket, but access to the beach is easier – and virtually free of pay-as-you-enter stretches of sand. From this part of the shore it is easy to reach **Camaiore** (to the Romans, Campus Maior), which is about 7km (4 miles) to the east.

Pietrasanta 3 is about 8km (5 miles) inland from the sea; its name, "Holy Stone", refers to the town's chief product, marble. This is the Tuscan centre for stone sculptors, who come here in droves to work the marble, ever since the days of Henry Moore and Joan Miró. As a result of all this artistic intensity, a fine white dust covers everything in Pietrasanta, even the wine glasses in the bars of the Piazza Carducci. Fortunately, there is some public sculpture on display, often presented to the town by the resident artists themselves.

This is the case with Colombian sculptor Fernando Botero, who lives in the resort for part of the year: "I like Pietrasanta, a beautiful town with a unique square, a cathedral worthy of a great city, and the Apuan Alps as a backdrop. What mountains, what greenery, what shade, what rivers, what fresh streams flow beneath chestnut trees and olive groves and orange orchards, all framed by marble quarries along the green." At the Enoteca Marcucci (see page 257) you can eat alongside sculptors and

Giacomo Puccini, composer of La Bohème, Tosca and Madama Butterfly, lived and died at Torre del Lago, where his villa is now a museum dedicated to his life and work.

TUSCANY'S BEST BEACHES

Tuscan beaches deliver both romance on the rocks and the regimented lines of beach umbrellas that most Italians consider to be beach-break heaven. In Forte dei Marmi, Versilia boasts the best-known beach resort for the chic set, while Viareggio remains the most popular big beach resort in Tuscany. The romantic, rocky cove of Cala Piccola, on Monte Argentario, arguably has the most aquamarine waters. Yachties will prefer to swim off chici Porto Santo Stefano and glitzy Porto Ercole. As for privacy and a back-to-nature remoteness, nothing beats Marina di Alberese, within the Parco della Maremma.

In the annual "beach charts", Tuscany has been triumphing for many years now. Every year Italian beaches get ranked by Green organisations, notably Legambiente's *Blue Guide*, which measures the cleanliness of the water, safety, quietness, eco-friendliness and sustainability. In 2014 a total of 269 Italian beaches passed the strict tests. Tuscany was judged to have an extremely clean coastline, with 18 beaches winning Legambiente's prestigious "blue flags", and it came second only to Liguria's 20 award-winning beaches.

In Versilia, the resorts awarded the best "blue flags" were chic Forte dei Marmi, Marina di Pietrasanta, Camaiore and bustling Viareggio. Near Pisa, family-friendly Tirrenia and Marina di Pisa are winners. Further south, on the Etruscan Riviera, the beaches do even better, with blue flags going to Castiglioncello, Vada, Marina di Bibbona, San Vincenzo, Cecina and Castagneto Carducci. In the Maremma, the best beaches include family-friendly Castiglione della Pescaia and most of the chic Monte Argentario peninsula's "Silver Coast". As usual, the region's best beach was deemed to be Castiglione della Pescaia (five "blue flags") in the Maremma, followed by beaches in Capalbio and on the islands of Capraia and Giglio (four "blue flags" each). Elba also fared very well, with awards for the popular beaches of Campo nell'Elba, Porto Azzurro, Marciana Marina and Capoliveri.

All of the winning Tuscan beaches mentioned tend to be holidaymakers' firm favourites whose Green credentials are sound. (For more information see: www.bandiera-blu.org and www.legambienteturismo.it)

Fresco by the 20th-century Colombian artist Botero, in Pietrasanta's church of Sant'Antonio.

The beach at Forte dei Marmi, with the Apuan Alps in the background.

painters, feasting on Tuscan *ribollita* soup, grilled meats and fine wines.

Luxurious villas

Further north, **Forte dei Marmi** ❹ is the favoured retreat of Italian celebrities and captains of industry, from the Agnelli dynasty, who helped to launch this chic resort, to Giorgio Armani and celebrity tenor Andrea Bocelli. Forte *is* snooty and cosmopolitan but also charming and old-fashioned: the *dolce vita* is cultivated according to time-honoured tradition, despite the influx of a brasher set ready to pay a fortune to sit under the right beach awnings.

Forte dei Marmi grew up around a fort built in 1788 by Leopold I of Tuscany – these remains dominate the main square today. The surrounding sleek boutiques and cafés manage to combine cosmopolitan chic with a small-town atmosphere, enhanced by a lack of high-rise buildings. The parasol pines are still the tallest markers around, framing discreet villa gardens overflowing with bougainvillea.

While catering to an elite, with its exorbitantly priced beach clubs and tropical-style bars, Forte still retains something of the seductive mood that once captivated bohemian writers and artists, from Thomas Mann to Henry Moore. When the gently sloping beaches pall, today's celebrity visitors happily hop on to vintage bicycles to potter down the coast to Pietrasanta.

Into the mountains

Given the mountainous nature of the interior, any inland trek along minor roads will inevitably be a leisurely trail along narrow, switchback roads, but with dramatic views and chance discoveries as compensation. This is "Slow Tuscany" so take Garfagnana and Lunigiana at a leisurely pace, ideally staying there – forays from the coast can also make a delightful diversion from the beach scene. If time is short, then bear in mind that it is quicker and easier to reach the area via Forte dei Marmi, Pietrasanta, Viareggio or Lucca than to travel as the crow flies.

Garfagnana

Castelnuovo di Garfagnana ❺, about 64km (40 miles) north of Lucca, is a convenient stepping stone to the Garfagnana. This fortress town once controlled the route from Genoa to Lucca and Pisa, and was ruled by the Este dukes of Ferrara until Italian unification. The town suffered during World War II, even if the Duomo survived, as did the town walls, and the church of San Michele, containing a 14th-century *Madonna*.

Other highlights are the **Rocca**, or governor's palace, which is now the town hall, and the medieval fortress at the top of the hill. But beyond the sights is the sense of a Tuscany off the tourist trail. This is exemplified by Il Vecchio Mulino, an engaging Slow Food inn run by the cherubic Andrea. If you prove *"simpatico"*, Andrea will lead you through a tasting of local dishes (see page 257).

Scenic routes

Northwest of Castelnuovo di Garfagnana, a scenic road runs from Poggio to Vaglia alongside the river Edron and **Lago di Vagli ❻**. The old stone houses and parish church in Vagli di Sotto are worth seeing, but the real draw is the partially submerged medieval village of **Fabbriche di Careggine**, covered by the creation of a dam in the 1940s. Sometimes seen peeking through the surface, the village is fully visible every 10 years when the lake is drained to service the dam. There are ambitious plans to construct a rope bridge over the lake and put a glass dome over the village to make it visible at all times, not only during maintenance periods.

The road winds its tortuous way through mountain scenery for about 18km (11 miles) to **San Pellegrino in Alpe ❼**, an ancient monastery housing the **Museo Etnografico Provinciale** (Apr–May 10am–1pm and 2–4.30pm, June–Sept 10am–1pm and 2–6.30pm, Oct–Mar weekdays 9.30am–1pm, Sun 10am-1pm and 2–4.30pm), whose display of peasant life is less compelling than the mountain views.

San Romano in Garfagnana offers a medieval castle and the stark peaks

TIP

At almost every turn there are more medieval villages, more castles, more breathtaking views. One of the best ways to see this rich and varied region is to take the little train between Aulla and Lucca on its slow journey through the mountains.

Castelnuovo di Garfagnana.

TIP

Barga's best bar is the historic Caffè Capretz (Piazza Salvo Salvi), a favourite meeting place for poets and politicians at the end of the 19th century. It has a terrace with a view at the back and tables laid out under the loggia at the front.

of the Alta Garfagnana, whose barren beauty is best appreciated with a visit to the **Parco dell'Orecchiella** ❽ (see page 68), now part of the Parco-Tosco-Emiliano (www.parcoappennino.it). This wilderness, laced with waymarked trails and cycling paths, is framed by the grandiose peaks of the Apennines.

A scenic route to the coast from Castelnuovo di Garfagnana goes along the spectacular Túrrite Secca through the Parco Naturale delle Alpi Apuane, via the **Marmitte dei Giganti** ("Giants' Cooking Pots") – 23 huge hollows (20 metres/65ft in diameter) made by Ice Age glaciers – and through the Galleria del Cipollaio, a long tunnel carved out of the marble. From here the road winds down to Seravezza and Forte dei Marmi on the Versilia coast.

Barga

To the south, pretty, arty, medieval **Barga** ❾ is by far the most beguiling town in the district. This quaint, surprisingly cosmopolitan place battles the problem of the rural exodus in its own way: many of those who left to make their fortunes abroad have returned, or keep a summer place here, including the Scots. The returning émigrés have brought a broader outlook to Barga, as seen in the kind of art galleries rarely found in a rural Tuscan outpost. The annual opera festival also brings the old town to life in July and August.

The sights, such as they are, are mostly about atmosphere, charm and stunning location, with lovely views at the very top. Leave your car outside the old city walls and head through the gate to explore the old town, with its narrow, winding streets lined with Florentine-style palazzi overlooked by the Romanesque Duomo, which commands wooded views of the Garfagnana from its hilltop position.

The Apuan Alps

From Barga, cross the Serchio valley to Gallicano. Just after the village, look out for signs to the 13th-century **Eremo di Calomini**, a gleaming white hermitage clinging to a rocky slope between the trees. Another 9km

SLOW FOOD IN 'SLOW TUSCANY'

Garfagnana is not just a hiking paradise. It is the domain of Slow Food.

The best place to start a tasting session is in Andrea Bertucci's Osteria Il Vecchio Mulino (tel: 0583-62192), a rough-and-ready inn and a temple to Slow Food. Here, as in other welcoming Garfagnana villages, you can discover *biroldo*, the local blood sausage, and a protected Slow Food delicacy. The popularity of salami and blood sausages is also linked to the proximity of Emilia Romagna, a region well-known for its penchant for pork products.

The most typical ingredient is spelt *(farro)*, one of the oldest known grains, dating back to Roman times. While spelt has disappeared from most regions, it takes pride of place in Garfagnana dishes, and finds its way into spelt soup, made with sage, garlic, red wine and pork rind. Spelt is also used to make local bread, pasta and savoury tarts and pies.

Whether roasted or boiled, chestnuts are also a feature of local cooking and are used in the so-called "paupers' bread". As in many mountain areas, polenta is a typical base for hearty rural dishes and is often combined with mushroom dishes. Polenta is also the base of chestnut cakes and in *castagnaccio*, the sweet local dessert. Instead, neighbouring Lunigiana specialises in *panigacci*, chestnut-flour pancakes cooked over an open fire and served with creamy cheese and home-cured meats.

If you would like to meet the cheese-makers and craftsmen, weavers and wine-makers, book a day's tour with Sapori & Saperi (tel: 339-7636 321, www. sapori-e-saperi.com). This small, local company runs food and craft adventures, introducing visitors to anything from ricotta-making to sourcing the best inns, the places that only insiders know. For instance you may engage in an exciting marzuolo truffle hunt with Riccardo and his hound and then taste the found truffles at Riccardo's house or learn how to bake potato bread in a wood-fired oven. These are culinary experiences, to meet Slow Food and wine producers and get a taste of their lives, far from the Chiantishire stereotypes.

(5.5 miles) of steep and winding road brings you to **Fornovalasco** and the **Grotta del Vento** ❿ (Cave of the Wind; www.grottadelvento.com; daily 10am–6pm; guided tours only, departing on the hour), in the Apuan Alps, a labyrinthine system of tunnels, caves and secret passages full of dramatic stalactites and stalagmites, underground lakes and echoing chambers. There are guided tours of one, two and three hours, with the three-hour itinerary (10am and 2pm Apr–Oct) the most dramatic. The cave complex, one of over 1,300 in the Apuan Alps, is chilly, even in summer.

Bagni di Lucca ⓫, once a fashionable spa town, played host to Shelley, Byron and the Brownings, who all bathed in these warm, sulphurous waters. Today, the **Bagni Caldi**, the "hot baths", are scenically shabby, including an intriguing time-warp spa, with maze-like passages carved into the rock, and steam-vapour grottoes. Rugged walking country beckons, including the white-water gorge of **Orrido di Botri**, an authentic wilderness with a canyon.

From Bagni di Lucca, the road winds along the banks of the River Serchio to **Borgo a Mozzano**' and the splendid, lofty five-arched bridge of Ponte della Maddalena, also known as the **Ponte del Diavolo** – Devil's Bridge.

Massa-Carrara

Bordering on Liguria, the province of Massa-Carrara has only been part of Tuscany since the mid-19th century, and still feels out on a limb, particularly in Lunigiana. Many of the locals talk of "going to Tuscany" as if it were a foreign land, which it is, in some ways. While Massa-Carrara's main towns and resorts are disappointing, the marble trails make up for it, as does the jagged backdrop. Expect pine-covered mountains, craggy ravines, remote castellated villages – and the majestic marble peaks of the Apuan Alps glittering deceptively like snow in bright sunshine.

The towns of Massa and Carrara have both prospered from the marble trade, but their Faustian pact leaves them blighted by industrial eyesores.

FACT

The impressive Ponte della Maddalena, which spans the Serchio just south of Bagni di Lucca, is also known as the Ponte del Diavolo, or Devil's Bridge. Legend has it that the bridge-builder appealed to the Devil for assistance. The Devil agreed, but in return demanded the soul of the first to cross the bridge. The shrewd builder kept his promise by sending a dog across.

The colourful facades of Barga's backstreets.

TIP

Between Carrara and
Marina di Carrara is a
marble museum, the
Museo Civico di Marmo
(Mon–Sat Oct–Apr
9.30am–1pm and
3.30am–6pm, May–Sept
9am–12.30pm and
2.30–5pm). Displays
include many varieties of
marble and granite,
geographical and
historical exhibits and
some modern sculptures.

*Eremo di Calomini in
the Apuan Alps.*

Marina di Massa is a popular resort, with fine wide, sandy beaches interspersed with groves of pine trees and a promenade of pretty pastel-shaded holiday villas. Ribbon development swallows up the port, from where ships carry marble all over the world.

Although somewhat lacklustre, **Massa** ⓬ has a well-preserved medieval centre, built by the dukes of Malaspina, who ruled Massa for three centuries, and were entombed in the cathedral. Massa is dominated by the magnificent Renaissance **Castello Malaspina** (Sat–Sun 3–7pm). Beyond the narrow old streets of the town, walk on up through leafy lanes past decaying villas dotted over the mountainside. The fortress walls provide marvellous views, and welded on to them is a graceful Renaissance palace, its delicate marble pillars providing a powerful contrast to the grim towers of the original castle.

The main evidence of the famous marble quarries in **Carrara** ⓭ is the river of white mud that flows through the town, which has a dusty, disaffected air about it. It is a working

town, not a monument to marble; there are few fine marble statues to be seen, even in the Pisan-style Duomo.

If time is short, ignore the town centre in favour of a visit to the marble-working quarries looming above the city. From the Carrara roundabout, decorated with a lofty marble sculpture, follow signs to **Fantiscritti**. The Vara bridges signal your arrival and are a striking sight, either in full sunlight or in moonlight, when the moon intensifies the shadows and the marble glows. After your marble tour, the descent back to the coast is via hairpin bends, viaducts and gorges, and a crawl through the marble tunnel, once part of the "marble railway" linking the three main quarrying fields.

Finally, in a scruffy area off the Via Aurelia, north of Carrara, there is **Luni**, the original Roman settlement from which marble was shipped. Beyond the amphitheatre and museum, excavations have revealed columns, capitals, mosaic floors and tomb fragments.

Just over the Ligurian border is **Sarzana**, a thriving market town colonised by artists. There is a large market

in the Piazza Matteotti, which is surrounded by Romanesque arcades sheltering smart little cafés.

Lunigiana

Luni gave its name to **Lunigiana**, "the land of the moon", an inward-looking, virtually undiscovered part of Tuscany. Lunigiana has always been a main trading route, however, and its many castles were built by the powerful Malaspina family who controlled the region to extract tolls from pilgrims and merchants.

Lunigiana was in the front line of fighting at the end of World War II, and this has left its mark. Since then there has been inevitable rural depopulation, with many people emigrating to the United States. Now, an enlightened attitude to tourism promises new hope for the area, with villages and castles being restored and the roads in a good state of repair.

It is a mountainous region of steep, winding roads, deep wooded valleys and sparkling streams. On the lower slopes of the hills, vines and olives grow. Narrow valleys are dotted with tiny villages; higher up are forests of oak and the chestnut trees that have provided a staple of the local diet for centuries, and there are deer and wild boar *(cinghiale)* in abundance. The terrain sweeps from the River Magra valley to the profound silence of deep river gorges.

The region's Romanesque churches, medieval villages and castles also attract an arty community of outsiders, with some castles taken over by eclectic sculptors, or turned into cultural centres. The inhabitants are notoriously proud and insular, in rural areas still growing most of their own food, wine and olives, and regarding other produce with suspicion. The locals will even buy in grapes from the Chianti, to make the wine themselves rather than buy a ready-made product from "foreigners".

Fortified villages

From Sarzana, **Fosdinovo** ⑭ is the first fortified village en route to Aulla. Its squares are shaded by chestnut trees, and the steep streets are dominated by the magnificent

TIP

In August, one of the most important Italian antique markets, "La soffitta nelle strade" (the open-air attic), is held in Sarzana, and in August the Cittadella hosts the National Antique Exhibition.

The Serchio River at Bagni di Lucca.

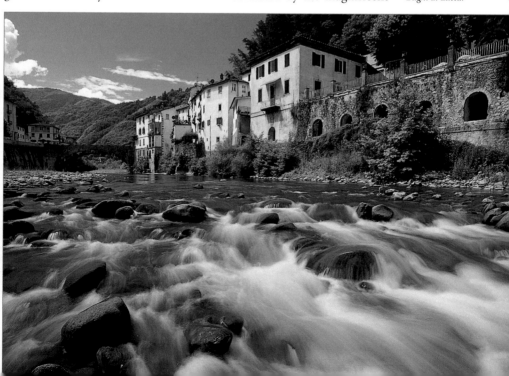

The fortress at Fosdinovo is one of the region's best-preserved castles.

13th-century Malaspina castle. It is one of the best-preserved castles in the region, despite wartime damage. The Germans had a command post here, exploiting its superb strategic position with views from all sides. Networks of corridors and loggias reveal beautiful frescoed walls (www. castellodifosdinovo.it; May–Sept Wed– Mon 11am–noon and 3.30–6.30pm, Oct–Apr Sat 3–5pm, Sun 11am– noon and 3–5pm).

Aulla itself is the gateway to Lunigiana, where the rivers Magra and Taverone meet. The brooding 15th-century fortress was restored earlier last century by Montagu Brown, the British consul in Genoa.

Fivizzano ⓫, a few kilometres east, is an attractive market town full of elegant Renaissance palaces. Nearby is the enchantingly restored castle of **Verrucola**, a fortified settlement on the banks of the river. Red-roofed houses cluster around the castle keep, with geraniums spilling from window boxes and gardens full of courgette, beans and tomatoes crammed right down to the river's edge.

To the northwest of Fivizzano is **Licciana Nardi** ⓰, a fortified town dating from the 11th century. Much of the town wall is still visible, with narrow passageways running through immensely thick walls into the village. In the Piazza del Municipio, the imposing 16th-century castle dominates the square, and is joined to the graceful Baroque church by a small bridge.

Comano is an important base for walking and riding, and nearby is the Castello di Comano, a ruined, malevolent-looking tower surrounded by a tiny farming community, with ducks and chickens wandering the streets, and steep steps up to the tower.

At the end of the valley is **Camporaghena**, the last outpost before the Apennines, where there is a sad war memorial in the church. When German soldiers came hunting for escaped prisoners of war and partisans, the priest rang the church bell as a warning and was summarily shot for his brave deed.

A 16km (10-mile) drive south of Fivizzano brings you to **Equi Terme** ⓱, a

MARBLE MOUNTAINS

The fine-grained pure white marble for which Carrara is renowned has been quarried here since Roman times. Italian medieval churches are decorated with it, and it has supplied artists from Michelangelo to Henry Moore with raw material. Marble is formed from limestone, hardened by great pressure and heat, and Carrara is still the world's single largest and most important source of the stone. About 200 of over a thousand original quarries are still functioning. They are scattered across three steep valleys: the Colonnata, Fantiscritti and Ravaccione. Here the villages cling to the mountainside that has been sliced away like a chunk of cheese. There are extraordinary views down into the quarries, where precarious-looking staircases are strung across the sides, and massive trucks trundle across the marble surface far below.

The best way to appreciate the majesty of the marble mountains and Carrara's "white gold" is to visit a couple of quarries and do a short marble tour, ideally at the **Fantiscritti historic quarries** that Michelangelo favoured. The master-sculptor apparently spent three

years looking for just the right block of marble to make Pope Julius II's tomb and found it here.

The Ravaccione section of Fantiscritti pioneered quarrying in the heart of the mountain and now runs fascinating 40-minute guided tours into the mountain (daily Apr and Sept 11am–5pm, May–June 11am–6pm, July–Aug 10am–6pm; follow signs to Fantiscritti from Carrara, via Miseglia; tel: 339-765 7470; www.marmotour.com). The main chamber in this working quarry is cavernous and genuinely feels like a "marble cathedral". During the tour a guide describes the techniques of cutting marble and presents the used equipment. Bear in mind that the temperature inside the cave is always about 15–17°C (59–62°F) so dress accordingly and wear sturdy shoes as well.

Recently, environmental campaigners have complained that the quarries contribute to dangerous levels of erosion and they are calling for much stricter measures to be imposed on the extraction of the marble. They are concerned that too much marble is being extracted from the mountains.

popular, if sulphurous, spa resort, with a lovely walk through a gorge, to the vaulted caves called **Grotte di Equi** (tel: 338-581 4482; www.grottediequi. it; tours Apr–Sept, rest of the year by appointment), where the remains of paleolithic men, dogs and even lions and leopards were found.

The Magra valley

A string of pretty castles and villages lines the main route (SS62) up the Magra valley between Aulla and Pontrémoli.

Bagnone ⓲ is an attractive town of Renaissance palaces, shady arcades and a honeycomb of houses, arches and passageways leading down to the river bank. Nearby **Filetto** is a symmetrical, square-walled village where almost every street is linked by covered overhead passages or bridges. Originally a defensive structure, it is now quite cosy, with cats snoozing in corners and village women passing the time of day.

Sleepy **Pontrémoli** ⓳ gives a good flavour of the Lunigiana, offering some of Italy's finest honey and

mushrooms, not to mention *testaroli*, the typical pancakes, served with local pesto or cheeses. There are rich medieval town houses, and the Church of the Annunziata has a 16th-century octagonal marble temple by Sansovino. The town was once divided in two to separate the warring factions of the Guelfs and Ghibellines, and the Castruccio fortress, built in 1332, similarly divides the town.

The hulking **Castello del Piagnaro** houses the **Museo delle Statue-Stele** (closed for restoration). Prehistoric statues or menhirs found in the area, the oldest of which date from 3,000 BC, are temporarily on display at the local Palazzo Comunale (Tue–Sun 9am–12.30pm and 2.30–5.30pm).

Don't leave town before sampling the local pastries in **Antica Pasticceria degli Svizzeri** (Piazza della Repubblica), a charming Art Nouveau café serving almond cake and *spongata*, a rich and tasty honeyed nut and raisin cake. The rustic specialities are low-key, quirky, old-world and engaging – much like Lunigiana itself.

Ruins of an aqueduct near Barga.

A Carrara marble quarry in the Garfagnana.

PISA AND THE ETRUSCAN RIVIERA

Beyond the iconic Leaning Tower and "Field of
Miracles", Pisa province has much to offer, from spa
centres to family-friendly beach resorts. Further south,
unsung Livorno province offers Etruscan ruins, scenic
coastal stretches, forgotten hill towns and great fish
restaurants – but give Livorno itself a wide berth.

With barely enough Renaissance art to enliven an overcast beach holiday, Livorno should be on the defensive. However, the province is as varied as its famed fish soup, *cacciucco*. The ingredients, a little of everything in the right proportions, apply to Livorno's seascapes. Captured in moody canvases by the Tuscan Impressionists, the rocky northern coast is as dramatic as the southern coast is soothing. The mainland stretches from wild, marshy Maremma to the rugged, hilly interior, or the Elban mountains.

Instead, Pisa province, despite its spas and beach resorts, means only one thing in the public imagination. The Leaning Tower draws tourists to Pisa like a magnet, many of them pausing to appreciate the religious architecture, others to enjoy the glorious art and history of this Tuscan city. Once a thriving Roman port, Pisa's harbour had silted up in the 15th century, and it now stands on the Arno River, 10km (6 miles) from the coast. Great sea battles were fought during the Middle Ages, with the city-state of Pisa becoming first an ally then a rival of a number of other states, including Genoa, Lucca, Venice and Florence. At its height, Pisa's power extended to Sardinia, Corsica and the Balearic Islands. Trade with Muslim Spain, North Africa and Lebanon meant

that Pisa even had a kasbah district for Arab and Turkish merchants. Arabic numerals were introduced to Europe through Pisa, and the city's major architectural monuments – the Leaning Tower, the Duomo and Baptistery – show the clear influence of Islamic architecture.

Pisa ❶ is split in two by the gently curving River Arno, its steep stone banks coloured by floating green algae. Elegant 16th-century palazzi along the banks hide the dilapidated areas in the narrow alleys behind.

Main Attractions
Campo dei Miracoli, Pisa
Torre Pendente, Pisa
Borgo Stretto Quarter, Pisa
Bagni di Pisa
Certosa di Pisa
Costa degli Etruschi
Castiglioncello
Bolgheri
Suvereto
Populonia

The Duomo in the "Field of Miracles".

152

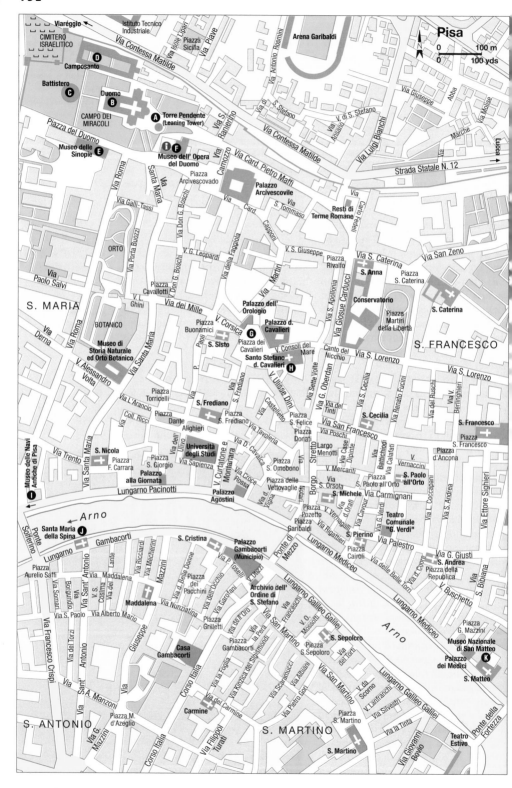

Pisa

0   100 m
0   100 yds

Viaréggio

CIMITERO
ISRAELITICO

Istituto Tecnico
Industriale

Via Isole Lipari

Piazza
Sicilia

Via Plave

Via Antonio Rosmini

Arena Garibaldi

Camposanto **D**

Via Contessa Matilde

Via di S. Stefano

Via Giuseppe

Abba

Via Molise

Battistero

Duomo **B**

C

CAMPO DEI
MIRACOLI

Torre Pendente
(Leaning Tower) **A**

Via S. Ranierino

Via di S. Stefano

Ansaldo

Via Luigi Bianchi

Marche

Lucca

Piazza del Duomo

Museo delle
Sinopie **E**

Via Roma

Via Santa Maria

Museo dell' Opera
del Duomo **F**

Camozzo

Via Card. Pietro Maffi

Via Contessa Matilde

Strada Statale N. 12

Piazza
Arcivescovado

Palazzo
Arcivescovile

Via
Card.

Via
S. Tommaso

Resti di
Terme Romane

Via
Carlo Fedeli

Via Galli-Tassi

ORTO

Via Porta Buozzi

Via Don G. Boschi

V. G. Leopardi

Via della Faggiola

Caltponi

V. S. Giuseppe

Piazza
Rivalfo

Via S. Caterina

Via San Zeno

Via
Paolo Salvi

Piazza
Cavallotti

V. L
Ghini

Via dei Mille

Piazza
Buonamici

V. Corsica

Proli

Via Martiri

Via S. Apollonia

Via Giosue Carducci

S. Anna

Conservatorio

Piazza
S. Caterina

S. Caterina

S. MARIA

BOTANICO

Museo di
Storia Naturale
ed Orto Botanico

Via Santa Maria

S. Sisto

Palazzo dell'
Orologio

Palazzo d.
Cavalieri **G**

Piazza dei
Cavalieri

Santo Stefano
d. Cavalieri **H**

V. Consoli del
Mare

Canto del
Nicchio

Piazza
Martiri
della Libertà

Via S. Lorenzo

S. FRANCESCO

Via
Derna

Via Roma

V. Alessandro
Volta

Piazza
Torricelli

Via L'Arancio

Coll. Ricci

Piazza
Dante
Alighieri

S. Frediano

Via S. Frediano

V. Ulisse Dini

Castelleto

V. Sette Volte

Via G. Oberdan

Via del
Tinti

Via S. Cecilia

Via Renato Fucini

Via dei Ruschi

Via V.
Berlinghieri

Via S. Lorenzo

Via S. Nicola

Piazza
F. Carrara

Università
degli Studi

Palazzo
alla Giornata

V. Curtatone e
Montanara

Via D. Cavalca

Via Tavolena

Piazza
S. Frediano

Piazza
Dotari

S. Felice

Via San Francesco

Via Poschi

Stretto

Largo
Menotti

Via Case
Dipinte

Via
Battichiodi

S. Cecilia

S. Francesco

Piazza
S. Francesco

Museo delle Navi
Antiche di Pisa **I**

Via Santa Maria

Piazza
S. Giorgio

Via Sapienza

V. Croce
Rossa

Piazza
S. Omobono

Via
Vettovaglie

Piazza delle
Vettovaglie

Borgo

Via
Mercanti

Via
S. Orsola

S. Paolo all'Orto

S. Michele

S. Paolo
all'Orto

V.
Vernaccini

Piazza
d'Ancona

Via
Coccapani

Via S. Andrea

Via Ettore Sighieri

Via Trento

Lungarno Pacinotti

Palazzo
Agostini

Via d.
Vigna

Piazza
Pozetto

V. Vernagalli

V. Oràfi

Via Cavour

Via Carmignani

Teatro
Comunale
"G. Verdi"

Arno

Ponte
Solferino

Santa Maria
della Spina **J**

Lungarno

Gambacorti

S. Cristina

Palazzo
Gambacorti
(Municipio)

Via P. Toselli

Ponte di
Mezzo

Piazza
Garibaldi

Via Rigatteri

S. Pierino

Piazza
Cairoli

Lungarno Mediceo

Via delle Belle Torri

Via G. Giusti

S. Andrea

Piazza della
Repubblica

V. Buschetto

S. Bibiana

Piazza
Aurelio Saffi

Via Sant' Antonio

Lante

Via Ricciardi

Via Mecherini

Mazzini

Via d. Belle Donne

Piazza
dei
Pacchini

Via dell'Occhio

Via Carofani

Archivio dell'
Ordine di
S. Stefano

Lungarno Galileo Galilei

V. O.
Mossotti

S. Sepolcro

Piazza della
Repubblica

Piazza
G. Mazzini

Museo Nazionale
di San Matteo

V.S.
Cosima

Via del

Maddalena

Via Nunziatina

Piazza
Grilletti

Via dell'Oro

Via San Martino

Via Francesco da

Piazza
S. Sepolcro

Lungarno Galileo Galilei

Palazzo
dei Medici **K**

S. Matteo

Via Torzi

Via S. Paolo

Via Alberto Mario

Giuseppe

Casa
Gambacorti

Corso Italia

Piazza
Gambacorti

Via la Paza

Via Krinica del Sigismondi

Via Scaramucci

Via Pietro Gori

Via Atbian

Via del Torri

Via S. Silvestri

V. Lanfranchi

Arno

Ponte della
Fortezza

Via Francesco Crispi

Via G.
Mazzini

Via
S.A. Manzoni

Via

Carmine

Via la Foglia

Via del Carmine

Corso Italia

Via Filippo
Turati

Piazza
S. Martino

S. Martino

Teatro
Estivo

S. ANTONIO

Piazza M.
d'Azeglio

S. MARTINO

Via la Tinta

Via Giovanni Bovio

The city's trump card is the budget airlines' choice of Galileo Galilei airport as their regional hub; but the town doesn't want to be Tuscany's airport lounge – Pisa needs visitors to come for more than just a photo of the Tower. No city in the world is as closely associated with one single monument as Pisa is with her tower. Even during the 1990s, when the marble miracle was in architectural intensive care and out of bounds to visitors, most still failed to notice that there was life outside the Campo. But after centuries of Pisan twilight, there are signs of a resurgence, especially around the arcaded Borgo Stretto area and the Arno, an area aspiring to a Left Bank feel. Centred on the prestigious university, a large student presence brings energy to the area, as does the enthusiasm of Pisan cyclists, who are among the most dedicated in Tuscany.

Crossing the original city bridge, Ponte della Citadella, the Via Nicola Pisano leads to the **Campo dei Miracoli** (Field of Miracles), a green swathe of manicured grass in the northwestern corner of the city walls – with perhaps the most perfect assemblage of religious buildings in Tuscany. The Campo dei Miracoli ticket office (daily Apr–Sept 8.30am–7.30pm, Mar 8.30am–5.30pm, Oct 8.30am–6.30pm, Nov and Feb 9.10am–5.10pm, Dec–Jan 9.30am–4.30pm), to the north side of the Leaning Tower, sells tickets to all the sites.

The Leaning Tower

Visitors flock from all over the world to marvel at the phenomenon of the **Torre Pendente Ⓐ** (advance bookings www.opapisa.it; daily Apr–Sept 9am–8pm, Mar 9am–6pm, Oct 9am–7pm, Nov and Feb 9.40am–5.40pm, Dec–Jan 10am–5pm; combined ticket; it may be possible to buy tickets on the day from the Campo dei Miracoli ticket office on the north side of the Tower, daily; no entry to children under eight, and children between eight and 12 must be held by the hand). The best place to catch your first sight of the 12th-century Campanile is through the archway of the Porta Santa Maria, otherwise known

Souvenir stalls near the Tower.

HALTING THE TILT

Pisa's Torre Pendente really does lean to a frightening degree, though less than it used to. The unstable subsoil that underlies the Piazza dei Miracoli has caused all the buildings to tilt and subside to dizzying effect.

Just to the right of the entrance to the Tower is a date stone inscribed ANDMI MCLXXIII (standing for Anno Domini 1173), the year in which building work started on the Campanile. But work stopped at the third stage because the building was already collapsing. A century later, three more stages were added, deliberately constructed to tilt in the opposite direction, so the Tower has a decided kink as well as a tilt. By 1989, the Tower was leaning to such a perilous degree that it was in danger of collapse. It was promptly closed to the public, and an international team of engineers spent the next two decades in a battle to save it.

During the first phase, completed in 2001, the tower was straightened by 40cms to avoid imminent collapse. In 1992 it was given a girdle of steel braces that were attached to a cunning counterweight system. A year later, the bells were silenced because of the damaging effect of vibration on the edifice. In 2011, work to stabilise the Leaning Tower was pronounced a success, and it was reopened to the public.

TIP

Pisa's annual Anima Mundi festival is a celebration of sacred music, with concerts by world-class musicians staged in the Duomo. This acclaimed event runs during the last two weeks of September. For information and bookings tel: 050-835 029; or visit www.opa pisa.it.

The Duomo and exterior of the Camposanto.

as the Porta Nuova. When the sun is shining, the whiteness dazzles; when raining, it glistens.

The Cathedral

The **Duomo B** (daily Nov–Feb 10am–12.45pm, 2–5pm, Mar 10am–6pm, Apr–Sept 10am–8pm, Oct 10am–7pm; free), built between 1068 and 1118, is one of the major monuments of Italy. The beautiful white-marble facade, the model for the Pisan Romanesque style, is set with mosaics, inlaid marble and glass pieces.

The tomb of Buscheto, the architect of the building, is above eye level on the left of the facade, designed by Rainaldo and built in the early 12th century. The 16th-century bronze doors are surrounded by frames enlivened by animals. The main entrance to the Duomo was intended to be through the bronze transept doors of the Porta di San Ranieri, near the Tower. The work of Bonanno Pisano, dating from 1180, they are decorated with 24 New Testament vignettes, including such delightful scenes as shepherds in

their conical caps playing their pipes to soothe the newborn child, and the figures of the Apostles under rows of swaying palm trees.

The rich complexity of the Cathedral interior is created by the forest of pillars rising to arches of banded white and grey stone, and the colourful mix of altar paintings and Cimabue's apsidal mosaic, from 1302. The beautiful marble pulpit by Giovanni Pisano (1301–11) is a masterpiece. Supported by figures representing prophets, sibyls and allegorical figures, its crowded and dramatic marble panels depict scenes from the *Life of Christ*.

Hanging from the westernmost arch of the great dome is Galileo's Lamp, so called because its pendulum movement is said to have inspired Galileo to discover the rotation of the Earth (in reality, the lamp wasn't here in Galileo's time).

The Baptistery

Across from the Rainaldo facade is the third building of the Duomo complex: the **Battistero C** (daily,

Apr–Sept 8am–8pm, Oct 9am–7pm, Nov–Feb 10am–5pm, Mar 9am–6pm; combined ticket), the largest baptistery in Italy, with richly decorated exterior niches and statues of saints. The interior is far plainer, but it has one great treasure: Nicola Pisano's pulpit of 1260, carved with scenes from the *Life of Christ*, clearly influenced by Ancient Roman art (the source for which we shall see next, in the Camposanto). Mary, for example, has the long neck, veil and ringlets typical of middle-aged matrons in Roman portraiture. You may be lucky enough during your visit to hear one of the attendants demonstrate the Baptistery's remarkable acoustics. As four or more individual notes are sung, the long echo allows them to build up to a complete chord that rings eerily round the dome.

Camposanto

The fourth element of the Duomo group is the **Camposanto D** (hours same as the Baptistery; combined ticket), one of the world's most beautiful cemeteries. The graceful white-marble cloister is paved with the grave slabs of medieval Pisans, carved with coats of arms or tools of their trade. Roman sarcophagi, imported from the Holy Land and reused as coffins for wealthy Pisans, line the walls, carved with the mythological scenes that inspired the pulpits of Nicola and Giovanni Pisano. Frescoes damaged by incendiary bombs during World War II have been restored to their original positions. They include a grim series of images (1360–80) inspired by the Black Death, on the themes of the *Last Judgement* and the *Triumph of Death*.

On the opposite side of the Campo dei Miracoli is the **Museo delle Sinopie E** (hours same as the Baptistery; combined ticket), where you can learn more about the Camposanto frescoes and how they were created by laying down a sketch on the plaster undercoat using red paint (called *sinopia* because the pigment came from Sinope on the Black Sea). When the final thin layer of white plaster was applied, the *sinopia* sketch showed through and guided the

Inside the Camposanto.

A relaxing way to see the city.

Attractive Piazza dei Cavalieri.

artists as they completed the fresco in full colour.

The fire that followed the bombing of the Camposanto destroyed some of the frescoes and left the others in so precarious a condition that it was necessary to remove them – but that was how the immense *sinopie* lying beneath the frescoes came to light and were salvaged, and are now carefully restored.

The Cathedral Museum

The final piece of the jigsaw is the **Museo dell'Opera del Duomo** Ⓕ (hours same as the Baptistery; combined ticket) – the Cathedral Museum. Room 1 contains casts of the foundation stones of each of the buildings and a chronology, which begins in 1064 with the start of work on the Cathedral, followed by the Baptistery in 1154, the Campanile in 1173, and the Camposanto a century later, in 1277. This short burst of fireworks was followed by swift decline as the city's harbour silted up. (Recent excavations have revealed Roman and medieval boats, complete with cargoes, preserved in the waterlogged silt, now exhibited in the maritime museum). By 1406, the city had been conquered by Florence and was about to be eclipsed culturally by that city's dogged determination to build even bigger and bolder monuments.

The museum is packed with 12th–15th-century sculptures and paintings: Giovanni Pisano's ivory *Virgin and Child* (1299) is one of the highlights, using the natural shape of the ivory tusk to give the Virgin her naturalistic stance. There are models to show the construction techniques used to build the domed Baptistery, and to explain the marble-inlay technique used to give all the buildings their intricate exterior decoration. Best of all, the rooms of the museum open out on to a quiet shady cloister, with a spectacular view of the Leaning Tower and the Cathedral.

New life in the old town

Students often congregate on the **Piazza dei Cavalieri** Ⓖ, one of the most attractive squares in the city.

This was the centre of activity in the Pisan Republic. It was in one of the towers of the Palazzo dell'Orologio (the building with the clock to the north of the square) – so we learn from Dante's *Inferno* – that Count Ugolino, wrongly convicted of treason in 1284, was left to starve to death with his sons.

The square is named after the order of knights *(cavalieri)* founded by Cosimo I (1561), to fight the Turks in the Mediterranean. The duke gave its members the Palazzo della Carovana, the former council chambers of the Pisan Commune. The magnificent *sgraffito* decoration (floral patterns, coats of arms, symbols) and the next-door church of **Santo Stefano dei Cavalieri** ⏺ (Oct–Mar Mon–Sat 11am–4.30pm, Sun 11.30am–5.30pm, Apr–Nov daily 9am–6pm) were based on plans by Vasari (1511–74). In 1606 Giovanni de' Medici added the marble facade and placed the knights' emblem above the great doorway. Displayed inside are trophies and spoils of war from Pisan naval victories against the Ottomans. Just

south, you can dine in an authentic early 13th-century tower-house in the **Osteria dei Cavalieri** (Via San Frediano 16; tel: 050-580 858; www. osteriacavalieri.pisa.it). This atmospheric "chivalric" inn serves hearty local dishes such as T-bone steak, cheese pie or beef with beans.

The lively warren of alleyways and shopping streets between the square and the Arno is known as the **Borgo Stretto quarter** and is the most elegant part of town. Lined with cafés and shops, the arcaded Borgo Stretto opens out at Piazza Garibaldi and the Ponte di Mezzo. Call into the **Pasticceria Federico Salza** (Borgo Stretto 46), the city's most delectable bar and pastry shop, set under the porticoes. It makes a tempting place for a light lunch, an afternoon coffee and cake, or evening cocktails.

Off the southern end of the Borgo Stretto, the arcaded **Piazza delle Vettovaglie** market area has been revamped, making it the haunt of Pisa University students who are drawn to the reasonably priced bars. Just beyond, the Arno River, with its boat

THE PISAN PARADOX

Since the glory days of the "Field of Miracles", some critics feel that Pisa has rested on its laurels, overwhelmed by the burden of its great history. It is as if, after pouring all its creative genius into one square, Pisa then slumbered for the next 500 years. Nor does it help that the Leaning Tower is so iconic that most visitors to the city see virtually nothing else.

There are no easy solutions because Pisa, unlike its Tuscan rivals, has no real centre. The Field of Miracles is set on the northern edge of the city, thus distorting the geography of tourism. Pisans themselves set great store by the River Arno as a dividing line, and a defining line, between different districts. But, unfortunately, much of the river is nondescript, with the Lungarno presenting a procession of blank, ochre facades that all merge into one another, matched by an equally unappealing and muddy-coloured river.

Pisa is not picturesque, and, for outsiders, simply doesn't tug the heartstrings like many other towns and cities in Tuscany. But there is a warmer side to the city. On the north bank, Piazza delle Vettovaglie welcomes

a bustling daily market, while the neighbouring arcaded Borgo Stretto is the most beguiling place for a coffee.

Visitors can best appreciate the Pisan sense of belonging at one of the heartfelt festivals held in the city, such as the Gioco del Ponte, the medieval tug-of-war fought on the Ponte di Mezzo on the last Sunday of June. During this festival, the Arno comes alive with boat races between Tramontana (north of the Arno) and Mezzogiorno (south of the river). Also in June are the celebrations in honour of St Ranieri, the city's patron saint. Known as the Luminaria, the night before the medieval regatta is a mesmerising festival that sees the banks of the Arno and the Leaning Tower bathed in candlelight.

In September the Duomo in the Piazza dei Miracoli hosts numerous events held as part of the prestigious Anima Mundi International Festival of Sacred Music. And November sees the Pisa Vini in the city's convent of Santa Croce; the festival celebrates the production of wine in the province of Pisa and features fine vintage wine and gourmet food tastings.

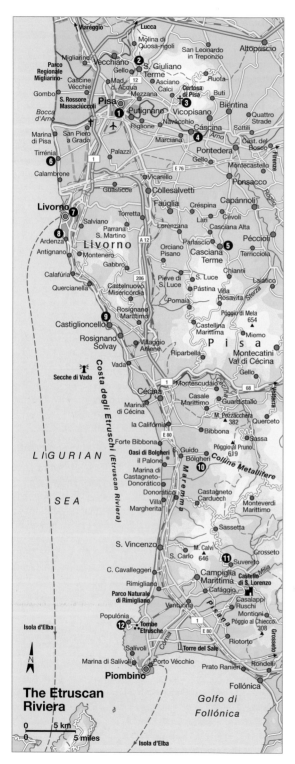

Viaréggio · Lucca · Molina di Quosa-rigoli · San Leonardo in Treponzio · Altopascio · Parco Regionale Migliarino · Migliarino · Vecchiano · Gello · S. Giuliano Terme · Cascine Vécchie · Mad. d. Acqua · Asciano · Ruota · Certosa di Pisa · Buti · Gombo · S. Rossore Massaciúccoli · Pisa · Mezzana · Calci · Biéntina · Bocca d'Arno · Putignano · Vicopisano · Quattro Strade · Riglione · Navácchio · Cáscina · Sottili · Marina di Pisa · San Piero a Grado · Marciana · Oast. del Bosco · Tirrénia · Palazzi · Pontedera · Calambrone · Gello · Montecastello · Vicarello · Ponsacco · Guasticce · Collesalvetti · Capánnoli · Livorno · Torretta · Faúglia · Créspina · Salviano · Lari · Cévoli · Parrana S. Martino · Lorenzana · Casciana Alta · Ardenza · Livorno · Orciano Pisano · Parlascio · Casciana Terme · Terricciola · Péccioli · Antignano · Montenero · Gabbro · Chianni · Calafúria · Pieve di S. Luce · S. Luce · Laiático · Quercianella · Castelnuovo Miséricórdia · S. Luce · Pástina Villa · Pisa · Pomaia · Rosavita · Rosignano Maríttimo · Póggio di Mela 654 · Castiglioncello · Castellina Maríttima · Miemo · Rosignano Solvay · Villaggio Arlene · Pisa · Vada · Riparbella · Montecatini Val di Cécina · Secche di Vada · Gello · Montescudáio · Cécina · Casale Maríttimo · Guardistallo · Marina di Cécina · M. Pezzáchera 382 · Querceto · la California · Bibbona · Sassa · Forte Bibbona · E 80 · Oasi di Bolgheri il Palone · Guido · Póggio al Pruno 619 · Bólgheri · Colline Metallifere · LIGURIAN · Marina di Castagneto-Donorático · Castagneto Carducch · SEA · Donorático · Villa Margherita · Monteverdi Marittimo · Sassetta · S. Vincenzo · M. Calvi S. Carlo 646 · Grosseto · Suvereto · C. Cavalleggeri · Campiglia Maríttima · Castello di S. Lorenzo · Rimigliano · Cafággio · Parco Naturale di Rimigliano · Venturina · Casalappi Ruschi · Montioni · Populónia · Póggio al Chiecco 308 · Tombe Etrusche · Riotorto · Isola d'Elba · Salívoli · Torre del Sale · Marina di Salívoli · Porto Vécchio · Prato Ranieri · Rondelli · Piombino · Follónica · The Etruscan Riviera · Golfo di Follónica · 0 5 km · 0 5 miles · Isola d'Elba · Costa degli Etruschi (Etruscan Riviera) · Maremma · Cornia

tours and festivals, is being touted as the Pisan "Left Bank".

Banks of the Arno

To the west, some distance along the river, the **Museo delle Navi Antiche di Pisa** ❶ (Museum of the Ancient Ships of Pisa; Lungarno Simonelli; closed for restoration and expansion) in the Medici Arsenale, the old Medici shipyards, houses the finds from the ongoing excavation of Pisa's ancient port, buried by silt in the 15th century. In 1998, workers expanding the railway station stumbled on the site, where the remains of 18 Ancient Roman ships and their contents (including the skeleton of a sailor) have been unearthed. These docklands, where the sea met the Arno, were probably composed of marshy flatlands and lagoon, very similar to Venice. Proclaimed a "marine Pompeii", excavations and restorations are ongoing and so the site has been labelled an "exhibition in progress" (Fri–Sun 10–noon, 2.30–3.30pm, guided tours, or by appointment tel: 055-512 1919). Two pavilions of this remarkable museum are scheduled to open in December 2015.

On the opposite bank of the Arno, across the Ponte Solferino, stands the church of **Santa Maria della Spina** ❸ (Apr–Sept Tue–Sun 10am–2pm and 3–6pm, Sat–Sun until 7pm, Oct–Mar Tue–Sun 10am–2pm). Don't worry if it is closed when you visit: it is the vivacious exterior that is the most important feature, a *tour de force* of Gothic pinnacles and niches, crowded with statues of saints carved by members of the Pisano family from 1230. Back in the days when Pisa was a port, before its harbour silted up, seafarers came to pray here before setting sail.

The chapel once guarded what was believed to be a thorn (*spina*) from the "crown" of Jesus, but that relic, plus the original statues, is now housed downriver, in the **Museo Nazionale di San Matteo** ❸

(Lungarno Mediceo; Tue–Sat 8.30am–7pm, Sun 8.30am–1.30pm). Set in rooms around the cloister of a medieval church, the museum contains such treasures as Masaccio's *St Paul* (1426), a contemplative man with a high brow, hooked nose and patriarchal beard; Donatello's bust reliquary for San Rossore; and a whole room of glowing Renaissance paintings by artists of the calibre of Gozzoli and Ghirlandaio.

Pisan country retreats

The Pisan countryside ranges from pretty to unprepossessing, with the magnificent Certosa di Pisa the main attraction, along with several charming spa resorts. Midway between Pisa and Lucca, at the foot of the Pisan mountains, is the charmingly faded spa town of **San Giuliano Terme** ❷. Olives, chestnuts and pines grow in the surrounding fertile countryside, wild horses roam the hills and ruins dot the valleys. San Giuliano is renowned for the curative powers of its thermal springs. Here, the best place to try out a thermal spa

treatment, or simply indulge in some pampering, is the atmospheric **Bagni di Pisa** spa resort, which, in its heyday, played host to the Romantic poets. These spa waters have been famous since Roman times, and are especially good for the treatment of rheumatism and arthritis. Montaigne, Byron and Shelley were among famous Grand Tourists.

Set in lush countryside, near Calci, 10km (6 miles) east of Pisa, stands the imposing **Certosa di Pisa** ❸ (Tue–Sat 8.30am–6.30pm, Sun 8.30am–12.30pm; part of the complex closed for restoration). The Charterhouse of Pisa was founded in 1366, but the finishing touches were only put to this Carthusian monastery in the early 18th century. The Carthusians were one of the strict new orders who believed that the increasing prosperity of the Cluniac orders was accompanied by a decline in religious observance. Their architecture reflected this stance; the monks lived in separate cells within a main enclosure. The centre of monastic life was the Great Cloister, of which the

The Arno cuts Pisa in two.

Certosa di Pisa has a particularly fine example. Work on the frescoes of the church walls began in 1701, and in 1718 workmen from Carrara carved the marble and renovated the church facade. In 1981 a part of the Charterhouse was allotted to the University of Pisa to house the **Museo della Storia Naturale e del Territorio** (daily 9am–7pm).

Lined with plane trees, the route to **Cascina** passes fields of sunflowers, grapevines and maize. Cascina is proud of its solid stone walls, dating from 1142, which are depicted in Vasari's energetic painting of the *Battle of Cascina*, now hanging in the Palazzo Vecchio in Florence. On Corso Matteotti, the tiny chapel of **Suore di Carmelitane di Santa Teresa**, on the left, has beautifully detailed frescoes. The nearby church of the saints Casciano and Giovanni, *c*.970, is a graceful building with a simple interior.

Casciana Terme , less than 40km (25 miles) southeast from Pisa, is surrounded by vineyards, olive groves and peach orchards. The appeal of the area lies in the gentle hills, mild climate, leisurely pace of life – and the spa culture. Casciana is a dedicated spa town, with its thermal waters attracting both earnest Italians "taking the cure" and holiday-makers seeking a break. At certain times, you can even try a "spa by night" experience, including a light dinner and drinks (tel: 0587-644 61; www.termedicasciana.it).

The Pisan coast

The pretty road from Pisa to the coast pauses here and there at railway crossings as it follows the Arno to the sea. About 6km (4 miles) southwest of Pisa, it passes **San Piero a Grado**, a magnificent basilica that would once have overlooked the sea. Legend has it that this is the spot where St Peter first set foot on Italian soil. The fresco cycle in the nave shows scenes from the Apostle's life.

The road reaches the sea at **Bocca d'Arno**, with moody views of fishing nets. Just south, the pleasant resort of **Marina di Pisa** makes a good stop for a stroll along the café-lined

Early morning fish market in Livorno port.

promenade. On a clear day, the islands of Gorgona and Capraia can be made out in the distance.

At **Tirrenia** ❻, 5km (3 miles) further down the coast, lies a stretch of Mediterranean pine forest – the one place where building has been prohibited. The trees act as a natural barrier against the *libeccio*, a strong southwesterly wind, reducing it to a light, scented breeze of pine and juniper that cools the air on hot summer days. Despite the appeal of this patch of coast, Tirrenia is a pleasant but underwhelming resort. The seafront stretch beyond the sand dunes is currently undergoing major development, with new residential areas, restaurants and a shopping and entertainment complex all centred on **Calambrone**. While rather charmless compared with more upmarket Forte dei Marmi or Marina di Pietrasanta, this emerging holiday resort is perfect for families looking for an active holiday, centred on the beach. Reasonably priced restaurants line the main route, while golf, tennis, horse riding, fishing, windsurfing, sailing and rowing are readily available. Each year colourful regattas and boat races are held, and the training centre for the Italian National Olympics is in Tirrenia.

Livorno city

The central coastal area of Tuscany is dominated by the busy comings and goings at the port of **Livorno** ❼, just south of Pisa. This is the Tuscan gateway to the sea and a city crossed by canals. As Italy's second-largest port after Genoa, it owes its existence to the silting up of Pisa in the 15th century; the Livornese joke that, unlike their rivals, the Pisans, they will never be so careless as to let the sea slip away from them. The rivalry between Pisans and Livornese is legendary and very much alive today. There is a saying in Livorno: *"Meglio un morto in casa che un Pisano all'uscio"* – "It is better to have a dead body in your house than a Pisan on the doorstep."

In 1421 the Florentines paid the Genoese 100,000 florins for Livorno, a vast sum for such a mosquito- and hence malaria-plagued village. It was

TIP

Trips to the sleepy volcanic island of Capraia are worth considering if you want to discover somewhere new. It's 64km (40 miles) off the coast of Livorno – a 2.5-hour boat ride from the port. Ferry services are run by Toremar (www.toremar. it). For more information on the seven islands of the Tuscan Archipelago, see page 172.

A view of Fortezza Vecchia.

Livorno is the birthplace of painters and composers, including Amedeo Modigliani, Pietro Mascagni, Giovanni Fattori and the Macchiaioli School, who influenced the development of art all over the world. It was also popular with British expatriates, such as Byron and Shelley, who anglicised the city's name to Leghorn.

Rocky Castiglioncello.

the enlightened Cosimo I who, in 1575, transformed Livorno into the greatest Medicean port. Cosmopolitan salons and elegant avenues made it a fashionable port of call for the Grand Tourists. But after 80 bombing raids in World War II, Livorno resembles a modern necropolis. Visitors soon realise that the city lives on commerce, not tourism. Few linger unless en route to the islands or the hills, but attractions there are. The Medicean port is unchanged. The red-brick **Fortezza Vecchia** is a patchwork of Livornese history, including Roman remains, medieval Pisan walls and a Romanesque tower. The **Fortezza Nuova** (Nov–Jan 8am– 5pm, Feb–Mar until 5.30pm, Apr and Oct until 7pm, May and Sept until 8pm, June–Aug until 8.30pm; free), built in 1590, completed the ambitious Medici fortifications. The murky canals encircling it once led to Pisa. Now restored, the New Fortress is landscaped as a park and is a popular spot for children's romps and summer festivals. The other main attraction is neighbouring

Piccola Venezia, dubbed "Little Venice" for its network of quiet canals.

The area of the port of Pisa and the **Navicelli canal**, between Pisa and Livorno, is currently undergoing a major development which will hopefully spur the revival of the Mediterranean short sea shipping. The canal through the marshes was opened in 1575 by the Medici, but fell into disuse and was partly destroyed in World War II. In the meantime, you can still do day and evening cruises on the Arno (contact Pisa tourist office, tel: 050-422 91).

The Etruscan Riviera

South of here is the area known as the Maremma Pisana – once a mosquito-infested swampland but now transformed – and the **Costa degli Etruschi**, the Etruscan Riviera. This is clever branding, even if it does conjure up incongruous images of beady-eyed Etruscans lounging under beach umbrellas, much as they do on their funerary urns.

Over 60 miles of coastline, Etruscan sites, medieval villages, hills, valleys and

wild woods make this lesser-known part of Tuscany unique. The coast is no architectural desert: a coastline of Pisan watchtowers and Medicean fortresses hides the occasional Roman villa or Etruscan necropolis.

The high coastal road from **Ardenza** ❽ to Castiglioncello offers some delightful scenic stretches as it hugs the cliffs' edge and dips in and out of tunnels. Ardenza, a fashionable resort flanked by palms and Art Nouveau villas, was home to what the Livornese called "Leghorn's British Factory". The sea views and the dramatic summer storms revived Shelley enough to enable him to write his famous *Ode to a Skylark*. Byron, also devoted to Ardenza, was a frequent visitor.

The coast becomes progressively more rugged, and the road winds past Medici castles, watchtowers and follies. Castello del Boccale, encircled by gulls and rocky paths to the shore, is a Medicean fort converted into a private villa. At **Calafuria**, an isolated Medicean tower and distorted rock formations provided the

Italian Impressionist painters with a dramatic setting. After Romito, the coastline becomes wild and wooded. As the small resort of **Quercianella** comes into view, pine woods run down to the water's edge; small coves, shingle beaches and a narrow harbour vie for space.

Quercianella is followed by the popular rocky resort of **Castiglioncello** ❾, which the Livornese seem to favour above the monotonous stretches of sand below Cecina. The Livornese also know that there are sandy bays tucked into the rocks. Cosimo's fort, built on the pine-clad promontory, was designed to keep pirates at bay, but since the 19th century it attracted all the great Italian Impressionists. In the 1930s, Castiglioncello was also very popular with film stars. It may not have much cachet today, but it's nice enough for a dip and a cheap lunch at one of the dockside bars.

For sightings of flamingos sheltering under umbrella pines, the **Parco Naturale di Rimigliano**, hugging the coast between San Vincenzo and Populonia, is where to head.

For a fabulous fish lunch with a sea view, this truck stop on the coastal road a few kilometres north of Quercianella is worth knowing about (see page 259).

TUSCANY BY TRAIN

The region abounds in scenic rail trips so do consider doing the occasional leg by train, including sampling the minor branch lines. These routes are not designed for speed but for savouring the countryside.

For arty sights and romantic scenery, the Pisa to Orvieto route is perhaps the finest introduction to the Tuscan and Umbrian landscape, which is dotted with hill towns and scenery depicted by the Renaissance masters. The route travels through the heart of Tuscany, revealing green hills striped with olive groves and vineyards, as well as historic towns studded with Renaissance art and architecture. Domesticated Tuscany melds with the hazy spirituality of Umbria's green hills. A variant on this rewarding route could take you from Pisa to Lucca, then Florence, Siena, Chiusi and possibly on to Orvieto.

Also from Pisa, you can follow the coastal route all the way to Liguria, stopping off at the oldest resort in Versilia, Viareggio, for the beach and to sip a coffee at one of the seaside cafés. And at Massa di Carrara you can visit the striking marble quarries of Fantiscritti, where Michelangelo himself came back in the day in search of the best marble

for his sculptures. From Chiusi, whose cathedral bell tower rewards visitors with breathtaking views of the Val d'Orcia, there is a delightful branch line that takes you on a plucky two-carriage train to sleepy Asciano, Siena and Buonconvento, with views of sunflowers, Montalcino shimmering in the distance, and a Sienese landscape straight out of a fresco by Lorenzetti. On the Pisa–Florence railway line the major stop is Pontedera, a hub from where many smaller localities in the Pisa province can be more easily reached by bus than from Pisa. The town is home to Piaggio, makers of the famous Vespa scooters, and the Piaggio Museum is worth a visit.

Lucca also makes a lovely rail base, with good onward services to Pisa (25 minutes), Viareggio (20 minutes) and Florence (1 hour 20 minutes). From Florence, the scenic journey into Garfagnana is also recommended; its picturesque mountains and valleys are still little affected by tourism and the town itself offers a rewarding escape from the hustle and bustle of Tuscany's major cities. Welcome to Slow Tuscany. Many of the best itineraries and rail holidays can be planned through Railbookers (www.railbookers.com).

The church of Santa Maria della Pietà in the pretty inland village of Bibbona.

Relaxing on the rocky coast south of Livorno.

Rural hinterland

But for a rewarding wine-tasting foray, leave the coast at **Cecina** and take the inland road to higgledy-piggledy **Bibbona** and wine-growing Bolgheri via **Casale Marittimo**. Quiet lanes trace through marshy countryside dotted with red farmhouses and occasional herds of placid white Maremman cattle, and spiral up into the hills.

The sun-baked hill town of Casale Marittimo offers views across the Livorno coast and out to Elba. Just south, medieval **Bolgheri** ❿ is a pocket of the Maremma fashionable for the so-called Super Tuscans, wines such as Sassicaia, Ornellaia and Antinori Solaia. To many wine experts, this is the future of Tuscan wine-making. Continue winding south through **Castagneto Carducci**, where the flatness is broken by low farmhouses, olive trees and the village vineyards, part of the wine trail bordering the Etruscan Riviera.

Sassetta, a bird's nest of a *borgo*, with a medieval castle, waits in the hills slightly further south. From here a winding road through olive groves, oleanders and woodland leads to **Suvereto** ⓫, another well-preserved village, with a crenellated town hall, an early Romanesque church, and a steep ascent through a rabbit warren of covered passageways. Many buildings are vividly decorated with the local red, brown or grey variegated marble, which has been quarried since medieval times. Suvereto's urban design, based on rising concentric circles, is simple but effective: each level corresponds to a street, from the church to the towering castle above. The sedate village pours on to the streets for the evening *passeggiata* and, in season, for the *sagra del cinghiale*, a wild-boar feast combining food and folklore. This area is **Val di Cornia**, an enchanting region of gently wooded hills, hot springs, lush valleys and old quarries.

The winding route south, towards the coast, leads to **Campiglia Marittima**, a hilly market and mining town known for its imposing castle and rustic cuisine based on sausages, chestnut polenta and bean soups.

Populonia

If the coast beckons, San Vicenzo's metallic sands and monotonous strip of beach bungalows can be sacrificed to **Populonia** ⑫, and the scenic ruins of the last of the 12 Etruscan cities to be founded, located behind the sweep of Baratti Bay (Tue–Sun 10am–6pm; free). The Etruscans, very considerately, had themselves buried beside a pine-fringed beach, reason enough to visit the only Etruscan city built on the coast. The ancient city was divided into two parts: the acropolis – the religious centre clustered high around the village – and the maritime and industrial centre around the bay. The necropolises cover the slopes that sit between the two centres.

Thanks to its proximity to Elba and to the metal-bearing Campigliese hills, Populonia became a rich industrial city. While Elban iron ore was smelted and then traded within the Etruscan League, minerals from Campiglia were shipped to Corsica, Sardinia and France. In the ancient "industrial zone", excavations have uncovered a blast furnace and sophisticated metalworking equipment dating back to the 6th century BC. Foreign slave labour was used to dig water channels, operate the furnace and mint coins. In the 6th century BC, Populonia was the first Etruscan city to mint gold, silver and bronze coins. Sadly, many tombs lie buried or collapsed under the weight of ancient slag heaps. Before setting out, check the Populonia archaeological park online (tel: 0565-226 445; www.parchivaldicornia.it) and also find time for the medieval village of Populonia. If catching a ferry to Elba from gritty Piombino, call in at the archaeological museum there, which displays the best Etruscan finds from Populonia (Piazza della Cittadella; tel: 0565-226 445; www.parchivaldicornia.it; erratic opening hours, check the website).

From Populonia there are smoky views of **Piombino**, a grimy, gritty city, where you can catch a ferry to **Elba** (see page 167). Best seen on foot, Piombino's genteel, down-at-heel charm lingers on in quiet squares and Art Deco bars.

> **FACT**
>
> October in Sassetta is a month of celebrations. A costumed Palio is held on the first Sunday of the month. The second sees a giant polenta cooked in the main square. The third Sunday is the Sagra del Tordo, a celebration of the thrush – this is a place where hunting is both a religious cult and a hobby, carried out in all seasons, legally or otherwise. A torch-lit procession is followed by a banquet of roast thrush served with chestnut-flavoured polenta.

Beach at Golfo di Baratti, near Populonia.

*Fisherman with fish trap,
Marciana Marina.*

ISOLA D'ELBA

Every August, the beaches of "Tuscany's island" are invaded by sun-worshipping Italians. For the rest of the year, its rocky roads, wooded slopes and sandy bays belong to intrepid tourists who make the short sea crossing in search of unspoilt nature, crystal-clear waters, Napoleonic landmarks and good food and wine.

Firenze

Known to the Etruscans as Ilva ("Iron") and to the Greeks as Aethalia ("Soot Island"), Elba has exploited its mineral wealth for more than 3,000 years. As the European powers occasionally took an interest in the island's attractive strategic position, waves of Romans, Pisans and Genoese were followed by Spanish, Turkish and French invasions. In 1548, the powerful and vainglorious Medici duke, Cosimo I, fortified the capital and named it Cosmopolis, after himself. His great military architect, Giovanni Camerini, designed the star-shaped defensive system and the two Medicean forts, Forte della Stella and Forte Falcone, to keep the Saracens at bay. Today, Portoferraio's horseshoe harbour, backed by a cluster of sun-baked pastel houses, is more welcoming than forbidding, as ferries, fishing boats, yachts and pleasure cruisers glide in and out of its embrace.

Napoleon's Elba

Portoferraio ❶ is inextricably linked to that other great imperialist, Napoleon Bonaparte. He made his official home in two converted windmills above the charming Forte della Stella. Under the terms of the Congress of Vienna in 1814, Elba became a principality of the fallen sovereign. Napoleon's great empire shrank to

his faithful "old guard", pragmatic mother and libertine sister Pauline. Most Elbans were proud to have him improve the administration, build new roads, develop the mines and expand the island's fleet. The foreign commissioners, however, rightly feared that the "Eagle" might spread its wings: after nine months, Napoleon flew, with the connivance of the Elbans. He escaped with no less than 1,000 troops, the Elbans' affection, his sister's diamond necklace and his mother's curt blessing: "Go and

Main Attractions
Palazzina dei Mulini
Marciana Marina
Marciana Alta
Monte Capanne
Capo Sant'Andrea
Capoliveri
Porto Azzurro
Rio Marina

The rugged coastline of Isola d'Elba.

Fishing boat on Elba.

fulfil your destiny." His **Palazzina dei Mulini** (Mon, Wed–Sat 8.30am–7.30pm, Sun 8.30am–1.30pm) was lined with silver and books from Fontainebleau, and furniture from his sister Elisa's house in Piombino. Most of its charm lies in the period furnishings and Italianate gardens.

The 17th-century Misericordia church on the Via Napoleone, a broad stairway nearby, displays one of Napoleon's bronze death-masks.

A few kilometres inland from Portoferraio is the emperor's country residence, **San Martino** (Tue–Sun 8.30am–7pm, joint ticket with the Palazzina), purchased with one of Pauline's handy diamond necklaces. The villa's classical facade was installed in 1851 by the Russian emigré Prince Demidoff. However, after the grand cypress-lined avenue and grandiose facade, the house itself seems a spartan affair. In one room, Napoleon's Nile campaigns of 1798–9 are recalled in the Egyptian-style frescoes, painted in 1814. In another, his tiny bed is a reminder of just how short he was. Information

on the emperor's life and times is thin on the ground here (though souvenir stands are not), but the fine garden, shaded by evergreen oaks and terraced vineyards, is pleasant to stroll through.

Portoferraio to Marciana

The scenic drive westward from Portoferraio to Marciana Marina passes a number of popular beaches. **Le Ghiaie**, the nearest beach to the town, is noted for its multicoloured pebbles, but it's worth going the extra distance to **Capo d'Enfola ❷**. The road to the cape ends at Porto di Sansone, a tiny isthmus flanked by two small pebble beaches and a couple of restaurants. Formerly restricted for military use, the cape itself remains closed to traffic, but is popular among walkers. Viticcio is another pretty cove, but sand-seekers head for **La Biodola ❸**, considered the chicest beach on Elba, dominated by expensive resort complexes filled with rich bronzed Florentines in Valentino swimwear. At La Biodola and **Procchio**, a more egalitarian paradise,

---

ELBA'S IRON HEART

Elba is a mineralogist's paradise and the island's metal heart creates a mysterious landscape that makes a lasting impression on visitors. Its mineral wealth has been fully exploited since Etruscan times and continues today: the swords wielded by countless Roman legionaries were famously made from Elban iron. The very name of Elba, Ilva for the Etruscans, means "iron" in Italian and the name of the island's largest city, Portoferraio, means "iron port".

In the Copper Age, colonisers mined copper, followed by the making of bronze and the mining of iron by Etruscan and Greek settlers. While ruling Elba, Napoleon reorganised the iron mines and was a serious steward of the island. But the last mine closed in 1984, and since then the island's economic mainstays have instead been tourism, agriculture and fishing.

To the east of Portoferraio is the scar across Elba's iron heart, where most of the mines and forges were located. In the hills around Rio nell'Elba, signs of Etruscan mining camps can still be seen. Neighbouring Rio Marina, now home to the mineralogical museum and the Parco Minerario (Mineral Park of Elba Island), was the set-off point where

the cargoes of metal were shipped overseas. At the Parco Minerario (Apr, May, Jun, Sept and und Oct 9.30am–12.30pm and 3.30–6.30pm; Jul–Aug 9.30am–12.30pm and 4.30–7.30pm), ardent rock hunters will feel in their element. The park offers trails on foot and by mountain bike in the Valle dei Mulini, excursions to the open-cast quarries in Rio Marina and Rio Albano and guided tours in Rio Marina. Their "Cercandoi Minerali" (Mineral Hunt) tour takes in a visit to a mining site where visitors can hunt for minerals and their "Trekking in Miniera" (Trekking in the Mines) excursion tours several major mining sites.

Further south, in Capoliveri, the black, iron-bearing lodestone still plays havoc with the compasses aboard passing ships. In this eastern part of the island, colourful semi-precious stones abound, from green quartz to black onyx and pink or pale-green beryl. The proper mineral name for most gem tourmalines is, in fact, "Elbaite".

In the resorts and mineralogical museums throughout the island there are ample opportunities for picking up pieces of rock or clunky jewellery that are now the last link with Elba's mining past.

the rocky ocean bottom means clear, sediment-free water.

Between Procchio and Marciana Marina is "La Paolina", an islet named after Napoleon's sister, whose passion for nude sunbathing would scandalise the natives.

Marciana Marina ➍ has evolved smoothly from fishing village to elegant resort, set amidst magnolias, palms and oleanders at the end of a long valley. The thin, pastel-coloured houses in the old quarter are reminiscent of those on the Ligurian coast. On 12 August the port explodes in a firework display to honour Santa Chiara, the patron saint.

Marciana Alta ➎, perched above, is Elba's best-preserved medieval town, where chestnut woods frame red-tiled rooftops, narrow alleys and the crumbling fortress. The local "Antiquarium" displays Etruscan sacred objects, Roman oil lamps and ivory statues found in shipwrecks.

Twin peaks

From the foot of Marciana, a cable car, the **Cabinovia del Monte**

Capanne (Apr–June, Oct 10am–1pm, 2.20–5.30pm, July–Sept until 6.30pm) lurches over crags and chasms up to the summit of **Monte Capanne** ➏. When not misty, the views are all-encompassing. Even in high summer, this wooded mountain area is wonderfully quiet and breezy. Depending on the season, patches of orchids, snapdragons and helianthemums are as common as the cedars and chestnuts. Even the coastal vegetation is more exotic than in the east: eucalyptus and magnolia rather than vines or maquis.

The high road from Marciana to the south side of the island winds past the quiet, neglected village of **Poggio** to Monte Perone nature reserve (for a scenic walk on the mountain, stop off at Poggio and follow the waymarked trail), vineyards and the plains behind Marina di Campo, the only part of the island flat enough for an airport.

The "Other Elba"

The northwestern corner of Elba is a protected area of wild, natural beauty,

Forno beach, on the Biodola Bay.

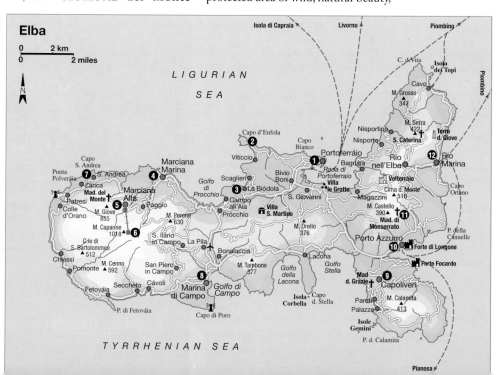

Cloud-covered Poggio.

The pretty resort of Marciana Marina.

with granite cliffs, thick holm-oak and chestnut woods, and dense maquis. Dubbed the "Other Elba", this craggy corner attracts the active and eco-conscious. The sea here is ideal for snorkelling, diving and kayaking, while the mountains are exploited by mountain bikers, birdwatchers, trekkers and climbers. A long, winding road leads down past houses and hotels to **Capo Sant'Andrea** ❼, a tight bay with a small port protected from westerly winds by the surrounding cliffs. This is an ideal base for exploring the area, starting with the walk from Capo Sant'Andrea to the next bay at Cotoncello.

The coastal road from Sant'Andrea to Marina di Campo clings to the edge of the island, an exhilarating and occasionally heart-stopping drive. Wherever you see a cluster of parked cars, chances are there's a rocky cove below, where those in the know gather to swim and sunbathe. This section of the coast is good for diving and snorkelling; most of the diving schools can be found in and around Pomonte.

As you round the southwestern corner, the first visible stretch of sand at **Fetovaia** comes into view – a pretty, child-friendly sweep of beach, edged by trees, that gets very crowded in summer. Between Fetovaia and Cavoli, another small, pleasant enough resort, the low rocks make perfect sunbathing platforms.

The south

With its expanse of golden sand, **Marina di Campo** ❽, in the south, is the largest, most buzzing resort on the island. While often overrun by German package tours in summer, it is still a good springboard to the medieval hamlets in the hills behind. Fortified by the Pisans in the 12th century, the hamlets of **San Piero in Campo** and San Ilario conceal Romanesque churches and hermitages.

Capoliveri ❾ is a traditional inland village, with a Roman and medieval past as dramatic as its location high on the southern promontory. Carved into the iron mountain of Monte Calamita, Capoliveri is also

an ancient mining village, where the mineral-rich soil is ideal for the production of sweet red Aleatico, reputedly the favourite wine of Napoleon Bonaparte. Often independent, Capoliveri was the only village to reject Napoleon in 1814. The story is that only the intercession of a local beauty saved the village. It soon became part of Napoleon's hunting estate, and to this day is noted for its dishes of woodcock, pheasant and hare.

The hills are covered with heath, fern and juniper; the enchanting scents of thyme and rosemary are never far away. Roads from the hills to the sea often turn into cart tracks but are worth pursuing unless specifically marked *strada privata*; this is often the only access to the loveliest beaches.

Innamorata is a sandy inlet linked to the romance between a nymph and a fisherman. Believing her lover drowned in a shipwreck, the nymph drowned herself; he survived and asked the gods to turn him into a seagull so he could seek her out.

From the east to the interior

Capoliveri also surveys fashionable **Porto Azzurro** ⑩, the main town on the east coast of Elba and once part of the Spanish protectorate. The vast Forte Longone, constructed in 1603 as a Spanish naval base, is now a top-security prison. Forte Focardo, its sister fortress across the bay, has uninviting ramparts running down a sheer cliff. By day, Porto Azzurro has a rather uninspiring seafront. In the evening, however, it comes to life with a leisurely promenade (the famous *passeggiata*), designer shopping and people-watching. It is also a top place for sampling seafood, including *cacciucco*, a seafood soup of octopus, scorpion fish, prawns and *riso nero* or "black rice" (risotto with dark cuttlefish ink), perhaps followed by *schiaccia briaca* ("drunken cake"), made with hazelnuts and Aleatico wine. After enough Elban wine, one's impressions of Porto Azzurro are of harbour lights, cheerful bustle and gently bobbing boats.

Behind Porto Azzurro is the most mystical spot on the island, the

TIP

Capo Sant'Andrea makes a good base for hiking, mountain biking, birdwatching, sea kayaking, snorkelling and other outdoor activities in the northwest of the island. For more information, go to www.visitelba.com, a useful website run by the owner/manager of the Hotel Ilio, who is a keen promoter of eco-tourism on the island. The tourist office produces a booklet, *Walking in the National Park*, which describes walks in the area.

Smooth rocky platforms attract sunbathers.

Divers heading to sea.

Portoferraio Lighthouse.

remote sanctuary of **Madonna di Monserrato** ⓫ (daily June–Sept, 9.30am–12.30pm and 3–7pm). It was built in the Toledan style by a Spanish governor, Ponce de León, in 1606. A steep, rocky track leads high up the mountain to the tiny red-domed church precariously balanced among the crags. Despite mountain goats cavorting on impossible ledges, the place has great solemnity and few visitors, and is the most important shrine on Elba. The Spanish facade and bell tower find echoes in the *Black Madonna* inside, which is a copy of an early Spanish painting. Every September, an Elban pilgrimage celebrates the Festa della Madonna with a walk past ravines and isolated grottoes to the church.

East of Portoferraio, the workaday town of **Rio Marina** ⓬ was once the centre of the mining activity. Surrounded by hills rich in ferrous oxide, the whole port has a pinkish hue, including the octagonal Pisan watchtower overlooking the harbour. More than 700 mineral exhibits are on display in the

Museo Mineralogico (tel: 0565-962 088; Mar–June, Sept–Oct 9.30am–12.30pm and 3.30–6.30pm, Jul–Aug 9.30am–12.30pm and 4.30–7.30pm). Only dedicated rock-hunters will continue to the **Parco Minerario**, set in a disused mine, where you can book a train tour or a hunt for minerals (book as above).

Inland, **Rio nell'Elba** is a strange, rather wild village perched on a couple of ledges among desolate mountain slopes and scattered remains of mines. A few kilometres west, on the road to Portoferraio, a steep road leads uphill to Volterraio and the ruins of an 11th-century Pisan fortress, perched on a rock.

From Rio nell'Elba to the small beach resort of **Cavo** in the northeast, the picturesque road cuts through woods and moorland. Paths trail through gorse, heather and the wild flowers of the maquis. Like the northwestern corner of the island, Elba's northeastern tip has quiet, unspoilt stretches of coast. Just north of Cavo, the remains of a Roman villa can be seen at Capo Castello.

ARCHIPELAGO

Elba is the largest island in a chain of seven between the Ligurian and Tyrrhenian seas, all loosely protected as part of the Arcipelago Toscano marine park. On a clear day, Pianosa, Gorgona, Montecristo and Capraia are visible from the island's highest reaches. Pianosa, just 14km (9 miles) from Elba, was a maximum-security prison until 1997 but is now a marine reserve. Gorgona, the smallest and most northerly island in the archipelago, is still a prison. Montecristo, 34km (21 miles) away, is a nature reserve, uninhabited but for its four guardians. So as not to disturb the fragile ecosystem, visitor numbers are restricted, but day trips are available from Porto Azzurro on Elba. Capraia, a miniature Elba without its history or architecture, is a two-hour ferry ride from Livorno and draws divers and those wishing to explore the marine grottoes.

Giglio, the second-largest island, and Giannutri are the southernmost islands. Giglio is popular with weekending Romans and divers. Both can be reached from Porto Santo Stefano on the Argentario peninsula. Frequent hydrofoils to Elba run from Piombino, on the mainland, to Rio Marina (45 minutes) to Portoferraio (1 hour). See Toremar ferries at www.toremar.it and www.arcipelago.turismo.toscana.it.

Rocky cove.

ORGANIC FOOD

VOLTERRA AND MASSA MARITTIMA

Perched on a windy plateau overlooking the Sienese hills, Volterra remains the most Etruscan of cities. The scenery sweeps from dry and desolate crags to the dense, eerie forests of the "Metal-bearing Mountains" – south to engaging Massa Marittima, the gateway to the Maremma.

One of the most important towns in Tuscany is **Volterra ❶**, which has a richly layered history with abundant evidence of its 3,000 years of civilisation. It commands a majestic, windswept position on a steep ridge 545 metres (1,780ft) above sea level. Walking round the ancient fortifications is an excellent way to view the medieval town, the Roman and Etruscan walls, and the wide sweep of countryside below.

Volterra was the Etruscan city-state of Velathri, one of the confederation of 12 city-states that made up Etruria. It became an important Roman municipality (Volterrae) when Rome annexed Etruria in 351 BC. It followed the new faith of Christianity, and at the fall of the Roman Empire, AD 476, it was already the centre of a vast diocese.

The modern city of Volterra sits within the walls of a much larger Etruscan predecessor. Wherever archaeologists dig in the city, they turn up new treasures. Sometimes they do not even need to dig, since parts of the city, built on tufa and undermined by subterranean springs, have been slipping slowly down the hillside for centuries, revealing the remains of an extensive necropolis.

Exploring Volterra

The **Porta all'Arco** (the Arch Gate) is the best-preserved Etruscan gateway in Italy, dating from the 4th century BC (though partly rebuilt by the Romans in the 1st century BC), with sides of huge rectangular stone blocks and three mysterious carved basalt heads above the gateway, thought to represent Etruscan gods.

From the arch, a pretty road winds its way uphill to the **Piazza dei Priori**. Evidence of the Middle Ages is to be found both in Volterra's urban structure and in its buildings, the most important of which are clustered around the main square. It is

Main Attractions
Piazza dei Priori, Volterra
Palazzo Incontri-Viti, Volterra
Museo Etrusco Guarnacci, Volterra
Teatro Romano, Volterra
Le Balze
Piazza Garibaldi, Massa Marittima
Massa Marittima Duomo
Citta Nuova, Massa Marittima
Museo della Miniera, Massa Marittima
Abbazia di San Galgano

Porta all'Arco.

Walk along the remains of Volterra's Etruscan walls, at the northwestern edge of town, for lovely views at sunset.

Piazza dei Priori.

dominated by the tall **Palazzo dei Priori** (1208), the oldest town hall in Tuscany, and said to be the model for Florence's Palazzo Vecchio. Across the square is the 13th-century **Palazzo Pretorio**, with its crenellated Torre del Porcellino (Tower of the Little Pig), named after its decorative relief of a boar. On the square, call into the wonderfully helpful tourist office (tel: 0588-87257) to pick up the Volterra audioguide. It is a model of its kind, providing judicious background on all the main sights, visited at your own pace.

To the south of the square, Via Turrazza leads to the 12th-century **Duomo** (Piazza San Giovanni; daily 8.30am–12.30pm and 3–8pm; free), which boasts works of art from the Middle Ages to the Renaissance. The sculpture of *The Deposition* is an extremely rare Romanesque wood-carving, simple in execution but bursting with pathos and drama.

The bishop's palace next door is now the **Museo d'Arte Sacra** (Via Roma; daily 9am–1pm, 3–6pm, Nov–mid-Mar 9am–1pm), a collection of gold reliquaries, church bells, illuminated manuscripts and some 13th-century sculptures of the Sienese school. The octagonal **Baptistery** opposite has an elegant marble doorway with a fine baptismal font sculpted by Sansovino.

As you head back towards the square, take Via Roma to Via Buonparenti and the Pisan-style **Casa Torre Buonparenti**, a pair of Gothic tower-houses.

At the top of Via Buonparenti, the **Pinacoteca e Museo Civico** in Palazzo Minucci-Solaini (www.volterratur.it; daily mid-Mar–Oct 10.30am–5.30pm, Nov–mid-Mar 10am–4.30pm) displays valuable paintings of the Sienese and Florentine schools, including an *Annunciation* by Signorelli and *Christ in Glory* by Ghirlandaio. The most famous painting in the collection is a masterly *Deposition from the Cross* by Rosso Fiorentino (1495–1540).

The **Palazzo Incontri-Viti**, on Via dei Sarti (tel: 0588-84047; www.palazzoviti.it; Apr–Oct 10am–1pm, 2.30–6.30pm, Nov–Mar by appointment only), is an impressive mansion whose facade is attributed to Ammannati, who worked on the Palazzo Pitti in Florence. Each salon is grander than the one before, adorned with art, porcelain and alabaster objects, a reminder that the palace once belonged to an alabaster merchant, whose heirs still live here. Renaissance buildings like these blend in surprisingly gracefully with the medieval Volterran houses. After exploring the patrician palaces, retreat to **Le Cantine**, the ancient cellars below Palazzo Incontri-Viti, for a drink in a cavern-like bar that contains a Roman cistern (see page 260).

The Etruscan museum and Roman theatre

The best of the city's ancient treasures are displayed in the **Museo Etrusco Guarnacci** (Via Don Minzoni; www.volterratur.it; daily mid-Mar–Oct 10.30am–5.30pm, Nov–mid-Mar

10am–4.30pm). This is packed with ancient Etruscan funerary urns, proof that Volterra has some of the best Etruscan art outside Rome. The alabaster sarcophagi run the gamut of Etruscan demonology and Greek mythology, featuring sea monsters, Greek gods, griffins and sirens. *The Married Couple* urn is a masterpiece of realistic portraiture, but even more stunning is the bronze statuette known as *L'Ombra della Sera (The Shadow of the Evening)*. Resembling a Giacometti sculpture but cast in the 5th century BC, this enigmatic elongated figure does indeed resemble the shadow of a boy thrown by the low beams of the setting sun. It blurs immortality and mortality in true Etruscan fashion.

After focusing so much on death, it's definitely a case of *carpe diem*: feast on Tuscan dishes in **Del Duca** (see page 260). Naturally, the restaurant terrace is built below the walls of the Etruscan acropolis. The spirit of the enigmatic Etruscans will accompany you throughout your stay in Volterra. Like the mystical *Shadow of the Evening* sculpture, the Etruscans knew how to live as well as how to die.

Volterra is dominated at its highest point by the **Fortezza Medicea**, a magnificent example of Renaissance military architecture – today it serves as a top-security prison. Intriguingly, the prisoners perform plays of a professional standard every summer but, to watch them, visitors need a certificate stating that they have no criminal record, which is not easily come by.

Nearby, on the site of the former Etruscan acropolis, the **Parco Archeologico** (mid-Mar–Oct daily 10.30am–5.30pm, Nov–mid-Mar Mon–Fri 10am–4pm) is an ideal spot for a picnic.

On the north side of town, just below the city walls, is the excavated **Teatro Romano** (mid-Mar–Oct 10.30am–5.30pm, Nov–mid-Mar 10am–4.30pm), the impressive remains of a complex built during the reign of Augustus, behind which lie the ruins of a 3rd-century Roman bathhouse. One of the loveliest walks runs along the city walls, from Porta Fiorentina to Piazza Minucci, and

Medieval Volterra.

FACT

The mountains south of Volterra are rich in metal ores, and for centuries provided Tuscany with the precious commodities of silver, copper, lead and zinc. However, by the end of the 19th century, mining and related industries had fallen into decline and now these hills are a remote and lonely region. The ruins of mines and factories engulfed in thick forest littered with heaps of coloured metals present a surreal picture.

affords compelling views of the theatre below.

Le Balze

The countryside around Volterra is one of gentle, undulating hills, interrupted in the west by the wild and awe-inspiring spectacle of abrupt crevasses known as **Le Balze** (The Crags). Over the centuries, these deep gullies, created by the continual erosion of layers of sand and clay, have swallowed up churches and settlements along with Etruscan and early Christian remains. Today, an 11th-century abbey, the Badia, sits on a precipice, awaiting its inevitable fate. For the perfect view of this dramatic landscape, exit through the western San Francesco Gate, passing the Borgo San Giusto and its remains until you reach Le Balze campsite (a 20-minute walk).

Metal mountains

The terrain south of Volterra goes from the crags of Le Balze to the dense, eerie forests of the "Metal-bearing Mountains". The wide vistas

The ruins of the Roman theatre.

of the dry, desolate terrain just south of town seem a world away from the cosy green hills of Chianti. In a remote area without significant sights, it is the journey that counts, an elemental voyage through a disconcertingly untamed Tuscany of gullies, mining gashes and belching fumaroles. Geothermic geeks will be in their element, but so, too, will open-minded adventurers. Fortunately, at either end of this surreal journey, whether Volterra or Massa Marittima, the cities are as beguiling and warmly welcoming as any in Tuscany.

At Saline di Volterra, an industrial suburb that developed around its salt mine, the SS439 leads south to Massa Marittima and the coast, cutting through the **Colline Metallifere**, or Metal-bearing Hills. Beyond the Upper Cecina valley, dense forests of chestnut, beech and oak are punctuated by fumaroles, cooling towers and gleaming silver pipelines, making for a strange and distinctly un-Tuscan picture.

The first noteworthy town on this surreal route is **Pomarance ❷**,

which retains vestiges of its prosperous past, including medieval town gates and the Romanesque church of San Giovanni. A short walk away, Via Roncalli is home to the **Bicocchi Museum** (tel: 0588-62306; May–Sept Sat–Sun guided tours at 4, 5 and 6pm and by appointment), a lavish early 19th-century home, whose decorations evoke the lifestyle of the wealthy mine-owning families. A little further along the road is the hamlet of **San Dalmazio**, and a short but steep walk (2km/1.25 miles) that culminates in commanding views from the ruins of the 11th-century castle, **Rocca di Sillana**.

Across the valley, the medieval hamlet of **Montecastelli Pisano** ❸ is dominated by the Torre dei Pannocchieschi. Like the Rocca Sillana, this fortified settlement was a pawn on the Tuscan chessboard, finally won by the Florentines in the 16th century. Follow the signs to **Castelnuovo Val di Cecina** and the "Buca delle Fate", a small but well-preserved 6th-century BC Etruscan tomb, just outside the village.

The road south from Montecastelli Pisano offers the best views of the medieval village of Castelnuovo Val di Cecina, which commands a steep ridge surrounded by woodland. A short walk east of the village leads through chestnut groves and down to the River Pavone, where you can swim in the rock pools, overlooked by two medieval bridges.

Steaming fumaroles

At the heart of this vast geothermic area, the industrial village of **Larderello** has been valued for its healing spring waters for centuries. But unless you're into industrial archaeology, move swiftly on to see geothermal activity in its more elemental form.

South along a back road from Larderello lie the hamlets of **Leccia** and **Sasso Pisano**, the latter of which commands a rocky outcrop above the Cornia River. The hamlets are linked by a narrow, winding route that cuts through a landscape of steaming fumaroles. Just outside Leccia are the ancient baths of **Bagnone**, a vast Etruscan-Roman complex

TIP

There are some excellent walks in the Forestali Berignone-Tatti, near Pomarance, especially in the autumn, when the leaves of the sweet chestnut turn golden-yellow and the forest becomes carpeted with bright pink cyclamen. Bicycle tours and horse-riding excursions can be booked through Pomarance's tourist office (in the car park on the SS439).

ALABASTER WORKSHOPS

Like everything in Volterra, alabaster carving is an Etruscan legacy. It is one of the many gifts the Etruscans have passed on to their descendants in this most Etruscan of cities. The ancient craftsmen made great use of alabaster from the 5th century BC onwards, primarily for their beautifully sculpted funerary urns.

Visit the Etruscan Museum before looking at alabaster objets d'art *in situ*, beginning with the grand collection created by Giuseppe Viti, the city's foremost alabaster merchant in the 19th century. Viti travelled the world to present his wares and, in India, sold his alabaster to the local rajah and, bizarrely, was then made Emir of Nepal. **Palazzo Incontri-Viti** displays superb pieces, including the grand candelabra in the ballroom, made for Emperor Maximilian, who was shot in 1867 before he could collect them. Admire the palazzo's floor, all white tesserae of hardened alabaster, and some decorative tables are adorned with alabaster mosaics.

Alabaster is sold in Volterra's workshops, as well as being exported. One of the most respected alabaster-crafting firms is the family-run **Ali, Alabastri Lavorati**

Italiani (Ali, Piazza Martiri della Liberta; tel: 0588-86078; www.alialabastro.it). Its showroom is the most elegant in town. Choose from lamps, sculpture, figurines, chess pieces, table tops, picture frames: so much can be carved from alabaster. Prices depend on the type, colour and veining of the alabaster, with colours ranging from creamy white to murky yellow. Visit one of the last remaining traditional alabaster craftsmen in his cramped workshop; **Giuliano Ducceschi** (Via Porta all'Arco 59) has been carving owls and fish, his favourite subjects, since the 1950s, and will continue until he drops.

Also call in at the alabaster museum, the **Ecomuseo dell'Alabastro** (Piazzetta Minucci, tel: 0588-87580; daily mid-Mar–Oct 9am–7pm, Nov–mid-Mar 10am–4.30pm). The museum tells the story of the alabaster craft, from the excavation of the stone to its artistic production and trade – from the Etruscan to the present times. On display are over 300 alabaster art works, mainly from the 18th and19th centuries, including female busts beautifully carved by Giuseppe Bessi.

TIP

A memorable experience – and a lot easier to see than Siena's Palio – is the traditional Balestro del Girifalco, every last Sunday in May and every second Sunday in August. The *terzieri* of Massa (old city, new city and the outer Borgo) hold a shooting contest using mechanical falcons with ancient crossbows.

Larderello, at the centre of geothermic activity.

from the 3rd century BC. The craggy medieval village of **Sasso Pisano** is a strangely appealing place, often shrouded in clouds of steam from the surrounding fumaroles, and the air is heavy with the smell of sulphur. The road through the village leads back to the SS439.

As the main road winds south towards Massa Marittima, it climbs up steeply wooded hillsides to the summits of the Colline Metallifere. It is an area of outstanding natural beauty, with dense forest and large open views across to Maremma and the Gulf of Follonica; on a fine day, the islands of Elba and Corsica can be clearly seen.

Massa Marittima

Massa Marittima ❹ is about 24km (15 miles) inland, despite its maritime name. It is one of the most astounding Tuscan cities, perched on top of a high hill on the edge of the Colline Metallifere. Although its relative remoteness from "picture-postcard Tuscany" has resulted in far fewer visitors than it deserves, Massa Marittima is finally coming into its

own. This underrated gem has preserved its gorgeous medieval core as well as gracious palaces, authentic regional restaurants, and a clutch of fine museums.

Massa Marittima grew up in the 10th century, after the decline of ancient Populonia, which was too exposed to coastal malaria and plundering by pirates.

Massa, once the second city of the Sienese Republic, prospered from copper and silver mines exploited since Etruscan times. Although the proud city spiralled into centuries of decline when the mines failed and malaria returned, its stagnation has proved a joy for visitors today. Massa feels authentic, harmonious, a picture of urban refinement.

The city's old republican pride is reflected in the concentration of public buildings around the cathedral. In the main square – the spectacular **Piazza Garibaldi**, one of the finest squares in Tuscany – are Palazzo Vescovile (seat of the bishop); Palazzo del Podestà (seat of the governor, now an archaeological museum);

Palazzo del Comune (town hall); Zecca Cittadina (the mint); Fonte Pubblica (public fountain); and Palazzo dell'Abbondanza (the public granary). Set on a pedestal, the Pisan-Romanesque **Duomo** boasts Gothic windows and marvellous reliefs of the *Madonna delle Grazie*, ascribed to Duccio di Buoninsegna (1316), as well as the *Arca di San Cerbone* (St Cerbone's Ark), a Sienese sculptural masterpiece. Return to the theatrical square in the evening, when you can drink or dine while admiring the cathedral facade by moonlight.

Leave the old **Citta Vecchia** area around the Cathedral for the so-called **Citta Nuova**, hardly new despite its name. The quaint **Via Moncini** climbs to this Gothic quarter clustered behind Sienese fortifications, and ends in Piazza Matteotti, beside the medieval clock tower, the **Torre del Candaliere**. Nearby, on Corso Diaz, is the **Museo di Arte Sacra** (Apr–Oct Tue–Sun 10am–1pm and 3–6pm, Nov–Mar Tue–Sun 11am–1pm and 3–5pm). This delightful museum of sacred art is in the

equally lovely complex of San Pietro all'Orta, a frescoed Romanesque-Gothic monastery. The art reflects Massa's period of medieval glory, with the highlight being Lorenzetti's *Maesta*, the Madonna in Glory. Sculptures taken from the cathedral facade are also on display here. Virtually next door is the intimate church of **San Agostino** and the **Museo Santa Cecilia** (tel: 0566-940 282; Mar–May 10am–1pm and 3–6pm, Jun–Sept 10am–1pm and 4–7pm, Oct–mid-Jan 10.30am–12.30pm and 3–6pm), which is more engaging for its mood and architecture than for its treasures on display.

There are two mining-related museums in town, with the best being the **Museo della Miniera** in Via Corridoni (tel: 0566-902 289; opening times are variable so call ahead; guided tours only), a short walk from the cathedral. Set in natural galleries and medieval mineshafts, this atmospheric mining museum saw service as an air-raid shelter in World War II. The child-friendly tour passes wagons, pneumatic drills and munitions stores

Houses in Massa Marittima.

The landscape around Volterra.

The Romanesque Cappella di Montesiepi.

Abbazia di San Galgano.

as it burrows deeper into the rock. The small display of minerals is a reminder that medieval Massa grew prosperous thanks to the discovery of silver and copper deposits nearby, followed by the mining of pyrites, found in veins of quartz.

Gothic ruin

Heading east from Massa Marittima along the Siena road leads to the Gothic ruins of **Abbazia di San Galgano** ❺ (Apr–Oct Mon–Sat 9am–7pm, Sun until 8pm, Nov–Mar Mon–Sat 9.30am–5.30pm, Sun until 6.30pm), best seen when the setting sun sends shafts of light through its windows. This roofless abbey, with grass for a nave and fragments of frescoes clinging to crumbling walls, feels a mystical spot. Once the finest French Gothic abbey in Tuscany, San Galgano is now a noble ruin, albeit one tended by Olivetan nuns, who allow concerts to be staged here in summer. Consecrated in 1288, the abbey of San Galgano was the Cistercian mother abbey that held sway over central Italy. Its abbot arbitrated in disputes between city-states,

while its monks oversaw the building of Siena Cathedral. In the mid-14th century, the abbey was ransacked by the English mercenary Sir John Hawkwood – an attack sanctioned by the Pope, who was fearful of the Order's influence. Decline set in and by 1576, San Galgano was occupied by one solitary monk "who didn't even wear a robe". A lightning strike during Mass in 1778 saw the collapse of the campanile and signalled the last service at San Galgano. Although it sounded the death knell for the abbey, San Galgano, like its mystical founder, never gives up the ghost.

On the neighbouring hillock is the circular Romanesque **Cappella di Montesiepi**, built on the spot where St Galgano had a vision and renounced soldiering to become a hermit, thrusting his sword into a rock. The sword remains in the church, protruding from the rock. The bizarre event is illustrated by the frescoes of Ambrogio Lorenzetti that adorn the adjoining chapel walls.

Siena is about 35km (22 miles) distant on the SS73.

THE "TWILIGHT" TOUR

Ever since Stephanie Meyer set her bestselling vampire novel in Volterra, droves of "vampire-ologists" have been visiting. The *Twilight* saga has sold millions of copies worldwide and *New Moon*, the second in the series, depicts the fictional home of the Volturi, a coven of elite vampires. Even if neighbouring Montepulciano was chosen for the filming (it has a larger main square), Volterra was the inspiration for the melodrama. Wildly popular vampire tours now visit the Piazza dei Priori where the heroine, Bella, rushes to save Edward, her vampire love. With its stern clock tower, the vampires' den can seem suitably chilling after dark.

The tour is not just for impressionable teenage girls, but is also a surreal way of discovering the dark side of Volterra, including candlelit caverns where you come face to face with cloaked vampires. In a secret wine bar with an Etruscan well you can drink local red wine masquerading as blood. Even if Volterra is probably vampire-free, a particular bronze in the Etruscan Museum would suggest otherwise – *The Shadow of the Evening* is reminiscent of the long shadow cast by a person at twilight.

(Book a vampire tour through the tourist office or tel: 0588-86099; www.newmoonofficialtour.com; and www.volteratur.it).

San Gimignano's towers.

SAN GIMIGNANO

This is quintessential Tuscany, taking in the medieval "skyscrapers" of San Gimignano, the quaint hill town of Certaldo, and the rolling hills between Siena and Florence – the harmonious vineyards, villas and wine estates dotted along the Chianti trail.

Famous for the sculptural quality of its skyline, **San Gimignano** ❶ is a spectacular sight. It may be a cliché to call this hill town a "Medieval Manhattan", but the famous towers do resemble miniature skyscrapers. Seen from inside, it is the unspoilt townscape that bowls you over: almost nothing seems to have changed since the Middle Ages. In its heyday, the city had a total of 76 towers, only 14 of which remain. After San Gimignano fell under Florentine control, it became an economic backwater, bypassed by the Renaissance – for which we are eternally grateful.

Exploring San Gimignano

The towers are concentrated around the **Piazza del Duomo** and **Piazza della Cisterna**, which is teeming with tourists all year round. The towers alone make a visit here worthwhile, but the town abounds in quirky sights, even if staying overnight is the only way to appreciate this medieval time capsule in peace.

The Romanesque **Collegiata** (Apr–Oct Mon–Fri 10am–7.30pm, Sat 10am–5.30pm, Sun 12.30–7.30pm, Nov–Mar Mon–Sat 10am–5pm, Sun 12.30–5pm but no visits during Mass; combined ticket for most town attractions) will detain you longest, as every inch of wall space is covered in frescoes. The north aisle has Bartolo di

Chiesa di Sant'Agostino, San Gimignano.

Fredi's dramatic scenes from the Old Testament (1367), while the opposite aisle has Lippo Memmi's *Life of Christ* (1333–41) and the nave the *Last Judgement* by Taddeo di Bartolo (1393–6). Contrast these Gothic-style narrative paintings with Ghirlandaio's lyrical Renaissance frescoes (1475) on the life of a local saint, in the chapel of Santa Fina.

Four museums

Next to the Collegiata, the **Museo d'Arte Sacra** (Apr–Oct Mon–Fri

Main Attractions
San Gimignano Cityscape
Collegiata, San Gimignano
Museo Civico, San Gimignano
Certaldo
Monteriggioni
Greve
Radda in Chianti
Badia a Coltibuono
Gaiole in Chianti
Castello di Brolio

TIP

To see San Gimignano at its best, stay overnight in one of the characteristic hotels. Then you can savour the peaceful beauty of the town in the evening and early morning, after the coach-trippers have gone.

10am–7pm, Sat 10am–5pm, Sun 12.30–7pm, Jan 1–15, Feb–Mar, Nov 1–15, Dec Mon–Sat 10am–4.30pm, Sun 12.30–4.30pm; combined ticket) contains a variety of sacred art from the 13th to the 15th century.

Alongside is the **Museo Civico** (daily Mar 10am–5pm, Apr–Oct 9.30am–6.30pm, Nov–Feb 11am–5pm; combined ticket), housed in the Palazzo del Popolo, a forbidding fortress that served as the town hall. Completed in 1311, its tower, the **Torre Grossa** (same hours as Museo Civico), is the tallest in the town (54 metres/175ft) and the only one you can climb; the views of the Val d'Elsa from the top are spectacular. Among the museum's many good paintings is a set of early 14th-century frescoes by Memmo di Filippucci – rare in that they depict secular rather than religious scenes. Known as the *Wedding Frescoes*, they show a young bride and groom sharing a bath and climbing into their nuptial bed – an intimate glimpse into the private life of medieval Italy.

On Via Folgore, the former convent of Santa Chiara is now home to the

Museo Archeologico (same hours as Museo Civico; combined ticket). Fascinating exhibits range from Etruscan finds to a 16th-century pharmacy displaying ceramic and glass vessels designed for herbal remedies and healing lotions and potions.

The nearby **Piazza della Cisterna** is a lovely triangular space with a 13th-century well and medieval palazzi. East of the square, on Via di Castello, is the **Museo della Tortura** (daily 10am–7pm), with a gruesome collection of medieval instruments of torture.

Every church in San Gimignano offers some reward, but perhaps the best is **Sant'Agostino** (Apr–Oct daily 10am–noon and 3–7pm, Nov–Dec until 6pm, Jan–Mar Tue–Sun 10am–noon and 3–6pm, Mon 4–8pm; free) to the north of the town (near Porta San Matteo). Here, in Gozzoli's faded frescoes on the *Life of St Augustine* (1465), you will find the same love of colour, rich clothing and exact portraiture as in Gozzoli's other frescoes, notably in *The Journey of the Magi* in the Palazzo Medici Riccardi in Florence.

Piazza del Duomo at dusk.

MEDIEVAL MANHATTAN

San Gimignano's towers were built in the 12th and 13th centuries by the *magnati*, or nobles, during the Guelf-Ghibelline conflicts. As well as defending the city, they served as status symbols: the higher the tower, the richer and more powerful its owner. The local 14th-century poet Folgore described the "earthly pleasures" he encountered in the city, including "silk sheets, sugared nuts, sweets and sparkling wine". The arrival of the Black Death in 1348 put an end to silk sheets in San Gimignano until the 20th century. While more civilised cities were exchanging towers for palazzi, this medieval backwater destroyed nothing and built nothing. The city's misfortune has made it the best-preserved medieval city in Tuscany.

On Via Costarella, call into the **Museo SanGimignano1300** (tel: 327 439 5165; www.sangimignano1300.com; Jan–Feb 10am–5pm, May–Nov 10am–6pm). The museum seeks to show how the city was in its 13th-century heyday, with reconstructions of the 72 tower-houses, fortifications, churches and convents. But what is remarkable is how much of this medieval cityscape remains in San Gimignano today.

A short walk along the city walls to the 14th-century fortress before leaving is worthwhile. This semi-derelict **Rocca** has views over tiered gardens and olive groves winding down to the Vernaccia vineyards, which produce the famous white wine that was even mentioned in Dante's *The Divine Comedy*. Just beyond the fortress, the **Museo del Vino** (tel: 0577-941 267; Apr–Oct daily 11.30am–6.30pm; free) is the place to sample a range of local wines.

The Val d'Elsa

A few kilometres north of San Gimignano, the windswept medieval hill town of **Certaldo** ❷ straddles the summit of a steep hill. To reach it, park in the unprepossessing lower town, Certaldo Basso, and take the funicular up the steep slope to the delightful upper town, which is closed to traffic. Certaldo Alto is a literary landmark as it was the home of Giovanni Boccaccio (1313–75), author of *The Decameron*, who died here in 1375. What is thought to have been his home was restored in 1823, bombed during World War II, and has now been rebuilt as the **Casa di Boccaccio** (Apr–Oct daily 10am–1.30pm and 2.30–7pm, Nov–Mar Wed–Mon, closes at 4.30pm). An allegorical garden, inspired by *The Decameron*, has recently been created here. Featuring a marble fountain, and dotted with references to Boccaccio, the garden is used for concerts and film screenings.

The red-brick town is crowned by the castellated **Palazzo Pretorio**, whose 15th-century facade is studded with terracotta coats of arms. Any wandering will reveal impressive medieval gateways that lead down to steep, narrow-approach lanes.

One of five circular towers along San Gimignano's city walls.

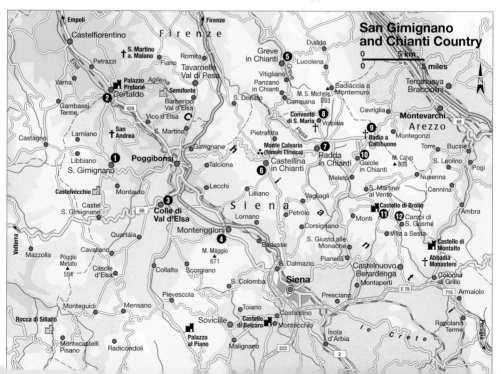

The Nectar of the Gods

Delightfully torn between tradition and creativity – like the contradictory Tuscans themselves – the wine scene allows for a duality between provenance and personality.

The know-how in the vineyards today compared with even a decade ago, is phenomenal," claims Lamberto Frescobaldi, whose Florentine family has been in the wine business for 700 years. For all its history, Tuscany remains at the forefront of the wine industry, which is still dominated by many of the original noble families.

Etruscan origins

Wine-growing dates back to Etruscan times, as evidenced by the goblet found in an Etruscan tomb at Castellina in Chianti, and surviving Etruscan frescoes that depict Bacchus, the Roman god of wine. Medieval monasteries established viticulture here – where Badia a Coltibuono and Antinori's Badia a Passignano remain beguiling wine estates today.

Vineyard below San Gimignano.

The avent of Chianti Classico

In the mid-19th-century, Barone Bettino Ricasoli capitalised on improvements in production and spearheaded the modernisation of wine-making, with the establishment of the Chianti Classico brand. Since then, a consortium, the Consorzio Chianti Classico, controls production, with the *gallo nero* (black cockerel) emblem guaranteeing quality. (Try Barone Ricasoli Castello di Brolio Chianti Classico 2006.)

To some outsiders, Tuscany is still synonymous with Chianti – to the chagrin of the region's other fine red-wine producers. Situated between Florence and Siena, the Chianti Classico heartland includes Barberino Val d'Elsa, Castellina, Greve, Gaiole, and San Casciano. However, the top Tuscan red is arguably Brunello di Montalcino, made from Sangiovese grapes grown on hillsides south of Siena. Brunello is a powerful yet refined red that ages superbly, with Rosso di Montalcino its more approachable younger sister, and the "princely" Vino Nobile di Montepulciano, loved by princes and popes since Medici times.

Maremma wines and the "Super Tuscans"

The wines of the Maremma are increasingly fashionable, and mostly made with Bordeaux varieties such as Cabernet Sauvignon, Franc and Merlot. These elegant wines have a crispness rarely found in New World Cabernets or Merlots.

Around Bolgheri, look out for great names such as Sassicaia and Ornellaia. Antinori Solaia, Frescobaldi Giramonte, Sette Ponti Oreno and d'Alessandro Syrah are other superb so-called "Super-Tuscans". Detractors claim that Super Tuscans lack a sense of place and are overpriced. Fans retort that these wines express the true creativity of the wine maker. The debate between native and French varieties pits provenance against personality, a sense of place against the creativity of the wine maker.

Beyond Chianti

Follow your nose: if Bordeaux blends don't appeal, there is ample choice among native grape varieties. That's without mentioning Vernaccia di San Gimignano, the characteristic white wine – crisp, full-bodied, golden-hued, and popular since Dante's day. Or dipping almond cantuccini biscuits into Vin Santo, Tuscany's amber-hued dessert wine: nectar of the gods indeed.

If hungry, stop at the **Osteria del Vicario** (Tue–Sat 12.30am–2.30pm, 7–10pm, Sun 12.30am–2.30pm). This frescoed, former monastery is now a delightful hotel and a Michelin-starred restaurant. Also be sure to drop into **Giuseppina** (Via del Castello 34, tel: (+39) 348 0034 869; www.cucinagiuseppina.com) to sample and buy local produce. It's worth booking a taster class in the eponymous owner's authentic cookery school, where you can learn how to make *ribollita* soup, *Sienese pici* pasta or crunchy almond cantuccini biscuits. The chef, Giuseppina herself, is helped by her wine-specialist son, who guides tastings at local vineyards or sets up truffle-hunting experiences for interested visitors.

South of San Gimignano, **Colle di Val d'Elsa ❸** is split between two sites. The lower "new" town is a busy, haphazard sprawl, whose centre of activity is the crystal factory – Colle is Italy's largest producer of crystal and fine glass, and there are plenty of shops selling it. The **Museo del Cristallo** (Via dei Fossi; May–Sept

Tue–Sun 10.30am–12.30pm and 4.30–7.30pm, Oct–Apr Tue–Fri 3.30–5.30pm, Sat–Sun 10.30am–12.30pm and 4.30–7.30pm) tells its story. Follow the signs up to the ancient upper town. Here the main street is lined with 16th-century palazzi of unusual refinement, and, at one point, the stately procession of buildings is interrupted by a viaduct from which there are splendid views of the surrounding landscape.

More spectacular sights await in nearby **Monteriggioni ❹**, just off the N2 to Siena. The fortified town, encircled by walls and 14 towers, was built in 1213 to guard northern Sienese territory. Like Montepulciano, this little hill village is emblematic of the Tuscan landscape. It is seen at its best first thing in the morning, when you can enjoy a coffee on the main square before the coach parties arrive.

The Chiantigiana

Spanning the hills between Florence and Siena, "Chiantishire" is a gentle vision of cypresses, vineyards and Medicean villa gardens. The rolling

FACT

In 1716, a decree issued by the Grand Duke of Tuscany defined the boundaries of the Chianti area and established the laws governing the production and sale of wine. Today, this region is the world's oldest wine-producing league. The Chianti Classico area includes the communes of Barberino Val d'Elsa, Castellina, Greve, Gaiole, San Casciano and Tavernelle Val di Pesa.

Fortified Monteriggioni.

Driving the Chiantigiana.

slopes are planted with olive groves that shimmer dark green and dusty silver. The Chianti is a spiritual rather than a geographical location. Its shifting borders reflect the fluctuations in Florentine and Sienese power, but, although it lies in Siena province, its soul remains where it has always been: on Florentine soil. It is a place whose turbulent history has shaped a scene of utter tranquillity, a harmony of tame hills and gentle people. In a place where nothing is essential viewing, everywhere is a glorious detour.

The SS222, known as **the Chiantigiana**, or Chianti Way, winds its picturesque way from Florence to Siena, through the heart of the region, offering archetypal scenes of cypress trees, olive groves and vineyards. First stop is the market town of **Greve in Chianti ❺**, with an impressive arcaded square, Piazza Matteotti, topped with wrought-iron balconies dripping with geraniums. The shops under the arcades are crammed with the usual assortment of local foods, crafts and wines. The

annual September Mostra Mercato del Chianti draws a large crowd.

An oft-missed jewel just five minutes' drive west of Greve is the tiny medieval walled town of **Montefioralle**, which was originally built as a feudal castle. Its narrow streets, stone houses and underpassages are beautifully preserved and splendid views are to be had from the various trattorias in the town.

Next on the SS222 is **Castellina in Chianti ❻**. Castellina overlooks symmetrical vineyards and wooded groves, a landscape dotted with low stone houses and Renaissance villas. New wine estates have been built from the remains of medieval castles. Villas have lazily domesticated the original castle or tower, but names like "La Rocca" or "La Torre" reveal the original function.

Castellina's name also reveals its medieval function as a Florentine outpost. In the late 13th century it was the first site of the Chianti League, a group of three Florentine feudal castles, each responsible for a third of the territory. The castle is now a fortified town hall hiding a small Etruscan

museum and a warren of atmospheric backstreets with half-glimpsed views of the Chianti hills.

Radda in Chianti

East of Castellina, **Radda in Chianti** ❼ retains its medieval street plan and imposing town hall. As in Castellina, the spontaneous rural architecture is more rewarding. Classical Medici villas with 16th-century windows and wells compete with romantic villas, constructed from castles or Etruscan ruins. One 17th-century masterpiece is Villa Vistarenni, a white beacon of sophistication. The elegant loggias and the openness of the architecture symbolise the increasing wealth of the countryside and its proximity to urban Florence. In the tranquil Chianti, the country is richer and more civilised than the town.

From Radda a tortuous road climbs to **Volpaia** ❽, a pretty medieval village with a ruined castle and Brunelleschi-style church. If Chianti villages and towns have little sense of identity and few artistic treasures, it is because they came into being with fully fledged Florentine and Sienese identities, while military outposts such as Radda had no time to develop artistically. Only the Chianti abbeys, which were endowed separately, had the independence to shape their own culture.

Abbey of the Good Harvest

Between Radda and Gaiole is the aptly named **Badia a Coltibuono** ❾ (Abbey of the Good Harvest; tel: 0577-746 110; www.coltibuono.com; tastings Apr–Oct daily), set among pines, oaks, chestnut trees and vines. Since the Dissolution of the Monasteries in 1810, this medieval abbey has belonged to one family. The lovely 15th-century cloisters, chapel and frescoed ceilings can be viewed as a guest of the cookery school or the bed and breakfast, while the 12th-century walls and bell tower are open to all. The cellars are filled with Chianti Classico, the abbey's traditional living. No less famous are the aromatic chestnut honey and olive oil, which can be bought on the premises.

A wine maker promotes his produce at the Chianti wine festival held in Greve in Chianti every September.

A fountain in Radda in Chianti.

The famous Chianti flask is no longer mass-produced for export. However, the nostalgic will be pleased to find rustic wicker fiaschi for sale throughout the region.

San Gimignano through the early morning mist.

Chianti castles

Gaiole in Chianti is a newer riverside settlement in a wooded valley. It is a popular summer escape for hot Florentines in search of family-run hotels, home cooking and the familiar *gallo nero* (black cockerel) wine symbol. History lies in wait at Meleto and Vertine, unusual castles, and Barbischio, a medieval village, is nearby. Tempting footpaths marked Sentieri del Chianti lead all the way to Siena. With vineyards rising up gentle slopes, tranquil Gaiole and sleepy Greve are traditional Chianti.

The countryside from Gaiole south to Siena and east to Arezzo is higher, wilder and wetter. The wooded peaks are green and fresh, with scents of thyme, rosemary and pine. Deep chestnut woods provide ideal cover for wild boar, recently reintroduced.

Of the many Florentine castles in the woods, **Castello di Brolio** ⓫ (Apr–mid-Oct daily, times and tours vary) is the most impressive – not least because of its views over the original Chianti vineyards stretching as far as Siena and Monte Amiata. On the medieval chessboard, every Florentine castle faced its Sienese shadow. If the surviving castles are Florentine, it is because Siena lost the match and all its pieces. While Sienese Cereto and Cettamura are small heaps, Florentine Brolio and Meleto are resplendent. As a Florentine outpost, Castello di Brolio's past spans Guelf-Ghibelline conflicts, sacking by the Sienese in 1529, and German occupation and Allied bombing in World War II. The medieval walls are the castle's most striking feature, along with the 14th-century chapel. Brolio has long been controlled by the Ricasoli, Chianti landowners since the 8th century. Baron Bettino Ricasoli, Italian premier in 1861, founded the modern Chianti wine industry, a business continued by the present family. (To visit the cellars, tour the estate, taste the wines, and see the family museum, tel: 0577-730 220; www.ricasoli.it).

The Chianti is a place for pottering and chance encounters, one of which could be tiny **Campi di San Gusmé** ⓬, just south of Brolio. A short climb leads to a Romanesque church and views of tumbledown castles and vineyards.

The view of the Chianti vineyards from Castello di Brolio.

THE CHIANTI WINE TRAIL

The Chianti Classico wine trail explores some of the most ancient and imposing wine estates, an experience combining countryside, castles, cuisine – and wine.

The Chianti covers an enormous region, spanning seven different wine "zones". At its heart, in the hills between Florence and Siena, is Chianti Classico, with the remainder – the Colli Fiorentini, Colli Senesi, Colline Pisane, Colli Aretini, Rufina and Montalbano – spread out over central Tuscany. The main centres in Chianti Classico are Greve, Panzano, Castellina, Gaiole, Fonterutoli and Radda. Easily accessible off the picturesque route SS222, the grandest, castle-like estates have often been run by the same families since medieval times, as is the case with the aristocratic Antinori, Frescobaldi, Mazzei and Ricasoli dynasties. Their vaulted castles, rolling vineyards and gastronomic restaurants encourage you to linger.

Contact the Chianti Classico consortium (tel: 055-82285; www.chianticlassico.com) for links to their producers. For a memorable experience, book a tasting *(degustazione)* combined with a tour of the vineyards and cellars.

The smaller barrels used to store the wine produced in the Chianti region are known as barriques; the larger barrels are known as botti.

The distinctive black cockerel logo of Chianti Classico.

The hills of Chianti are blanketed with vineyards; many of th wine estates are hundreds of years old and have been run by the same families for generations.

Chianti grapes.

RECOMMENDED WINE ESTATES

Badia a Coltibuono
Gaiole in Chianti; tel: 0577-746 110; www.coltibuono.com
This wine estate, run by the Stucchi Prinetti family, markets
itself as a "wine resort" – stay overnight; dine in the stables;
do a cookery course – within the former Romanesque abbey.
Guided tours Apr–Oct daily 2.30, 3.30 and 4.30pm; tastings
Apr–Oct Tue, Wed and Fri 11am or by appointment.

Badia a Passignano
Tavarnelle Val di Pesa; tel: 055-807 1278;
www.osteriadipassignano.com
Book a tour at this estate and sample iconic Antinori wines,
such as Tignanello, Guado al Tasso and Solaia, as well as
Chianti Classico Riserva Badia a Passignano. After the cellar
visit, enjoy an oil tasting, followed by lunch in
the Michelin-starred Osteria.

Castello di Brolio
Gaiole in Chianti; tel: 0577-730 220; www.ricasoli.it
Baron Ricasoli, whose descendants now run
the castle (Apr–mid-Oct daily 10am–7pm), first
designated the grape mixes to be used in
Chianti wine. Explore the castle gardens
and cellars before a tasting and lunch
(best to book).

Castello di Fonterutoli
Castellina in Chianti; tel: 0577-741 385;
www.mazzei.it
Owned by the Mazzei family since 1435,
Fonterutoli's award-winning wines are
matched by their grappa, olive oil and
Tuscan cuisine. Wine tours several
times a day, reservations are
recommended.

A bottle of Castello di Brolio Chianti.

*...hough chestnut was the traditional wood of the region,
...ianti normale is now usually kept in oak barrels for several
...nths to mature.*

*...ate owners are usually proud to show off their wines and
...lain their particular methods of wine-making.*

Palazzo Pubblico and the Piazza del Campo glowing pink at sunset, Siena.

SIENA

Siena is a classic case of a city that Italians call "*a misura d'uomo*" – meaning a city "made to the measure of man". Siena is, indeed, a Gothic city built on a human scale, and is effortlessly civilised, harmonious and at ease with itself.

F rom its striped marble Cathedral to its tunnelled alleys, brilliant Campo and black-and-white city emblem, Siena is a chiaroscuro city. In its surging towers it is truly Gothic. Where Florence is boldly horizontal, Siena is soaringly vertical; where Florence has large squares and masculine statues, Siena has hidden gardens and romantic wells. Florentine art is perspective and innovation, while Sienese art is sensitivity and conservatism. Siena is often considered the feminine foil to Florentine masculinity.

For such a feminine and beautiful city, Siena has a decidedly warlike reputation, nourished by sieges, city-state rivalry and Palio battles. The pale theatricality in Sienese painting is not representative of the city or its inhabitants: the average Sienese is no ethereal Botticelli nymph, but dark, stocky and swarthy.

A brief history

In keeping with Sienese mystique, the city's origins are shrouded in myths of wolves and martyred saints. According to legend, the city was founded by Senius, son of Remus, hence the she-wolf symbols you will encounter throughout the city. St Ansano brought Christianity to Roman Siena and, although he was promptly tossed into a vat of hot tar and beheaded, he has left a legacy of mysticism traced

through St Catherine and St Bernardino to the present-day cult of the Madonna. The power of the Church came to an end when the populace rose up against the Ecclesiastical Council and established an independent republic in 1147. The 12th century was marked by rivalry in which the Florentine Guelfs usually triumphed over the Sienese Ghibellines.

In 1260, the battle of Montaperti routed the Florentines and won the Sienese 10 years of cultural supremacy, which saw the foundation of the

Main Attractions
Il Campo
Palazzo Pubblico
Duomo
Museo dell'Opera
  Metropolitana
Santa Maria Della Scala
Pinacoteca Nazionale
Fortezza Medicea

A Sienese backstreet café.

University and the charitable "fraternities". The Council of the Twenty-Four – a form of power-sharing between nobles and the working class – was followed by the Council of Nine, an oligarchy of merchants that ruled until 1335. Modern historians judge the Nine self-seeking and profligate, but under their rule the finest works of art were either commissioned or completed, including the famous amphitheatre-shaped Campo, the Palazzo Pubblico and Duccio's *Maestà*.

The ancient republic survived until 1529, when the reconciliation between the pope and the emperor ended the Guelf-Ghibelline feud. The occupying Spanish demolished the city towers, symbols of freedom and fratricide, and used the masonry to build the present fortress. The final blow to the republic was the long siege of Siena by Emperor Charles V and Cosimo I in 1554.

After the Sienese defeat, the city of Siena became absorbed into the Tuscan dukedom. As an untrusted member of the Tuscan Empire, impoverished Siena turned in on itself until the 20th century. Still today, Siena's tumultuous history as arch-rivals of Florence is written in the streets and squares, and resonates in the passionate souls of the Sienese. Of all Tuscans, the Sienese have the longest memories and there are local aristocrats who still disdain to visit Florence.

Change is anathema to the city: traditional landowning, financial speculation, trade and tourism are more

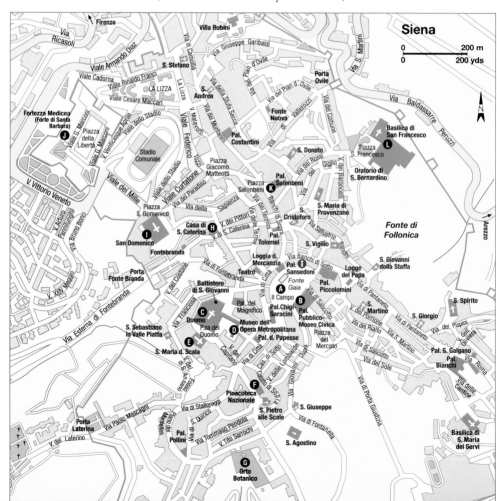

appealing than the introduction of new technology or industry. Siena has made a virtue of conservatism; stringent medieval building regulations protect the fabric of the city; tourism is decidedly low-key; old family firms such as Nannini, Siena's most famous café, do a roaring trade with locals (and also produced Gianna Nannini, one of Italy's best-known female singers). Siena is Italy's last surviving city-state, a city with the psychology of a village and the grandeur of a nation.

Il Campo

All roads lead to **Il Campo** Ⓐ, the huge main central square, shaped like an amphitheatre – the Sienese say that it is shaped like the protecting cloak of the Virgin, who, with St Catherine of Siena, is the city's patron saint. From the comfort of a pavement café on the curved side of the Campo, you can note the division of the paved surface into nine segments, commemorating the beneficent rule of the "Noveschi" – the Council of Nine that governed Siena from the mid-13th century to the early 14th, a period of stability

and prosperity when most of the city's main public monuments were built.

The Campo is tipped with the Renaissance **Fonte Gaia** (Fountain of Joy). The marble carvings are copies of the original sculptures by Iacopo della Quercia, which are on display in Santa Maria della Scala. Beneath the fountain lies one of Siena's best-kept secrets – a labyrinth of medieval tunnels extending for 25km (15.5 miles), constructed to channel water from the surrounding hills into the city. The underground aqueduct has two main tunnels: one leads to the Fonte Gaia and the other to the Fonte Branda, the best preserved of Siena's many fountains. Parts of this subterranean system can be visited and explored on a guided tour (enquire at the tourist office for more information).

At the square's base is the **Palazzo Pubblico** Ⓑ, the dignified Town Hall with its crenellated facade and waving banners, surmounted by the tall and slender tower. The Town Hall, which has been the home of the commune since it was completed in 1310, is a Gothic masterpiece of rose-coloured

Chiocciola contrada; traditionally, its residents worked as terracotta makers.

Romulus, Remus and the she-wolf: Remus' son is said to have founded Siena.

"CONTRADE" PASSIONS

Siena's cultural aloofness owes much to the *contrade*, the 17 city wards designated for now-defunct administrative and military functions during the Middle Ages, which continue to act as individual entities within the city. To outsiders, the only real significance of the *contrade* seems to be in connection with the Palio, but their existence pervades all aspects of daily life. Despite its public grandeur, parts of Siena are resolutely working class and attach great weight to belonging to a community. Events such as baptisms are celebrated together, while traditional Sienese will only marry within their *contrada*.

All over the city, the importance of the various *contrade* is evident. Little plaques set into the wall indicate which *contrada* you are in (such as snail unicorn, owl, caterpillar, wolf or goose). Each neighbourhood has its own fountain and font, as well as a motto, symbol and colours. The last are combined in a flag, worn with pride and seen draped around buildings for important *contrada* events, notably a Palio triumph. To gain an understanding of this secret world, book a private Palio tour (tel: 0577-280 551) that takes you to the individual museums, churches and stables associated with individual *contrade*, all in the heart of the city, or visit www.ipalio.org.

The interior of the Duomo, a magnificent Gothic structure of banded black-and-white stone, with a superb floor of inlaid marble depicting biblical and pagan themes.

Contrada procession in the Campo, by Vincenzo Rustici.

brick and silver-grey travertine. Each ogival arch is crowned by the *balzana*, Siena's black-and-white emblem representing the mystery and purity of the Madonna's life.

The distinctive **Torre del Mangia** (daily Mar–mid-Oct 10am–7pm, mid-Oct–Feb until 4pm) – named after the first bell-ringer, Mangiaguadagni, the "spendthrift" – is 87 metres (285ft) high, and it's a 500-step climb to the top to enjoy glorious views of the pink piazza and Siena's rooftops. At the bottom of the tower, the Cappella in Piazza (Chapel in the Square) was erected in 1378 in thanksgiving for the end of the plague.

The city museum

Although bureaucrats still toil in parts of the **Palazzo Pubblico**, as they have for some seven centuries, much of the complex is now dedicated to the **Museo Civico** (daily mid-Mar–Oct 10am–7pm, Nov–mid-Mar until 6pm), which displays some of the city's greatest treasures.

Siena's city council once met in the vast **Sala del Mappamondo**, although the huge map that then graced the walls has disappeared. What remains are two frescoes attributed to the medieval master Simone Martini: the majestic mounted figure of *Guidoriccio da Fogliano* and the *Maestà*. Martini's *Maestà*, a poetic evocation of the Madonna seated on a filigree throne, has a rich, tapestry-like quality. The muted blues, reds and ivory add a gauzy softness. Martini echoes Giotto's conception of perspective, yet clothes his Madonna in diaphanous robes, enhancing her spirituality in dazzling decoration.

Opposite is the iconic *Guidoriccio*, the haughty diamond-spangled *condottiero* (mercenary) reproduced on calendars and *panforte* boxes. But in recent years, despite Sienese denials, doubts have been cast on the authenticity of the fresco. Art historians maintain that a smaller painting uncovered below the huge panel is Martini's original, and the Guidoriccio we see was executed long after the artist's death.

In the next room is a genuine civic masterpiece, Ambrogio Lorenzetti's *Effects of Good and Bad Government*,

painted in 1338 as an idealised tribute to the Council of the Nine. Its narrative realism and the vivid facial expressions used on this impressive painting give the allegory emotional resonance to observers. A wise old man symbolises the common good, while a patchwork of neat fields, tame boar and busy hoers suggests order and prosperity. By contrast, *Bad Government* is a desolate place, razed to the ground by a diabolical tyrant, the Sienese she-wolf at his feet.

The Cathedral

Exiting the Campo, turn left and head up the hill via one of the winding streets to the Piazza del Duomo. The **Duomo** ⓒ (www.operaduomo.siena.it; Mar–Oct Mon–Sat 10.30am–7pm, Sun 1.30–6pm, Nov–Feb 10.30am–5.30pm, Sun 1.30–5.30pm; combined ticket) is Siena's most controversial monument, either a symphony in black-and-white marble, or a tasteless iced cake, depending on your point of view. It began in 1220 as a round-arched Romanesque church, but soon acquired a Gothic façade festooned

with pinnacles. Bands of black, white and green Tuscan marble were inlaid with pink stone and topped by Giovanni Pisano's naturalistic statues.

The Cathedral interior is creativity run riot – oriental abstraction, Byzantine formality, Gothic flight and Romanesque austerity. A giddy chiaroscuro effect is created by the black-and-white walls reaching up to the starry blue vaults.

The inlaid floor is even more inspiring, and the Duomo is at its best between August and October when the intricate marble-inlaid paving is on display. Outside these times, to preserve the well-restored floor, many of the most captivating scenes are hidden. Major Sienese craftsmen worked on the marble *pavimentazione* between 1372 and 1562. The finest scenes are Matteo di Giovanni's pensive sibyls and the marble mosaics by Beccafumi. Giorgio Vasari called these "the most beautiful pavements ever made".

Nicola Pisano's octagonal marble pulpit is a Gothic masterpiece: built in 1226, it is a dramatic and fluid progression from his solemn pulpit in

TIP

The Duomo's museum allows access to the parapets, which offer dazzling views of Siena – a more accessible alternative to the Torre del Mangia's panorama.

The fan-shaped Campo.

TIP

Siena is not the cheapest place to shop, but it is full of enticing shops, galleries and boutiques selling quality goods, often handmade. The main shopping streets are Via Banchi di Sopra and Via di Città. Opening hours are generally 9.30am–1pm and 3–7pm. Many shops close on Mondays.

Pisa Cathedral. Off the north aisle is the decorative **Libreria Piccolomini** (times as for the Duomo; combined ticket), built in 1495 to house the personal papers and books of Pope Pius II. The frescoes by Pinturicchio (1509) show scenes from the life of the influential Renaissance pope, a member of the noble Sienese Piccolomini family and founder of the town of Pienza.

The **Crypt** is an extraordinary discovery, with recently revealed frescoes attributed to Duccio's school. Because the frescoes were perfectly concealed for so long, the intensity of the colours shines through in a vivid array of blue, gold and red. Given that the frescoes date from 1280, the "modern" expressiveness is all the more remarkable.

In the unfinished eastern section of the Cathedral is the **Museo dell' Opera Metropolitana** ● (times as for the Duomo; combined ticket) and Pisano's original statues for the facade. In a dramatically lit room above is Duccio's *Maestà*, the Virgin Enthroned, which graced the High Altar until 1506. Siena's best-loved work, the largest known medieval panel painting

ever, was escorted from the artist's workshop to the Duomo in a torch-lit procession in 1311. The biggest panel depicts the Madonna enthroned among saints and angels, and, since the separation of the painting, facing scenes from the Passion. Although Byzantine Gothic in style, the *Maestà* is suffused with melancholy charm. The delicate gold and red colouring is matched by Duccio's grace of line, which influenced Sienese painting for the next two centuries. The Sienese believe that Giotto copied Duccio but sacrificed beauty to naturalism. The small panels do reveal some of Giotto's truthfulness and sense of perspective.

Around the Cathedral

Opposite the cathedral on the piazza, **Santa Maria della Scala** ● (www. santamariadellascala.com; mid-Mar–mid-Oct daily 10.30am–6.30pm, mid-Oct–mid-Mar Mon, Wed 10.30am–4.30pm, Thur–Sun 10.30am–6.30pm) is often described as a city within a city. It began as a hospital a thousand years ago and continued as one until its reincarnation as a museum in the year 2000. The far-sighted foundation originally functioned as a pilgrims' hostel, a poorhouse, an orphanage and a hospital, but is now a magnificent museum complex, embracing frescoed churches, granaries and an archaeological museum. Symbolically, the hospital door never had a key, demonstrating its role as a sanctuary to all-comers. The Pilgrims Hall, depicting care for the sick, is frescoed by Siena's finest 15th-century artists. The scenes portrayed, of wet-nurses, alms-giving and abandoned children, reveal a human side of the city absent from the luminous sacred art. The complex is also a venue for major medieval and Renaissance art exhibitions.

The city's **Museo Archeologico** (times as above; combined ticket) is also here, with its significant collection of Etruscan and Roman remains. The vaulted, former granaries make a moody setting for the display of

A backstreet leading towards the Duomo.

Etruscan treasures, including funerary urns and sarcophagi from Sarteano.

A set of steps behind the Duomo leads down to Piazza San Giovanni, a small square dominated by the **Battistero di San Giovanni** (times as for the Duomo; combined ticket), built beneath part of the Cathedral. Inside are frescoes and a beautiful baptismal font by Jacopo della Quercia.

Two art museums

There are two art museums in the vicinity of the Cathedral complex, at opposite ends of the scale of their content. The **Pinacoteca Nazionale** ⑦ (Via San Pietro 29; Tue–Sat 8.15am–7.15pm, Mon–Sun 9am–1pm) contains the finest collection of Sienese "Primitives" in the suitably Gothic Palazzo Buonsignori. The early rooms are full of Madonnas, apple-cheeked, pale, remote or warmly human. Matteo di Giovanni's stylised Madonnas shift to Lorenzetti's affectionate *Annunciation* and Ugolino di Neri's radiant *Madonna*. Neroccio di Bartolomeo's *Madonna* is as truthful as a Masaccio.

As a variant, the grisly deaths of obscure saints compete with a huge medieval crucifix with a naturalistic spurt of blood. The famous landscapes and surreal Persian city attributed to Lorenzetti were probably painted by Sassetta around a century later. But his *Madonna dei Carmelitani* is a sweeping cavalcade of vibrant Sienese life.

Those suffering from a surfeit of medieval sacred art can visit the **Palazzo delle Papesse** (Via di Città 126; Tue–Sun noon–7pm), a contemporary art gallery with changing exhibitions, which also offers a 360-degree view of Siena from its loggia.

For some outdoor space and greenery, turn left out of the gallery and head south to the **Orto Botanico** ⑥ (Via P.A. Mattioli 4; Mar–Aug, mid-Sept–mid-Oct daily 9.30am–5pm, early Sept until 6.30pm, mid-Oct–Feb until 4.30pm), a small botanical garden just inside the city walls. Opposite the Orto Tolomei is another little garden, with a lovely view over the countryside and a sculpture that – although not obvious at first glance – outlines the shape of the city.

Siena's ornate cathedral.

TURF WARS

The Palio horse race is the symbol of the Sienese's attachment to their city, and outsiders challenge it at their peril. One of the piazza's tight turns, the Curva di San Martino, set at a 95-degree angle, has often been the cause of fatalities among horses. Animal-rights activists have long protested against the event and Michela Brambilla, when she was Minister for Tourism in 2009–11, refused to allow the race to be put forward for Unesco World Heritage status. She argued the "the shame of 48 horse deaths since 1970 marks the Palio of Siena, and a current investigation will shed light on accusations of doping in some horses. This damages the image of one of the most beautiful cities in the world." The Sienese beg to differ.

St Catherine trail

Slightly outside the historic centre, on Vicolo del Tiratoio, is the **Casa di Santa Caterina da Siena**  (Costa di Sant' Antonio; daily 9.30am–7pm; free), the home of Catherine Benincase (1347–80), canonised in the 15th century by Pope Pius II and proclaimed Italy's patron saint in 1939, along with St Francis of Assisi. The house, garden and her father's dye-works now form the "Sanctuary of St Catherine". Although never taking holy orders, Catherine was an ascetic, and lived like a hermit in a cell, reputedly sleeping with a stone as her pillow. If it didn't sound too smug, the Sienese would admit to spiritual superiority. Apart from producing two saints and fine religious art, the city still venerates the Virgin.

Sienese panforte.

Inside the nearby **Basilica di San Domenico** ❶ (May–Oct 7am–7pm, Nov–Apr 9am–6pm; free) – a huge fortress-like church founded by the Dominicans – a reliquary containing the saint's head is kept in the Cappella Santa Caterina. The chapel is decorated with frescoes depicting

Shopping for sweet treats in a deli.

events in the saint's life, the majority completed by Il Sodoma in the early 16th century. The view from outside the Basilica across to the Duomo is spectacular.

The Fortress

From here it's a short walk to the Forte di Santa Barbara, also known as the **Fortezza Medicea** ❶, built by Cosimo I after his defeat of Siena in 1560. The red-brick fortress now houses an open-air theatre, provides glorious views of the countryside and contains the **Enoteca Italiana** (tel: 0577-228 811; www.enoteca-italiana.it; Mon–Tue noon–7.30pm, Wed–Sat noon–midnight). The latter, a wine exhibition and shop, allows for guided tastings from a wide range of Tuscan wines. This is also the best place to study and savour Sienese wines, from Chianti Classico to Vino Nobile di Montepulciano, Brunello di Montalcino and Vernaccia di San Gimignano.

Via Banchi di Sopra, lined with fine medieval palazzi, is one of the three main arteries of the city centre (the

---

SIENESE SWEETS

Sienese pastries are so renowned that they even have their own saint watching over them, San Lorenzo. Exotic spices reached Siena along the Via Francigena pilgrimage route, and many find their way into the medieval recipes still used today. *Panforte*, a rich, filling cake, dates back to 1205, and is often eaten with sweet Vin Santo. The intense flavours are created by a mix of honey, almonds, hazelnuts, candied orange peel, and a secret blend of spices such as cinnamon and nutmeg. *Panpepato*, a spicier version, predates it. The delicacy was originally the preserve of Sienese nuns, who guarded their secret recipes, which were also a source of revenue. Such was *panforte*'s popularity that even in the 14th century, it was being exported. Originally a festive treat, *panforte* is now eaten all year round. *Ricciarelli*, small almond biscuits, are also typically Sienese, and far lighter.

The most famous place for *panforte* is **Nannini** (Banchi di Sopra 24; www.grupponannini.it), a bar and pastry shop, but **Pasticceria Bini** (Via Stalloreggi 91) is even more illustrious, occupying what was supposedly Duccio's workshop. Carved into the former stables of a patrician palace, **Antica Drogheria Manganelli** (Via di Citta 71) is another exotic shop for Sienese delights.

other two being Via Banchi di Sotto and Via di Città). It links the Campo with the splendid **Piazza Salimbeni**  at its northern end. The grand palazzi flanking the square are the head office of the Monte dei Paschi di Siena, one of the oldest banks in the world. Founded in 1472 and still an important employer, it is known as "the city father".

Basilica of St Francis

From the square, Via dei Rossi leads east to the **Basilica di San Francesco** ⬤ (7.30am–noon, 3.30–7pm; free). Now housing part of the University, the vast church exhibits fragments of frescoes by Pietro and Ambrogio Lorenzetti. Next door, the 15th-century **Oratorio di San Bernardino** (Mar–Oct 9.30am–7pm, Nov–Feb 10.30am–5.30pm), dedicated to Siena's great preacher, contains frescoes by the artists Il Sodoma and Beccafumi.

Here, as at all its far reaches, the city has well-preserved walls and gateways. Siena's compactness makes these easy to explore, inviting you to wind through the sinuous medieval streets and stumble across secret courtyards, fountains and surprisingly rural views. This perfect, pink-tinged city is a delight to discover on foot, from the shell-shaped Campo to the galleries full of soft-eyed Sienese madonnas. In the backstreets, the city history is laid out before you, with noble coats of arms above doorways, or *contrada* animal symbols defining where their citizens belong. Everywhere leads back to the Campo, at its most theatrical in the late afternoon, after a day spent in the shadows of the city walls and inner courtyards.

But to escape the crowds, walk along the walls, or take the countrified lane of **Via del Fosso di Sant'Ansano**, which runs behind Santa Maria della Scala. Or stroll to **Santa Maria dei Servi** to lap up equally lovely views en route to a sublime church.

Given its impossibly narrow alleys threading between tall rose-brick palaces, Siena is mostly pedestrianised. Although the city is closed to traffic, visitors with hotel reservations are generally allowed to drive in, if only to park in a designated spot.

Statue of Sallustio Bandini, founder of Siena's library, on Piazza Salimbeni.

Strolling the walls of Fortezza Medicea.

THE PASSION OF THE PALIO

In little more than a minute, the Campo is filled with unbearable happiness and irrational despair as centuries-old loyalties are put to the test.

It is strange how a race that lasts just 90 seconds can require 12 months' planning, a lifetime's patience and the involvement of an entire city. But Siena's famous Palio does just that, as it has done since the 13th century, when an August Palio made its debut. At that time, the contest took the form of a bareback race the length of the city. The bareback race around Siena's main square, the Piazza del Campo, was introduced in the 17th century. Today the Palio is held twice a year, in early July and mid-August. The Palio, which has been run in times of war, famine and plague, stops for nothing. In the 1300s, criminals were released from jail to celebrate the festival. When the Fascists were gaining ground in 1919, Siena postponed council elections until after the Palio. In 1943, British soldiers in a Tunisian prisoner-of-war camp feared a riot when they banned Sienese prisoners from staging a Palio; Sienese fervour triumphed.

Although, as the Sienese say, *"Il Palio corre tutto l'anno"* ("The Palio runs all year"), the final preparations boil down to three days, during which there is the drawing by lots of the horse for each competing ward (*contrada*), the choice of the "jockeys" and then the six trial races – the last of which is held on the morning of the Palio itself.

The ruthless race lurches around the Campo three times. If a riderless horse wins, the animal is almost deified: it is given the place of honour in the victory banquet and has its hooves painted gold.

A highlight of the Palio pageantry is the spectacular display of the flag-wavers, famous throughout Italy for their elaborate manoeuvres.

Palio band.

Proud members of the Oca (goose) contrada.

THE POWER OF THE *CONTRADE*

In Siena the *contrada* rules: ask a Sienese where he is from and he will say, *"Ma sono della Lupa"* ("But I'm from the Wolf *contrada*"). The first loyalty is to the city in the head, not to the city on the map.

Ten out of Siena's 17 *contrade* take part in each Palio: the seven who did not run in the previous race and three more who are selected by lot. Each *contrada* appoints a captain and two lieutenants to run their Palio campaign. In the Palio, the illegal becomes legal: bribery, kidnapping, plots and the doping of horses are all common occurrences.

Each *contrade* has its own standard, many of which are displayed around the city during the Palio and play an important role in the ceremonial aspect of the event.

Flags, or standards, are a central theme of the Palio event. In fact, the *palio* itself – the trophy of victory for which everyone is striving – is a standard: a silk flag emblazoned with the image of the Madonna and the coats of arms of the city, ironically referred to by the Sienese as the *cencio*, or rag. The *contrada* that wins the event retains possession of the prized *palio* standard until the next race takes place.

The Historical Parade, which is staged in the run-up to the main race, retraces Siena's centuries of struggle against Florence, from the glorious victory against its rival in 1260 to the ghastly defeat in 1560.

...a's Campo becomes extremely crowded during the race so ... screens are set up in the contrada squares. After the race, ...ts are held to celebrate, or to commiserate, the result.

The words "C'è terra in piazza" ("There's earth in the Campo") are the signal to remove the colourful costumes from Siena's museums to feature in the great Historical Parade.

SOUTH OF SIENA

The route through the dramatic Crete region delivers you to the heart and soul of Tuscany. Pienza, Montalcino and Montepulciano are must-sees, but countless other lesser-known towns await discovery, while the hidden beauty of the Val d'Orcia river valley and the tortuous roads of Monte Amiata beckon the intrepid.

Main Attractions

Abbazia Monte Oliveto
  Marriore
Pienza
Montepulciano
Val d'Orcia
Bagno Vignoni
Chiusi
Monte Amiata
Montalcino
Sant'Antimo

A timeless Tuscan landscape.

The area just south of Siena is a primeval landscape of stark beauty. Appropriately called **Le Crete**, it is a moonscape of interlocking pale-clay hummocks and treeless gullies. In winter it is cold, bleak and even more crater-like. In summer the curvaceous terrain is softened by a deep green blanket. Sienese city-dwellers love this barren landscape and are successfully discouraging local farmers from accepting European Union funds to flatten the land and grow wheat.

There is an extraordinary range of wildlife in the area: by day, wild deer roam beside the Ombrone River; by night, porcupines and foxes are about in the woods. If intrepid walkers venture out on a late autumn evening they may meet a strange character with a couple of dogs, a torch and a harness. He is a truffle hunter, sniffing out truffles in the dampest ditches. More legal are the Sardinian peasants selling cheese. Unlike many Tuscans, Sardinians are prepared to live in remote, infertile places.

The best route through the Crete is the SS438 to Asciano, and the SP451 to Monte Oliveto Maggiore – empty roads through a barren landscape, dotted with striking hilltop farmhouses and lone cypresses. Known as the Accona Desert in medieval times, it retains its spiritual remoteness.

Monte Oliveto Maggiore

After so much pale, undulating land, the red abbey of **Monte Oliveto Maggiore** ❶ (daily 9am–noon, 3–6pm, winter until 5pm; free) is glimpsed through a wood of pines, oaks and olive trees. If the land appears to fall away from the abbey, it is not far from the truth: land erosion and frequent landslides provide a natural defence to the abbey's mystical centre. In 1313 Tolomei, a wealthy Sienese, abandoned the law for a life of prayer in the wilderness, taking with him two fellow hermits. After a vision of white-robed monks, Tolomei established an

Olivetan Order under Benedictine rule. The monks followed St Benedict's precept that "a real monk is one who lives by his own labour". Fortunately, a meagre diet, fervent prayer and lack of conversation stimulated the monks to artistic endeavour in the form of woodcarving, sculpture and manuscript design. As a noted artistic centre, the abbey invited Luca Signorelli and Il Sodoma to decorate the cloisters with scenes from St Benedict's life.

The excitement of Il Sodoma aside, Monte Oliveto is a spiritual retreat. The austere refectory, the library cluttered with ancient manuscripts and books, the exquisite marquetry work of the choir stalls are as peaceful as the hidden walks deep into the woods. Today, there is a restaurant, and a lovely shop selling honey, oil and liqueurs made by the monks, as well as wine tasting in vaulted cellars. The former monastic cells are also available for overnight visitors (tel: 0577-707 652; closed in winter).

Situated on a plain in the heart of the Crete, **Buonconvento** is worth a brief stop, if only to admire the imposing red 14th-century walls and massive medieval city gates of iron-bound wood. In 1366 Siena rebuilt the walls because, as a Sienese outpost, Buonconvento had been devastated. Today, the town is essentially a place for a leisurely introduction to truffles or game, or for a summer picnic in the peaceful gardens beside the town walls.

Pienza

Pienza ❷ is an exquisite Renaissance showpiece, slightly suffering from its over-popularity. Although created by a humanist pope, Pius II, Pienza is almost too perfect to be human and too precious to be spiritual. Every fountain, piazza and painting is harmonious. Model citizens walk through streets as romantic as their names – Via dell'Amore, Via del Bacio, Via della Fortuna – streets of "love", "kiss" and "fortune".

Pienza's origins date back to 1458. When E.S. Piccolomini was elected pope, he could not resist playing God in his home village, Corsignano. He chose the noted Florentine architect Bernardo Rossellino to ennoble the

A view of Pienza.

TIP

The pretty walled village of Monticchiello offers fine views of Pienza, just 4km (2.4 miles) away. It is also renowned for the Teatro Povero – an annual play written and starring the villagers about life in rural Tuscany.

hamlet in accordance with humanist principles. When the first masterpiece in modern town planning emerged late and over budget, the Pope reduced his fraudulent architect to tears with his words, "You did well, Bernardo, in lying to us about the expense involved in the work… Your deceit has built these glorious structures; which are praised by all except the few consumed with envy."

Bernardo Rossellino was rewarded with a scarlet robe, 100 ducats and some new commissions. The decision to build a cathedral enabled the pope to rechristen Corsignano the village as Pienza the city. The result is what locals call a *città d'autore*, a city inspired by one vision. After Pienza, other cities in Tuscany or elsewhere are liable to look chaotic.

Much of the symmetry lies in the cathedral square, **Piazza Pio II**, and the slightly listing Duomo adds to the charm. Despite a Renaissance facade, the interior is late Gothic and decorated with mystical paintings from the Sienese school. In one central alcove is a chilling *Assumption* by Vecchietta, in which St Agatha holds a cup containing

Chapel in a golden field outside Pienza.

her breasts, torn off by the executioner. The Duomo's facade, the gracious arches, the well and the Palazzo Piccolomini, the pope's home, are just as Pius left them when he set off to fight the Crusades, never to return.

Palazzo Piccolomini (Tue–Sun mid-Oct–mid-Mar 10am–4.30pm; mid-Mar–mid-Oct until 6.30pm; guided tours only), now a museum, is lined with both grand and homely treasures, including a library and arms collection. In the pope's bedroom, the intriguing book-holder, as cumbersome as a church lectern, is proof that the pope did not read in bed. The library opens on to a tranquil loggia with Etruscan urns, hanging gardens and a panorama stretching across the Orcia valley as far as Monte Amiata.

On the opposite side of the square, the **Museo Diocesano** (Wed–Mon 10am–1.30pm and 2.30–6pm, Nov–mid-Mar Sat–Sun only 10am–4pm) has a rich collection of medieval paintings, tapestries, and ornate gold- and silverware.

Just outside Pienza is the **Pieve di Corsignano**, a simple but coherent

Romanesque church where Pope Pius II was baptised.

Montepulciano

The winding road from Pienza up to Montepulciano ❸ – visible for miles around, with houses clustered on the sides of the hump of a hill on which it is built – is lined with *vendita diretta* signs, offering pecorino and wine. After Pienza, Montepulciano's asymmetrical design and spontaneous development give it the architectural tension that the earlier city lacks. If Pienza belongs to Rossellino, Montepulciano is Antonio da Sangallo's masterpiece.

Just outside and below the city walls, at the end of a long line of cypresses, lies Sangallo's **San Biagio**, the Renaissance church most at ease with its setting. The building's isolation focuses attention on the honey-coloured travertine, the Greek Cross design, the dome and the purity of the line. Sangallo's design skills rival Bramante's, not just in the church, the elegant well and the porticoed Canon's House, but elsewhere in the city. The airy interior has a deeply classical feel, more akin to the Roman Pantheon than to a small Tuscan church.

Traffic is banned within the city walls, but you can park outside San Biagio, from where it's a short but steepish walk into town. Alternatively, park in one of the many car parks at Montepulciano's eastern end and enter through the Porta al Prato. Here, Piazza Savonarola is guarded by a statue of the Marzocco lion, the symbol of Florentine

TIP

Tuscany Pass
(www.tuscanypass.com) is
a reliable website that
offers an events
calendar and some of
the best day trips in
Tuscany. Choose from
day-long Tuscan cookery
courses to Vespa trips to
the wine country; or arty
walking tours.

One of the more spiritual aspects of the St Benedict frescoes.

power. From here the princely Via di Gracciano nel Corso leads up to the main square. Its lower end is lined with noble palaces. The Renaissance **Palazzo Bucelli**, at no. 73, is decorated with a mosaic of Etruscan urns and pots, a reminder of the city's ancient origins. The road continues upwards to Piazza Grande, both the highest part of town and the highpoint culturally.

Florentine design has shaped the grand facades on Piazza Grande, but earlier Sienese Gothic touches are present in the interiors, double arches and doorways. Both styles reflect Montepulciano's buffeting between the two city-states and the eventual supremacy of Florence. On one side, the 15th-century **Palazzo Comunale** (Town Hall) has a Florentine Michelozzo facade adorning Sienese turrets. The **Tower** (Apr–Oct daily 10am–1pm, 2–6pm), modelled on that of Florence's Palazzo Vecchio, surveys the whole province: from Monte Amiata to Siena and across to Lake Trasimeno in Umbria.

Sangallo's **Palazzo Contucci**, on the other side of the square, still belongs to the aristocratic Contucci family, who produce Vino Nobile. In the **Cantine Contucci** (wine cellars; www.contucci.it; Mon–Fri 9.30am–12.30pm, 2.30–6.30pm), Ginevra Contucci will be delighted to expand on the noble wine heritage of her family, the virtues of their silky *Riserva*, and the maze of secret tunnels underneath the palace. Vino Nobile, a smooth red wine with a hint of violets, was "ennobled" in 1549 when Pope Paul III's sommelier proclaimed it "a most perfect wine, a wine for lords".

Between the two grand palazzi, at the top of wide steps, stands the **Duomo** (daily 9am–noon, 4–6pm), which contains a masterpiece of the Siena school: the huge *Assumption* triptych by Taddeo di Bartolo (1401) shines out above the high altar in the vast, gloomy nave. If you need cheering up, call into the labyrinthine cellars of **Cantine del Redi** (Via Ricci), where part of the *Twilight* vampire series was filmed (see page 182).

A circular tour

Scattered among the rolling landscape of Siena province are some beautiful

villages, each with a separate identity and architectural treasures espied almost incidentally over the brow of a hill. A circular itinerary from Montepulciano unites a group of tiny villages once ruled by the Cacciaconti barons.

Montefollonico ❹, 8km (5 miles) northwest of Montepulciano, has a 13th-century frescoed church and one of the best restaurants in Italy, La Chiusa (see page 262).

Petroio ❺, set on a rocky, wooded promontory, is a grand fortified village on an old pilgrim route. In recent years it has been undergoing a revival thanks to its terracotta – examples of which adorn the city walls, Palazzo Pretorio and the medieval towers. Look out for the Canon's House, which contains a remarkable *Madonna and Child* by Taddio di Bartolo. Near the village is the intact **Abbadia a Sicille**, built by the Knights Templar as a refuge for knights on the way to the Holy Land. The adjoining Romanesque church is decorated with two Maltese crosses, but an Olivetan coat of arms marks the abolition of the Templars.

Set among farmland and woods, **Castelmuzio** is a medieval village wrapped up in itself, its Museum of Sacred Art and its direct line to San Bernardo. Narrow shops in winding streets sell honey, salami and cheese made by an ageing population of churchgoers.

Once a Cacciaconti fortress, aristocratic **Montisi ❻** commands a view over two valleys, a view that is even more stirring when seen from the basket of a hot-air balloon (www.ballooning intuscany.com). Even discounting the ballooning base in the village, Montisi offers lofty views, intriguing alleys, earthy inns, and two tiny Romanesque churches, one featuring a Scuola di Duccio crucifix. A few apparently stark, uninviting farmhouses conceal wonderful frescoes and the occasional private chapel so are worth investigating.

One can return to Montepulciano via **Sinalunga**, a dual-personality town with a hideous "low town" but a pleasant "old town". Its original name, Asinalunga, echoes its shape, "the long donkey". But in the lively market, pigs, not donkeys, are in evidence in the

FACT

The Strada del Vino Nobile di Montepulciano is an association that promotes the local wines. As well as organising tours of the local vineyards and cellars, it offers a range of cultural tours including visits to the Garden of Villa La Foce, the Montepulciano spa, and Siena's pottery workshops. Its office is on Piazza Grande (Mon–Sat 10am–1pm, 3–6pm; tel: 0578-717 484; www.stradavinonobile.it).

The Chiesa San Biagio in Montepulciano.

Montepulciano's Etruscan origins are evident everywhere.

form of *porchetta*, the local speciality of roast pig flavoured with rosemary.

Val d'Orcia

The **Val d'Orcia** is a beguiling rural area south of Le Crete, but within sight of hulking Monte Amiata. Although these villages suffered from depopulation in the 1950s, today they are reaping the benefits of an intact urban and rural landscape. **San Quirico d'Orcia** ❼ is a dignified valley town still waiting for its heyday. It survived both an attack by Cesare Borgia's troops in 1502 and a World War II bombardment.

The Romanesque **Collegiata**, made from sandstone and local travertine, has three remarkable portals and columns supported by two stony lionesses. The lovely park, the **Horti Leonini**, is a model 16th-century Italian garden, complete with geometric beds. Stern, 17th-century **Palazzo Chigi** has now opened its frescoed rooms for inspection (daily 8am–6.30pm), and, round the corner, a bijou boutique hotel is flourishing. It seems that San Quirico might well be enjoying a belated renaissance.

Just south of San Quirico, off the SS2, **Bagno Vignoni** ❽ is a tiny but lively spa station, at its most evocative at dusk. The steam rises from the hot springs, and the yellowish light of the lanterns dimly illuminates the stone facades of the buildings lining the square, which is in fact a stone pool of sulphurous water, where both Lorenzo de' Medici and St Catherine once bathed. The hot springs were used by the Romans but became public baths in medieval times. Bathing is now forbidden, but the baths of Hotel Posta Marcucci are open to non-residents for a fee, and are also open at night on summer weekends.

From the relaxation of the pool, all senses are fulfilled at once: outside the pool of light, the sound of sheep and crickets reverberates; the softness of the hot, chalky water dissolves tiredness; and the smell of sulphur evaporates into the night air. After a swim, a short *passeggiata* around the old baths shows the well-restored square at its most romantic.

In the vicinity are three medieval fortresses – Ripa d'Orcia, Rocca

d'Orcia and Castiglione d'Orcia. After the turning to Bagno Vignoni, **Ripa d'Orcia**, an enchanted castle (now a hotel; tel: 0577-897 376; www.castellori padorcia.com) set among cypress groves, comes into view.

Rocca d'Orcia ❾, a fortified village once owned by the warring Salimbeni clan, has an impressive castle open to visitors. **Castiglione d'Orcia** offers more of the same: an atmospheric, cobblestoned centre, a ruined fortress and wonderful views. The abbey of Sant'Antimo can be reached from here. The mountain roads in the area are tortuous but beautiful, as are the walks.

Chiusi

Although set among attractive low hills, **Chiusi** ❿ comes across as a rather unprepossessing town, somewhat devoid of Renaissance charm. The "low town" is a commercial centre and the shabby "high town" is endearing but overwhelmed by its glorious Etruscan past.

Then, as now, the Chiusini were farmers, merchants and craftsmen, a spirit that predominates over artistry. Yet, with a little Etruscan knowledge and much curiosity, the town is as fascinating as any in Tuscany. It boasts a complete underground city; an unrivalled collection of female cinerary urns; and the only tomb paintings in their original setting in all of Tuscany.

As one of the greatest city-states in the Etruscan League, Chiusi, or "Kamars", controlled the area from Lago di Trasimeno to Monte Amiata. After reaching its zenith as a trading centre in the 7th century BC, Etruscan Kamars became submerged by Roman Clusium and then by medieval Chiusi. The old city now survives on three levels of civilisation: the Etruscan necropolis beneath the city hills; the Roman street-grid system below the Cathedral; and the medieval city above it.

The **Museo Archeologico Nazionale** (tel: 0578-20177; daily 9am–8pm) has one of the finest collections of its kind in Italy, which attests to the vitality of Kamars and shows a distinct bias in the outstanding female Canopic jars, cinerary urns and rounded *cippi* tombstones. The containers have

Montepulciano is bathed in a russet glow at sunset.

Val d'Orcia

The Val d'Orcia combines the most crowd-pleasing elements in one small valley: castles and country walks; spas and superb inns; iconic scenery and intoxicating settings.

The valley's prime location on the Via Francigena pilgrim route partially explains the surprisingly noble architecture and grandiose Romanesque churches; medieval insecurity accounts for the cluster of castles built to watch over the Orcia valley. But nothing quite explains why these elements come together so well.

A special bond with the land

Landscaped since time immemorial, the Val d'Orcia represents quintessential Tuscany: clusters of cypresses, ribbons of plane trees, sloping vineyards and farms perched on limestone ridges. But it was not this alone that won the area Unesco World Heritage status in 2004. It was as much to do with the harmonious relationship between the custodians and their landscape, a

Vineyards below Sant'Antimo.

bond that has survived to the present day, leaving the countryside cultivated but unscathed. This harmony extends to the hilltop hamlets, the Romanesque churches, the isolated farmhouses and the contemplative abbeys. All entities are anchored in this mystical yet pragmatic patchwork: they serve a purpose yet transcend it. This happy partnership has produced an idealised landscape that is at once the continuation of the natural order and the best that man and nature can achieve in unison.

Partly boosted by its Unesco recognition, Pienza, in particular, has become very popular, almost as much for its superb pecorino cheeses as for its perfect architecture and splendid views of Monte Amiata.

But it's not a case of the valley selling its soul. If spas can be mystical, then Bagno Vignoni comes close, not just because St Catherine of Siena enjoyed bathing there. The ancient abbey of Sant'Antimo continues to inspire visitors: the Romanesque church reels you in with its carved capitals, its Gregorian chant and Cistercian spirit.

Orcia trails

This soft mysticism extends to the landscape, where the rambles around Sant'Antimo are among the loveliest in Tuscany. A waymarked trail links the abbey with Montalcino on a gentle, 9.5km (6-mile) walk that unravels views over Monte Amiata and the whole of Val d'Orcia. A far more challenging 18km (11-mile) trail connects the abbey with Bagno Vignoni, via the medieval fortress of Ripa d'Orcia. En route are views of the Brunello vineyards, the soft hills around Pienza and the looming presence of Monte Amiata.

Train travel

Alternatively, the so-called Nature Train (Treno Natura; www.trenonatura.terresiena.it) provides a similar atmosphere. This service runs through countryside, covering routes where towns are peripheral. The Nature Train generally does the Val d'Orcia run on Sundays in spring and autumn. At other times of the year, the train service focuses on quirky local festivals, including the olive-oil festival in San Quirico d'Orcia, or the pork festival in Vivo d'Orcia. During the autumn white truffle season, one special train travels round the Crete moonscape to San Giovanni d'Asso (http://museo tartufo.museisenesi.org), culminating in truffle tasting over lunch.

Egyptian-style lids resembling human or animal heads. The Etruscans borrowed freely from the Greeks and Egyptians; the imitation Greek vases are less rational but more vigorous than the originals.

A speciality of Chiusi is *bucchero*, glossy black earthenware, often in the form of vases with figures in relief. This pottery has a sophisticated metallic finish that cannot be reproduced by modern craftsmen. Although much of the domestic pottery has a naturalness verging on the commonplace, the sarcophagi, the cinerary urns and the crouching sphinxes reveal an underlying obsession with death and the appeasement of shadowy spirits.

A visit to the **Etruscan tombs**, 3km (2 miles) outside town, can be arranged with the museum staff or pre-booked (tel: 0578-20177). The tombs contain sarcophagi, cinerary urns and, in the case of the **Tomb of the Monkey**, rare wall-paintings of athletic games and domestic scenes.

Three civilisations are visible at once in Chiusi's **Duomo**: the Romanesque Cathedral is built from Etruscan and Roman fragments. The **Museo della Cattedrale** (Feb–Mar Tue, Thur, Sat 9.45am–12.45pm, Sun also 3–5.15 pm, Apr–May, mid-Oct–Dec Mon–Sat 9.45am–12.45pm, Sun 4–6.30pm, Jun–mid-Oct daily 9.45am–12.45pm, 4–6.30pm) is of limited appeal, but your ticket entitles you to a tour of a fascinating labyrinth beneath the Cathedral. The recently excavated tunnels are part of an Etruscan water system cut into the rocks, which provided natural filtration. After being led through tunnels to a large Roman cistern dating from the 1st century BC, you emerge, blinking, at the bottom of the Cathedral bell tower. Climb to the top to gaze at Monte Amiata, the Val d'Orcia, and even Lake Trasimeno.

The entrance to Chianciano Terme.

Chianciano Terme

After underground Chiusi, **Chianciano Terme** ⑪ is a breath of fresh air. Italians have flocked to this spa town since Roman times to enjoy the unique powers of Acqua Santa. The innovative **Terme Sensoriali** is just one of a new breed of swish thermal day spas that have appeared across

The thermal pool in Bagno Vignoni.

FACT

In her book *War in Val d'Orcia*, Iris Origo, an Anglo-Florentine who lived in the Orcia valley, painted a dramatic picture of the Tuscan battlefield. As a young woman, Origo was part of D.H. Lawrence's artistic circle, but her understanding of the Tuscans set her apart.

The famous cypress-lined road leading to La Foce.

Tuscany in recent years, replacing the more old-fashioned clinical baths.

Although better known for its spa than for its culture, a new museum aims to put Chianciano on the artistic map. The **Museo d'Arte di Chianciano** (280 Viale della Liberta, 0578-60732; www.museodarte.org) presents a collection by the Realists, Surrealists and Post-Impressionists, as well as staging international exhibitions.

Southern Siena province is positively bursting with Etruscan remains, and digging produces a continual flow of exciting finds. In Chianciano, well-marked walks lead to several recently discovered tombs and temples, and an excellent **Museo Etrusco** (tel: 0578-30471; www.museoetrusco.it; Apr–Oct Tue–Sun 10am–1pm and 4–7pm, Nov–Mar Sat–Sun same hours) contains an intact monumental tomb of a princess, lined with bronze and adorned with gold and bronze artefacts. The museum also features the remains of a spa complex dating from the 1st century BC, which was discovered in Chianciano and is thought to be the sacred magic spring that cured

Emperor Augustus in 23 BC from a life-threatening stomach ailment.

Around La Foce

Near the town are some of the loveliest walks and drives in Tuscany. Many walks start from **La Foce** , a 15th-century farmhouse that overlooks the fertile Val di Chiana and the desolate craters of the Val d'Orcia. The superb gardens here (guided tours only: Mar–Oct Wed 3pm, 4pm, 5pm and 6pm, Sat–Sun 11.30am, 3pm and 4.30pm) were designed by the famous British landscape gardener Cecil Pinsent. There are views across an Etruscan site to Monte Amiata and Monte Cetona. Its excellent strategic position meant that its owners, the Anglo-Italian Origos, allowed it to be used as the partisans' refuge during World War II. Excavations on the property have uncovered some 200 Etruscan tombs. From here, a rough track leads to Petraporciana, the partisans' hidden headquarters, and to a primeval forest full of giant oaks, cyclamens, wild orchids or snowdrops: a perfect short spring or autumn walk.

Beside La Foce is **Castelluccio**, a castle – and summer concert venue – that commands the best-loved view in the province: a sinuous line of cypresses plotting an Etruscan route across the craters. When Prince Charles stayed at La Foce, proud locals were not surprised to see him painting this view.

A short walk leads to **Pocce Lattaie** and prehistoric caves with dripping stalactites shaped like teats or nipples. These pagan caves were used in fertility rites and when propitiatory offerings were made to the gods. Be prepared to hire a guide (and a torch) from Chianciano.

Around Monte Cetona

From Chianciano, an idyllic rural drive leads via La Foce to Sarteano and Cetona, two small medieval and Etruscan towns. These views of desolate *crete*, fortified farmhouses and hazy Monte Amiata are captured by Paolo Busato in his celebrated photographs. It is worth sacrificing a hired car to the dirt roads, but the nervous can take the more direct route to Sarteano.

Castiglioncello sul Trionoro is a tiny village with a *castello* and a church containing a Trecento Madonna. The village is set amid vast expanses of abandoned countryside in which Etruscan remains are regularly uncovered.

Spilling over its double ring of city walls, **Sarteano** ⑬ is a popular spa centre that has retained its traditional identity. The town offers Etruscan remains, a grandiose 13th-century Rocca and crumbling Renaissance palazzi built into the city walls. There is an interesting **Museo Etrusco** (tel: 0578-269 261; Apr–Oct Tue–Sun 10.30am–12.30pm, 4–7pm, Nov–Mar Sat–Sun same hours) but, contrary to rumours, the tomb of the Etruscan king Porsenna has never been discovered. In August each year, Sarteano holds a famous *Giostra* or jousting tournament.

Cetona ⑭ clings to a richly wooded hill. The grand 18th-century houses on the plains are a relic of past prosperity, but Cetona is a refreshingly authentic Tuscan community. The broad traffic-free square is filled with locals going about their daily lives, free (as yet) of the quaint wine, food and craft shops that predominate in touristic towns such as Pienza. Although Cetona is noted for its textiles and copies of Etruscan vases, it now relies on *agriturismo* to keep its population from leaving. A short stay in a local farm with mountain walks, local cheeses and *bruschetti* drenched in olive oil is highly recommended.

A very scenic route, the Via della Montagna, goes from Cetona to the spa town of **San Casciano dei Bagni** ⑮ (take the high road north out of town and follow signs to Mondo "X"). En route, it's worth stopping at the beautifully restored **Convento di San Francesco**. It now houses a rehabilitation centre (Mondo "X"), but if you ring the bell, one of the occupants of the *comunità* will be happy to show you round.

The **Fonteverde spa resort**, on the edge of San Casciano dei Bagni, is one of Tuscany's most alluring destination spas, with the Medici villa at the heart of the stylish resort. Fortunately, you

TIP

Monte Cetona (1,148 metres/3,800ft) is crisscrossed by woodland lanes and open tracks for walking, cycling and horse riding. A map of the network of mountain trails is available from the tourist offices of Cetona, San Casciano dei Bagni and Sarteano.

A bather at Bagni San Filippo.

A Sienese shepherd.

The view towards Abbadia San Salvatore.

can also use it as a day spa, and wallow in the hot pools while gazing over a sea of greenery (www.fonteverdespa.com).

Routes up to Monte Amiata

The journey to Monte Amiata, southern Tuscany's highest peak, is at least as rewarding as the arrival. The fast Pienza to Abbadia San Salvatore route allows for a detour to the thermal baths at **Bagni San Filippo**, where you can float along on faded charm in a friendly, affordable time-warp spa, or dine in the good-value restaurant (www.termesanfilippo.it)

The alternative route, via Sarteano and **Radicofani** ⑯, was the one taken by both Dickens and Montaigne to a location second only to Volterra for natural drama. While the mountain villages have walking and food trails to thank for their revival, the villages on the edge of Amiata seem to be in permanent limbo, trapped rather than enhanced by a medieval identity. Dickens found Radicofani "as barren, as stony, and as wild as Cornwall, in England". Perched on a craggy basalt rock, it is the only place in Italy to possess a

triple Medicean wall. The town overlooks *"Il Mare di Sassi"*, the "Sea of Stones", suitable only for very hardy sheep. Although an 18th-century earthquake destroyed much of the town, enough atmosphere remains.

The drive from Radicofani up to **Abbadia San Salvatore** ⑰ is via Le Conie, a tortuous road known as "Amiata's sentry". For those not interested in skiing, mountain walks and disused mercury mines, Abbadia is best known for its overrated **Abbazia** (abbey) and its medieval "high town". The Romanesque **San Salvatore** (summer Mon–Sat 8am–5pm, Sun 8.30am–6pm, winter until 5pm; free) is all that remains of a once-magnificent abbey, but it has been clumsily restored. A 12th-century *Crucifix* and the crypt with 36 columns remain relatively unspoilt. Geometric symbols, grapes, palm leaves, animals and Gordian knots decorate the pillars.

From Abbadia, a winding road with sharp bends and sheer drops leads to the top of **Monte Amiata**, 1,738 metres (5,700ft) high. The wooded area around the extinct volcano has

attractive walks. The Fosso della Cocca, a leafy tunnel, is the best place to spot unusual wildlife and vegetation.

Castel del Piano, set among pine forests and wild raspberries, is the oldest settlement in the area, but **Piancastagnaio** is a better base. Perched among chestnut groves, the town has a newly restored Rocca and Franciscan monastery.

Arcidosso ⑱ was the birthplace of David Lazzaretti, "The Prophet of the Amiata". In the 19th century, Lazzaretti created a revolutionary social and religious movement with its headquarters on **Monte Labro**, a lonely peak. Now a nature reserve where deer, chamois and wolves roam, the park is best visited in autumn, when the crowds have left and the wild mushrooms appear.

Santa Fiora is particularly delightful, and has fine works of art in the 12th-century Santa Fiora and Santa Lucilla churches, including some della Robbia ceramics.

Montalcino

In both temperament and identity, **Montalcino** ⑲ is certainly the most Sienese town in the province. In essence, its history is a microcosm of Sienese history. From a distance, Montalcino even looks like a Sienese Trecento painting: the landscape could be a background to a saint's life; in the foreground would be the fortress and scenes of rejoicing and celebration after a historic victory.

Montalcino has been known as "the last rock of communal freedom" since its time as the Sienese capital-in-exile between 1555 and 1559. After the fall of Siena, exiles gathered around Piero Strozzi and the Sienese flag. As a reward, Montalcinesi standard-bearers have the place of honour in the procession preceding the Palio in Siena.

The magnificent 14th-century **Fortezza** (Tue–Sun 9am–6pm) is the key to Montalcino's pride. The approach is through olive groves and the slopes famous for Brunello wine. But the asymmetrical fortress, astride a spur of land, dominates the landscape. From its gardens, there is a sense of boundless space and absolute freedom. In winter, the wind howls over the massive walls and

A view of Montalcino.

Brunello di Montalcino is one of Italy's best wines. Opportunities abound to taste and buy Brunello and the younger Rosso di Montalcino.

The Romanesque abbey of Sant'Antimo.

drives visitors to a different type of fortification in the *Enoteca* bar inside. This "National Wine Library" naturally serves Brunello, a magnificent wine whose reputation is slightly tarnished after some producers were charged with illegally blending it with other grapes.

Architecturally, Montalcino offers a neoclassical cathedral, a Gothic loggia, a Romanesque church and myriad intriguing alleys. The Duccio and della Robbia schools are well served by the Civic and Sacred museums. Most significant is the Palazzo Comunale, a mass of *Fiorentinità* finished off by a Sienese tower to prove that the Sienese always surpass the Florentines.

In spring, the area is very green, but yellow rapeseed, poppies, sunflowers and grapes soon take over. Before leaving, try *pici*, home-made spaghetti, in the Grappolo Blu (see page 262) or sweet *sospiri* ("sighs") in a *fin-de-siècle bar*.

Sant'Antimo

Nearby is **Sant'Antimo** ⓴ (Mon–Sat 10.15am–12.30pm and 3–6.30pm, Sun 9.15–10.45am and 3–6pm; free), the remains of a Romanesque abbey founded by Charlemagne, set amidst cypress trees in a peaceful valley. Designed in the French and Lombard style, the abbey is built from local travertine, which resembles alabaster or onyx. The interior has a translucent quality that, as the light changes, turns luminous shades of gold, white and brown.

The community of Augustinian monks who tend the church sing the Gregorian chant at Mass every Sunday afternoon throughout the year. From here there are several superb marked trails through timeless countryside.

Not far away, **Sant'Angelo in Colle**, a fortified hilltop village, once cast a dramatic shadow over Grosseto and other enemies. Until 1265, it was a Sienese outpost, but the tower is all that remains. Today it is a quiet medieval village.

Modern Siena province ends just there. As a frontier castle, Sant'Angelo looked down on to the plain that falls into Grosseto. After Siena province, Grosseto can look deceptively flat.

Montalcino at dusk.

The tufa town of Sorano.

THE MAREMMA AND MONTE ARGENTARIO

Grosseto province has some of the most beautiful
stretches of coast and wilderness areas in the region.
The Maremma, "the marsh by the sea", is Tuscany's Wild
West, where cowboys and long-horned cattle roam.
Inland, the marshy plains give way to densely wooded
hills, where towns seem to grow from the tufa.

Tuscany's southwestern corner offers a wonderfully varied landscape, ranging from the flat coastal plains to the wooded, snow-capped peak of Monte Amiata, or to the gentle hills bordering Siena province. The coastline has an unrivalled mix of Mediterranean flora and fauna, but the region is dominated by the marshy plain of the Maremma, stretching from the Piombino headland to Tuscany's border with Lazio. Backed by striking hills, this coastal marshland is famous for its horse-breeding, wild-boar hunting, Etruscan sites and austere inland villages, not to mention its rich cuisine.

Abundant remains reveal that the Etruscans thrived in this area, cultivating the land and exploiting the mineral wealth on Elba. However, while the Romans continued to mine Elba for the iron they needed to make swords, they allowed the drainage and irrigation systems the Etruscans had put in place on the mainland to decay. By the Middle Ages, the Maremma had become a malarial swamp and the population had migrated to the hills. It wasn't until the mid-19th century, with the draining of the swamps and land reclamation, that the revival of these evocative lowlands began, spearheaded by the return of the *butteri* (Tuscany's tough cowboys) with their herds of long-horned cattle.

The harbour at Porto Ercole.

Grosseto

The provincial capital, **Grosseto ❶**, is a commercial and administrative centre, with little to recommend it, unless you are passing through and have an interest in things Roman and Etruscan. The **Museo Archeologico e d'Arte della Maremma** (Piazza Baccarini 3; http://maaam.comune.grosseto. it; Apr–May, mid-Sept–Oct Tue–Fri 10am–5pm, Sat–Sun 10am–1pm and 4–7pm, June–mid-Sept Tue–Fri 10am– 5.30pm, Sat–Sun 10am–1pm and 5–8pm, Nov–Mar Tue–Fri 9am–3pm,

The pink-and-white candy-striped facade of Grosseto's Cathedral overlooks Piazza Dante, the hub of the town.

Sun 10am–1pm and 4–7pm) is one of the richest museums in the area. It has a fine collection of pre-Etruscan, Etruscan and Roman artefacts from the archaeological sites of Roselle, Vetulonia, Talamone, Pitigliano and Saturnia to the south.

The excavations at **Roselle ➋** (daily Nov–Feb 8.30am–5.30pm, Mar–Apr and Sept–Oct until 6.30pm, May–Aug until 7pm; follow signs to the ruins, not the town of Roselle), about 10km (6 miles) northeast of Grosseto, reveal one of the most important Etruscan cities in northern Etruria. The paved streets, ruins of Etruscan taverns and workshops, and the nearly intact circuit of Romano-Etruscan walls, as well as the outlines of the Roman forum and amphitheatre, are all very evocative. Most of the finds are on display in Grosseto's archaeological museum.

On the other side of the old Roman Via Aurelia (also less romantically known as the N1), about 20km (12 miles) north of Grosseto, the hilltop village of **Vetulonia ➌** lies above another ancient Etruscan city, Vetluna. The small excavated area (the *Scavi Città*) is more Roman than Etruscan. More interesting are the tombs (Oct–Feb 10am–4pm, Mar–May until 6pm, June–Sept 10am–2pm and 4–8pm; archaeological park same hours), 3km (2 miles) from the *Scavi Città*.

The coast

This stretch of coast ranges from the mundane to the magical, often with little in between. South of the rural delights of the Maremma reserve, the decidedly chic Monte Argentario peninsula is dotted with charming coves and small beaches. Instead, north of Castiglione della Pescaia, the Gulf of Follonica represents tawdry, cheap-and-cheerful tourism aimed at the local market. Ignore the unprepossessing **Marina di Grosseto** in favour of the old fishing village of **Castiglione della Pescaia ➍**.

The boat-lined harbour is believed to be the Etruscan Hasta, or Portus Traianus in Roman times. Overlooking the port is the Rocca Aragonese, with its walls and towers dating back to the 14th century. This low-key resort has pleasant, family-friendly

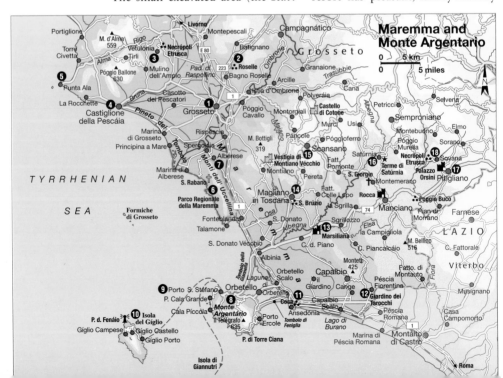

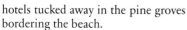

hotels tucked away in the pine groves bordering the beach.

The coastal stretch from Castiglione della Pescaia south to the Parco della Maremma is bordered by a magnificent forest of umbrella pines known as the **Pineta del Tombolo**. You can leave your car by the roadside and take any of the footpaths through the umbrella pines to the lovely beach.

From here the road leads north to the brash Gulf of Follonica. The gulf's southern promontory is occupied by **Punta Ala ⑤**, an elite summer resort with a flashy marina, upmarket hotels, golf clubs, horse riding and polo facilities. It's an attractive spot, and offers an amusing window on the lemming-like habits of moneyed Italians at leisure.

If you are in Bay of Follonica area and yearning for the seaside, **Cala Violino** is a quiet bay just before the resort. Alternatively, there are some good beaches between Follonico and Piombino. Otherwise, at this point you're better off heading inland to **Massa Marittima**, or back south to the beautiful Parco della Maremma.

Parco Regionale della Maremma

Also known as the Parco dell'Uccellina, the **Parco Regionale della Maremma ⑥** covers an area of around 60 sq km (150 sq miles), including about 20km (12 miles) of coastline.

Evidence of human settlement here can be seen in the remains of a castle, the Benedictine monastery of **San Rabano**, and lookout towers used for the unfortunate soldiers posted here to watch for Saracen pirates and Spanish galleons.

The main entrance to the park is at **Alberese ⑦**, where you have to leave your car. The helpful visitor centre (tel: 0564-407 098; www.parcomaremma.it; daily Oct–mid-Mar 8.30am–1.30pm, mid-Mar–Sept 8am–5pm), where you buy your entrance ticket, is full of information on the flora and fauna, and activities within the park. With your ticket you'll be given a map of clearly explained waymarked trails you can follow, of various levels of difficulty and duration, from gentle two-hour walks to day-long treks. Shuttle buses into the park leave from outside the visitor centre at regular intervals, but be sure

The Maremma's increasing reputation as a centre for wine-making and gastronomy has been endorsed by high-profile French chef Alain Ducasse. He has transformed a former ducal residence near Castiglione della Pescaia into an elegant hotel with a superb restaurant. Wine and olive oil are produced by the estate, which is surrounded by ancient olive groves and vineyards.

Beach at Castiglione della Pescaia, with Rocca Aragonese above.

TIP

The beaches within the Parco dell'Uccellina are among the most beautiful and unspoilt in Tuscany. To preserve this wilderness, the number of visitors is limited during the summer, and apart from the road to Marina di Alberese, cars are not permitted in the park. Transport from Alberese is arranged on buses. Visiting in the height of summer is ill-advised, as the weather becomes hot and humid, and there are tiny insects, *serafiche*, whose bite is painful.

to check the time of the last bus back down.

Activities within the nature park include canoeing on the Ombrone River, sailing along the coast, riding across the mountains, birdwatching beside the salt marshes, and visiting the noble ruins of San Rabano and other towers strung out along the mountain tops and overlooking the sea, each with its story of marauding pirates and hidden treasures, going back to the times of the Saracens and the Spanish galleons.

If time is limited or you'd rather not walk, you can take the one access road (you still need a ticket) from Alberese to **Marina di Alberese**, a 6km (4-mile) stretch of beach.

Just outside the southern boundaries of the park is the walled village of **Talamone** (18km/11 miles from Alberese), a low-key resort with decent hotels and restaurants. You can gain access to local trails around here from nearby Caprarecce.

Monte Argentario

It's a short drive from Talamone along the Aurelia-Etrusca (Grosseto–Rome

highway) to **Monte Argentario ❽**, a craggy peninsula that was once an island, thought to have been occupied by Roman money lenders in the 4th century – *argentarius* in Latin is money lender. From 1556 until 1815, Argentario existed as a separate state from the Grand Duchy of Tuscany, under Spanish rule. This kingdom encompassed the whole promontory and the existing ports of Orbetello, Talamone and Porto Azzurro, on the island of Elba. The Spanish legacy lingers on in the medieval watchtowers that still hug the coast.

Monte Argentario gradually became attached to the land by two long sandbanks: Tòmbolo della Giannella and **Tòmbolo di Feniglia**. Both have fine beaches, but while Giannella is backed by a main road, Feniglia is traffic-free and backed by protected pine forest. It's a 7km (4-mile) walk or bike ride to the mainland.

Like two outstretched arms holding on to the mainland, the sandbanks embrace a lagoon, an important wintering spot for migrating birds. The lagoon is cut in half by a central

PARCO DELLA MAREMMA

As the last virgin coast on the Italian peninsula, Tuscany's most beguiling park is extraordinarily precious and thus well cared for. The landscape ranges from salt marshes, sand dunes and open plains to rocky mountains, sheer cliffs, pine forests and Mediterranean maquis – dense scrubland characterised by rosemary, broom, sea lavender and holm oaks. Wild deer, boar and small mammals thrive in the undergrowth, while it is incredibly rich in birdlife. Wading birds flock to the marshes around the mouth of the Ombrone River, and birds of prey circle the hills. The park is also an important resting place for birds migrating between Europe and Africa. Depending on the habitat and the season, you can see flamingoes, falcons, ospreys, herons and black-winged stilts.

Down on the open fields and low-lying olive groves, herds of long-horned cattle and horses graze. They are reared by *butteri*, the tough Tuscan cowboys who settled in the region in the 19th century, after the swamps were drained and the land could be used for cattle grazing.

One of the loveliest marked routes leads to a high

cliff overlooking a forest of umbrella pines cascading all the way down to a sea, and beach, that looks almost Caribbean.

The park headquarters in Alberese (Via del Bersagliere, tel: 0564-407 098, www.parco-maremma.it) has recently launched a series of new itineraries, notably a scenic cycling trail (8.5km/5 miles) from Alberese to Marina di Alberese. There are also specific marked horseriding trails. The park offers birdwatching canoe trips and there is even a night-time trip during which you can listen to animal sounds under the stars. For those not eager or unable to walk, the park organises horse-drawn carriage excursions as well.

The park is open year round. However the information centre in Talamone and the Talamone Aquarium, which concentrates on the Orbetello lagoon sealife, are open Mar–Oct only (tel: 0564-887 173).

Last but not least, there is a tasting zone where visitors can try selected local produce for free, including wine, honey and cheeses. (Naturalmente Toscana, tel: 0564-407 269, www.naturalmentetoscana.it).

causeway that links Argentario to the town of **Orbetello**, which juts into the lagoon. The town's Baroque architecture reflects its history as a 16th-century Spanish garrison, where the sea laps the city walls. Visitors come from afar for the excellent fish restaurants found here and on Monte Argentario.

The rugged peninsula rises to a height of 635 metres (2,000ft) and is cloaked in Mediterranean maquis, olive groves and vineyards. Apart from **Porto Santo Stefano** ❾, the mountain has been spared from the property developers, but the exclusive villas outside the port towns remain the preserve of the rich. Sadly, most of this delightful coastline is inaccessible, unless, of course, you are the owner of a yacht. The best way to enjoy Argentario is to stay in a hotel with a private beach. Otherwise, of the few beaches with public access, the nicest are Le Cannelle (roughly opposite Isola Rossa) and the beach to the left of the luxury hotel Il Pellicano, near Porto Ercole.

Porto Santo Stefano's busy harbour is crowded with fishing boats and yachts. It is an atmospheric town,

lined with upmarket boutiques, bars and fish restaurants. For a breathtaking and often hair-raising drive, the scenic coastal road from here (follow signs to La Panoramica) takes you along the clifftops.

Porto Ercole is Santo Stefano's smaller, more exclusive sister, but what was once a quiet fishing village is often overwhelmed by all the traffic that converges on it from sea and land. Its main attractions for landlubbers are the *centro storico* and the 16th-century Spanish fortress overlooking the harbour.

Island excursions

Santo Stefano has ferry connections with Giannutri and Giglio, two of the seven islands in the Arcipelago Toscano. The archipelago was declared a nature reserve in 1996 – not that all the regulations are interpreted as strictly as one might imagine. Crescent-shaped **Giannutri** is a tiny, flat, virtually uninhabited island 22km (14 miles) away, where day-trippers go to visit the ruins of a Roman villa – columns, mosaics, baths and a private pier.

Umbrella pines line many of the long, straight roads through the Maremman plains.

Porto Santo Stefano.

TIP

An annual rodeo is held in August, which brings American cowboys to Alberese. Other local festivals include the Sagra del Cinghiale (Boar Fair) in Montepescali; the Sagra dello Struzzo (Local Gastronomic Fair) in Manciano; and the Sagra della Trippa (Tripe Fair) in Montemerano.

The harbour at Porto Ercole.

Giglio , an hour's sail from Porto Santo Stefano, has more to offer. It is a playground for sailors and divers, and the second-largest island in Tuscany after Elba. It has an almost impenetrable coastline, with only one easily accessible port, Giglio Porto. A rocky road uphill leads to Giglio Castello, which dominates the landscape. Set among vineyards (which produce grapes for the very strong, distinctive local wine, Ansonica), it is a picturesque settlement, with archways, alleyways and stairs carved from the rock. Giglio abounds in sandy beaches on its western side and is covered in typical Mediterranean vegetation: aromatic herbs and plants, and orange and lemon groves.

Cosa to Capalbio

Back on the mainland coast, across the Aurelia from the town of **Ansedonia** are the important Roman remains of **Cosa** ⑪ (www.cosaexcavations.com; daily May–Sept 9am–7pm, Oct–Apr 9am–5pm; site free, small museum charge) built on top of an Etruscan settlement. Excavations have revealed a main street, a forum, a walled acropolis and *capitolium* with magnificent views out to sea. After a long break which saw the site get overgrown, new excavations have begun there.

Below the promontory is the silted-up Roman port and the Tagliata Etrusca, the Etruscan Cut – a canal in fact built by the Romans to drain the **Lago di Burano** reserve.

Inland lies **Capalbio**, one of the first towns on the hills bordering Lazio. Capalbio is a fashionable, foodie haunt among wealthy Italians. Nearby is the magical **Giardino dei Tarocchi** ⑫, or Tarot Garden (tel: 0564-895 122; www.nikidesaint phalle.com; daily Apr–mid-Oct 2.30–7.30pm), created by French sculptor Niki de Saint-Phalle, who died in 2002, and inspired by the arcane symbolism of the Tarot. The park displays 22 fantastic, brightly coloured sculptures covered in mirror and mosaic, glinting in the sun among the flowers and fountains.

Fortified towns

Across the densely wooded hills

north of Capalbio is the drained Albegna plain, which leads to the castle of **Marsiliana** ⓫, once an Etruscan town and now the only property left belonging to the Corsini family, who originally owned the entire area. Most of these swamps were expropriated by the state, drained and then distributed to small landowners.

North of here lies **Magliano in Toscana** ⓮, a fortified medieval village perched above olive groves. Both civil and religious architecture shows a strong Romanesque influence, with Gothic and Renaissance additions. A perfect example of the blend of styles is San Giovanni Battista, a Romanesque church with Gothic side windows and a Renaissance facade.

A few kilometres further inland, **Scansano** ⓯, a breezy hill village with a fortified section (*oppido*), was once the summer capital of the province, when the administrative powers were moved from malarial Grosseto during the hot season. Now famous for the fine wine Morellino di Scansano, there are several *cantine* for wine tasting.

Spa resort

Travelling eastwards across hills and moors inhabited by *butteri* (cowboys) and Maremman cattle, you come to Montemerano, another typically Tuscan walled town, with 15th-century fortifications. From here you can head to the ancient Roman spa centre of **Saturnia** ⓰. On the approach to the town, around a sharp curve, you will glimpse the **Cascate del Gorello**, a steaming waterfall where you can bathe in hot sulphur springs. Alternatively, soak car-weary limbs in the upmarket thermal swimming pools of Terme di Saturnia (see page 274). Saturnia, drowsy under the weight of its Etruscan and Roman past, is centred around a large oak-ringed piazza with one or two notable trattorias.

Tufa towns

Pitigliano, Sovana and Sorano are three southern Tuscan jewels situated above dramatic cliffs of soft, porous tufa covered in a thick jungle of fern, ivy and evergreen trees. The roads here, hewn out of the hills, are an

Bathing in the Cascate del Gorello.

SPA THERAPY

Tuscany has an ancient spa tradition. Etruscans worshipped water and were believers in water rituals and herbal cures, but it was the Romans who perfected water cures, pioneering the virtues of moving between the hot and cold of the *caldarium*, *tepidarium* and *frigidarium*. The steaming thermal waters that gush from the ground are channelled into spa pools. These waters stimulate, re-mineralise, relax and revive the body, with sodium and magnesium nourishing bones, while the therapeutic mud is collected at the source of the spring and used in natural face and body treatments. The top Tuscan spas are pampering as well as curative. (For a list of Tuscany's best spas, see page 274).

Ciborium of the 8th or 9th century inside Sovana's exquisite Romanesque church of Santa Maria.

Pitigliano at night.

experience in themselves. The winding stretch between Sovana and Pitigliano, which rises spectacularly above it, is particularly memorable.

In the middle of the 18th century, **Pitigliano** ⑰ was one of the most important settlements in southern Tuscany. This majestic town is built on a hill of volcanic tufa and straddles a vast aqueduct with wine and olive-oil cellars carved out of the hillside below. The town is centred around a magnificent medieval citadel built by the Orsini. Laid out around two parallel streets, Pitigliano is crossed by countless atmospheric alleys.

Pitigliano used to be called "little Jerusalem", as it was a refuge for Jews fleeing from religious persecution in the Papal states. Even today, the Jewish quarter of the city, which has the oldest Italian synagogue, remains distinct. It is one of the few places in Italy where you can find kosher cakes, from a Jewish bakery no less. The **Museo Ebraico (Jewish Museum)** (via Zuccarelli; Sun–Fri Apr–Sept 10am–1pm, 2.30–6pm, Oct–Mar 10am–noon and 3–5pm) is utterly compelling.

Although resident in the former ghetto, Pitigliano's Jewish community were never persecuted. Before leaving town, dip into a Slow Food inn and enjoy a glass of Bianco di Pitigliano from the tufa wine cellars.

Sovana ⑱, situated a few kilometres away, is a perfectly formed one-street village with two outstanding proto-Romanesque churches. The surrounding area is scattered with Etruscan tombs, hidden in the woods, as well as evocative Etruscan streets, carved, like deep gorges, into the rock. These are best seen with a guide (tel: 0564-633 099).

Situated above a deep ravine with a roaring stream and waterfall is medieval **Sorano**, which is also built on a tufa outcrop.

Visible from all corners of the Maremma on a clear day, is **Monte Amiata**, the highest peak in Tuscany south of Florence. It is a dormant volcano, with hot geysers and underground waters that supply the spa at Saturnia. Monte Amiata is a refreshing escape during the summer months and a ski resort in winter.

Monte Amiata.

View of Poppi.

AREZZO AND EASTERN TUSCANY

Known for its gold, art and antiques, Arezzo can feel removed from tourism. The province is also blessed with prosperous farms, castles and abbeys tucked into deep woods. For all its wealth, there is a spirituality in the air that feels more akin to mystical Umbria.

A rezzo province is rugged, with steep, thickly wooded valleys that shield its towns and villages from view. The source of the Arno is here, too, in an area of great natural beauty known as the Casentino. This remote, northern area of chestnut woods, vineyards and monasteries leads to the farms of the fertile Val di Chiana. To the west, across the Pratomagno ridge, lies the Arno valley. At the heart of the province, its capital, Arezzo, was one of the most important towns in the Etruscan federation, thanks to its strategic position on a hill at the meeting point of three valleys. Today, it is one of Tuscany's wealthiest cities, as witnessed by the proliferation of jewellers, goldsmiths and antique shops on the city's streets.

Arezzo city

Arezzo ❶ abounds in monuments and works of art from all eras, but tourism is mostly muted. The old, hilly part of the city is the most picturesque, with its massive main square, the **Piazza Grande Ⓐ**, barely on an even keel. On the first Sunday of every month, this square welcomes an antiques market, the largest of its kind in Italy. Stalls cover the square, run around the base of the Duomo, and spill into the cobbled **Corso Italia**, the city's main shopping street. After

Giostra del Saracino, Arezzo.

being tempted by the jewellery shops, linger over a leisurely lunch around Piazza Grande, ideally at **La Torre di Gnicche** (Piaggia di San Martino, tel: 0575-352 035), a rustic inn serving salami, cheese platters and stuffed pasta (see page 264).

Spiritual duties await in one of the loveliest Romanesque churches in Tuscany. Rising from the southern side of the square, sitting on the Corso, is the **Santa Maria della Pieve Ⓑ** (daily 8am–1pm and 3–7pm; free), with its "tower of a hundred holes", so

Main Attractions

Piero della Francesca Frescoes, San Francesco, Arezzo
Sansepolcro
Monterchi
The Casentino Countryside
Monastero di Camaldoli
Castello dei Conti Guidi, Poppi
Lucignano
Cityscape, Cortona
Museo Diocesano, Cortona

FACT

Some great intellectuals hailed from Arezzo – Maecenas, Roman patron of the arts who encouraged the work of Virgil and Horace; Petrarch, classical Italian poet; Guido d'Arezzo, the inventor of musical notation; and Giorgio Vasari, the 16th-century painter, architect and art historian.

named because of the filigree pattern of arches that pierces the belfry.

A spiritual trail

Just west stands the cavernous church of **San Francesco** ⓒ (Mon–Fri 9am–6pm, Sat until 5.30pm, Sun 1–5.30pm; free) which contains Piero della Francesca's restored *Legend of the True Cross* (1452–66) (advance booking necessary; tel: 0575-352 727). This haunting fresco cycle weaves together a complex story in which the wood of the *Tree of Knowledge* (from which Adam and Eve ate the apple) becomes the wood of the cross on which Christ died, and which was later discovered by the Empress Helena, mother of the Emperor Constantine the Great, who converted to Christianity and made it the state religion of the Roman Empire, AD 313. What matters more is the spirituality that suffuses his art, a transcendent quality that elevates his work beyond the mere mastery of perspective and space. Look for his graceful figures framed by idealised depictions of Arezzo and Sansepolcro.

Medieval monuments cluster together in the northern part of the

The Corso.

city, where you will find the **Duomo** ⓓ (daily 6.30am–12.30pm and 3–6.30pm; free), sheltered by the encircling walls of the Grand Duke Cosimo's 16th-century Fortezza, now a park with fine views of the town and the Casentino beyond. The lofty Duomo, dating from the late 13th century, boasts a Gothic bell tower but still feels stranded on its hilltop site. Inside you can see 16th-century stained-glass windows and the 14th-century tomb of Guido Tarlati, which flanks the *St Mary Magdalene* fresco by Piero della Francesca. This work can be contemplated in comparative peace, unlike the frescoes in San Francesco. The **Museo Diocesano** (daily 10am–6pm), behind the Cathedral, contains medieval crucifixes and some Vasari frescoes.

Vasari trail

Further west is the **Casa del Vasari** ⓔ (Mon, Wed–Sat 9am–7pm, Sun 9am–1pm), the attractive house that Giorgio Vasari – Mannerist painter, architect and author of *The Lives of the Artists* (1550) – built for himself and decorated with frescoes painted by the artists he

most admired. The 500th anniversary of his birth was celebrated with much pomp in Arezzo in 2011, including the painstaking restoration of a Vasari altarpiece before visitors' very eyes.

Close by is the **Museo Statale d'Arte Medievale e Moderna** (Tue–Sun 8.30am–7.30pm), housed in the 15th-century Palazzo Bruni. Its varied collection includes an excellent display of majolica pottery, a selection of frescoes and fine examples of the Arezzo goldsmiths' work, featured alongside paintings by Vasari and modern works by local artists.

Roman Arezzo

Last but not least, in the flat southern part of the city, you will find the **Anfiteatro Romano** (daily 8.30am–7.30pm, request to be accompanied by museum custodian). The Roman Arretium was originally an Etruscan city, but in 294 BC it became a Roman settlement, a convenient resting post on the Via Cassia between Rome and Florence. The site was later plundered to build the city walls and churches, and the perimeter wall is all that remains.

A section of the amphitheatre walls was incorporated into an Olivetan monastery (near the station), now occupied by the excellent **Museo Archeologico** (daily 8.30am–7.30pm). This museum features the Aretine ware for which Arezzo has long been famous. This Roman pottery once competed with the more famous Samian ware as the crockery of choice on the dinner tables of Roman aristocrats.

Piero della Francesca trail

East of Arezzo, the Upper Tiber valley is tightly enclosed at its northern end by the Alpe di Catenaia and the Alpe della Luna. Two important towns for Piero della Francesca enthusiasts are here. **Sansepolcro** is famous for two things: as the town where Buitoni pasta is produced; and as the birthplace of the great Renaissance artist. The old town, huddled behind crumbling ramparts, is an important artistic centre. The quiet, narrow streets are linked by four ancient gates, the best preserved of which is the Porta Fiorentina.

Piazza Grande is the scene of the Giostra del Saracino, a historic jousting tournament held twice a year, in June and September.

The Loggia Vasari in Arezzo.

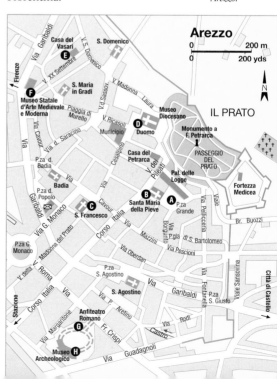

FACT

Piero della Francesca's 1463 masterpiece, *The Resurrection*, was hailed by Aldous Huxley as "the best picture in the world".

In the town centre, at the junction of Piazza Torre di Berta and Via Matteotti, is the **Duomo** (daily 8am–12.30pm, 3–6.30pm; free). Dedicated to St John the Evangelist, it began life in the 11th century as a monastic abbey. A wide range of excellent artworks cover the walls of the interior, including a tabernacle by the della Robbia school. Perugino's *Ascension of Jesus* is also here.

However, the reason most people make the pilgrimage here is to see Piero della Francesca's greatest work, *The Resurrection*. The fresco, created in 1463, was nearly destroyed by the Allies during World War II as they bombarded Sansepolcro, believing the Germans were still occupying the town. The fresco was thankfully saved from destruction by the villagers,

who surrounded it with sandbags. Today, this intense, brooding work is displayed in the **Museo Civico** (daily mid-June–mid-Sept 10am–1.30pm, 2.30–7pm, mid-Sept–mid-June 10am–1pm, 2.30–6pm), in Via degli Aggiunti, alongside the *Madonna della Misericordia*, another Piero della Francesca masterpiece.

Also stop to admire the 16th-century Palazzo delle Laudi (the Town Hall) and the Gothic Palazzo Gherardi, both in Via Matteotti, and the Palazzo Pretorio opposite Piazza Garibaldi.

From Sansepolcro, the Piero della Francesca trail leads south to **Monterchi ❸**, where a former schoolhouse displays his striking *Madonna del Parto* in the **Museo Madonna del Parto** (Apr–Oct 9am–1pm and 2–7pm, Nov–Mar

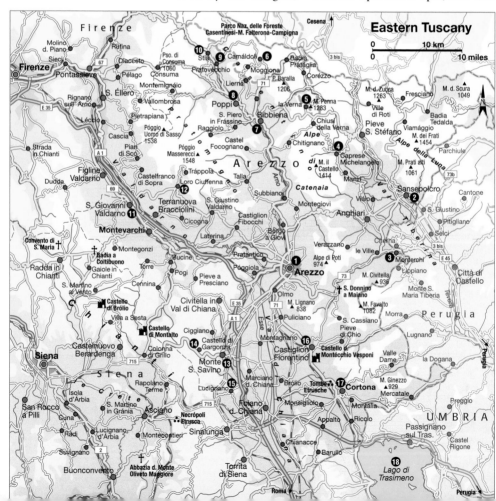

Eastern Tuscany

0   10 km
0   10 miles

until 5pm). The Madonna, heavily pregnant and aching, has unbuttoned the front of her dress for relief, while above, two angels hold up the entrance to the tent in which she stands.

Michelangelo's birthplace

Northwest of Sansepolcro, on a steep slope above the Tiber, is the hamlet of **Caprese Michelangelo ❹**, birthplace of Michelangelo. Protected by an almost complete set of walls, this cluster of rustic buildings – which includes the Buonarroti house, the old town hall where Michelangelo's father was the Florentine governor, and the tiny chapel in which Michelangelo was baptised – are interesting more for their connections than for their contents. The views over Alpine countryside explain why Michelangelo attributed his good brains to the mountain air he breathed as a child.

The Casentino

The Casentino is the name given to the little-known region of the Upper Arno valley that runs from the eastern side of the Consuma Pass down to the source of the river just north of Arezzo. It is an area of great natural beauty, enclosed by high mountains, cloaked in fir, chestnut and beech woods, and concealing ancient monasteries and farming villages. The narrow, winding, rural roads are slow going, and with views at every turn, the temptation to stop and admire them is hard to resist.

At its remoter edges, this region is rooted in the 13th century, when St Francis took to a desolate crag on the wooded slopes of **Monte Penna** at **La Verna ❺**, using a niche between two huge boulders as a hermitage. On this spot in 1224, St Francis is supposed to have received the stigmata while he was praying. Today, in the middle of the ancient forest, a Franciscan sanctuary still occupies the rock. Assembled around a tiny piazza is a collection of monastic buildings, including one large church containing yet more examples of della Robbia terracotta sculptures.

Sixteen kilometres (10 miles) northeast of La Verna, high in the spectacular woodland cut by mountain streams and waterfalls, is another more ancient monastery, **Camáldoli ❻** (daily 9am–1pm, 2.30–7pm; summer until 7.30pm; tel: 0575-556 012; www.camaldoli.it; free). It was founded in 1012 by San Romualdo (St Rumbold), a former member of the Benedictine Order, who founded a strict community of hermits. The monastery is still inhabited, and the monks run a welcoming café here. The old cloister pharmacy (9am–12.30pm, 2.30–6.30pm), with its mortars and crucibles, now sells soaps and liqueurs made by the monks.

Another 300 metres (1,000ft) up the mountain (a beautiful hour-long walk), above the monastery, is the **Eremo**, a hermitage comprising a small Baroque church and 10 cells, each surrounded by a high wall and a tiny kitchen garden. Here the hermits still live in solitude and silent contemplation. The church and St Rumbold's cell are open to visitors (Mon–Sat 9am–noon and 3–5pm; summer until

The Resurrection, by Piero della Francesca.

The view across Poppi from the Palazzo Pretorio.

Fiat's classic Cinquecento "Bambino" is still a much-loved runaround, perfect for the narrow streets of small towns such as Poppi.

In Tuscany, shop decoration is an art form.

6pm; tel: 0575-556 021), but access to the monks' quarters is closed.

After the silence and isolation of Camáldoli, noisy **Bibbiena ❼** will bring you sharply back to the modern world. Although hidden by urban sprawl and best known for its tobacco industry and salty salami, Bibbiena is still a typical Tuscan hill town at heart. Buildings of note in the historic centre include the church of **San Lorenzo** (daily 8am–6pm), which has some richly decorated della Robbia panels, and the church of **Sant'Ippolito Martire** (daily 8am–7pm), which has a fine triptych by Bicci di Lorenzo.

Nearby is the Renaissance Palazzo Dovizi, home of Cardinal Dovizi, who, as Cardinal Bibbiena, became the secretary of Pope Leo X. Bibbiena's central piazza offers distant views to Camáldoli and Poppi – the latter is the gateway to an interesting area for castles and fortified towns.

Casentino castles

This region was continually fought over by the Guelf Florentines and the Ghibelline Aretines. A decisive battle in 1289, which firmly established the dominance of the former over the latter, is marked by a column on a site called Campaldino, just between Castel San Niccolò and Poppi.

Poppi ❽ surveys the surrounding countryside from its hilltop perch, dominated by the brooding **Castello dei Conti Guidi** (mid-Mar–Oct daily 10am–6pm, Jul–Aug until 7pm, Jan–mid-March, Nov–Dec Thur–Sun 10am–5pm; www.castellodipoppi.it), the most important medieval monument in the Casentino. Built in the 13th century for the ruling Guidi counts, the castle's design was inspired by the Palazzo Vecchio in Florence, and it is thought likely that Arnolfo di Cambio was the architect. The courtyard and stairway are impressive, and the Florentine frescoes may be viewed on request. The ancient streets of this quiet town are lined with arcades linked by steep steps and decorated with finely carved capitals and stone seats. There is a Romanesque church and a few shops here selling locally made copper pots.

Off in the distance, on a hill above the village of **Pratovecchio ❾**, birthplace of Paolo Uccello, is the 11th-century **Castello di Romena** (mid-Mar–June, Sept–Oct 10am–1pm, 2–6pm, July–Aug 10am–7pm or by appointment; tel: 338 523 1501), another Guidi castle. The noble family gave refuge to Dante here after his expulsion from Florence at the beginning of the 14th century. Of the 14 towers that Dante would have seen at the castle, only three remain.

Standing on a lonely slope, a stone's throw from the castle, **Pieve di Romena** (visits by appointment with the custodian; tel: 0575-582 060; free) is one of the most important Romanesque churches in Tuscany. Beneath its apse, which dates from 1152, excavations have revealed the remains of an Etruscan building as well as two earlier churches. The finely carved capitals atop the gigantic granite columns in the nave make reference to the four Evangelists and to St Peter.

Back down in Pratovecchio, you'll find the headquarters of the **Parco Nazionale delle Foreste Casentinesi** (Casentino national park) (Via G. Brocchi 7; tel: 0575-50301; www.parco forestecasentinesi.it; free).

To the north and guarding the source of the Arno (Monte Falterona) is the medieval town of **Stia** ⑩, with a pretty porticoed piazza. Here stand the ruins of the **Castello di Porciano** (www.castellodiporciano.com; May–Oct Sun 10am–noon, 4–7pm, or by appointment; tel: 337 671 277; free), another Guidi stronghold that once watched over the Arno valley.

The **Castello di Romena** is visible from up here. Whereas most monuments are easily accessible, the fortified remains at Castel Castagnaia, with the nearby ruined Roman temple, both to the west of Stia, are harder to reach. The road peters out, and they can only be reached on foot through rough, stony countryside.

Remains of yet another Guidi castle can be seen in the tiny village of Montemignaio. There's not much left to see, but the village church does have Ghirlandaio's *Virgin and Child with the Four Church Elders*.

On the slope of the forested Pratomagno ridge, south of Bibbiena, is the restored castle at **Chitignano**. The medieval remains were rebuilt in the 18th century. There are other ruined castles located at Talla and Subbiano.

The Valdarno

The most scenic route to Florence skirts the Pratomagno ridge on the eastern side of the Arno. It's full of twists and turns, but the views are rewarding. In the Middle Ages, the Valdarno was bitterly fought over by the Ghibellines and the Guelfs. At the close of the 13th century pressure was exerted on the Florentines by the warlike Aretine bishops, who controlled powerful strongholds in the Arno valley. In an effort to resist them, the Florentines built three fortresses, which were really fortified towns, at San Giovanni Valdarno, Terranuova and Castelfranco di Sopra.

Halfway between Florence and Arezzo, **San Giovanni Valdarno** ⑪ was fortified as a bulwark against the

BED, BORGHI AND WINE

Tuscany excels at rescuing medieval hamlets *(borghi)* and turning them into country retreats, often with a castle or wine estate attached. Set in the hills near Arezzo, **Il Borro** (tel: 055-977 053; www.ilborro.it) is part of a patchwork of cypresses, sunflowers, olive groves and vineyards that once inspired Leonardo da Vinci. The setting may feature in fashion shoots, but the Ferragamo fashion dynasty are serious hoteliers and wine producers. As Salvatore Ferragamo says, "It's a wine estate, not Disneyland. The medieval village was in ruins after the war but my father and I had a vision of turning it into a rural resort and wine estate for trail-blazing Super Tuscans rather than traditional Chianti Classico." Formerly owned by the Savoia, Italy's former royal dynasty, the estate is unstarry, with craft workshops set up for a goldsmith, carpenter, ceramicist, glassmaker and, of course, a cobbler, a reminder of Ferragamo's shoemaking heritage.

Set in the Val d'Orcia, **Castiglion del Bosco** (tel: 0577-1913 001; www.castigliondelbosco.com) is another medieval borgo converted into a chic country estate, as smooth as its Brunello vintages. It boasts a prestigious 18-hole golf course designed by one-time British Open winner Tom Weiskopf. **Castello del Nero** (tel: 055-806 470; www.castellodelnero.com) represents rural luxury, with frescoed, vaulted suites, views of vineyards and olive groves, as well as a top of the range spa. **Laticastelli** (tel: 0577-724 419; www.laticastelli.com) is a simpler affair, set in a fortified hamlet outside Rapolano with probably the best panoramic pool in Tuscany. In the Chianti, **Castel Monastero** (tel: 0577-570 570; www.castelmonastero.com) boasts frescoed bedrooms, superb wines, a luxury spa and cookery courses in a former monastery. Just north, **Borgo di Vescine** (tel: 0577-741 144; www.vescine.it) is a medieval hamlet converted into a Chianti wine estate and country resort offering wine-tasting and cooking classes. Near Colle di Val d'Elsa, the latest boutique bolthole is **Castello di Casole** (tel: 0577-961 501; www.castellodicasole.com), combining castle suites with farmhouse hideaways, complete with an excellent spa, pool and fitness centre.

TIP

East of the Arno, and skirting the western edge of the high Pratomagno ridge, is the panoramic road known as the Strada dei Sette Ponti, or Road of the Seven Bridges. The winding route passes through several medieval towns, including Castelfranco di Sopra, Loro Ciuffena to the south and the abbey at Vallombrosa to the north.

Piazza Collegiata, Lucignano.

Aretines, but little evidence remains of its former military function. The central piazza and arcaded **Palazzo Comunale** were designed by Arnolfo di Cambio. The nearby church of **Santa Maria della Grazia** (daily; free) contains a *Virgin and Child with the Four Saints* by Masaccio, who was born here in 1401. Just outside the town, the Renaissance monastery of Montecarlo houses an *Annunciation* by Fra Angelico.

In prehistoric times, the Arno basin was one big lake, and farmers today frequently dig up fossil remains and bones of long-extinct animals. At **Montevarchi**, south of San Giovanni Valdarno, is a castle housing the **Accademia Valdarnese** (tel: 055-981 1227; Thur–Sun 10am–1pm and 3–6pm), an important museum of prehistory. It is home to an impressive collection of fossilised remains of the Pliocene period discovered in this stretch of the Arno valley.

Unlike San Giovanni Valdarno, **Castelfranco di Sopra**, across the Arno (also fortified for the Florentines by Arnolfo di Cambio), retains its military character: the Porta Fiorentina

gate is as forbidding as it ever was, and many of the 14th-century streets and buildings have survived.

About 10km (6 miles) south of Castelfranco, on the scenic **Strada dei Sette Ponti** (Road of the Seven Bridges), is **Loro Ciuffenna ⑫**, a medieval village positioned on a chasm cut by the Ciuffenna river. A couple of kilometres away is the rural Romanesque church of Gropina, dating from the early 13th century, noted for the carvings of animals, figures and geometrical patterns on the pulpit and columns. From here the picturesque route to Talla, where you'll find another ruined castle, crosses into the Casentino.

Val di Chiana

Surrounded by hills and charming towns, the fertile **Val di Chiana** plains south of Arezzo supply Florentine restaurants with the raw ingredient of *bistecca alla Fiorentina*. **Monte San Savino ⑬**, on the edge of the Val di Chiana, has been a citadel since Etruscan times, although the existing fortifications date from the Middle Ages. In 1325 the inhabitants were unable

to fend off a ruthless Aretine mob, who razed the town as punishment for their Guelf sympathies. It was subsequently rebuilt. Its once large Jewish community was wiped out – many were burnt at the stake – for resisting the French army in 1799. "Progress" has hardly touched Monte San Savino; it retains medieval and Renaissance houses, of which the **Palazzo Comunale**, with a facade by Antonio da Sangallo the Elder and a fine museum (Nov–Mar Wed–Fri 9am–1pm, Sat–Sun also afternoons 4–7pm, Apr–Oct Tue 9am–1pm, Wed–Fri 9am–1pm and 4–7pm, Sat–Sun until 7.30pm; free), is the most important.

Other important landmarks here include the Loggia del Mercato by Sansovino, and the churches of Santa Chiara and Sant'Agostino.

The wild hills northwest of the town shelter a feudal retreat, the **Castello di Gargonza** ⑭. This 13th-century *borgo*, or walled village, on the western slope of Monte Palazzuolo dominates the Chiana valley and is the centre of a vast wooded estate producing oil and wine. The walled settlement has been converted into a hotel and restaurant complex (www.gargonza.it). The adapted cottages, tiny cobbled streets, a chapel, a baronial tower, attractive gardens and a magnificent view down to the Chiana all make Gargonza a very pleasant retreat.

South of Monte San Savino is **Lucignano** ⑮. Originally an Etruscan stronghold, the concentric arrangement of streets around a fortress make it unique among Tuscan hill towns. With a few exceptions, Lucignano's buildings (13th–18th-century) are perfectly preserved, as is the Gothic church of San Francesco. The 14th-century **Palazzo Comunale** (Fri–Sun 10.30am–1pm, 2.30–6pm, winter until 5.30pm) contains frescoes from the Sienese and Aretine schools, as well as some examples of finely worked gold ornaments for which the province of Arezzo has long been famous, including the beautiful 14th-century *Tree of Lucignano*, richly embellished with jewels.

Fortified villages

Marciano della Chiana 6km (4 miles) northeast, another tiny village

The church and square in Lucignano, known for its unique concentric street plan.

The white Chianina cattle are prized for their beef.

VAL DI CHIANA CATTLE

The Val di Chiana, the most extensive valley in the Apennine range, is rich in farmland that is mainly used for cattle-rearing.

Here graze herds of one of Italy's most prized breeds of beef cattle – the Chianina, which is native to Tuscany. (Its only rival is the Razza Piemontese from Piedmont.) The cream-coloured Chianina cow grows quickly to a large size, so that it is butchered when the steer is a grown calf.

The meat is firm and tasty, with a distinctive flavour. For any beef-loving Italian, *bistecca alla Fiorentina* – a huge, tender Val di Chiana T-bone steak, grilled over an open fire and seasoned with nothing more than crushed peppercorns, salt, and a hint of garlic and olive oil, served very rare – is the ultimate steak.

of great character, was also fortified in the Middle Ages. Much of the castle remains intact, as do the walls and a gateway that has a clock tower built into it. Three kilometres (2 miles) to the southeast is the octagonal chapel of Santa Vittoria, designed by Ammannati to mark the spot where the Florentines defeated the Sienese in battle in 1554.

Foiano della Chiana clings prettily to the side of the hill. Much of it dates from the 15th–16th centuries, though traces of medieval defences can be seen around the edge of the town. At **Cisternella**, about 3km (2 miles) to the northeast of the centre, are the remains of what is believed to have been a Roman bathhouse.

From here, looming large in the distance, is the fortified village of **Castiglion Fiorentino** , bounded by thick walls and dominated by the **Cassero Fortress** (Fri–Sun 10am–1pm and 4–7pm or by appointment). This well-preserved medieval settlement has an unusually high number of churches. The oldest of these, the **Pieve Vecchia** (the oldest church), has

a Signorelli fresco of the *Deposition of Christ* (1451), and the 13th-century church of San Francesco also contains a sculpted version.

Other sacred works and gold, and silverware from the surrounding churches can be seen in the **Pinacoteca Comunale** (tel: 0575-659 457, by appointment). On the old market square Vasari's famous loggias can be found. Their stone arches frame a fine vista of the rooftops and surrounding countryside.

Just outside the village is the fine octagonal temple of **Santa Maria della Consolazione**. Looming beyond the village, and visible from the Cassero Fortress, are the battlements of the **Castello di Montecchio** (tel: 338 352 1165; Tue–Sun 10–11am, 3–4pm). This crenellated medieval castle once belonged to the legendary English *condottiero* John Hawkwood.

Cortona

Close to the Umbrian border, 30km (18 miles) south of Arezzo, **Cortona** is one of the most enchanting hill towns in Tuscany. It was founded by the Etruscans, colonised by the Romans, and, after being sold to the Florentines in 1409, thrived under the Grand Duchy of Tuscany. The success of the celebrity-studded Tuscan Sun festival, and the book by Frances Mayes, mean that Cortona's quaintly crooked, cobbled streets can be awash with summer visitors.

Cortona is perched majestically on a ridge of Monte Sant'Egidio, dominating the Val di Chiana. The approach road winds its way through terraced olive groves and vineyards, past villas, farms and monasteries. But Cortona's main attraction lies in the steepness of its crooked streets, linked by stone staircases, which work their way painfully to the Medici fortress at the top.

The town is entered from the relatively flat Piazza Garibaldi and Via Nazionale, which lead to Piazza Signorelli, with its 13th-century **Palazzo Comunale** (Town Hall) and the

The lofty heights of Cortona.

Museo dell'Accademia Etrusca (www.cortonamaec.org; Apr–Oct daily 10am–7pm, Nov–Mar Tue–Sun until 5pm). The highlights are the lovely fresco of Polymnia, generally considered to be a fine Roman painting of the *Muse of Song* until recent research proved it to be an 18th-century forgery; and a genuine Etruscan chandelier dating from 300 BC.

At the bottom of the hill, a new archeological park, the **Parco Archeologico del Sodo**, showcases the Etruscan Sodo Tombs, including a sculpted sacrificial altar.

West of the piazza is the 16th-century Cathedral and its companion, the **Museo Diocesano** (Apr–Oct 10am–7pm, Nov–Mar Tue–Sun until 5pm), which contains some rare masterpieces by Fra Angelico, Lorenzetti and Luca Signorelli.

Before leaving town, seek out **Via Janelli** for its row of brick buildings with overhanging upper storeys – some of Tuscany's oldest surviving medieval houses. Other picturesque streets include the Via Ghibellina and Via Guelfa. It's a steep climb up to the

Basilica di Santa Margherita, dedicated to the local saint and follower of St Francis. The citizens of Cortona still make pilgrimages up the winding stone-flagged streets to her tomb to offer her prayers during hard times. The **Medici Fortress** above is overgrown and rarely open, but the views from up here are splendid, and it's a fine spot to stop for a picnic.

One side of Cortona's public gardens opens to a belvedere with sweeping views south, enveloping the **Lago di Trasimeno** ⑱, Italy's fourth-largest lake, which lies in neighbouring Umbria. Its shallow waters are surprisingly clean and popular with swimmers, boaters and windsurfers. There was a day, though, in 217 BC, when the lake waters ran red with the blood of the Roman legions, more than 16,000 of whom were slaughtered by Hannibal's troops.

Today, the scene is considerably more peaceful, especially on the southern shore, with Castiglione del Lago the place to toast farewell to underrated Arezzo province over a lakeside fish feast.

FACT

Frances Mayes' books, *Bella Tuscany* and *Under the Tuscan Sun* (also a lavishly shot film), have elevated Cortona, where she lives, to celebrity status.

Castiglion Fiorentino.

Classic Tuscan road.

TRAVEL TIPS
TUSCANY

TRANSPORT

GETTING THERE AND GETTING AROUND

By Air

From the UK, low-cost airlines such as Ryanair and easyJet operate from many of Italy's smaller provincial airports, making travel between the UK and Italy easy, as well as opening up Italian routes to greater competition.

In addition to the national airline, Alitalia, many major scheduled airlines run direct flights to Italy, as well as charter flights, which tend to offer lower fares and often fly to more convenient provincial airports.

From the US, the main carriers are Alitalia, Delta, United and US Airways, which fly to Rome, Milan and Venice. European airlines such as British Airways and Air France also fly to Italy, with a stopover.

The country has two airports designed for intercontinental flights: **Roma Leonardo da Vinci** (known as Fiumicino) and **Milano Malpensa**.

Pisa's Galileo Galilei Airport is the usual airport for most international visitors to Florence. Getting from Pisa to Florence is easy and cheap.

Florence's Peretola-Florence Airport (also known as Amerigo Vespucci) is 4km (2 miles) northwest of the city centre. Some international flights land here, but these tend to be more expensive than flights to Pisa. Meridiana operates regular flights between Florence and the UK (www.meridiana.it). CityJet airlines have introduced a direct flight from London City Airport to Florence (www.cityjet.com). **Bologna Airport** is a further alternative; it is conveniently located for Florence

and Tuscany (there's a direct train to Florence and Arezzo).

By Rail

Rail travel is a slow but scenic option, although Italy has improved the speed and quality of its inter-city trains in recent years. (Florence is now only 36 minutes from Bologna and 1 hour 45 minutes from Milan). And the rise of "slow travel" makes rail an appealing option, travelling through Alpine scenery, avoiding the airports, and arriving in the heart of the city. It's both civilised and eco-friendly.

For those under 26, travel is far cheaper if you sign up to the InterRail scheme (providing a month's unlimited rail travel in Europe). When travelling from Great Britain via Paris (the usual route when travelling to Florence), it is necessary to change in Paris (from Gare du Nord to Gare de Lyon).

ES (Eurostar), EC (EuroCity), IC (Inter City) and TEE (Trans Europe Express) trains are top-of-the-range, running between the main Italian and European cities. A supplement is charged and seat reservation is obligatory. You can check your route or book tickets online on the official Italian railway website: www.trenitalia.it.

In the UK, consider booking through **Railbookers** (tel: 020-3780 2222; www.railbookers.com). A week's break includes an independent rail tour staying in Florence, Siena and Lucca.

Alternatively, for train bookings, contact **Rail Europe** tel: 08448-485 848; visit the travel centre and ticket office at 1 Piccadilly, London W1J 9EU, Mon–Fri 10am–6pm, Sat until 5pm; or consult www.raileurope.co.uk.

Visitors from the US and Canada can also buy tickets and passes in advance through Rail Europe, or holidays through Railbookers. Visit www.raileurope.com or tel: 1-800-622 8600 in the US and 1-800-361 7245 in Canada.

By Road

When calculating the cost of travelling to Italy by car, allow for the price of motorway tolls as well as accommodation en route and petrol. The quickest cross-Channel car ferries are from Dover to Calais. The Channel Tunnel transports cars on the train between Folkestone and Calais (Eurotunnel, tel: 08443-353 535; www.eurotunnel.com). The usual route from France to Italy is via Paris and the Mont Blanc Tunnel (between Chamonix and Courmayeur), or from Switzerland through the Gran San Bernardo Tunnel (between Bourg St-Pierre and Aosta). Some of the Alpine passes are seasonal, so check the viability of your route with the tourist board or a motoring organisation before setting off.

To take your car into Italy, you will need your current driving licence, your vehicle registration document and insurance certificate. You are also required to carry a warning triangle in case of breakdown. Headlights should be illuminated at all times. Some petrol stations require payment in cash, not credit card. Keep cash handy for *autostrada* tolls, too.

The AA and RAC in the UK give up-to-date advice on Channel crossings, with or without a car, and also driving on the Continent.

In the US, the AAA provides information on travel in Italy.

By Coach

Travelling to Italy from the UK by coach is not much cheaper than flying. National Express Eurolines runs coaches from London Victoria, via Paris and Mont Blanc, to Aosta, Turin, Genoa, Milan, Venice, Bologna, Florence and Rome. To book from London, contact: National Express (www.nationalexpress.co.uk).

GETTING AROUND

On Arrival

Pisa Airport: The international airport, Galileo Gallilei (tel: 050-849 111) has its own railway station. Trains take five minutes into Pisa Centrale and one hour for the 80km (50 miles) to Florence (www.trenitalia. com). A CPT bus (www.cpt.pisa.it) also links the airport with Pisa Centrale rail station. You can pre-book on the 70-minute coach transfer between the airport (departing outside Arrivals) and Florence's Santa Maria Novella train station (tel: 055-235 2595; www.terravision.eu). Car hire is available from the airport, and so are taxis. A toll-free *superstrada* links Pisa airport with Florence. **Peretola (Amerigo Vespucci) International Airport** (tel: 055-306 1700) in northwest Florence is also connected by Terravision bus (15-minute transfer) to central Florence.

By Air

Alitalia offers a huge range of internal flights from Florence and Pisa airports. These are supplemented by Meridiana's domestic services, which are usually a bit cheaper.

By Rail

For information, visit www.trenitalia. it. The state-subsidised railway network is a relatively cheap and convenient form of transport for travelling between major cities in Tuscany. The principal Rome–Milan line is convenient for Bologna (36 minutes), Florence and Arezzo, while the Rome–Genoa line serves Pisa, Livorno and Grosseto. The Florence–Siena route is much faster by coach than by train.

Note that Pisa and Florence both have several train stations: **Pisa Centrale** station serves Pisa city, while **Pisa Aeroporto** serves the airport. In Florence, **Santa Maria Novella** is the main station

for the city, although the second station, **Rifredi**, is served by several Eurostar trains. In Florence, a controversial additional station for high-speed routes designed by Norman Foster is scheduled to open in 2015.

Categories of Trenitalia Trains

Eurocity: these trains link major Italian cities with other European cities – in Germany and Switzerland, for instance. A supplement is payable on top of the rail fare.
Le Frecce: these swish, high-speed Frecciarossa (330kmh/186mph; four classes of carriages; supplements payable), Frecciargento (250kmh/155mph) and Frecciablanca (200kmh/125mph) trains connect major cities across Italy.
Intercity: this fast service links medium-sized and major Italian cities. Intercity Plus is the latest fleet of plush, new fast trains. A supplement is payable; reservations required.
Interregionali: these inter-regional trains link cities within different regions (eg Tuscany and Umbria) and stop fairly frequently.
Regionali: these trains link towns within the same region and stop at every station.
Intercity night: couchettes or sleepers; possibly the best way to travel long-distance in Italy.

In 2012 privately-owned NTV (Nuovo Trasporto Viaggiatori) started operating Italo high-speed trains (three classes of service), competitive to Trenitalia's Frecciarossa, between major Italian cities; www.italotreno.it.

Santa Maria Novella train station, Florence.

Tickets

Booking

Reservations are mandatory for superior trains (such as Eurostar and Eurocity) and tickets should be purchased in advance. Other tickets with compulsory supplements should be purchased at least three hours in advance. You must date-stamp *(convalidare)* your rail ticket before beginning the journey at one of the small machines at the head of the platforms, or you may be fined. If you wish to upgrade to first class or a couchette, you can pay the conductor the difference.

To avoid long lines for tickets at major stations, book online with Trenitalia or, for a small charge, buy from local travel agencies. There are automatic ticket machines at major stations, although these are often out of order. Payment can be made either by cash or by credit card.

Wagons Lits/Carrozze Letto (sleeper cars) are found on long-distance trains within Italy, as well as on trains to France, Austria, Germany, and Switzerland. Reservations are essential.

Special Offers

There are a wide variety of train tickets and special offers available, which vary constantly and with the season. Some of the more established are:
The Eurail Italy Pass: available for foreign visitors, it allows between 3, 4, 5 or 8 days of unlimited travel on the Italian State Railway network, within a one month's period.

TRANSPORT

EATING OUT

ACTIVITIES

A – Z

LANGUAGE

Group fares: groups of between 6 and 24 people can benefit from a 20 percent discount.
Youth fares: students aged between 12 and 26 can buy a yearly Carta Verde – "green card". This season ticket entitles them to a 10 percent discount on national trains and a 25 percent discount on international trips.
Children's fares: children under four travel free; children aged between 4–12 are eligible for a 50 percent discount on all trains but must pay the full supplement for Intercity and Eurocity trains.
Pensioners' fares: the over-60s can buy a Carta d'Argento (free for over 75s). Valid for a year, this "silver card" entitles them to a 10–25 percent discount on certain train tickets.

Railway Stations

The main railway stations are open 24 hours a day and are integrated with road and sea transport. They provide numerous services, including telecommunications, left luggage, food and drink, tourist information and porters (luggage trolleys are hard to find).
Florence: The train information office at Santa Maria Novella station is next to the waiting room. The train reservation office is just inside the building (daily 6am–10pm). There is a left-luggage counter, where pieces of luggage are left at your own risk. The station also has an air terminal where you can check in for Pisa airport. There are bars and a pharmacy in the main hall, and shops on the lower level.
Siena: The railway station has an information office, counter for left luggage (and bicycles), and restaurant. Immediately outside the station is a bus ticket office and a tourist office.

The ferry at Livorno.

However, Siena's railway station is outside the town centre. More useful, and with faster services and a greater range of local destinations, is the coach service, with coaches leaving from Piazza San Domenico to Florence and various other Tuscan towns.

By Coach

Coaches are very comfortable and often quicker than trains. Especially convenient is the Rapida bus to Siena, running several times a day. Provincial bus companies include (websites in Italian only, except for Sita and sena):
cpt, Pisa; tel: 050-505 511 or free phone line: 800-012 773; www.cpt. pisa.it (for travel in Pisa Province).
cap, Piazza Duomo 18, Prato; tel: 0574-6081; www.capautolinee.it (for travel in Tuscany and elsewhere).
Lazzi, Piazza Stazione 3r, Florence; tel: 0573-1973 900; www.lazzi.it (for travel in Tuscany).
Sita, Via S. Caterina da Siena 15, Florence; tel: 800-001 311; www.sita bus.it (for travel in Tuscany and Italy in general).
sena, Sottopassaggio (Underpass) la Lizza, Siena; tel: 0861-199 1900; www.sena.it (travel to and from Tuscany, great for Siena–Rome).

Tuscan Island Ferries

Numerous ferries ply the waters between the mainland and the islands of the Tuscan archipelago (Elba, Giglio, Capraia, Gorgona and Pianosa). Services from Piombino to Elba are regular throughout the day – every half-hour in the summer – but during the peak months, especially August, you should book in advance. At other times you can turn up and buy your

ticket direct from the harbour office. The journey time for the car ferry is under an hour. Hydrofoil services for foot passengers only are less frequent but take around 35 minutes.
The biggest operator is **Toremar**, which connects Piombino to Portoferraio, Porto Azzuro, Rio Marina and Cavo. For information and online bookings, go to www.toremar.it and see www.elba.org. Alternatively, book Toremar services through www. traghetti-toremar.com; tel: 0565-31100 (Piombino office). **Moby Lines**, the other main operator, runs a regular service between Piombino and Portoferraio. For information and bookings, see: www.moby.it.
If you are booking from the UK, or you want to compare the two main ferry operators to Elba, consult www.ferry savers.com, tel: (UK only) 0844 371 8021. Toremar also operates services from Livorno to Capraia and Gorgona, from Piombino to Pianosa, and from Santo Stefano on the Argentario peninsula to the island of Giglio.

City Transport

Local Buses/Trams
Buses within each province are cheap and plentiful. Tickets can be bought at designated offices, tobacconists, bars and newspaper stands. They are purchased in booklets (of usually 10) or as singles, and have to be stamped by a machine on the bus at the start of a journey. Failure to do so risks a fine. All provincial bus services are routed past the railway station in every town.
In **Florence**, a range of tickets for the city's buses and new tram system is available from the ATAF office (Piazza Stazione; tel: 800-424

500). One of the handiest options is the three-day Firenze Card (see page 90), which includes museum access and public transport on buses and trams, including the tram to the Cascine Park and Scandicci.

Rather confusingly for English-speakers, **Siena's** city/regional bus service is called TRA-IN.

Pisa province bus times are displayed on a board in Pisa's APT office on Piazza Garibaldi. Just outside Pisa Centrale Station, on the left, is a window for bus tickets.

Sightseeing Buses
Numerous sightseeing tours are offered in all the main cities.

Florence: **City Sightseeing Italy** (Piazza Stazione 1; tel: 055-290 451; www.city-sightseeing.it) offers a tour to Fiesole and a tour to Piazzale Michelangelo, both with multilingual commentary. Given the gradual pedestrianisation of parts of the city, the route is subject to change. Tickets are valid for 24 hours, allowing you to hop on and off at numerous points around the city. However, far more interesting are the thematic Florence walking tours booked through the Link guiding service (see page 92).

Taxis
Taxis are plentiful in all towns and tourist resorts. They wait in special ranks at railway stations and main parts of the city but can be contacted by telephone. If you book one by phone, the cost of the journey begins then. (In Florence, tel: 055-4242, 055-4390 or 055-200 1326). Meters display fares: the fixed starting charge varies and extra charges are payable for night service, Sunday service and public holidays, luggage and journeys outside the town area. In Florence, there are taxi ranks in Via Pellicceria, Piazza di San Marco and Piazza Santa Trinità, and outside Stazione di Santa Maria Novella.

Cycling and Mopeds
Mopeds and bicycles are the most efficient way to get around the narrow streets of Florence, Siena and Lucca. They can be hired in the main cities. Try to find one with good brakes and a stand. You may have to leave an identity card or passport as security. **Florence:** The **Bike Sharing** initiative, www.bicifirenze.it, allows cyclists to borrow bikes at very reasonable prices from six distribution points in the city centre. You can also can rent a bike from Florence by Bike, Via San Zanobi 54r; tel: 055-488 992; www.florencebybike.it or **Alinari**, via San

Zanobi 38r; tel: 055-280 500. **Siena:** Perozzi, Via del Romitorio 5 (near the Lizza park); tel: 0577-280 839; www.perozzi.it. Amici della Bicicletta di Siena, c/o Comitato Associazioni Sportive Sensei, Via G. Di Vittorio 12; tel: 0577-333 333; www.adbsiena.it.
Lucca: Rent Bike Lucca in the square in front of the railway station (www.touristcenterlucca.com); Barbetti, Via Anfiteatro 23; tel: 0583-954 444; Cicli Bizzarri, Piazza S. Maria 32; tel: 0583-496 682.

Driving
To ease traffic, many city centres are closed to most vehicles. Since cities such as Florence, Montepulciano and Pistoia have introduced partial or complete city-centre driving bans (at least for non-residents), it makes sense to leave the car in the car parks on the edge of the historic centre. Florence, in particular, has extended its pedestrianised areas to include Via de Tornabuoni, the Palazzo Pitti area and parts of the Oltrano.

State highways in Tuscany include the No. 1 "Aurelia", which runs north–south, to the west of Pisa. National motorways *(autostrade)*: the A11, the "Firenze–mare", and the A12, the "Sestri Levante–Livorno". Both of these are toll roads. The two *superstrade* (Florence–Siena and the Florence–Pisa–Livorno) are toll-free.

Car Hire
The major rental companies (Hertz, Avis, Europcar, etc.) have representation in most cities and resorts. The smaller local firms offer cheaper rates but cars can only be booked on the spot. Booking online, or in advance, often as part of a fly-drive package, is usually cheaper than hiring on arrival.

Rates normally allow unlimited mileage and include breakdown service. Basic insurance is included but additional cover is available at fixed rates. Most firms require a deposit and often take and hold a credit-card payment until the car is returned. You will usually be asked to return the car with a full tank; do so, as if the rental company has to fill it, they charge a premium for the petrol.

Licences and Insurance
Licences: Drivers must have a driving licence issued by a nation with a reciprocal agreement with Italy. The pink EU licence does not need an Italian translation. All other licences do need a translation, obtainable (free) from motoring organisations

and Italian tourist offices. You are legally required to keep documents related to the car and driver on you. **Insurance:** If you are bringing your own vehicle, check that your insurance covers Italy. A Green Card, obtainable from your insurance company, is not obligatory within the EU and does not provide extra cover, but it is internationally recognised, which may be useful if you have an accident.

Rules of the Road
Italy drives on the right. Road signs are international, with a few local differences:
Road signs: ALT is a stop line on the road for road junctions; STOP is for a pedestrian crossing.
Precedence: At crossroads, motorists must give precedence to vehicles on their right, except on recently built roundabouts, when those already on the roundabout have priority. If a motorist approaching a crossroads finds a precedence sign (a triangle with the point downwards) or a Stop sign, he/she must give precedence to all vehicles coming from both the right and left.
Parking: Outside cities and towns, parking on the right-hand side of the road is allowed, except on motorways, at crossroads, on curves and near hilly ground not having full visibility. Illegally parked vehicles will be towed away, and incur a hefty fine. To understand the parking options in Florence, look at the clear advice and map on www.visitflorence.com. To find a car park in an Italian town online, look on www.parcheggi.it; for Florence go to www.firenzeparcheggi.it. There is a *parcheggio scambiatore* in Viale Europa (south Florence) – drivers can park their cars here and get a bus, hire a bike or take part in the car-sharing scheme to get into the centre. Special "tourist" rates (24 hours and nightly tickets) are available at the "Parterre" (Piazza della Libertà), "Oltrarno" (Porta Romana), and "Beccaria" garages.
Breakdowns and accidents: In case of a breakdown, dial 116. On motorways, telephones are 2km (1 mile) apart, with buttons to call for the police and medical assistance. Both have to be contacted if an accident involves an injury.

Motorways
Access signs to the motorways, unlike in other European countries, are in green, not blue. Motorway tolls can be high. There is rarely a hard shoulder on motorways, and often there are only two lanes. Accidents are frequent, so take care.

EATING OUT

BEST RESTAURANTS, BARS AND CAFÉS

Tuscan cuisine is highly revered throughout food-focused Italy. In general, the food is rustic and simple, relying heavily upon fresh vegetables, legumes (pulses), meat and game.

WHERE TO EAT

Italy has three traditional types of place to eat: a *trattoria*, a *ristorante* or an *osteria*. At first they may appear to be similar, and this is increasingly true, but to Italians they signify different types of dining experiences. A *trattoria* is more casual, serving basic regional dishes in an informal setting. *Trattorie* are often family-owned and have no frills. A *ristorante* implies somewhat fancier décor, more formal service, and more elaborate and expensive food. To make things more confusing, the *osteria* is historically a tavern-like wine shop where you can buy a glass of wine and perhaps a hunk of cheese, but the word is now used almost interchangeably with *ristorante* or *trattoria*.

Yet another type of eating establishment is the *tavola calda* or *rosticceria*, both of which are cafeteria-style places where several selections of hot dishes are prepared daily and served from a counter. You generally pay in advance and show the receipt to someone working behind the counter, who prepares a plate for you.

Although pizza has become a national dish, it is not one for which Tuscany is particularly famous. Eating in a *pizzeria* costs considerably less than in a *ristorante* or *trattoria*, and they generally serve only pizza and appetisers.

In general, a *ristorante* or *trattoria* serves both lunch and dinner. Lunch is generally from 12.30 to 3pm, and dinner from 7.30 to 11pm. Most establishments close one day a week and occasionally for lunch or dinner immediately preceding or following that day. Most Italian eating establishments close for holidays *(ferie)* once or even twice a year. Many restaurants close for at least two weeks around 15 August and sometimes another week or two in the winter.

WHAT TO EAT

You will notice that just about all menus are divided into more or less the same categories: *antipasti* (appetisers), *primi* (first courses), *secondi* (second courses), *contorni* (side dishes) and *dolci* (desserts).

Antipasto means 'before the meal', and these selections are usually served in small portions. Restaurants offer an *antipasto misto* (mixed appetiser) that is often served buffet-style from a table laden with such dishes as *melone con prosciutto* (ham and melon) or grilled vegetables, and *insalata caprese* (mozzarella, tomatoes and basil). Typical Tuscan *antipasti* are *crostini*, tomatoes or liver pâté on toast; *prosciutto di cinghiale*, ham from wild boar; *finocchiona*, pork and fennel sausage.

Il primo is the first course, and in Tuscany that generally means hearty soup or pasta (increasingly you will also find risotto). Typical Tuscan *primi* include: *acquacotta*, onion soup that is a speciality of Arezzo; *minestrone alla fiorentina*, a vegetable soup with beans; *panzanella*, a bread salad often found on summer menus, whose ingredients also include tomatoes and basil; *pappardelle con lepre* or *con cinghiale*, broad noodles topped with a rich sauce made from hare or wild boar; *ribollita*, a rich vegetable soup with bread mixed into it; *cacciuco*, a rich fish soup that is reason in itself to travel to Livorno.

Il secondo is the main dish of meat or fish, usually meat, and often beefsteak, pork, rabbit or game birds. Some typical dishes are *porchetta*, roast suckling pig; *cinghiale*, wild boar; *fritto misto*, a mixed grill including lamb chops and sweetbreads; *anatra*, duck; and *girarrosto*, a spit of roast game birds; *trippa alla fiorentina*, tripe with tomato sauce; *baccala alla livornese*, salt cod, a speciality of Livorno; and *bistecca alla fiorentina*, a T-bone steak grilled rare.

Il contorno is the vegetable course. It's always ordered separately. *Fagioli*, beans, are a favourite. Salads *(insalate)* are straightforward and come in two varieties: green *(insalata verde)* or mixed *(insalata mista)*.

Il dolce is dessert, a course that is not among Italy's greatest culinary achievements, but ice cream *(gelato)* is reliably delicious when it is home-made, and *biscotti* are sweet biscuits, often almond flavoured, that are dipped in *vinsanto*, a sweet wine. Most restaurants offer *tiramisù* and the town's own sweet specialities.

Enjoying food and wine at Golden View.

FLORENCE

Restaurants

Acqua al Due
Via della Vigna Vecchia 40r
Tel: 055-284 170
www.acquaal2.it €€
A popular dining experience, so book ahead for a chance to dine at this atmospheric spot. Try the *assaggio di primi* (five pasta dishes as chosen by the chef) followed by the *assaggio di dolci* (a selection of the desserts of the day).

Alle Murate
Via del Proconsolo 16r.
Tel: 055-240 618
www.allemurate.it €€€€
Romantic, dinner-only spot in a historic guild-house with original frescoes, including one of Dante, and a Roman cistern. Superb Tuscan-meets-Southern gastro cuisine in a relaxed but stylish setting. Led by top restaurateur Umberto Montano, this is one of the city's best restaurants. Cheaper snacks in the bar. Closed Mon.

Benedicta
Hotel Rivoli
Via della Scala 33
Tel: 055-264 5429
www.ristorantebenedicta.it €€
Dependable Tuscan dishes, from steak to pasta, with a quietly creative touch in a contemporary-looking setting, despite being in a former Franciscan convent. It is close to Santa Maria Novella.

Buca Lapi
Via del Terbbio 1r
Tel: 055-213 768
www.bucalapi.com €€€
Set in the wine cellars of the Antinori palazzo, this claims to be the oldest restaurant in town. Highly traditional Tuscan cuisine. Eve only Mon–Sat.

Cantinetta Antinori
Piazza Antinori 3
Tel: 055-292 234
www.cantinetta-antinori.com
www.antinori.it €€€
Restaurant in a 15th-century palazzo, serving typical Tuscan snacks and meals with wines from the well-known Antinori estates. A good place for a light lunch at the bar or a fuller meal in the elegant dining room. Closed weekends and Aug.

Cantinetta dei Verrazzano
Via dei Tavolini 18–20
Tel: 055-268 590
www.verrazzano.com €
Old-fashioned wood-panelled wine bar serving rustic lunch sandwiches and wines from the owners' Chianti estate; closed Sun, and closed after 9pm.

A meal at stylish Gustavino.

La Casalinga
Via dei Michelozzi 9r
Tel: 055-218 624 €
One of the best-value eateries in town, close to Piazza Santo Spirito. Plentiful helpings of home cooking attract locals as well as visitors. It is family-run and highlights include the *bollito misto* and the Limoncello sorbet. Closed Sun.

Il Cibrèo
Via Andrea del Verrocchio 8r
Tel: 055-234 1100
www.cibreo.com €€€€
Justly famed, elegant but relaxed restaurant, one of the most popular in the city. Pure Tuscan cuisine, with a creative twist. No pasta, but a selection of superb soups and other *primi* (first courses). Closed Sun and Mon.

Coco Lezzone
Via del Parioncino 26
Tel: 055-287 178 €€
Traditional bustling trattoria of the highest quality, especially the meat dishes. The menu is seasonal. Closed Sun and Aug.

Enoteca Pinchiorri
Via Ghibellina 87
Tel: 055-242 777
www.enotecapinchiorri.com €€€€
Elegant dress and a jacket are required at "Italy's finest restaurant" (three Michelin stars). It occupies a 15th-century palace with a fine courtyard for alfresco meals. Expect excellent nouvelle-meets-Tuscan cuisine, rare wines, and a hefty bill. Reservation essential. Closed Sun, and Mon–Wed lunchtime.

Dei Frescobaldi
Via dei Magazzini 2r
Tel: 055-284 724
www.deifrescobaldi.it €€
Tasty Tuscan cuisine off Piazza della Signoria, including grilled Tuscan meats and pumpkin ravioli, washed down with Frescobaldi wine. Or snack on Tuscan "tapas" (salami, cheese, salads) in the adjoining wine bar.

Golden View Open Bar
Via de Bardi 58r
Tel: 055-214 502
www.goldenviewopenbar.com €€€
Touristic by day, fashionable jazz bar by night. Great view of Ponte Vecchio, with live jazz almost every night and good food, although not cheap.

Gustavino
Via della Condotta 37r
Tel: 055-239 9806
www.gustavino.it €€
Stylish contemporary restaurant with an open kitchen so you can watch the chefs in action. The food is creative without being too fussy and is beautifully presented, with a fine choice of wine. You can also just have a drink in the wine bar. Closed Mon.

Mario
Via Rosina 2r
Tel: 055-218 550
www.trattoriamario.com €
Intimate and down to earth, this is a great place to experience earthy Tuscan food, from *ribollita* soup to grilled chicken and a variety of steaks. Only lunch Mon–Sat. Closed Aug.

Le Mossacce
Via del Proconsolo 55r
Tel: 055-294 361
www.trattorialemossacce.it €
Trattoria between the Duomo and the Bargello, serving pasta dishes and basic Tuscan fare. Popular with

PRICE CATEGORIES

Prices for a three-course meal per person with a half-bottle of house wine:
€ = under €30
€€ = €30–45
€€€ = €45–65
€€€€ = over €65

office workers at lunchtimes. Closed Sat–Sun.

Napoleone
Piazza del Carmine 24
Tel: 055-281 015
www.trattorianapoleone.it €€
This trattoria in the trendy Oltrarno neighbourhood features simple Tuscan fare with Mediterranean influences. Same owners as the popular Da Zà Zà. Open for dinner.

Da Nerbone
Mercato di San Lorenzo
Tel: 055-219 949 €
Authentic, very good market eatery as old as the market itself. Dishes such as tripe and *lampredotto*, as well as the usual trattoria fare. There are few tables. Closed evenings and Sun.

Omero
Via Pian dei Giullari 11r
Tel: 055-220 053
www.ristoranteomero.it €€
Located in the hills just outside the city centre, this restaurant specialises in Florentine cuisine. Great view and good wine selection. Closed Tue.

Opera et Gusto
Via della Scala 17r
Tel: 055-288 190 €€
Eclectic dining club where you can listen to opera, blues or jazz while tucking into Tuscan cuisine. The setting is a theatrical red-and-black "stage".

Osteria Caffè Italiano
Via dell'Isola delle Stinche 11/13r
Tel: 055-289 368/289 080
www.caffeitaliano.it €€€
Under the same management as Alle Murate (above). Short menu but high standards and superb Tuscan cuisine near Santa Croce. 10am "till late", closed Mon.

Osteria de' Macci
Via de Macci 77

The dining room at Da Zà Zà.

Tel: 055-241 226 €
Typical, dependable Tuscan trattoria with no frills, good food but perfunctory service.

Pane e Vino
Piazza di Cestello 3r
Tel: 055-247 6956
www.ristorantepaneevino.it €€
Situated close to the river, on the Oltrano side, this is a pleasant, informal restaurant with an interesting menu (including a daily tasting menu) and excellent wine. Closed Sun.

La Pentola dell'Oro
Via di Mezzo 24–26r
Tel: 055-241 808
www.lapentoladelloro.it €€
As well as being unique, this is one of the friendliest restaurants in the city. Chef Giuseppe Alessi is more than willing to explain the dishes; the recipes – published in the restaurant's book – are inspired by medieval and Renaissance cookery. Closed Sun.

Il Pizzaiuolo
Via de Macci 113r
Tel: 055-241 171 €
The pizzas are wonderful, but there's plenty more besides. Try the *antipasto della casa*. Popular. Closed Sun and Aug.

Relais Le Jardin, Hotel Regency
Piazza Massimo d'Azeglio 3
Tel: 055-245 247
www.regency-hotel.com €€€€
Top-notch but light interpretations of Tuscan cuisine in an exclusive hotel restaurant, overlooking a garden. Dine on the summer veranda. Elegant dress and reservation required.

Ristorante Le Carceri
Piazza Madonna della Neve
Tel: 055-247 9327
www.ristorantelecarcere.it €
An amiable pizzeria, trattoria and wine bar set in the former prisons of Le Murate, which are now a cultural complex off Via Ghibellina.

Ristorante Terrazza Bardini
Costa San Giorgio 4a
Tel: 055-200 8444
www.moba.fl.it €€€
Set in a panoramic spot in the Villa Bardini complex, this elegant fish restaurant is matched by La Terrazza, which serves cocktails and light Tuscan meals on the summer terrace. Art exhibitions and jazz. Tue–Sun evenings only.

Da Ruggero
Via Senese 89
Tel: 055-220 542 €€
Excellent restaurant just outside the Porta Romana. Popular with the locals, so best to reserve. Great

ribollita and other Tuscan fare. Closed Tue, Wed and 3 weeks in July/Aug.

Santa Lucia
Via Ponte alle Mosse 102r
Tel: 055-353 255 €
Authentically Neapolitan, no-frills trattoria, serving the best pizzas in town. Good seafood, too. Booking essential. Closed Wed and Aug.

Il Santo Bevitore
Via Santo Spirito 64r
Tel: 055-211 264 €€
Moody, mid-priced, stylish wine bar and restaurant with great appeal, atmosphere and sound creative cuisine; worth waiting for a table as it's deservedly popular.

Da Sergio
Piazza San Lorenzo 8r
Tel: 055-281 941 €
Big, airy trattoria, hidden behind a row of stalls. A haunt of market workers and discerning tourists. There's a short, simple, seasonal menu. Try the spelt soup (*minestra di farro*) and the steak. No desserts served. Lunch only; closed Sun.

Targa Bistrot
Lungarno Cristoforo Colombo 7
Tel: 055-677 377
www.targabistrot.net €€€€
Very pleasantly situated restaurant on the north bank of the Arno, some way from the centre, with a wood-panelled interior. Imaginative take on Tuscan dishes. Closed Sun and 3 weeks in Aug.

Taverna del Bronzino
Via delle Ruote 25/27r
Tel: 055-495 220 €€€€
Classically comfortable restaurant in a quiet side street, some way from the centre. Elegantly served traditional food. The black tortellini, flavoured with truffle, is a must. Closed Sun and Aug.

Il Teatro del Sale
Via de Macci 111r
Tel: 055-200 1492
www.teatrodelsale.com €€
Hedonistic dining club run by celebrity chef Fabio Picchi (of Cibrèo, below). A filling Tuscan buffet is offered before live blues, jazz or theatre; membership essential but cheap, as is the good-value buffet dinner, which includes wine and entertainment.

PRICE CATEGORIES

Prices for a three-course meal per person with a half-bottle of house wine:
€ = under €30
€€ = €30–45
€€€ = €45–65
€€€€ = over €65

Trattoria Cibrèo (Il Cibreino)
Via de Macci 122r
Tel: 055-234 1100
www.cibreo.com €€
Annexe of the famous Il Cibrèo, but with meals at half the price. Few frills, but the food is basically the same as in the main restaurant. No bookings. Closed Sun and Mon. Caffè Cibrèo (Via del Verrocchio) is even cheaper, for snacks.

Il Vegetariano
Via delle Ruote 30r
Tel: 055-475 030 €
The imaginative use of fresh vegetables in its dishes makes Il Vegetariano the city's best vegetarian eatery. The laid-back, informal atmosphere is halfway between a diner and a cafeteria. Closed Mon, weekends at lunch.

Le Volpi e le Uva
Piazza de Rossi 1r
Tel: 055-239 8132
www.levolpieluva.com €
Welcoming and well-run wine bar for a light lunch or supper of superb wines, cheeses, cold cuts and bruschetta; closes 9pm.

Da Zà Zà
Piazza del Mercato Centrale 26r
Tel: 055-215 411
www.trattoriazaza.it €€
Good quality, earthy food and delicious pasta e *fagioli* soup and puddings. The riotous atmosphere is enjoyed by locals and tourists alike, along with the warm, rustic brick-and-beam dining rooms.

Bars, Cafés and Ice-cream Parlours

A hot chocolate or *aperitivo* at **Rivoire** (Piazza della Signoria) is worth experiencing just once. **Dei Frescobaldi**, at the end of the square, has a moody bar that is perfect for relaxing over Tuscan "tapas" and wine from one of the most famous *vino* dynasties. Piazza della Repubblica, the rival major square, is the place for people-watching in the grand, time-warp cafés of **Paszkowski**, **Gilli** or **Giubbe Rosse**. Alternatively, **Café Giacosa** (Via della Spada 10) is a historic café that's had a makeover by designer Roberto Cavalli, whose own estate wines feature highly.

Far more relaxed, **Le Volpi e le Uva** (Piazza de Rossi 1r) is an addictive wine bar for a light supper of cheeses, cold cuts – and superb wines. **Fusion Bar** in Gallery Hotel Art (Vicolo dell'Oro) is for posing while nibbling on Asian finger food. **Cibrèo Caffè** (Via del Verrocchio) is a peaceful café for delicious, but inexpensive, Tuscan treats from the celebrated restaurant over the road. Satisfy your sweet tooth at **GROM** (Via delle Oche), whose *gelati* reflect the seasons. **Vivoli** (Via delle Stinche), between the Bargello and Santa Croce, is another popular ice-cream parlour. Towards the Arno, **Moyo** (Via de Benci) is a slick *aperitivi* bar. The elegant bars lining the river are where Florentines go to be seen. On the south bank, sip wine at **Caffè Pitti** (Piazza Pitti) or have a cocktail at the ever-popular **Il Rifrullo** (Via San Niccolò). **Zoe** (Via dei Renai) is an all-day (and late-night) arty café in Oltrarno that takes a trendy crowd from brunch to cocktails and beyond. **Negroni**, in the same street, attracts a quieter, more sophisticated set. End the evening at trendy **Dolce Vita** (Piazza del Carmine), an arty club in the bohemian Oltrarno quarter.

Grand charm in Gilli on Piazza della Repubblica.

AROUND FLORENCE

Restaurants

Artimino
Biagio Pignatta
Paggeria Medicea, Viale Papa Giovanni XXIII
Tel: 055-875 1406
www.artimino.com €€–€€€
This restaurant is part of a four-star hotel, Paggeria Medicea, which occupies the former stables of a Medici villa. Dishes with historical origins a speciality. Closed Wed evening and Thur lunch.

Da Delfina
Via della Chiesa 1
Tel: 055-871 8074
www.dadelfina.it €€–€€€
High-quality ingredients served in an elegant setting, overlooking the Medici villa. Tuscan food, often with a twist. Closed Mon, Tue lunch, and Oct–May Sun evening.

Barberino di Mugello
Cosimo de' Medici
Viale del Lago 19
Tel: 055-842 0370 €€
A well-respected restaurant, serving Tuscan and international food of a consistently high standard. Closed Sun evening and Mon.

Borgo San Lorenzo
Ristorante degli Artisti
Piazza Romagnoli 1
Tel: 055-845 7707
www.ristorantedegliartisti.it €€€
Not far from Scarperia, this restaurant in the hills features delicious Tuscan fare. Traditional dishes include wild hare, wild boar, served with fresh, seasonal vegetables. Closed Wed, most of Jan, 3rd week in Aug.

Cerbaia, Val di Pesa
La Tenda Rossa
Piazza del Monumento 9/14
Tel: 055-826 132
www.latendarossa.it €€€€
One of the best restaurants in the Florence area, serving elegant and creative food in modern, refined surroundings. Excellent wine list. Worth the trek. Closed Mon lunch, Sun and Aug.

Fiesole
La Reggia degli Etruschi
Via San Francesco 18
Tel: 055-59385
www.lareggia.org €€–€€€
The patio of this restaurant has a wonderful view over Florence. The food, if not quite as breathtaking as the view, is reliable, from the cold cuts to the handmade spaghetti, risotto and steaks. Oct–May closed Tue.

Pizzeria San Domenico
Piazza San Domenico 11
Tel: 055-59182 €–€€
This is a simple spot for pizzas, pastas and friendly service. Also recommended are the big salads followed by a *coppa della casa*, the house dessert. Closed Mon outside summer months.

Vinandro
Piazza Mino 33

Tel: 055-59121
www.vinandrofiesole.com €
Tiny rustic wine bar that offers simply
prepared meals and good wine.
Reservations recommended. Open air
seating. Closed Mon.

Galluzzo
Bibe
Via delle Bagnese 1r
Tel: 055-204 9085
www.trattoriabibe.com €€
Above-average rustic trattoria in
this typical suburb, with a delightful
garden for alfresco meals. Closed
Mon–Fri lunch and all day Wed.

Prato
Il Baghino
Via dell'Accademia 9
Tel: 0574-27920 €–€€
This traditional establishment in the

historic heart of Prato serves local
specialities to a faithful clientele.
Closed Aug, Sun, and Mon lunchtime.
Osvaldo Baroncelli
Via Frà Bartolomeo 13
Tel: 0574-23810 €€€
Acclaimed restaurant that mixes
traditional and innovative choices.
Has a good wine list. Booking
advised. Closed Sat lunch and Sun.

San Casciano in Val di Pesa
Trattoria Mamma Rosa
Via Cassia per Siena 32
Tel: 055-824 9454 €–€€
Off the beaten track, this
unpretentious but elegant trattoria
serves some of the best Tuscan food,
using locally sourced ingredients.
Excellent wines. The proprietor-chef
also runs a cooking school in the Il
Borghetto hotel. Closed Wed.

San Miniato
Il Convio – San Maiano
Via San Maiano 2
Tel: 0571-408 114
www.ristoranteilconvio.com €€
A pleasant, rustic restaurant with
views over the hills and outdoor seats
in summer. Traditional Tuscan fare.
Closed Wed.

Firenze Settignano
La Capponcina di Settignano
Via San Romano 17r
Tel: 055-697 037
www.capponcina.com €–€€
Set in the hills just outside
Florence, this restaurant has great,
reasonably priced food. The terrace
offers an outstanding view of
Florence. Closed Mon in autumn/
winter.

LUCCA AND PISTOIA

Restaurants

Abetone
Da Pierone
Via Brennero 556
Tel: 0573-60068 €€
Rustic restaurant. Good cooking
based on traditional mountain fare.
Closed Mon, 15–30 June, 20 Oct–
early Nov.

Lucca
All'Olivo
Piazza San Quisico 1
Tel: 0583-496 264
www.ristoranteolivo.it €€€
Traditional yet innovative Tuscan fare
of meat and fish dishes. Seasonal
menus. There are four different rooms
to choose from.

Buca di Sant'Antonio
Via della Cervia 1/3
Tel: 0583-55881
www.bucadisantantonio.it €€€
Renowned restaurant serving
Lucchese and Garfagnana classic
dishes (try the fettuccine with pigeon
sauce), alongside dishes with a
more modern slant. Closed Sun
evening, Mon and periods in Jan
and July.
Cantine Bernardini
Palazzo Bernardini,
Via del Suffragio 7
Tel: 0583-494 336
www.cantinebernardini.com €€
Feast on chickpea soup, steak, wild-
boar terrine, Pecorino cheese, and
pasta stuffed with artichokes. The
dishes represent the best of Lucca

and Garfagnana. These vaulted
cellars, along with the restaurant,
wine bar and deli, belong to the
patrician Bernardini family, who also
sell wines from their estates.
Gli Orti di Via Elisa
Via Elisa 17
Tel: 0583-491 241
www.ristorantegliorti.it €
Good choice for a quick lunch: a busy
trattoria with a wide choice of pasta
and pizzas, plus a self-service salad
bar. Closed Wed dinner and Sun.
Ristorante Giglio
Piazza del Giglio 2
Tel: 0583-494 058
www.ristorantegiglio.com €€
Charming restaurant specialising in
fish and Tuscan meat dishes, with
tables spill out on to the piazza. One
of Lucca's best restaurants, and
very popular with locals. Closed Wed
lunch, Tue and 2nd half of Nov.
**San Colombano Ristorante/
Caffetteria**
Baluardo San Colombano 10
Tel: 0583-464 641
www.caffetteriasancolombano.it €€€
Excellent restaurant on the city walls
with superb views over the city.
Typical Lucchese dishes change with
the season. The café serves good
snacks throughout the day and is a
lovely spot for an *aperitivo*. Closed
Mon. Reservations recommended.

Montecatini Terme
Enoteca Da Giovanni
Via Garibaldi 25
Tel: 0572-71695
www.enotecagiovanni.it €€€–€€€€

Alfresco dining on Piazza Anfiteatro, Lucca.

A caffè in Lucca's backstreets.

The wine list is extensive, but the food is the main attraction. Excellent meat and fish. Closed Mon and last 2 weeks in Feb and Aug.

Pescia
Cecco
Via Forti 84
Tel: 0572-477 955
www.ristorantececco.com €€
Mushrooms, asparagus and truffles feature here, and the fish is also good in this historic and welcoming trattoria. Closed Mon in winter.
Monte a Pescia

Località Monte a Pescia
Tel: 0572-490 000 €€
This trattoria specialises in meats grilled over an open fire. Lovely terrace overlooking olive trees and hills. Closed Wed.

Pistoia
L'Arrosticino da Pietrino
Via Dalmazia 462
Tel: 0573-403 219 €€
Succulent grilled meats and vegetables accompanied by excellent house wines.
La Bottega Del Pizzaiolo
Viale Belvedere 10a

Tel: 0573-400 664 €
Very tasty pizza and great *dolcino* in a simple decor.
Ristorante l'Cice
Via Tasselli 233
Tel: (+39) 366-712 5747 €€
Be tempted by the seafood spaghetti and ravioli with fish sauce. Closed Sun.
La Limonaia
Via di Gello 9a
Tel: 0573-400 453
www.osterialalimonaia.it €
Appealing, rustic trattoria a little way from the centre of town. Unusual herbs and flavourings pep up the Tuscan food. Closed Mon evenings and Tue.
La Ti.gre
Via Porta San Marco 245/247
Tel: 0573-358 794 €€
Cosy restaurant specialising in homemade tortelli with various sauces and pizza. Traditional local cuisine at its best.
Trattoria dell'Abbondanza
Via dell'Abbondanza 10–14
Tel: 0573-368 037 €€
Traditional restaurant focusing on recipes from the surrounding region, including the delicious *farinato* (a hearty Tuscan soup). Closed Wed and Thur lunch.

VERSILIA, GARFAGNANA AND LUNIGIANA

Restaurants

Bagni di Lucca
Corona
Via Serraglia 78
Tel: 0583-805 151
www.coronaregina.it €€–€€€
Overlooking the Lima River, this restaurant specialises in local cuisine and seafood. Outdoor terrace. Closed Wed and mid-Jan–mid-Feb.

Barga
Caffe Capretz
Piazza Salvo Salvi
Tel: 0583-723 001 €
A traditional café, bar and pastry shop in the centre of Barga, with a terrace view over the countryside.

Carrara
'L Purtunzin d'Ninan
Via Lorenzo Bartolini 3
Tel: 0585-74741 €€€€
This is sophisticated gourmet dining. The current chef, Claudio Folini, is a worthy successor to Marco Garfagnini, and has won a Michelin star for his excellent Tuscan cuisine. Bookings essential. Closed Mon.

Il Trillo
Via Bergiola Vecchia 30,
Località Castegnetola
Tel: 0585-46755
www.iltrillo.net €€
A restaurant in the hills above industrial Massa, 7km (4 miles) south of Carrara, set in a lemon grove with sea views. The food is traditional and plentiful. Closed Sun and Mon lunch in summer, Mon in winter.

Castelnuovo di Garfagnana
Osteria Il Vecchio Mulino
Via Vittorio Emanuele 12
Tel: 0583-62192 €
Run by Andrea Bertucci, the local leader of the Slow Food movement, the inn has hams hanging from the beams and shelves piled with spelt. Lunch on local salami and cheese before sampling one of the 10 varieties of coffee on offer.

Marina di Massa
Ristorante La Peniche
Via Lungo Brugiano 3
Tel: 0585-240 117 €€€

Upmarket restaurant in a lovely setting, with some tables on a barge on the water (booking essential). Excellent, beautifully presented haute cuisine.

Forte dei Marmi
Lorenzo
Via Carducci 61
Tel: 0584-84030 €€€€
Expensive, chic Michelin-starred restaurant specialising in fish. Popular with well-heeled Milanese. Must book. Closed Mon and lunch July–Aug.

Pietrasanta
Enoteca Marcucci
Via Garibaldi 40
Tel: 0584-791 962

PRICE CATEGORIES

Prices for a three-course meal per person with a half-bottle of house wine:
€ = under €30
€€ = €30–45
€€€ = €45–65
€€€€ = over €65

www.enotecamarcucci.it €€–€€€
Fashionable wine bar and inn with
a vast choice of wines. The food
is simple but superb, and Enoteca
Marcucci is one of British fashion
designer Paul Smith's favourite
restaurants. Must book. Closed
Mon, lunchtime (except July–Aug)
and Nov.

Pontrémoli
Cà del Moro
Via Casa Corvi 9
Tel: 0187-830 588
www.cadelmororesort.it €€–€€€
Charming restaurant serving Tuscan
specialities. Popular with golfers.
Also has rooms. Closed Sun evening
and Mon, two weeks Jan and Nov.
Osteria da Busse
Piazza Duomo 31
Tel: 0187-831 371 €€
Owned by a local farmer, the inn
features his vegetable tarts, home-
cured salami and lasagna made from
local chestnut flour. Try the *zuppa con
ragu*, the filling house soup.
Osteria Oca Bianca
Via Cavour 27
Tel: 0187-833 219 €

The menu is short but tempting in
this cosy inn. Try the local speciality:
testaroli, pancakes served with a
pesto sauce, the stuffed ravioli or
the roast cooked in a terracotta pot.
Lunch only Mon–Fri, but lunch and
dinner at the weekend.

Torre del Lago
Butterfly
Belvedere Puccini 24/26
Tel: 0584-341 024
www.hotelbutterflytoscana.it €€
A hotel restaurant with rooms
overlooking the lake. Sardinian
dishes feature alongside Tuscan
and fish specialities. Good value.
Closed Fri.

Viareggio
Cabreo
Via Firenze 14
Tel: 0584-54643 €€
Pleasant family-run restaurant with
an emphasis on the "catch of the
day". Closed Mon and Nov.
**Gran Caffè Ristorante
Margherita**
Via Regina Margherita 30
Tel: 0584-581 143 €€

This legendary Art Nouveau café has
moved with the times and serves
versions of classic Tuscan dishes,
either in the historic dining room, or
the garden. Also a bookshop.
Nitens
Piazzetta Viani 16
Tel: 0584-370 585 €€€
Stylish restaurant with a great
selection of wines and efficient
service. The focus here is on local
dishes with a twist. There is a limited
number of seats so reservations are
recommended.
L'Oca Bianca
Via Coppino 409
Tel: 0584-388 477
www.oca-bianca.it €€€–€€€€
Possibly Viareggio's finest
restaurant, with a creative seafood
menu. Exquisite service; exceptional
wine list. Near the port. Closed
Tue (except July–Aug) and lunch
Fri–Sun.
O' Sole Mio
Via Mazzini 160
Tel: 0584-944 850 €€
No-frills restaurant with a wide
selection of pizzas. Good value for
money. You can watch the pizzas
being prepared.

PISA AND THE ETRUSCAN RIVIERA

Restaurants

Pisa
Da Bruno
Via Bianchi 12
Tel: 050-560 818
www.anticatrattoriadabruno.it €€–€€€

*Fresh pasta, fresh pesto – the simpler
the better.*

Tuscan and Pisan flavours are the
hallmarks of the cuisine in this
atmospheric and popular
restaurant. Closed Mon evening
and Tue.
Il Campano
Via Cavalca 19
Tel: 050-580 585 €€
Set in a quiet spot beside the
marketplace, this restaurant dating
back to medieval times specialises in
fish, seafood and pasta. In summer
its terrace is a pleasant setting for
dining alfresco. Good wine list. Closed
Wed and Thur lunch.
A Casa Mia
Via Provinciale Calcesana 10, Ghezzano
(just outside Pisa)
Tel: 050-879 265 €€
Pleasant, family-run restaurant set in
a little villa. It serves creative Tuscan
cuisine using the freshest ingredients.
Closed Sat lunch and Sun, 1–7 Jan
and Aug.
La Clessidra
Via del Castelletto 26/30
Tel: 050-540 160 €€
Typical Tuscan flavours feature at
this pleasing and popular restaurant
in an elegant part of town. Booking
advised. Closed Sat lunch, Sun,
Christmas–early Jan and Aug.

Osteria dei Cavalieri
Via San Frediano 16
Tel: 050-580 858
www.osteriacavalieri.pisa.it €€
Modern restaurant near Piazza dei
Cavalieri where fish is the speciality.
A simpler menu is offered at
lunchtime. Excellent value. Booking
essential. Closed Sat lunch, Sun
and Aug.
Osteria del Porton Rosso
Vicolo del Porton Rosso 11
Tel: 050-580 566 €€
A brother-and-sister team create
excellent fish dishes in the centre of
Pisa. Booking recommended for this
rustic and gastronomic find. Closed
Sun.

Marina di Pisa
Bagno Italia
Via Litoranea 10

PRICE CATEGORIES

Prices for a three-course meal per
person with a half-bottle of house
wine:
€ = under €30
€€ = €30–45
€€€ = €45–65
€€€€ = over €65

Tel: 050-34095
www.ristorantebagnoitalia.it €€€
Enjoy superb dishes, especially
fish, taking in the lovely sea
view. Busy, so booking is
recommended.

Da Gino
Via delle Curzolari 2
Tel: 050-35408 €-€€€
Excellent fish restaurant near the sea;
dishes simply prepared and delicious.
Popular with both locals and tourists.
Closed Mon and Tue and Sept.

Foresta
Via Litoreana 2
Tel: 050-35082
www.ristoranteforesta.it €€€
Overlooking the sea, this little family-
run restaurant serves gourmet
cuisine. The speciality is fish and
other seafood. Must book as covers
are limited. Closed Sun evening and
Thur.

Antignano
Il Romito
Via del Littorale 274, 3km (1.7 miles) from
Antignano
Tel: 0586-580 520 €€
Roadside restaurant suspended
above the sea, with fabulous views
from its spacious semicircular
terrace. Service is brisk, but the
dishes, predominantly fish-based, are
presented with pride. Closed Wed in
summer.

Trattoria in Caciaia in Banditella
Via Puini 97
Tel: 0586-580 403 €-€€
Set on a quiet piazza, this pleasing
trattoria offers a great selection of
typical Livornese fish dishes. Closed
Mon and Tue, weekday lunchtimes
and 1 week in Sept.

Ardenza
Ciglieri
Via Ravizza 43
Tel: 0586-508 194 €€€€
The warm, inviting decor is matched
with excellent cuisine using only
seasonal specialities. Must book.
Closed Wed.

Oscar
Via Oreste Franchini 78
Tel: 0586-501 258
www.ristoranteoscar.it €€€
Historic restaurant with modern
"designer" ambience and a pleasant
garden for alfresco dining. Fish
predominates, with cacciucco
a speciality (must be ordered in
advance). Extensive wine list. Closed
Mon and 20 days from 27 Dec.

Castagneto Carducci
Osteria San Michele
Via Aurelia 199

Open kitchen at Lunasia, Green Park Resort.

Tel: 0565-774 478
www.osteriasanmichele.it €€
Excellent food served in a homely
atmosphere. The owner is very
knowledgeable about local wines.
Closed Mon.

Livorno
Da Galileo
Via della Campana 20
Tel: 0586-889 009 €€
Trattoria specialising in fish and
authentic Livornese cuisine at very
reasonable prices. Book ahead.
Closed Sun evening and Wed, and
last two weeks in July.

Ristorante Montallegro
Piazza Montenero 3
Tel: 0586-579 030 €€-€€€
Set in a spot with panoramic views
near the Sanctuary of Madonna di
Montenero. Cacciucco features every
day of the year, with other traditional
specialities. Pleasant frescoed
dining room and terrace for warmer
weather. Closed Tue in winter. Book
ahead.

Trattoria Antica Venezia
Via dei Bagnetti 1
Tel: 0586-887 353 €
A typical Tuscan trattoria in the heart
of Livorno's Venezia neighbourhood.
Offers traditional Livornesi recipes
including possibly the best cacciucco
(seafood soup) in town.

San Giuliano Terme
Dei Lorena
Hotel Bagni di Pisa, Largo Shelley
Tel: 050-88501
www.bagnidipisa.it €€€-€€€€
Set in a lovely resort between Pisa
and Lucca, this restaurant is a
celebration of Tuscan cuisine. Enjoy
distant views of the Leaning Tower
while tucking into giant Pisan steak,

Tuscan bouillabaisse (cacciucco),
truffled pasta and Antinori wines.
Separate menus for vegetarians and
dieters – resist. Do have a drink in the
bar, once a stylish salon frequented
by Shelley.

San Vincenzo
Il Sale
Via San Bartolo 100
Tel: 0565-798 015 €€€€
Possibly the best restaurant in San
Vincenzo with delightful dishes
prepared by a chef who likes to
interact with his diners. Booking
recommended. Lunch and dinner
daily.

Tirrenia
Dante e Ivana
Viale del Tirreno 207c
Tel: 050-32549
www.danteeivana.com €€€
Pleasant fish restaurant with an open
kitchen and a tank from which to
choose your feast. Closed Sun and
Mon, 20 Dec–end Jan.

Green Park Resort
Via dei Tulipani 1, Calambrone 56018
Tel: 050-313 5711 €€-€€€
www.softlivingplaces.com
Behind the dunes, dine either in
the romantic, candlelit Lunasia
gourmet restaurant (creative cuisine,
including seafood in a pot, or prawn,
pecorino and broad bean salad), or
in the family-oriented Le Ginestre
(reinterpretations of classic Tuscan
dishes). Both places are excellent.
Charming staff.

La Terrazza
Viale del Tirreno 313
Tel: 050-33006 €
Bustling, reliable, family-friendly
pizzeria that is packed in summer;
service is slow.

ISOLA D'ELBA

Restaurants

Capo d'Enfola
Da Giacomino
Localita Viticcio
Tel: 0565-915 381
www.ristorantedagiacomino.it €-€€
A small, family-run trattoria, a short
drive from the island capital. Sunsets
from the terrace across the bay are
memorable. Pizzas served in the
evening. Closed Tue lunch, Oct-Easter.
Ristorante Emanuel
Porto di Sansone
Tel: 0565-939 003 €-€€
The road to Capo d'Enfola promontory
ends at a pebble beach with a couple
of restaurants. Emanuel is a good
option for a snack lunch, and one
of few places to offer a vegetarian
menu. Closed Wed Sept-Oct and
Nov-Easter.

Marciana Marina
Affrichella
Via Santa Chiara 7
Tel: 0565-996 844 €€-€€€
Intimate restaurant, tucked down a
backstreet away from the seafront
bustle, offering an inventive fish-
based menu.
Borgo al Cotone
Via del Cotone 23
Tel: 0565-904 390 €€-€€€
Romantic harbourside restaurant

where fish and shellfish come
grilled and gratinated, or in more
adventurous concoctions such as
lasagne with chickpeas and clams.
Closed Oct-early Mar.
Ristorante Capo Nord
Localita La Fenicia
Tel: 0565-996 983 €€€-€€€€
The island's top restaurant, where you
will be fed exquisite Tuscan food by
impeccably dressed and deferential
waiters. Dress up and book. Ask for
table 5 or 6. Closed Mon in autumn
and Nov-Easter.

Marina di Campo
La Lucciola
Viale Nomellini 64
Tel: 0565-976 395
www.lalucciola.it €€€
Brush the sand off your feet and step
on to the wooden-decked terrace of
this relaxed beach bar/restaurant,
where you can enjoy a drink, a big
summer salad, or go for the catch of
the day. Closed Tue and mid-Apr-Oct.
Booking recommended.

Poggio/Marciana Alta
Publius
Piazza Castagneto 11
Tel: 0565-99208
www.ristorantepublius.it €€-€€€€
Nestled on the mountainside, Publius
has a well-established reputation on

the island, and offers fine views from
the terrace. Elban wines, fish and
game dishes. Closed Mon.

Porto Azzurro
I Quattro Gatti
Piazza del Mercato 4
Tel: 0565-95240 €€-€€€
A cosy and convivial restaurant
decorated with copper pots, beaded
lamps, old wirelesses and other
knick-knacks. The menu is equally
eclectic, with offerings such as
herrings with apple, carpaccio of cod
and fish ravioli. In a resort town full of
bright and brash restaurants, this is a
real find. Closed Mon in low season.

Portoferraio
Da Lido
Salita Falcone 2
Tel: 0565-914 650
www.ristorantelido.org €€
Set back from the port area, this
consistently good and constantly
bustling trattoria is one of
Portoferraio's best. Closed Sun in low
season, mid-Dec-mid-Feb.
Enoteca della Forteza
Via Scoscesa
Tel: 335-839 3722 €€
Tasty local food and wine served in
a Medici fortress. Great views of the
town plus friendly service make this
a winner.

VOLTERRA AND MASSA MARITTIMA

Restaurants

Volterra
Le Cantine del Palazzo
Via dei Sarti 39
Tel: 0588-80033 €-€€
The moody wine cellars below
Palazzo Viti are used for wine
tasting and light meals (of Sienese
salami, pecorino cheese and
bruschette) in a labyrinth that
includes an Etruscan well and a
Roman cistern.
Del Duca
Via di Castello 2
Tel: 0588-81510 €€-€€€
The city's best restaurant is in a
medieval building at the foot of
an Etruscan acropolis, with wine
cellars carved into the tufa walls.
The menu celebrates Volterran
specialities and features local
truffles, stuffed pasta, Tuscan
T-bone steaks. Barbecue in the
courtyard garden every Wed.

Il Pozzo Degli Etruschi
Via delle Prigioni 28-30
Tel: 0588-80608
www.ilpozzodeglietruschi.com €
The simple medieval backdrop of
this appealing eatery is echoed in the
unpretentious and delicious Tuscan
fare. In summer the shady inner courtyard is also open for dining. Closed Fri.
La Sosta del Priore
Vicolo delle Prigioni 2
Tel: 0588-97447 €
A very small place with delicious, fresh
Tuscan sandwiches and good local
wine.
La Vecchia Lira
Via Matteotti
Tel: 0588-86180
www.vecchialira.it €-€€
Justifiably popular rustic-looking
spot on the main street: it's a
good quality self-service place at
lunchtime but a proper restaurant
in the evening. Friendly staff and a
varied selection of regional dishes,

ranging from grilled meats to
cacciucco and *baccala alla livornese*
(dried salted cod Livorno-style).

Massa Marittima
La Massetana
Via Marconi 24
Tel: 0566-940 314 €
Predominantly local, traditional
food including delicious *tortelli
maremmani* (ricotta and spinach)
and *tagliatelle alla boscaiola* (porcini
sauce). Plentiful helpings. Closed
Mon.

PRICE CATEGORIES

**Prices for a three-course meal per
person with a half-bottle of house
wine:**
€ = under €30
€€ = €30-45
€€€ = €45-65
€€€€ = over €65

Le Mura
Via Norma Parenti 7
Tel: 0566-940 055 €€€
This large and busy restaurant has
panoramic views towards Follonica
and Elba, from both inside and out.
The extensive menu incorporates
typical Tuscan ingredients from the
nearby wooded hills and fresh seafood
from the coast beyond. Closed Tue.
Osteria Da Tronca
Vicolo Porte 5

Tel: 0566-901 991 €€
A reasonably priced and popular
family-run restaurant offering
simple, well-prepared dishes cooked
to traditional recipes. Booking
recommended. Closed Wed.
La Padellaccia Del Viggia
Piazza Cavour 1
Tel: (+39) 329-729 5464 €€
A simple eatery which shows you can
eat well and local without spending
a fortune. *Pizza arrotolata* is a

speciality. In summer open daily, in
winter closed Wed.
La Tana del Brillo Parlante
Vicolo del Ciambellano 4
Tel: 0566-901 274 €€€
The best approach in this tiny
restaurant – there are just four
tables – is to ask what's available.
The dishes are lovingly prepared
and seasonal, and there's a good
selection of fine wines. Booking
essential. Closed Wed.

SAN GIMIGNANO AND CHIANTI COUNTRY

Restaurants

Also try the restaurants at wine
estates on the Chianti Trail (see
page 194).

Castellina in Chianti
Albergaccio
Via Fiorentina 63
Tel: 0577-741 042
www.albergacciocast.com €€
The dishes change, but the quality
of the food – which is Tuscan with
flair – remains the same. Booking
advisable. Closed Sun, summers also
Wed at lunch.
La Torre
Piazza del Comune
Tel: 0577-740 236 €€
Restaurant with terrace outside
the fortress. Extensive menu
of predictable Tuscan fare, but
reasonable. Closed Fri.

Certaldo Alto
L'Antica Fonte
Via Valdracca 25
Tel: 0571-652 225
www.tavernaanticafonte.it €€
Small, simple restaurant offering
Tuscan specialities in a friendly and
relaxed atmosphere. In summer
there's additional seating in the
garden, with views across the Val
d'Elsa. Booking essential. Closed Jan
and Feb.
Osteria del Vicario
Via Rivellino 3
Tel: 0571-667 809 €€€
www.osteriadelvicario.it €€€
Charmingly set in Romanesque
cloisters, this Michelin-starred
restaurant serves inventive variations
on Tuscan cuisine, including dishes
inspired by ancient recipes. Closed
Sun dinner, Mon.

Gaiole in Chianti
Badia a Coltibuono
Loc. Badia a Coltibuono
Tel/fax: 0577-749 031
www.coltibuono.com €€€

Part of a glorious rural wine estate,
complete with 11th-century abbey.
Specialities include home-made
pasta with wild-duck sauce and
antipasto della Badia. Popular stop
on the Chianti trail. Closed Mon
except May–Oct.
Il Carlino d'Oro
Località San Regolo
Tel: 0577-747 136
www.carlinovacanze.com €
Family-run trattoria, far removed from
typical underperforming restaurants
on the well-beaten Chianti trail. Lunch
only; closed Mon.
**Ristorante Il Pievano (Castello di
Spaltenna)**
Località Spaltenna 13
Tel: 0577-749 483
www.spaltenna.it €€€€
Magnificent restaurant in a hotel
converted from a fortified monastery.
Dishes use fresh local ingredients,
and food is cooked in a wood-burning
stove. Closed Nov–Mar.

Greve in Chianti
Bottega del Moro
Piazza Trieste 14r
Tel: 055-853 753
www.labottegadelmoro.it €€
Restaurant serving good-quality
traditional Tuscan fare. Try the *coniglio*
(rabbit) or *trippa alla Fiorentina* (tripe)
after a fresh pasta dish. Closed Mon.

Monterrigioni
Il Pozzo
Piazza Roma 20
Tel: 0577-304 127
www.ilpozzo.net €€
Famous restaurant full of foreigners
in summer, but deservedly popular, in
a gem of a tiny walled town. Closed
Sun evening, Mon, most of Jan and
period in Aug.

Panzano in Chianti
Enoteca Baldi
Piazza Bucciarelli 25
Tel: 055-852 843 €

Enoteca (wine bar/inn) with
impressive wine selection. Open for a
light lunch or afternoon snack.

Radda in Chianti
La Terrazza dei Glicini
Via Pianigiani 9, Relais Vignale hotel
Tel: 0577-738 094
www.vignale.it €€–€€€
This hotel-restaurant, set in a
converted farm, serves refined and
imaginative Tuscan cuisine. Be
warned though, prices are steep
and the clientele is mostly tourists.
Booking essential.
Le Vigne
Podere le Vigne Est (1km/0.6 miles outside
town)
Tel: 0577-738 301 €€–€€€
Located among vineyards, and
serving great food, this is a treat.
Reasonably priced rooms for rent
above the restaurant. Closed mid-
Nov–Feb.

San Gimignano
Dorandò
Vicolo dell'Oro 2
Tel: 0577-941 862
www.ristorantedorando.it €€€€
Stylish restaurant specialising in
recipes from the past. Closed Mon
(except Easter–Nov) and 9 Dec–20
Feb.
Osteria delle Cantene
Via Mainardi 18
Tel: 0577-941 966 €€
New-wave trattoria where traditional
and contemporary ideas successfully
co-exist. Try the local Vernaccia wine.
Closed Wed and Jan.

Volpaia
La Bottega
Piazza della Torre 2
Tel: 0577-738 001
www.labottegadivolpaia.it €€
Gorgeous lunch spot with a maple-
shaded terrace and valley views.
Quality varies, but the service and
location make up for it. Closed Tue.

SIENA

Restaurants

Al Mangia
Piazza del Campo 42
Tel: 0577-281 121
www.almangia.it €€€–€€€€
In a great position on the Campo, this popular restaurant serves classic Tuscan cuisine. Seating outside in the summer. Closed Wed Nov–Feb.

Antica Osteria Da Divo
Via Franciosa 25/29
Tel: 0577-286 054
www.osteriadadivo.it €€€
Haute Tuscan cuisine set in a vaulted Etruscan room. Extensive wine list. The menu changes regularly but truffle dishes are a must.

Antica Trattoria Botteganova
Via Chiantigiana 29
Tel: 0577-284 230 €€€–€€€€
Refined restaurant serving fine Sienese cuisine. Specialities include local delicacies, fish and tasty puddings. Closed Sun, period in Jan, early Aug.

Il Canto
Strada di Certosa 82
Tel: 0577-288 180
www.certosadimaggiano.com €€€€
This restaurant in a Carthusian monastery-turned luxury hotel, Certosa di Maggiano, serves gourmet food in a magical setting: a courtyard overlooking Siena. It's one of San Pellegrino's World's 50 Best Restaurants. Closed Tue.

Da Guido
Vicolo del Pettinaio 7
Tel: 0577-280 042 €€–€€€
Veritable Sienese institution, set in medieval premises and popular with visiting VIPs. Traditional Sienese cuisine. Closed Wed and Jan.

Osteria del Castelvecchio
Via Castelvecchio 65
Tel: 0577-47093 €€
Converted from ancient stables, this perennially popular hostelry creates contemporary dishes with traditional flavours, including vegetarian dishes. Interesting wine list. Closed Tue.

Osteria Il Boccon del Prete
Via San Pietro 17
Tel: 0577-280 388 €
Family-run restaurant serving Sienese dishes in a pleasing setting. Closed Sun.

Hosteria Il Carroccio
Via Casato di Sotto 32
Tel: 0577-41165 €
Well run, tiny trattoria serving local dishes. Closed Tue dinner, Wed, Feb and 1 week in Nov.

Osteria La Chiacchiera
Costa di San Antonio 4
Tel: 0577-280 631
www.osterialachiacchera.it €
Small, rustic inn offering Sienese fare – try the local pasta, *pici* (thick spaghetti), and the pork casserole. Dine outside in summer. Closed Tue.

Osteria La Taverna di San Giuseppe
Via G. Dupré 132
Tel: 0577-42286
www.tavernasangiuseppe.it €–€€
Delicious Tuscan fare in an atmospheric cavern with wooden furnishings. An antipasto is a must; delicious dishes using pecorino. Closed Sun.

Osteria Le Logge
Via del Porrione 33
Tel: 0577-48013 €€–€€€
Set in a 19th-century pharmacy, with authentic dark-wood and marble interior. One of a few gastronomic Siena eateries, it offers dishes such as ravioli with mint and pecorino, duck and fennel, or stuffed guinea fowl *(faraona)*. Montalcino wines from chef's estate. Closed Sun and Jan.

Pizzeria di Nonno Mede
Via Camporegio 21
Tel: 0577-247 966 €
Serves good pizza and great desserts. Splendid view of the Duomo, which is well lit in the evenings. Book ahead.

Trattoria Papei
Piazza del Mercato 6
Tel: 0577-280 894 €€
Ideal place for sampling genuine Sienese home cooking in large portions. Closed Mon (except public holidays) and end July.

Tre Cristi
Vicolo di Provenzano 1–7
Tel: 0577-280 608
www.trecristi.com €€–€€€
Elegant restaurant with frescoed walls and a contemporary Mediterranean menu. Booking advised. Closed Sun in Aug.

Bars and Cafés

Nannini's (Via Banchi di Sopra) is an obligatory coffee stop on Siena's main shopping street. Opposite is **Caffè del Corso** – chic by day, boisterous by night. **Caffè le Logge** (Via Rinaldini, at the end of Banchi di Sotto) is a non-touristic place to drink cappuccino. On Il Campo, to the left of the Palazzo Pubblico, **Gelateria Caribia** (Via Rinaldini) offers a multitude of ice-cream flavours. **The Tea Room** (Via Porta Giustizia; closed Mon) is cosy for tea and cake, or a cocktail with live jazz. Further from the centre, **Il Masgalano** (Via del Camporegio, next to San Domenico) is a friendly place for coffees, light lunches or an *aperitivo*.

SOUTH OF SIENA

Restaurants

Montalcino
Osteria di Porta al Cassero
Via Ricasoli 32
Tel: 0577-847 196 €
This is a local favourite. Be sure to try the restaurant's polenta with wild-boar sauce, a regional speciality.

Taverna Il Grappolo Blu
Scale di Via Moglio 1
Tel: 0577-847 150 €€–€€€
Intimate, well-run inn with a rustic atmosphere, charming service and excellent cuisine that spans the full range of Tuscan dishes. Typical dishes include filling soups, rabbit dishes and pasta with *porcini*. Excellent wine list. Reserve.

Trattoria L'Angolo
Via Ricasoli 9
Tel: 0577-848 017 €
Among the pricey restaurants of Montalcino, this well-known trattoria remains a down-to-earth and fairly priced option. Particularly good is the bean soup and home-made pasta. Closed Tue.

Montefollonico
La Chiusa
Via Madonnina 88
Tel: 0577-669 668
www.ristorantelachiusa.it €€€€
One of Tuscany's fanciest restaurants, set in an old oil mill on the outskirts of Montefollonico, with glorious views of the countryside. Seasonal dishes

PRICE CATEGORIES

Prices for a three-course meal per person with a half-bottle of house wine:
€ = under €30
€€ = €30–45
€€€ = €45–65
€€€€ = over €65

are lovingly prepared according to traditional recipes, using locally sourced ingredients and vegetables grown in the adjoining kitchen garden. Dine on duck with wild fennel or tagliatelle with truffles. 15 rooms to rent. Come here for a special occasion. Closed Tue.

Monte Oliveto
La Torre
Monte Oliveto Maggiore
Tel: 0577-707 022 €€
Tourists fill every table on the lovely shaded terrace of this restaurant beside the Benedictine abbey, but the food is surprisingly good. Service is brusque but efficient. Picnic tables nearby. Closed Tue.

Montepulciano
Caffè Poliziano
Via di Voltaia del Corso, 27
Tel: 0578-758 615
www.caffepoliziano.it €-€€
Lovingly restored Art Nouveau café-restaurant in the historic heart of Montepulciano. It's a landmark, often full, but worth trying to get a table, even just for a coffee. Glorious panoramic balcony.
La Grotta
Località San Biagio 16

Tel: 0578-757 479 €€€
www.lagrottamontepulciano.it €€€
Once the home of architect Sangallo, and right next to his stunningly positioned church of San Biagio. Rustic Tuscan dishes, with French influences. *Alfresco* dining in summer. This is where locals go for a special occasion. Closed Wed and Jan–Feb.
Osteria Acquacheta
Via del Teatro 22
Tel: 0578-717 086 €-€€
Authentic *osteria* serving uncomplicated but tasty dishes such as *pici* (the chunky local pasta) with wild boar *ragù* and tagliatelle with white truffles. Wine is sloshed into glass tumblers and your bill will be scribbled on the tablecloth. Excellent value, but book or be prepared to wait.

Monticchiello
La Porta
Via del Piano 1
Tel/fax: 0578-755 163
www.osterialaporta.it €€
Pleasant inn just outside the walled town of Monticchiello. Stop here for the sweeping views, a glass of wine and a choice of both traditional and more inventive dishes. Closed Thur, most of Jan.

Pienza
La Buca delle Fate
Corso il Rossellino 38/a
Tel: 0578-748 448 €
Simple trattoria and bar in the lovely 16th-century Palazzo Gonzaga, on the main thoroughfare through town. One of the best of Pienza's many eateries. Closed Mon.

Proceno
Trattoria La Dogana
Via Cassia Km 141
Tel: 0763-734 092
www.ladogana.eu €€
Real Tuscan food cooked mainly in the open fire. Try *bistecca fiorentina* and *tagliatelle* with truffles. Very homely and welcoming atmosphere. Open daily.

Sinalunga
Le Coccole dell'Amorosa
Località l'Amorosa 2km (1 mile) south
Tel: 0577-677 211
www.amorosa.it €€€-€€€€
Superb restaurant, romantically set in the stables of a medieval estate. The food is a mix of traditional and new, with a good choice. There is no better place to eat a *bistecca chianina* (farmed locally). Book well in advance. Closed Mon and Tue lunch.

THE MAREMMA AND MONTE ARGENTARIO

Restaurants

Capalbio
Il Fontanile dei Caprai
7km (4.5 miles) from Capalbio on the Marsiliana road
Tel: 0564-896 526 €€
This country restaurant and its jovial owner are full of Tuscan rustic charm. Tasty Maremman dishes made from locally sourced ingredients are lovingly prepared and served. Weekends for lunch and dinner, and from mid-June–mid-Sept, 26 Dec–8 Jan in the evenings, too.

Castiglione della Pescaia
La Griglia
Via delle Rocchette
Tel: 0564-941 402
www.lagriglia.org €€
A modest but reliable trattoria that offers customers its fantastic speciality – a mixed platter of fresh and tasty grilled-fish.
La Terrazza
Corso Della Libertà 49
Tel/fax: 0564-933 835 €
Reliable restaurant and pizzeria. Spring and summer only.

Grosseto
Il Canto del Gallo
Via Mazzini 29
Tel: 0564-414 589 €€
A tiny trattoria set in the old town walls that favours organic, local produce for its dishes. Closed Sun and two weeks in Feb.

Montemerano
Da Caino
Via della Chiesa 4
Tel: 0564-602 817
www.dacaino.it €€€€
One of the best restaurants in all of Tuscany. Serves exquisite and creative food, specialising in wild mushrooms and truffles. Booking essential. Closed Wed, Thur lunch, late Jan–late Feb and 2 weeks in July.

Orbetello
Osteria Il Nocchino
Via Lenzi 64
Tel: 0564-860 329 €€
Squeeze yourself into this tiny fish restaurant and enjoy tucking into such dishes as salt cod and chickpeas or the seafood risotto.

Open in the evenings only. Closed Tue and weekend lunchtimes during winter.
La Posta di Torrenova
Strada Provinciale della Parrina 56
Tel: 0564-862 479
www.torrenova.eu €€€
This restaurant by the pool serves tasty grilled fish and octopus mains, as well as squid salads, all beautifully presented. Wine tasting available too.

Pitigliano
Hostaria Il Ceccottino
Piazza San Gregorio VII 64
Tel: 0564-614 069
www.ceccottino.com €€
Set on a lovely square in the old town, this Slow Food inn lives up to its good reputation. In summer, dine on the terrace, sipping a chilled glass of Bianco di Pitigliano. On the seasonal menu are dishes including pumpkin ravioli, Florentine steak, pasta with porcini or truffles, and apple-and-cinnamon tart.
Trattoria del Grillo
Via Cavour 18
Tel: 0564-615 202 €

Authentic trattoria, beside the aqueduct, mixing Tuscan classics with local flourishes. So you might follow good old *bruschetta* or *pici*, with escalopes in Pitigliano wine. Honestly priced and packed with locals. Closed Tue.

Porto Santo Stefano
Il Moletto
Via del Molo
Tel: 0564-813 636 €€
The last in a long line of fish restaurants along the marina's main drag. Share a seafood platter while watching the port activity. Closed Wed.

Saturnia
Due Cippi da Michele
Piazza Vittorio Veneto 26/A
Tel: 0564-601 074 €€–€€€
Better known simply as Da Michele, this is an inn serving Maremman dishes in a patrician palazzo. Tasty Tuscan dishes are offered across the board, from steaks to pasta and the range of antipasti. Closed Tue.

Sovana
Taverna Etrusca
Piazza del Pretorio 16
Tel: 0564-616 183
www.tavernaetrusca.info €€

The best restaurant in town, and not just for the quality of the local specialities on offer. Meals are served in an atmospheric medieval dining room with exposed beams and a terracotta floor. Closed Wed and July.
Ristorante dei Merli di Sovana
Via del Duomo 5
Tel: 0564-616 531
www.albergoscilla.net €€
This bright and elegant restaurant inside Hotel Scilla has a more contemporary feel than the Taverna Etrusca (above) and offers a vegetarian menu. Closed Tue.

AREZZO AND EASTERN TUSCANY

Restaurants

Arezzo
Antica Osteria L'Agania
Via Mazzini 10
Tel: 0575-295 381
www.agania.it €–€€
Very pleasant and hugely popular family-run trattoria serving good, homely Tuscan fare, including the *Chianina* steak. Excellent value. Closed Mon, except June–Aug.
Buca di San Francesco
Via San Francesco 1
Tel/fax: 0575-23271 €€
A famous cellar restaurant adjoining San Francesco church, with trecento frescoes and a Roman-Etruscan pavement. The medieval atmosphere is matched by rustic cuisine. Closed Mon evening and Tue.
Il Cantuccio
Via Madonna del Prato 76
Tel/fax: 0575-26830 €€
Vaulted basement restaurant run by the Volpi family, who produce their own wine and olive oil. Try the *bistecca*, perhaps with deep-fried *porcini* mushrooms. Closed Wed.
Il Torrino
Strada dei Due Mari 1
Tel: 0575-360 649 €€€
Eight km (5 miles) along the San Sepolcro road, this restaurant is worth seeking out for the good food and view. Truffles in season. Closed Mon.
La Lancia d'Oro
Piazza Grande 18/19
Tel: 0575-21033 €€–€€€
Excellent Arezzo cuisine features in this pleasing, central restaurant. In summer you can dine alfresco. Closed Sun evening, all day Mon and 5–25 Nov.
La Torre di Gnicche
Piaggia San Martino 8

Tel: 0575-352 035 €
Just off the northern corner of the main square, this tiny wine bar is an excellent choice for a cheap and simple meal – a hearty *ribollita* soup or a cheese platter – and some wine from its long and excellent selection. Popular with the antique-dealing fraternity. Closed Wed.

Cortona
Il Falconiere
Loc. San Martino 370 (4km/2.5 miles north of Cortona)
Tel: 0575-612 679
www.ilfalconiere.it €€€€
In a lovely setting in the hills, this hotel makes you feel as though time stands still. The imaginative cuisine of fish and meat dishes, combined with the excellent service, is deserving of its one Michelin star. Lovely panoramic terrace. Reserve in advance.

Restaurants on Piazza della Repubblica, Cortona.

La Grotta
Piazzetta Baldelli 3
Tel: 0575-630 271
www.trattorialagrotta.it €€
A well-established family-run trattoria with local food and a warm welcome. Alfresco dining in summer. Popular with tourists. Closed Tue.
Osteria del Teatro
Via Maffei 2
Tel: 0575-630 556
www.osteria-del-teatro.it €€–€€€
Simple but delicious food, located in a 15th-century palazzo, and friendly service. One of Cortona's nicest eateries. Closed Wed.

Lucignano
Osteria da Totò
Piazza del Tribunal 6
Tel: 0575-836 763
www.trattoriatoto.it €–€€
Run by well-known chef Lorenzo Totò, dishes are inspired by traditional Italian cooking. Closed Tue.

Mercatale di Cortona
Mimmi
Via Pietro della Cortona 29
Tel: 0575-619 029 €
A wonderful experience: arrive early to enjoy plentiful home-made Tuscan cuisine, cooked in a wood-fired oven. Vegetables from the kitchen garden and local wines. Closed 1 week in Nov.

PRICE CATEGORIES

Prices for a three-course meal per person with a half-bottle of house wine:
€ = under €30
€€ = €30–45
€€€ = €45–65
€€€€ = over €65

ACTIVITIES

THE ARTS, SIGHTSEEING, NIGHTLIFE, FESTIVALS, SPORTS AND SHOPPING

THE ARTS

Archaeological Sites

There are various places of archaeological interest in Tuscany. These include **Etruscan** (8th–2nd century BC) sites at Volterra, Fiesole, Arezzo, Chiusi, Vetulonia and on the island of Elba. There is an archaeological museum in Florence, and other museums in Volterra, Chiusi, Cortona, Asciano, Grosseto and Massa Marittima.

Notable **Roman** (8th century BC–5th century AD) remains can be seen at Fiesole, Cosa, Roselle, Volterra and Arezzo.

Art and Architecture

Art

Renaissance art is, of course, what Tuscany is most famous for. The most outstanding Renaissance collections are in Florence, in the Uffizi Gallery, the Pitti Palace and the San Marco Museum.

Works of art from the late Renaissance and Mannerist periods, the Baroque, the neoclassical and Romantic, and also the 21st century are exhibited at most galleries and museums in the main cities of the region.

The exciting La Strozzina gallery, in the restored cellars of the Palazzo Strozzi, has finally put Florence on the contemporary-art map. The Palazzo Strozzi itself is a major exhibition site focusing on high-profile art exhibitions (see page 93).

Architecture

Tuscany is a treasure trove of architectural history (see page 58).

Churches and civil buildings from the Romanesque period can be found at Pisa, Florence, Lucca, Siena, Pistoia and Arezzo. The most important Gothic buildings are in Florence, Siena, Pisa, Pistoia and Arezzo. Tuscany also abounds in religious and secular Renaissance buildings, Florence being the most important centre.

SIGHTSEEING

Details of important museums and art galleries are in the Places section of this book. Be sure to take advantage of multi-entrance tickets, especially in Florence.

Florence

There are stands in shops and cafés where free leaflets detailing events and exhibitions can be picked up.

Amici dei Musei Fiorentini (The Friends of Florentine Museums Association; Via Folco Portinari 5a; tel: 055-293 007) arranges a wide variety of events including guided museum visits, lectures, and recitals accompanying exhibitions.

If you plan to visit a lot of museums in Florence, consider a membership to Amici degli Uffizi (Via Lorenzo Il Magnifico 1; tel: 055-479 4422), which allows free entrances and no queues. (See www.amicidegliuffizi.it)

It is advisable to reserve Uffizi and Accademia tickets in advance, or face lengthy queuing (see pages 104 and 110).

The **Firenze Card** covers three days of museums and public transport (see page 90). Entry prices for museums and galleries vary greatly, with the Uffizi the most expensive. State museums

are closed on Monday, while most other museums close on Tuesday or Wednesday. Most museums also close on 1 May.

Every year, in the spring, Florence has a "culture week" (*La Settimana di Beni Culturali*), when all the state museums are free. Enquire at the tourist office for more information.

Florence on foot: Walking tours are an excellent way to gain more insight into the city. **Link** (tel: 055-218 191; www.linkfirenze.it) is a Florentine-based guiding service that covers personalised thematic tours, ranging from arty walking tours to nature rambles and gastro-tours that visit the markets and Chianti wine estates. All the guides can be recommended, with Guido perfect for art and history, and Marina the best for foodie experiences.

Florence by rickshaw: Tre Rote; tel: (+39) 338-638 9245; www.pedicab firenze.it

Florence by Segway: www.segway.it

Florence by horse-drawn carriage: from Piazza Duomo or Piazza della Signoria.

Florence by Vespa: Tuscany Vespa Tours (tel: 055-3860 253; www.tuscany-vespatours.com) offers Vespa trips to the Chianti.

Pisa

The main sites can be easily visited on foot or by local bus. Buy a joint ticket to see all the sights on the Campo dei Miracoli. A horse-and-carriage ride is a pleasant introduction to the city; prices are negotiable.

Siena

The tourist office can provide a list of authorised guides. With one week's notice, you can visit any of the *Contrada* (district) museums that celebrate the Palio and the ancient city traditions: the numbers are available on www.ctps.it.

Themed Tours

ABTOI, the Association of British Tour Operators to Italy (www.loveitaly.co.uk) is a good place to start when planning holidays to Italy, and for booking unusual themed itineraries ranging from art trails to adventures, such as foodie, wine and walking trails.

Sapori + Saperi (UK tel: +44 (0)7768-474 610; Italy tel: +39 339-763 6321; www.sapori-e-saperi. com) specialises in Slow Travel and Slow Food in Northern Tuscany. These are culinary adventures to meet the local wine and food producers and get a taste of their lives, far from Chiantishire stereotypes.

Tuscany Pass (www.tuscanypass. com) is a reliable website that offers an events calendar and some of the best day trips in Tuscany. Choose from day-long Tuscan cookery courses to Vespa trips to the wine-growing Chianti; arty Florentine walking tours and designer shopping excursions.

Link (tel: 055-218 191; www.link firenze.it): Tuscan tours (as above)

The entrance to the Odeon.

Wine & Cookery Courses

Italy abounds in foodie courses but these are two of the best, which remain small, authentic, professional and memorable:

The Florence Chefs (tel: (+39) 347 800 7419; www.theflorencechefs. it) is a collaborative project of Silvia Maccari (Camilla in Cucina) and Barbara Desderi (La Pentola delle Meraviglie). The two renowned chefs give private cooking classes at their homes and run a regular cookery school where they teach how to cook the Italian way, not forgetting about cultural and historical traditions.

Cucina Giuseppina (tel: (+39) 348 0034 869; www.cucinagiuseppina. com) is a warm yet authentic cookery school in medieval Certaldo, not far from San Gimignano. The chef, helped by her wine-specialist son, guides you through regional recipes. The school also offers wine appreciation and truffle-hunting experiences.

Listings

The Florentine is the city's free bi-weekly English-language newspaper. Issues can be found around town or downloaded from its website (www.theflorentine. net). Articles cover current events in Florence and event listings. The monthly publication, *Firenze*

Spettacolo, also has complete listings of city events; although in Italian, the listings are usually straightforward. Also check the entertainment pages of *La Nazione*, the regional newspaper, or the Tuesday edition of the national, *La Repubblica*. Also see the city website: www.comune.fi.it.

Music, Ballet and Opera

Florence

The **Maggio Musicale Fiorentino** music festival (www.maggiofiorentino. com), held from the end of April to the end of June, is a big event with top names in music, ballet and opera performing in various venues throughout the city. Major performances are staged in the new **Teatro del Maggio Opera di Firenze**, Florence's opera house and auditorium (tel: 055-2779 350; www.operadifirenze.it), which opened close to **Teatro Comunale** (Corso Italia 16). In summer, concerts are also given in cloisters, piazzas and the Boboli Gardens. Louder (and free) rock concerts are held in **Le Cascine park**.

During the **Estate Fiesolana** – Fiesole's summer festival – concerts, opera, ballet and plays are presented in the **Roman amphitheatre**, and in many city churches.

The **Estate Fiorentina** summer music festival, held in July and August, takes over the newly restored **Ampitheatre** at Le Cascine park; the new contemporary space at **Le Murate**; as well as city squares, courtyards of major palaces and churches. Rock concerts are relegated to Le Cascine park, while Le Murate becomes an open-air cinema.

Chamber music is often performed in **Teatro della Pergola**, Via della Pergola (tel: 055-226 41; www.fond azioneteatrodellapergola.it), a superb example of a 17th-century theatre (inaugurated in 1656). Concerts are

generally given at weekends, and are well publicised.

The Fiesole Music School in San Domenico also gives a concert series (tel: 055-597 8527; www.scuolamusica.fiesole.fi.it) and the Orchestra Regionale Toscana's lively concert series runs December–May.

Florence's **Teatro Verdi**, Via Ghibellina 99 (tel: 055-212 320; www.teatro verdifirenze.it) is the venue for light opera, ballet, jazz and rock concerts.

Teatro del Maggio Opera di Firenze: a new era for the opera company in its new location.

The **Orchestra da Camera Fiorentina** gives bi-monthly classical concerts in the Bargello and the church of Orsanmichele. Their schedule is available at www.orcafi.it.

The **Florence Dance Festival**, held in July, features well-known national and international names along with up-and-coming dancers and choreographers (tel: 055-289 276; www.florencedance.org for information).

Lucca

Lucca's summer festival (www.summer-festival.com) in July attracts big-name international artists to a range of venues.

"Puccini e la sua Lucca" is a permanent festival dedicated to Giacomo Puccini, with concerts in the Basilica di San Giovanni. Tickets available at the church on performance days from 6pm; www.puccinielasua lucca.it (see page 128).

Pisa

Pisa's opera season runs at the Teatro Verdi from October to February. Tel: 050-941 111 or visit www.teatrodipisa.pi.it.

Pistoia

Held every July, the Pistoia Blues Festival (www.pistoiablues.com) hosts big-name blues, jazz and rock artists for three days of concerts.

Siena

Public performances of rare, unpublished and new music are held in July each year during the Sienese Music Week.

Arezzo

Every July, the Arezzo Wave Love Festival (www.arezzowave.com) brings a variety of Italian and world-famous musicians to Tuscany to perform free concerts in a five-day music fest.

Theatre

In addition to the main theatres, Teatro della Pergola and Teatro Verdi (Via Ghibellina 99; tel: 055-212 320; www.teatroverdionline.it), there are numerous smaller companies performing regularly in Florence, but most productions are in Italian.

Ticket Sales

Useful ticket agencies in Florence are Box Office Toscana, Via delle Vecchie Carceri 1; tel: 055-210 804 (Mon–Fri 10am–7pm, Sat 10am–2pm) and many more locations; branches throughout Tuscany in Siena, Piza, Lucca and several other places.

Cinema

Almost all films are dubbed into Italian, but there are a few cinemas that occasionally show original versions, screenings by organisations such as the British Institute, and the odd film festival or special season that will use subtitles rather than dubbing. The main cinema for foreigners is the **Odeon** (Piazza Strozzi; tel: 055-214 068; www.odeonfirenze.com), which shows recent films in English and is packed with foreign students and expatriates. During the summer, a number of films are shown in the open air, including at Le Murate.

Enjoying drinks at Dolce Vita.

NIGHTLIFE

Tuscany's cities offer a wide variety of music and entertainment, especially in the summer when there are any number of festivals around the region. In Florence, bars and clubs are set up in the warm weather in several piazzas, often with live music. There are a number of late-night bars and clubs dotted around town, but most of the bigger clubs are on the outskirts. Nightclubs come and go, so it's best to ask around for recommendations. The following places are all in Florence. Elsewhere, your hotel or local tourist office may advise about clubs, bars and events. Note that most clubs close on Monday; and very few get going before 10pm on other nights.

Bars and Live Music

Astor
Piazza del Duomo 20r; tel: 055-239 9318, www.astorcafe.com. Cocktail bar with dance floor, frequented by Americans.

Il Caffè
Piazza Pitti 9; tel: 055-239 9863, www.caffepitti.it. Chic and refined: a cosy spot to chat to friends, day or evening.

Caffè Cibreo
Via del Verrocchio 8r; tel: 055-234 1100. Atmospheric annexe to the famous restaurant, ideal for anything from a morning coffee to a late-night *digestivo*. Closed Sun and Mon.

Cantinetta dei Verrazzano
Via dei Tavolini 18r; tel: 055-268 590, www.verrazzano.com. Old-fashioned wine bar serving rustic lunch snacks and wines from the owners' Chianti estate; closed 9pm.

Caffè Giacosa
Via della Spada 10; tel: 055-277 6328, www.caffegiacosa.it. Historic café given a hip makeover by designer

Roberto Cavalli, whose own estate wines are served there.

Dei Frescobaldi
Via dei Maggazini 2r; tel: 055-284 724, www.deifrescobaldi.it. Snack on Tuscan antipasti (salami, cheeses, salads) in this new wine bar founded by the famous Frescobaldi wine dynasty. Their adjoining restaurant is more elegant.

Dolce Vita
Piazza del Carmine 6r; tel: 055-284 595; www.dolcevitaflorence.com. Arty, full-on, fashion-conscious bar in the bohemian Oltrarno quarter that appeals to the Happy Hour and late-night crowd.

Fusion Bar
Vicolo dell'Oro 3; tel: 055-2726 6987, www.lungarnocollection.com. Swanky bar in the Gallery Hotel Art, perfect for tea, cocktails, sushi and showing off.

Harry's Bar
Lungarno A. Vespucci 22r; tel: 055-239 6700, www.harrysbarfirenze.com. Casual but elegant bar with excellent cocktails.

Jazz Club
Via Nuova dei Caccini 3; tel: (+39) 339-4980 752. Relaxed basement bar with live music daily. Small charge to become a member.

Moyo
Via dei Benci 23r; tel: 055-247 9738, www.moyo.it. Smart cocktail bar in the Santa Croce area with outside seating and delicious cocktails.

Negroni
Via dei Renai 17r; tel: 055-243 647, www.negronibar.it. Celebrated bar whose drinks are famous since the 1920s.

Slowly
Via Porta Rossa 63r; tel: 055-0351 335, www.slowlycafe.com. Trendy cocktail bar with a great aperitif buffet.

Teatro del Sale
Via de Macci 111r; tel: 055-200 1492, www.teatrodelsale.com. Hedonistic dining club run by celebrity chef Fabio Picchi. A Tuscan buffet before live blues, jazz or theatre; membership essential but cheap, as is the good-value buffet dinner.

I Visacci
Borgo Albizi 80r; tel: 055-263 9443. Pleasant arty café with friendly staff, relaxed music and a good selection of wines and cocktails.

Le Volpi e le Uva
Piazza de Rossi 1r; tel: 055-239 8132, www.levolpieluva.com. Elegant but friendly wine bar for a light supper of superb wines, cheeses, cold cuts and bruschetta; closes 9pm.

Zoe
Via dei Renai 13; tel: 055-243 111. All day (and late-night) arty,

contemporary café in trendy Oltrarno that takes you from brunch to cocktails and beyond.

Nightclubs

Blue Velvet
Via del Castello D'Altafronte 16; tel: 055-215 521, www.bluevelvetfirenze. it. Disco, restaurant and blue velvet couches, of course. Fri–Sun.
Central Park
Via del Fosso Macinante 1, Parco delle Cascine; tel: (+39) 366-478 7655. Dinner, disco, House music. Tue–Sat.
Club TwentyOne
Via Cimatori 13; tel: (+39) 328 729 0848. Dance floors and bars. Popular among Italian and foreign students alike. Wed–Sat.
Dolce Zucchero
Via de Pandolfini 36/38r; tel: 055-247 7894. One of the few clubs in the city centre, it operates a drinks card whereby you pay on exit. Tue–Sun.
Space Club Firenze
Via Palazzuolo 37, tel: 055-293 082, www.spaceclubfirenze.com. Disco and bar frequented by young people of all nationalities. Daily.
Tenax
Via Pratese 46; tel: 055-308 160, www.tenax.org. Popular club and live-music venue. Fri–Sat.
YAB
Via Sassetti 5r; tel: 055-215 160; www.yab.it. Established disco-pub.

FESTIVALS

Arezzo

Last Sunday in June and first Sunday in September: Giostra del Saracino – Jousting match in which mounted knights attack a wooden effigy of a Turk.

Chianciano Terme

September: The Chianciano Biennale is a celebration of contemporary art, staged in uneven years (www.museodarte.org)

Cortona

June: The Tuscan Sun Festival features concerts, stars, wine and food events, and art exhibitions (www.tuscansunfestival.com).
Mid-August: Sagra della Bistecca – "Feast of the Beefsteak".
End of August/beginning of September: antiques fair.

Florence

Easter Day: Scoppio del Carro, the Explosion of the "Carriage" (actually fireworks on a float). Colourful musical processions.
Ascension Day: Festa del Grillo, Festival of the Crickets in the Cascine park. Sale of crickets and sweets.
End of April: Flower Show, Parterre, near Piazza Libertà – a riot of colour.
End of April, May and June: Maggio Musicale Fiorentino – performances of opera, ballet and classical music.
Saturday in late June: Notte Bianca in Oltrarno – all-night festivities, music and food in and around Piazza Santo Spirito.
July–August: Estate Fiorentina – Florence's summer festival.
June–September: Estate Fiesolana in Fiesole (just outside Florence) – music, dance, opera, cinema and theatre.
24 June: San Giovanni – Florence's patron saint's day, with a holiday in the city and an evening firework display near Piazzale Michelangelo.
June: Calcio in costume (Calcio Fiorentino) – football in medieval costume in Piazza Santa Croce.
7 September: night festival of the Rificolona (lanterns) – procession of carts, lanterns and singers.
First three weeks of December: German Christmas Market – Piazza Santa Croce becomes a festive German market with decorations, mulled wine, sausage and beer, and other German specialities. For Florence events, see www.comune.fi.it.

Lucca

July: One of Tuscany's best festivals – with big-name international bands in Piazza Anfiteatro and a range of venues around town.
September – first weekend. Festival of Flowers.
September: Luminara di Santa Croce – a religious procession.

Lucignano

Last two Sundays in May: Maggiolata Lucignanese festival that includes a procession of carts decorated with allegorical scenes in flowers.

Massa Marittima

Sunday following May 20 and the second Sunday in August: Balestro del Girifalco – crossbow competition.

Montalcino

Last Sunday in October: Sagra del Tordo – Thrush Festival. Pageant, costume ball, banquet and archery at the fortress.

Monticchiello

End of July–early August: Il Teatro Povero – "The Poor Theatre" presents a performance written by locals about locals.

Pienza

First Sunday of September: Fiera del Cacio – a fair devoted to Pienza's famous cheese.

Pisa

May and June: concerts at various annual festivals and fairs, especially during the Gioco del Ponte on the last Sunday of June.
16–17 June: Luminaria di San Ranieri – thousands of candles light up buildings along the Arno. Boat race in the evening of the second day.
Last Sunday in June: Gioco del Ponte.
September: The annual Anima Mundi International Festival of Sacred Music takes place in Pisa Cathedral. Tel: 050-835 029; www. opapisa.it.

Pistoia

25 July: Giostra dell'Orso – a mock battle between a wooden bear and 12 knights in costume on Piazza del Duomo.

San Gimignano

July–September: Summer Fair, Estate Sangimignanese – varied programme of events, including ballet, concerts and cinema.

Siena

28–30 April: Feast of St Catherine.
2 July and 16 August: Il Palio traditional horse race. For tickets and hotel bookings, plan six months in advance (www.ilpalio.org).
July: Sienese Music Week – performances of opera, symphonies and chamber music.
End of July: Incontri in Terra di Siena – chamber-music festival featuring top-quality concerts held in stunning settings south of Siena.
13 December: Festa di Santa Lucia – ceramics festival.

Torre del Lago

July and August: Puccini Opera Festival, Torre del Lago, near the composer's villa on Lake Massaciuccoli (www.puccinifestival.it).

Viareggio

February: Carnevale – one of the best carnivals in Italy.

Volterra

First Sunday in September: Torneo di Tiro con la Balestra – crossbow tournament.

OUTDOOR ACTIVITIES

Sources of Information

For information about green tourism and outdoor activities, contact the nearest office of ENIT, the Italian national tourist board (see page 279). Also check the Tuscan Regional Tourism website, www.turismo.intoscana.it.

In English, the most comprehensive guide to green tourism is *Wild Italy* (by Tim Jepson, Sheldrake Press, 2005).

Hiking

Hiking (usually called "trekking" in Italian) is a popular activity in Tuscany. The region is well served by tough, long-distance trails for serious hikers. But more casual (or less-experienced) hikers should be wary of embarking on any trail without fully researching it, especially given the idiosyncrasies of some Tuscan signposting and maps. At the easy end of the spectrum, the region abounds in short walks, whether along the Versilia seafront or in regional parks, such as the Maremma. The middle spectrum of mixed-ability walkers, those wishing for a walking holiday of at least several days, softened by great scenery, food and wine, are better served by a dedicated walking-tour operator.

Specialist UK tour operators

Whether opting for a self-guided or accompanied walking holiday, booking through a specialist often ensures a better deal, along with tried-and-tested routes, not subject to the vagaries of regional maps or to "lost in translation" itineraries. These tours follow the operator's wonderfully detailed route, and generally include

the transporting of your luggage to the following hotel, which can be luxurious, or a simple farm-stay.

Make the most of walks that combine hills, history and cosy inns by booking through a specialist offering a portfolio of Tuscan trails:
Collett's (tel: +44 1799-513 331; www.colletts.co.uk)
Gusto tours (tel: +44 07515-941 879; www.gustocycling.com)
Inntravel (tel: +44 01653-617 001; www.inntravel.co.uk)
Headwater (tel: 01606-828 431; www.headwater.com)
Hedonistic Hiking (tel: +44 1858-565 148; www.hedonistichiking.com.au)
Long-distance hiking: Serious hikers can follow the Italian Alpine Club (CAI or Club Alpino Italiano: www.cai.it) paths, which crisscross the region. There is a branch of the CAI in Florence (tel: 055-612 0467; www.caifirenze.it).

Two long-distance paths, Apuane Trekking (a four-day trek) and the Grande Escursione Apenninica (GEA, taking 25 days, end to end, along the ridges of the Apennines), have well-marked trails and can be joined at various points. Shorter waymarked trails (such as those in the Maremma or Chianti regions) tend to be less well signposted, so take good local maps (such as those produced by CAI).

All walkers should bear in mind that there is no public right of way across private property. Be particularly vigilant during the hunting season, especially on Sundays. If travelling without a car, forward planning is required. City-to-city transport is generally fine (often quicker by bus than train), but rural transport is poor: either of the "two buses a day" variety, or simply nonexistent.

Areas to Explore

The following are guidelines to some of the more accessible areas of natural beauty. Also see: www.parks.it (Italian Parks and Nature Reserves).
Abetone and the Tuscan-Emilian border
Abetone makes a good base for exploring this forested mountain region, also known as the Alto Appennino. The town has a profusion of Swiss chalet-style hotels. The picturesque medieval centres of Fiumalbo and Cutigliano make good alternative bases but have fewer facilities and lack Abetone's more dramatic Alpine views.
Transport: by public transport, it is quicker to reach Abetone by bus from Modena (in Emilia-Romagna) than by other routes.

Hiking trail in the Apuan Alps.

Apuan Alps (Alpi Apuane)
Maps and information on mountain refuges are available from Massa, Carrara and most coastal tourist offices. Numerous one-day hikes are available through the Alps, with typical starting points being the villages of Stazzema and Levigliano on the western flanks of the mountains. Almost as appealing is a car journey along the winding mountain roads towards the interior.
Arezzo/Pratovecchio
The Parco delle Foreste Casentinesi (www.parks.it) straddles Tuscany and Emilia-Romagna. The park headquarters is at Pratovecchio, Via G. Brocchi 7; tel: 0575-50301. Alternatively, contact the Arezzo tourist office for more information.
Lunigiana and Garfagnana
Serious hikers should request the Trekking in Lunigiana map, with long-distance trails beginning in Aulla, Fosdinovo, Frignoli and Sassalbo. To appreciate the rural atmosphere, avoid staying in such fashionable coastal resorts as Forte dei Marmi. Instead, choose the Garfagnana hinterland, where Castelnuovo di Garfagnana is picturesque, and Barga, the main town, makes a gorgeous base. Both are convenient for **Parco dell'Orecchiella**, the national park, 15km (9 miles) north of Castelnuovo di Garfagnana. San Pellegrino in Alpe, 16km (9.5 miles) northeast of Castelnuovo, is appealing in summer and winter.
Transport: coastal transport is good, with transport into the Garfagnana hinterland less so. If you are planning to explore Garfagnana and Lunigiana by train or bicycle, a small branch line connects Lucca with Aulla and allows bicycles on the train.
The Maremma
If you want to be by the sea, stay in Santo Stefano, Talamone, Orbetello or Castiglione della Pescaia. Otherwise, opt for a ranch or farm near the

park. **Transport:** visitors using public transport should go to Orbetello (by bus or train) or to Monte Argentario (by bus from Grosseto). To visit the nature reserve is trickier: by train to Alberese station (only a couple of trains a day, from Grosseto), then a taxi.

The Mugello

The best website is www.mugello toscana.it. Avoid staying in Borgo San Lorenzo, the main town, which is not very attractive, or in the semi-industrialised valleys. Instead, choose the countryside or such villages as Vicchio. **Transport:** for those who wish to explore the Mugello by train or bicycle, the Faenza–Florence train service stops at stations along the Apennine ridge (Vicchio, Marradi, Ronta), ideal places to begin trekking.

The Val d'Orcia, Montalcino, San Gimignano, Volterra

Expect a range of dreamy trails in the Val d'Orcia that combine rolling hills and fortified villages with a mystical atmosphere. Hiking trails linking San Gimignano and Volterra are superb, including several by Headwater (www. headwater.com).

The Via Francigena pilgrimage route passes through some of the loveliest areas, including the Chianti, Lucca, and the Sienese countryside around Montalcino – en route to Rome and Canterbury (www. viafrancigena.com).

Green Sites

These include nature reserves, caves, botanical gardens and museums of rural life. The classification of Italian conservation areas is chaotic and confusing. (See: www.parks.it, the website of Italian Parks and Nature Reserves).

Abetone

On the Tuscan-Emilian border, Abetone is the main ski and summer resort in the northern Apennines (see page 137). It is also the centre for infor-mation on GEA long-distance trails and shorter botanical rambles. For details, contact the Abetone tourist office.

The Apuan Alps and Lunigiana

The Frignoli Botanical Gardens, near Sassalbo (tel: 055-949 688; June–Sept daily 10am–6pm) have an arboretum and display the full range of plants grown in the Apuan Alps. In Aulla, in Lunigiana, there is an interesting natural-history museum and ecological centre set in historic Brunella castle (tel: 0187-409 077; www.fortezzadellabrunella.it; Tue–Sun Nov–Feb 9am–noon, 2–5pm, Mar–May and Oct 9am–noon, 3–6pm, Jun–Sept 9am–noon, 4–7pm),

as well as neighbouring botanical gardens. From Aulla, visitors can organise tours of glacial moraines, karst gorges and caves.

Garfagnana

Here, **Parco dell'Orecchiella**, 15km (9 miles) north of Castelnuovo di Garfagnana, is the chief regional park in the Lucca stretch of the Apennines. The main entry point is Corfino. There are also botanical gardens nearby, at Villa Collemandina, Pania di Corfino (tel: 0583-644 911). The local visitors' centre (tel: 0583-619 002) includes a civilised mountain refuge and nature trails. Contact the Comunità Montana Garfagnana (tel: 0583-644 911) or the tourist office in Barga, the region's main town. The Orrido dei Bottri reserve is a narrow gorge with sheer cliff faces that can be crossed by serious hikers.

The Maremma

In the Maremma region, the Centro Visite Parco della Maremma (tel: 0564-407 098) is closed to traffic. Entry points are Marina di Alberese (the coast and lovely beach) or Alberese (the landward side, with the park ticket office, shuttle bus, guiding service and free tasting of local produce and wine). The Alberese entrance provides access to the park on foot or by means of the park shuttle bus. In addition to short trails, there are longer trails of 5 or 4km (3 or 2.5 miles, lasting about three hours). The waymarked paths are not wholly reliable. It is advisable to take drinking water and a picnic. In Alberese, canoes can be hired to explore the canals, and horse riding is also available.

The Mugello

In the Mugello, the hamlet of Grezzano has Casa d'Erci, which is a farmhouse converted into a museum of rural life and peasant culture. Check opening times on tel: (+39) 338-688 0647.

Cyclists on the Chianti route.

Cycling

Cycling is increasingly popular in Tuscany, especially on the Chianti route, and in key cities such as Florence, Pisa and Lucca, where bike hire is easy.

Cycling in the city

Lucca: hire a bike at the Rent Bike Lucca in the square in front of the railway station (www.tourist centerlucca.com) or at Barbetti, Via Anfiteatro 23; tel: 0583-954 444 and Cicli Bizzarri Piazza S. Maria 32; tel: 0583-496 682. Also see the advice in the chapter on Lucca (see page 133).

Florence: there is the **Bike Sharing** initiative, www.bicifirenze.it, operating in Florence and offering bike rental at very reasonable prices. Also contact: **Alinari**, via San Zanobi 38r; tel: 055-280 500; www.alinari rental.com or Florence by Bike, Via San Zanobi 54r; tel: 055-488 992; www.florencebybike.it.

Gusto tours (www.gustocycling.com) rents bicycles, including racers, to villas, hotels, and individual holiday-makers anywhere in Tuscany.

Cycle routes

These are great for families as an alternative to a day on the beach. **Viareggio:** from Parco di Migliarino and Torre del Lago, where Giacomo Puccini lived.

Viareggio to Marina di Massa: an easy 23km cycle along the seafront.

Viareggio seafront to Lido di Camaiore, Marina di Pietrasanta and Forte dei Marmi.

Pisa (a harder ride): from the seafront to the top of Monte Serra, crossing nature reserves and passing Etruscan sites and medieval castles (www.turismo.pisa.it).

In the Maremma, see www.natural mentetoscana.it.

Wildlife-watching

In theory, the Arcipelago Toscano (Tuscan Archipelago, including Elba and the other islands) is a marine park, but in reality much remains unprotected. Illegal hunting continues in the larger parks. The best-run sanctuaries tend to be the smallest, often those administered by the Worldwide Fund for Nature (WWF, www.wwf.it/oasi) or by LIPU, the Italian bird protection society (for which there is a great need). For more information on parks, see Wild Tuscany chapter and A Walk in the Park, page 65.

Dolphin-watching: dolphins live in the waters off Versilia. Between April and September visitors can join research groups that look for dolphins and whales. Contact the CETUS centre in Viareggio (www.cetusresearch.eu) and Versilia tourist office (www.aptversilia.it)

Wildlife sanctuary: the **Oasi di Bolgheri** is the best bird and wildlife sanctuary, a mixture of scrub, lakes and marshy grasslands. This WWF reserve is home to native and migratory birds and small mammals such as wild boar. The reserve lies 10km (6 miles) south of Cecina and is reached by train to Bolgheri. Contact Marina di Cecina or Livorno provincial tourist offices for details.

Bird-watching: Bottaccio Wood, outside Castelvecchio di Compito, in Lucca province, is a marshland nature reserve good for birds and best visited in spring (tel: 0583-56008).

The lakeside habitat at **Lago di Massaciuccoli** is home to migratory and wintering wildfowl as well as native species, including flamingoes, geese, ducks, cranes and tern. The region's lone surviving lagoon has suffered from intensive shooting but survives nonetheless. For details of opening times and tours, contact Pisa provincial tourist office.

Lago di Burano (tel: 0564-898 829) in the Maremma, south of Alberese, offers one of the best bird-watching opportunities in Tuscany. This is the southern-most of two lagoons beside the peninsula of Monte Argentario. This WWF lagoon is home to falcons, cormorants, the black-winged stilt, purple and grey herons, with peregrines, ospreys and marsh harriers using the lagoons as feeding grounds. (By road, the reserve is at the Capalbio Scalo exit on the SS1; by rail, travel to the small Capalbio station.) For details of opening times, contact the Parco della Maremma (as above).

Horse riding

There are over 40 centres belonging to the National Association of Equestrian Tourism (Fitetrec Ante; Largo Lauro de Bosis 15, 00135 Rome; tel: 06-326 50231; www.fitetrec-ante.it) or to the Federazione Italiana Sport Equestri (Viale Tiziano 74, 00196 Rome; tel: 06-3600 3753; www.fise.it).

Here are some suggestions for riding near Tuscany's main cities:

Maneggio Belvedere, Località. Filetta 58010 Sorano (Grosseto province); tel: 0564-615 465; www.maneggiobelvedere.it.

Club Ippico Senese, Località Pian del Lago, Siena; tel: 0577-318 316; www.clubippicosenese.it.

Equestrian Escapes (tel: +44 01829-781 123; www.equestrian-escapes.com) offers tailor-made riding holidays on the Tuscan–Umbrian border.

For horse-riding centres elsewhere in Tuscany, call the **Centro Ippico Toscano**, Via Vespucci 5r, Florence; tel: 055-315 621.

Fishing

For freshwater fishing, foreigners need a temporary membership of FIPS (Federazione Italiana della Pesca Sportiva) and a government licence issued by the Provincial Administration. Sport fishing can be practised both from the shore and from a boat. In some ports, a special permit is required from the Harbourmaster's Office.

Golf

There are some decent courses, often with spas attached; the best include: Golf Club Ugolino, Via Chiantigiana, Grassina; tel: 055-230 1009; www.golfugolino.it
Montecatini Golf and Country Club (18 holes), Via dei Brogi 32, Località Pievaccia, Monsummano Terme; tel: 0572-62218; www.montecatini golf.com
Cosmopolitan Golf and Country Club, Viale Pisorno 60, Tirrenia-Pisa; tel: 050-33633; www.cosmopolitangolf.it
Golf Club Punta Ala; tel: 0564-922 121; www.puntaala.net/golf

Skiing

Tuscany has a major ski resort at Abetone in the Apennines, north of Pistoia, extending over four valleys with 30km (19 miles) of trails. For information on ski passes and pistes, call Abetone tourist office; tel: 0573-630 145 or visit www.abetone.com.

Watersports and Diving

At all Tuscan sea resorts it is possible to water-ski and row with hired boats. Yacht-chartering facilities are also available in the resorts of Marina di Pisa and Tirrenia, and Porto Azzurro, **Elba** (www.aptelba.it).

Diving is very popular in Tuscany, the best areas being around the Argentario on the southern coast, and the islands Giglio, Giannutri, Elba and Capraia. There is red coral, a huge variety of Mediterranean underwater flora, and even a couple of wrecks off Giannutri. Many of the seaside ports have diving clubs that take boats out regularly.

Elba Diving Centre, Marciana Marina; tel: 0565-904 256; www.elba diving.it
Giglio Diving Club, Via della Torre Campese; tel: (+39) 348 582 8426; www.gigliodiving.it.

Swimming Pools

Many Tuscan hotels, villas and *agriturismo* (farm-stay) places have pools, and there are public pools in most towns, although these often have limited opening hours.

Public swimming pools in Florence: Piscina Le Pavoniere, Viale della Catena 2; tel: 055-362 233. During the summer. There is also a bar and pizzeria here.
Piscina Nannini, Lungarno Aldo Moro 6; tel: 055-677 521. Olympic-size pool that is open-air during the summer months.

Siena has its own Piscina Comunale, Piazza Amendola; tel: 0577-47496.

Spectator Sports

Football is the national sport. Almost every city and village has a team and the most important national championship is the "Serie A" (Premiership), the winner of which is eligible to play in the Champions League, against other top European teams. The season runs from September to May. Florence usually does well but has fierce battles with Juventus, its loathed rival. Matches here tend to be safe, family affairs. If you want to see a game, ask your hotel concierge to help.

Horse racing is also popular and there is a racecourse in Florence's Cascine park: Ippodromo le Cascine; tel: 055-4226 076.

TRANSPORT

EATING OUT

ACTIVITIES

A – Z

LANGUAGE

For tickets to any sporting event, consult the local tourist office or, alternatively, buy the pink *Gazzetta dello Sport* newspaper, which gives the lowdown.

SHOPPING

What to Buy

The quality is exceptionally high, especially in terms of craftsmanship, but prices are generally reasonable. Suggested buys are:
Fashion: dresses, suits, hats, gloves, linen, silk ties and shirts, scarves, knitwear, designer labels and jewellery.
Leather goods: prices are not rock-bottom but the quality is often excellent and the designs appealing. Shoes and handbags are particularly good buys, but there are also boxes and belts, luggage, briefcases and wallets.
Fabrics: silk, linen, wool and cotton.
Handicrafts: lace and tablecloths; pottery, ceramics and porcelain; gold- and silverware; alabaster and marble objects; woodwork; straw and raffia goods; glass and crystal work; art books and reproductions; marbled paper; rustic household goods; prints; antiques; reproduction furniture.
Alcohol: regional wines – along with the well-known Chianti, Montalcino and Montepulciano, wines from the coastal Maremma such as Sassicaia and Ornellaia are celebrated Super Tuscans; also try Vin Santo, Tuscan dessert wine.
Food: extra-virgin olive oil, herbs, locally made pasta, farmhouse cheeses, bottled vegetables, truffles, dried mushrooms, cured ham, salami etc.

Shopping Hours

Food stores and general shops open 8.30am–1pm and 3.30 or 4–7.30pm. They stay open a little later in the summer. Many of the bigger supermarkets stay open through lunch and close at around 8pm. Department stores and other shops in bigger cities stay open all day (9.30am–7.30/8pm), and there is now limited Sunday trading in some places. Many clothes shops are closed on Monday mornings.

Where to Shop

Chain stores such as Oviesse and Standa can be found in most towns in Tuscany, and the upmarket Rinascente is in Florence.

Open-air markets are held once or twice a week in almost all tourist resorts and towns.
Supermarkets are found in most big centres but are otherwise more scarce.
Tobacconists (called *tabacchi*) sell bus tickets, stamps, cigarettes and tobacco.

Outlet Shopping

The Arno Valley is the cradle of many clothes factories for some of Italy's top designer labels. They tend to be located between Pontassieve and Incisa Val d'Arno, and have retail outlets with huge discounts. Avoid weekends. The best retail outlets, within easy reach of Florence and Arezzo, include:
The Mall, Via Europe 8, Leccio Regello; tel: 055-865 7775; www.themall. it. Gucci, Cavalli, Giorgio Armani, Sergio Rossi, Yves Saint Laurent, Bottega Veneta, Loro Piana, Agnona, Tod's, Hogan, La Perla, Salvatore Ferragamo, Ungaro, Ermenegildo Zegna, Valentino, Alexander McQueen, Balenciaga, Burberry, Fendi, Stella McCartney, Yohji Yamamoto. Best for bags and shoes. Take the free shuttle from your hotel.
Fendi, Via Pian dell'Isola 66, Rignano sull'Arno; tel: 055-834 981. Best for accessories.
Barberino, Via Meucci snc, Barberino del Mugello; tel: 055-842 161, www.mcarthurglen.it/barberino. Outlet of over 100 stores including designer fashion: Bottega Verde, Bruno Magli, Coccinelle, D&G, Furla, Guess, Missoni, Prada, Puma.
Dolce e Gabbana, Via Santa Maddalena 49, Santa Maria Maddalena; tel: 055-833 1300. Everything from accessories and clothes to household designer goods.
Prada and Miu Miu, Località Levanella, Montevarchi; tel: 055-978 9481. A limited selection, but great for bags, shoes and accessories – if you get there early, or queue.

For more information on outlet shopping, go to www.outlet-firenze. com. Dedicated fashionistas may consider investing in a copy of *Lo Scopri Occasioni* (published in English as Designer Bargains in Italy), which has over 1,000 outlet addresses.

Shopping in Florence

Despite tourism, consumerism and high labour costs, Florence still has a reputation as a city with high standards of craftsmanship, from silver jewellery to marbled paper. If you wish to visit craftsmen at work, check the craft list on www.turismo.

intoscana.it or request the leaflet from the tourist office. It lists the main craftspeople, including the Santa Croce leather school, on Piazza Santa Croce, a popular place to watch skilled Florentine leather-workers.

Most artisan workshops can be found in the Oltrarno neighbourhood, near the Pitti Palace and Piazza Santo Spirito.

Antiques

There are two main areas for antiques shops: Via Maggio and the surrounding streets in the Oltrarno and Borgo Ognissanti, west of the centre. There is a wide choice of goods, but you are unlikely to find a bargain.

Books

Feltrinelli Internazionale, Via de'Cerretani 30/32; tel: (+39) 199 151 173. The best bookshop in Florence, with a range of foreign-language books and guides.
Seeber-Melbookstore, Via Cerretani 16r; tel: 055-287 339; www.melbook store.it. A range of books and music as well as a café.
The Paperback Exchange, Via delle Oche 4r; tel: 055-293 460; www.papex.it. Just south of the Duomo, this is no ordinary bookshop: it stocks just about every book ever written on Florence. It also has a vast stock of quality second-hand English and American paperbacks.

Boutiques

Florence is full of top designer boutiques. The most elegant street is the newly pedestrianised Via de' Tornabuoni where Gucci, Valentino and other big names in fashion have their outlets. Other exclusive streets are the Via Calzaiuoli and Via Roma (for leather goods), Via della Vigna Nuova and Via del Parione.

The top designer shops are:
Giorgio Armani, Via de' Tornabuoni 48r; tel: 055-219 041. For a more affordable Armani, visit Emporio Armani, Piazza Strozzi 14–16r; tel: 055-284 315.
Cavalli, Via de' Tornabuoni 83r; tel: 055-239 6226. The Florentine designer's store, with a stylish café, Giàcosa.
Dolce e Gabbana, Via della Vigna Nuova 27r; tel: 055-281 003. Sexy, stylish, often outrageous.
Enrico Coveri, Lungarno Guicciardini 19; tel: 055-287 676. Flamboyant, colourful.
Ferragamo, Via de' Tornabuoni 4r/14r; tel: 055-292 123. The famous Florentine shoemakers have now branched out into accessories

and clothes. Upstairs, the Ferragamo Museum (www.ferragamo.com; daily 10am–7.30pm) hosts various historical shoe exhibitions.
Gucci, Via de' Tornabuoni 73r; tel: 055-264 011. The range has expanded, but belts and handbags remain its trademark.
Max Mara, Via de' Tornabuoni 66/68/70r; tel: 055-214 123. Haute couture clothes and accessories.
Prada, Via de' Tornabuoni 51–55r and 67r; tel: 055-283 439. Gorgeous accessories and shoes.
Emilio Pucci, Via de' Tornabuoni 20–22r; tel: 055-265 8082. Famous for its retro prints, beautiful scarves and dresses.
Raspini, Via Martelli 5/7r; tel: 055-239 8562. Upscale boutique carrying top brands.
Valentino, Via dei Tosinghi 52r; tel: 055-293 142.
Also worth checking out are:
Ethic, Borgo Albizi 37; tel: 055-234 4413. One of few fashionable boutiques to offer clothing at reasonable prices.
Christian Dior, Via de' Tornabuoni 1r; tel: 055-266 9111.
Hogan, Via de' Tornabuoni 97r; tel: 055-274 1013.
Trussardi, Via de' Tornabuoni 34/36; tel: 055-219 902.

Ceramics

Sbigoli Terracotte, Via Sant' Egidio 4r; tel: 055-247 9713. Good choice of hand-painted ceramics in traditional and contemporary designs.

Fabrics

Antico Setificio, Via L. Bartolini 4; tel: 055-213 861; www.antico setificiofiorentino.com. Fabrics made traditionally, above all silk, still woven on 18th-century looms.
Casa dei Tessuti, Via de' Pecori 20–24; tel: 055-215 961; www.casa deitessuti.com. Fine silks, linens and woollens in a historic Florentine store.

Gloves

Madova, Via Guicciardini 1r; tel: 055-210 204; www.madova.com. Every kind of gorgeous glove imaginable.

Jewellery

There is still a flourishing jewellery trade in Florence (particularly on the Ponte Vecchio and in Oltrarno, on the south side of the river), though most gold jewellery is now made in Arezzo. The following traditional goldsmiths and silversmiths remain:
Brandimarte, Via U Foscolo 6; tel: 055-230 411. Hand-crafted silver and jewellery.

Donato Zaccaro, Sdrucciolo de' Pitti 12r; tel: 055-212 243.
Gatto Bianco, Borgo SS Apostoli 12r; tel: 055-282 989. Contemporary designs in gold and silver.
Maurizio Casprini, Via Rosso Fiorentino 2a; tel: 055-710 008. Silversmith.

Exclusive Jewellery
If you can afford to push the boat out, these are some major names:
Buccellati, Ponte Vecchio 2r; tel: 055-215 502.
Bulgari, Via de' Tornabuoni 56r; tel: 055-218 012.
Torrini, Piazza del Duomo 10r; tel: 055-230 2401.

Leather

Quality ranges from hand-tooled creations to shoddy goods aimed at undiscerning tourists. For top-of-the-range quality (and prices), start with the designer boutiques in the Via de' Tornabuoni or in streets around the Piazza della Repubblica. Try the following outlets:
Il Bisonte, Via del Parione 31r; tel: 055-215 722. Leather goods at high prices.
Furla, Via dei Calzaiuoli 47r; tel: 055-238 2883. Bags and accessories in contemporary designs.
Raspini, Via Martelli 5/7r; tel: 055-239 8562. Superb leather bags and coats.

For more down-to-earth prices, head for the San Lorenzo market northwest of the Duomo, where numerous street stalls sell shoes, bags, belts and wallets; you can also try the Santa Croce area.

Marbled Paper

Marbled paper is very closely associated with Florence and many of the designs echo ancient themes or Medici crests. With their beautiful colours, vibrant patterns and particular smells, the shops are a joy to visit.

Jewellery shop on Ponte Vecchio.

Giulio Giannini e Figlio, Piazza Pitti 37r; tel: 055-212 621. Florence's longest-established marbled-paper shop.
Il Papiro, Via Cavour 49r; tel: 055-215 262; Piazza del Duomo 24r; tel: 055-281 628.
Il Torchio, Via de' Bardi 17; tel: 055-234 2862. Cheaper than some other shops, you also see the artisans at work.

Markets

Many neighbourhoods have a weekly market. Try the following:
Straw Market (Mercato del Porcellino): hand-embroidered work, Florentine straw, leather goods, wooden objects and scarves; the most touristic market.
Flea Market (Mercato delle Pulci, Piazza dei Ciompi): basically junk, but great fun.
Sant'Ambrogio (Piazza Ghiberti): food, fruit and vegetables (cheaper than San Lorenzo).
San Lorenzo Market (Mercato di San Lorenzo, Piazza San Lorenzo): the fascinating covered market sells vegetables, fruit, meat and cheeses etc, while the surrounding streets are filled with stalls selling clothes, shoes, leather goods and jewellery.
Cascine Market (Mercato delle Cascine, Tuesday mornings only): fresh produce, household goods and clothing.
Artisan Market (Piazza Santo Spirito, 2nd Sun of the month, Sept–June): craft market with some organic food.

Pharmacy

Officina Profumo Farmaceutica di Santa Maria Novella, Via della Scala 16; tel: 055-216 276. Housed in a frescoed chapel, this fascinating perfumery and herbalist was founded by monks in 1612. It sells herbal remedies and beautifully packaged perfumes.

Shoes

Florence is still a good place to buy shoes at reasonable prices.
Cresti, Via Pietrapiana 75; tel: 055-240 856. Beautiful shoes at much lower prices than at Ferragamo.
Ferragamo, Via de' Tornabuoni 4r/14r; tel: 055-292 123. Italy's most prestigious shoemaker, providing hand-tooled shoes and beautifully crafted ready-to-wear collections.

The roads leading from the Duomo to Santa Maria Novella station have a good range of slightly cheaper shoe shops.

Shopping in Siena

Clothes and Shoes

The main shopping streets in Siena are Banchi di Sopra and Via di Città. They are lined with chain stores and individual stores selling a range of clothes and footwear.

Crafts

A wide choice of wrought-iron and copper, ceramics, crystal and stained glass. **Giorgi Leonardo & Co**, at Antica Siena e Martini Marisa, Piazza del Campo 28 (tel: 0577-46496; www.anticasiena.it) sells beautiful blue and yellow porcelain, while **Il Papiro** (Via di Città) sells handmade paper and gifts. **Acquerelli Originali** (Via Monna Agnese 14–16), a tiny store near the Duomo, sells hand-painted watercolours.

Food and Wine

Siena is known for its pastries and cakes, particularly *panforte*, which is made from a sweet dough, flavoured with vanilla and full of candied citrus fruits. The most famous maker of such specialities is **Bar Pasticceria Nannini** at Via Banchi di Sopra 24 and **Nannini Toselli**, at Viale Toselli 94a (www.gruppOnannini.it).

Siena Province produces superb wines including Chianti, Brunello di Montalcino and Vino Nobile di Montepulciano. The **Fortezza Medicea** (tel: 0577-228 811; www.enoteca-italiana.it) displays and sells regional wines in the fortress (Mon–Tue noon–7.30 pm, Wed–Sat noon–midnight). **Gino Cacino**, Piazza Mercato 31 (tel: 0577-223 076) sells superb cheeses, salami and hams.

Shopping in Volterra

Crafts

Ali, Piazza Martiri della Liberta; tel: 0588-86078; www.alialabastro.it.

This is one of the oldest and best alabaster workshops in town. Admire the wide range of picture frames, chess pieces, mosaics, vases, table lamps and sculptures – all made by local craftsmen.

OTHER ACTIVITIES

Children

Tuscany has much to offer children of all ages, from medieval castles to ice creams galore and plenty of child-friendly restaurants. There are several good parks, nature reserves and numerous opportunities for horse riding, cycling and swimming. Much of the coast of Tuscany, particularly the well-equipped resorts near Viareggio and the beaches on islands such as Elba, is also great for children.

Tuscan festivals can be fun, especially the Lenten carnivals, the horse races, the jousting, boat pageants, and all the tiny food festivals that take place throughout the region. To find out what's on, above all in summer, check the listings in *La Repubblica* or *La Nazione*, as well as enquiring at the tourist offices. If you read Italian, buy *Firenze Spettacolo*, which has a good children's section: *Città & Ragazzi*.

Some of the suitable places in Tuscany for children are:
The Boboli Gardens (Giardini di Boboli) in Florence are fun for children to clamber around. There is an amphitheatre, strange statues and grottoes, and a handy café.
The **Museo dei Ragazzi in Palazzo Vecchio** offers special children-friendly tours of the Palace led by actors in costume, as well as activities and workshops.
The Cascine, Florence's other main park with a tiny zoo.
Giardino dei Tarrocchi (tel: 0564-895 122, near Capalbio) is a bizarre garden full of Niki de Saint-Phalle's colourful fantasy figures.
Ludoteca Centrale, Via Fibbiai 2, Florence; tel: 055-247 8386, is a fun children's centre with games, music and audiovisual equipment for the under-sixes.
Pinocchio Park (Parco di Pinocchio) at Collodi, near Pisa, is an obvious, if old-fashioned choice for children (tel: 0572-429 342; www.pinocchio.it; Mar–Oct daily 8.30am–sunset, Nov–Feb holidays and days before holidays 10am–sunset).
Pistoia Zoo, Via Pieve a Celle, Pistoia; tel: 0573-911 219;

www.zoodipistoia.it. Compact zoo, but one of the region's best.
Zoo Fauna Europa, just south of Poppi; tel: 0575-529 079. A conservation centre for such breeds as the lynx and the Apennine wolf. 9am–sunset.

Spas

Tuscany has a large number of authentic thermal spas, offering a range of health and beauty treatments from mud baths to hydro-massage, or just the opportunity to relax in hot springs. Check www.turismo.intoscana.it (look at the Terme e Golf section). The Consorzio Terme di Toscana, presso Terme di Montecatini (Via Manzoni 5; tel: 0572-910 357; www.termeditoscana. com) also provides information.

Here is a list of Tuscany's top thermal spas:
Bagni di Pisa, San Giuliano Terme; tel: 050-88501; www.bagnidipisa. com. Atmospheric spa resort, with distant views of the Leaning Tower – a romantic retreat.
Grotta Giusti Spa Resort, Monsummano Terme; tel: 0572-90771; www.grottagiustispa.com. Historic spa resort around an elegant villa that is proud of its restorative spa caverns and innovative treatments; golf course nearby.
Fonteverde Natural Spa Resort, San Casciano dei Bagni; tel: 0578 57241; www.fonteverdespa.com. A lovely rural setting. The spa is equally strong on Mediterranean and oriental treatments. One of the best spas in the country.
Petriolo Spa & Resort, Pari-Civitella Paganico; tel: 0564-9091; www.atahotels.it/petriolo. Timeless resort near Siena, offering everything from an Ayurvedic massage to sweating in a dry-ice cave.
Terme di Saturnia Spa & Golf Resort, Saturnia; tel: 0564-600 111; www.termedisaturnia.it. Fed by historic springs, this exclusive pampering resort boasts a peaceful setting in the Maremma. The sulphurous spa boasts hot springs, waterfalls and a recreation of Ancient Roman baths. Elegant suites and an 18-hole golf course.
Terme Sensoriali, Parco Acqua Santa, Chianciano Terme; tel: 848 800 243; www.termesensoriali. it. Innovative spa with an eclectic approach, from classic treatments based on the healing powers of the thermal springs to therapies inspired by Ayurveda.

TRANSPORT

A – Z

A HANDY SUMMARY
OF PRACTICAL INFORMATION

EATING OUT

ACTIVITIES

A – Z

LANGUAGE

A

Accommodation

The quality and choice of accommodation in Tuscany is extremely varied. Visitors can choose between a city palazzo, grand country villa, or a historic family-run hotel, a rented apartment or villa, a bucolic farm-stay holiday *(agriturismo)* or even, in the most popular cities, a private home stay. (This is not known as bed and breakfast since breakfast is not usually provided.)

Hotel rooms generally need to be booked well in advance in Florence and Siena. During local summer festivals, particularly the Sienese Palio and Arezzo's Giostra, it can become very difficult to find a room.

Attractive accommodation in the centre of Volterra and San Gimignano is popular, so early booking is advisable.

There is a huge variation in what you get for your money. A moderately priced hotel in Florence may be somewhat underwhelming, whereas the same money could buy you a luxurious 4-star room in a grand country house off the tourist track.

Generally speaking, "high season" in Tuscany is May to September. However, in towns this does not necessarily include August. In Florence, for instance, many of the more expensive hotels reduce their prices during this month. It can sometimes pay to bargain.

Many hotels with restaurants insist on a half- or full-board arrangement, especially in the high season. This ploy is particularly prevalent on the islands (eg Elba), in seaside resorts (eg Forte dei Marmi), in spa resorts (eg Montecatini Terme and Chianciano Terme), and where accommodation is in short supply.

Private Home Stays

This is a fairly new development in Tuscany, but it is a good way of meeting the locals while paying modest prices. In Florence and Siena, the homes are carefully graded from simple to luxurious.

In Florence, contact www. firenzealloggio.com for B&B accommodation booked online directly with the owners, and no booking charge. For B&B accommodation in Florence, Lucca, Pisa and Siena, book online through the reliable American website: www.bedandbreakfast.com. Also try **ANBBA** (Associazione Nazionale Bed & Breakfast e Affittacamere): www.anbba.it.

In Siena, request the *Affittacamere* (private lodgings) booklet of addresses from the tourist office (APT, Piazza Campo 56, Siena; tel: 0577-280 551). The list includes private accommodation in the whole of Siena Province, including San Gimignano, Montalcino and the Sienese Chianti.

Agriturismo

Farm stays *(agriturismo)* are an excellent way of experiencing the Tuscan countryside while staying on a farm or a wine estate. Standards vary widely from simple, rustic accommodation at low prices to relatively luxurious surroundings, complete with swimming pool. Before booking, check the website if they have one, or insist on a description or a photo, since many may be modern and fail to match up to the visitor's romantic image of Tuscany. Some farms, however, are genuine

16th-century wine and oil estates. There is usually the opportunity to buy local produce on site and meals are sometimes provided. For obvious reasons, you will normally need a car to make the most of a farm stay.

Reservations: During peak season, it is best to book in advance. Official accommodation tends to be booked for a minimum of one week, but individual arrangements for weekends and overnight stays are often possible, especially during mid- and low season.

Every local tourist authority produces farm-stay booklets. Or you can browse the following websites: www.agriturismo.com; www.agriturismo. net; and www.agriturist.it. Also try Terranostra, tel: 064-899 3209; www.terranostra.it; and www.toscana. campagnamica.it.

Rural Stays

These overlap with farm stays but can include country houses or even entire restored medieval villages (such as Sovicille, near Siena). In general, there is a working farm attached to the accommodation, or at least the opportunity to sample or buy wine, oil and local produce grown on the estate. As with farm stays, the accommodation offered can vary from simple rooms to self-contained apartments. The owners often use the profits from letting to reinvest in the restoration of the family estate or village. With rural stays, the emphasis is on country living in traditional buildings rather than in luxurious villa accommodation.

Many of the owners may speak basic English, French or German, but at least a smattering of Italian is appreciated. Always request detailed descriptions and directions.

Local tourist offices are a good source for recommendations (see page 280). Extensive listings, supported by images, can also be found on www. agriturismo.com and www.agriturismo. net. The following are some typical examples of rural stays, but are just a handful among countless options:

La Ripolina, Località Pieve di Piana, 53022 Buonconvento, Siena Province; tel: 0577-282 280; www.laripolina.it. Most of the holiday apartments are in converted farmhouses; one is in a fortified abbey with a 10th-century wall. Fresh farm produce available.

Agriturismo Podere San Lorenzo, Via Allori 80, 56048 Volterra, Pisa; tel: 0588-39080; www.agriturismo-volterra.it. Podere San Lorenzo is a working olive farm that has nine guest apartments in the farmhouse. Organic produce from its garden is used in the preparation of delicious meals served in an old Franciscan chapel. Cooking classes are available and there is a chemical-free swimming pool.

San Savino, Val di Chio, Località Santa Lucia 89/a, 52043 Castiglion Fiorentino, Arezzo province; tel: 0575-651 000; www.agriturismo-sansavino. it. This restored 11th-century monastery overlooks, a lake, olive groves and woods and offers several apartments (plus pool and stables).

Villa Igea, Torre Alta, 55060 Ponte del Giglio, Lucca province; tel: 0583-353 122; www.villa-igea.biz. This charming traditional Tuscan villa and cottage is set among woodland and olive groves overlooking a valley. Home-produced extra-virgin olive oils and tastings.

La Parrina, km 146 Via Aurelia, Località Parrina, 58010 Albinia, Grosseto province; tel: 0564-862 626; www.parrina.it. This long-established agricultural estate is set among vineyards, olive groves and orchards. The rooms and dining rooms are decorated with an unfussy elegance that makes you feel right at home. To prove you're on a working farm, you may be woken early by the sound of tractors. Rooms and apartments; swimming pool; chapel; farm shop; restaurant and wine tasting; and bicycles.

Villa and Apartment Rentals

One of the most popular ways of visiting Tuscany is to stay in a rented villa or apartment. They do not come cheap, but you have the benefit of independence, and the freedom to cook for yourself using delicious fresh Tuscan produce. Prices vary enormously, depending on the season and the luxuriousness of the accommodation. The following agencies deal with rentals:

To Tuscany: UK: (+44) 12128-67 782, e-mail: dympna@to-tuscany.com. US/Canada: (toll-free) 888 768-4401; email: dick@to-tuscany.com, www.to-tuscany.com. This recommended, well-established company is well known for its customer service. Specialising in the Chianti, it offers cottages, villas with pool and entire estates, and has both a US and a (main) UK office.

The Best in Italy, tel: 055-223 064; www.thebestinitaly.com. A Florence-based lettings agency offering luxurious villas and palazzi with pools, tennis courts, stables, domestic staff and other such luxuries.

Caffelletto, www.caffelletto.it, info@ caffelletto.it. This Italian company offers a selection of villas, castles, stylish country manors and city apartments, some on a bed-and-breakfast basis, others self-catering.

Cottages to Castles, tel: (+44) 01622-775 217; www.cottagestocastles.com. UK-based and established.

Cuendet: tel: (+39) 041-251 6100; www.cuendet.com. A good selection of Tuscan villas and apartments.

Hello Italy, tel: (+44) 01983-508 923; www.helloitaly.co.uk: recommended for the Lunigiana region.

Casa Glyn, Cotto, Lunigiana, tel: 0585-92098; www.merrioncharles. com. Lovely setting with striking views of the Apuan Alps and the Carrara hills. A tempting base for walks in the Apennines and foodie forays to Lucca. Unwind in a modest family retreat with great character and comfort. Pizza oven, pool, gardens and south-facing terrace.

Humilis Caellaccia: Val d'Orcia, tel: (+44) 01803-290 958; www. globalartichoke.co.uk. Restored farm sleeps 19 in contemporary style. A lovely pool and great kitchen where local cook Marcella Libertini can be hired. She supposedly inspired the late River Café founder Rose Gray. Foodie forays to Pienza for pecorino cheese and oil, and Montalcino and Montepulciano for red wines.

Villa Rignana: Via di Rignana 7, Greve in Chianti, Chianti; tel: 055-852 137; www.villarignana.com. Set among vineyards, this former monastery is now a villa retreat with the air of a minor stately home, dotted with heirlooms. Sleeps 20, with a chapel that makes it popular for wedding parties.

Castles and Monasteries

Accommodation is available in a variety of castles and palaces. Standards will vary from very simple to luxurious. Many convents, monasteries and other religious institutions offer simple accommodation for tourists and pilgrims. Monte Oliveto Maggiore is just one example. Each provincial tourist office should be able to supply you with a full list.

Youth Hostels

A list of youth hostels is available from ENIT (Italian National Tourist Offices (see page 279) and places can be booked through them or through local Tuscan tourist offices. Alternatively, contact the Associazione Italiana Alberghi per la Gioventù, Via Nicotera 1, 00195 Rome; tel: 06-487 1152; www.aighostels.it.

Camping

For a free list of campsites, contact the Confederazione Italiana Campeggiatori, Via Vittorio Emanuele 11, 50041 Calenzano, Florence; tel: 055-882 391; www.federcampeggio.it

C

Climate

The Tuscan climate is pleasantly mild in the spring and autumn, cool and wet in the winter, and very hot near the sea and on low-lying land in the summer, with a pleasant warmth in the hills. There is very little wind except for on the Tyrrhenian coastline around Marina di Pisa and Tirrenia, but surprise storms can be very heavy at any time of the year, and flooding in a number of places has caused severe damage in the past. The rainfall in Tuscany is generally higher than in most other parts of Italy. The temperature is slightly lower than in other areas, making it more agreeable in summer but somewhat colder in winter.

The weather in Florence can be extreme. The city is situated in a bowl, surrounded by hills, with the Arno cutting through it, and this accounts for the high degree of humidity that is often a feature of midsummer. The worst of the humidity is likely to occur between mid-July and mid-August, with temperatures climbing well into the 30s Celsius (90s Fahrenheit).

Crime and Safety

Although violent crime is rare, in recent years, much crime in the north has tended to be gang- or drug-related. With increasing numbers of immigrants in Italy, the harassment of so-called "foreigners" (essentially immigrants from former Yugoslavia, Eastern Europe, Albania or Africa) is unfortunately on the increase in a country traditionally unused to dealing with immigrants.

The main problem for tourists is petty crime, from pick-pocketing and bag-snatching to the theft of objects left unattended in cars; it is wise to have insurance coverage against this and to take basic, sensible precautions against theft. If driving, lock your car and never leave luggage, cameras or other valuables inside. This applies particularly in major cities.

If you are the victim of a crime (or suffer a loss) and wish to claim against your insurance, it is essential to make a report at the nearest police station as soon as possible and get documentation to support your claim. When you need a policeman, dial **113** (or **112** for the *Carabinieri*, the national police force). Or, in Florence, call the Tourist Aid Police, 055-203 911.

Customs Regulations

Examination of luggage, passports, currency and hand baggage may take place on both entering and leaving Italy at airports, ports and borders. Formalities may also be carried out on trains. Registered luggage may be sent to towns with Customs Offices: examination takes place at the destination.

It is no longer possible to buy duty-free or tax-free goods on journeys within the EU; VAT and duty are included in the purchase price. Shops at ports and airports will sell goods duty- and tax-paid to those travelling within the EU; in practice, many shops have chosen not to pass on price increases since the sale of duty-free goods within the EU was abolished.

There are no longer any limits on how much you can buy on journeys within the EU, provided it's for your own personal use. But there are suggested limits, and if you exceed them Customs may seize your goods if you can't prove they are for your own use.

Emergency Numbers

Fire Brigade: 115.
Medical Aid/Ambulance: 118.
Police Immediate Action: 112.
General Emergency: Fire, Police or Ambulance (replies are in foreign languages in the main cities): 113.
Automobile Club d'Italia (ACI): 24-hour breakdown: 803-116. 24-hour information line: 1518.

The guidance levels are: 3,200 cigarettes or 400 cigarillos or 200 cigars or 1 kg of smoking tobacco; 10 litres of spirits; 20 litres of fortified wine; 90 litres of wine; 110 litres of beer.

Duty-frees are still available to those travelling outside the EU.

Professional photographers must carry an ata Carnet (issued in the UK through the London Chamber of Commerce, 33 Queen Street, London EC4R 1AP; tel: 020-7248 4444) for temporary importation of equipment.

D

Disabled Travellers

Despite difficult cobbled streets and poor wheelchair access to many tourist attractions and hotels, many people with disabilities visit Florence and Tuscany every year.

However, unaccompanied visitors will usually experience some difficulty, so it is best to travel with a companion.

Conditions and disability awareness are improving slowly in Tuscany (as well as in Italy in general), although the situation is certainly not ideal, and access is not always easy. More museums now have lifts, ramps and adapted toilets; newer trains and buses are accessible (although wheelchair users may need help when boarding); and recent laws require restaurants, bars and hotels to provide the relevant facilities. These laws, however, do not always cover access to those facilities. In 2004, Siena became the first Italian city to have an itinerary for the deaf. The brochure, *Siena in Lingua dei Segni*, is available from the tourist information centre, as is information about the facilities offered at sights and museums.

The Accessible Guide to Florence, by Cornelia Danielson, provides very detailed information on museums, restaurants, hotels and more for disabled travellers to Florence. Also, visit www.sagetraveling.com, the site of the European Disabled Travel Experts, tel: (+44) 2033-564 884 (UK), +1-888-645 7920 (US), where you can order bespoke comprehensive guides to Florence, Siena, Livorno and the Tuscany region.

For drivers with disabilities, there are plenty of reserved parking places in towns, and these are free.

In the UK, you can obtain further information from Disability Rights UK, Ground Floor, CAN Mezzanine, East Road 49-51, London N1 6AH; tel: 020-7250 8181; www.disabilityrights

uk.org. In the US, contact SATH, 5th Avenue, Suite 605, NY 10016; tel: 212-447 7284; www.sath.org.

E

Electricity

Italy uses 220v and two-pin plugs. Adaptors for British three-pin appliances can be purchased from airports or department stores in the city. You will need a transformer to use 100–120 volt appliances.

Embassies

Australian Embassy: Via Antonio Bosio 5, 00161 Rome; tel: 06-852 721.
UK Embassy: Via XX Settembre 80a, 00187 Rome; tel: 06-4220 0001.
UK Consulate: Lungarno Corsini 2, 50123 Florence; tel: 055-284 133.
US Embassy: Via Vittorio Veneto 121, 00187 Rome; tel: 06-46741.
US Consulate: Lungarno A. Vespucci 38, 50123 Florence; tel: 055-266 951.

Emergencies

Useful Florence Contacts

Ambulances *(Misericordia)* – tel: 118
Italian Red Cross Medical Service – Ungarno Soderini 11; tel: 055-293 801.
Tourist Medical Service (Guardia Medica Turistica), with English-, German- or French-speaking doctors: Piazza del Duomo; tel 055-212 222, no need to book if 8am–8pm (normal cases) or call any time for emergencies.
Lost Property, Via Circondaria 19; tel: 055-328 3942/43; but first report to the Police (Questura, tel 055-49771).

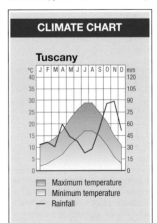

CLIMATE CHART

Tuscany

Maximum temperature
Minimum temperature
Rainfall

Automobile Club d'Italia (ACI) tel: 055-24861.

Car breakdown, call ACI Road Service, tel: 116.

Car pound – if your car is towed away – tel: 055-422 4142.

Police Headquarters (Questura) – the place to visit in the event of thefts, stolen cars, lost passports, etc., Via Zara 2; tel: 055-49771 and 055-497 7602.

Tourist Police *(Polizia Assistenza Turistica)* are at Via Pietrapiana 50r (Piazza dei Ciompi); tel: 055-203 911, and have interpreters on hand to assist.

Associazione Volontari Ospedalieri, Florence; tel: 055-234 4567. This group of volunteers will translate (free) for foreign patients.

Useful Siena Contacts

Siena Hospital Nuovo Policlinico di Siena, Località le Scotte, Viale Bracci; tel: 0577-585 111.

Police Station *(Questura)*, Via del Castoro 6; tel: 0577-201 111 – 24 hours a day.

Pronto Soccorso *(Misericordia)*, Via del Porrione 49; tel: 0577-21011, or dial 118 in an emergency.

Lost Property Via Casato di Sotto 23; tel: 0577-292 230.

Associazione Volontari Ospedalieri tel: 0577-247 869.

See the Siena Town Hall website for all key numbers: www.comune.siena.it

Etiquette

Tuscans are generally friendly and will appreciate efforts to speak the language. Any attempt to rush or pressurise them, however, will be regarded as the height of bad taste, and whatever you want will take longer. Almost everything is done on the basis of personal favours or contacts, so any personal recommendations you can muster will always come in useful.

H

Health and Medical Care

UK visitors are entitled to medical treatment in Italy provided they have a European Health Insurance Card (tel: 0300-330 1350; visit www.nhs.uk; or obtain an application form from the post office). There are similar arrangements for citizens of other European Union countries. As few Italians have faith in their own state health service, it may be

advisable to take out insurance for private treatment in case of accident.

Visitors from outside the EU are strongly advised to take out adequate holiday and medical insurance to provide full cover during their stay abroad.

In high summer, the weather can be very hot; sunscreen, shady hats and mosquito repellent are recommended.

Medical Services

Pharmacies: The staff in chemists *(farmacie)* are usually very knowledgeable about common illnesses and sell far more medicines without prescription than in some other countries (even so, most drugs still require a prescription). Pharmacies are identified by a cross, often red or green and usually in neon.

Normal pharmacy opening hours are Mon–Fri 9am–1pm and 4pm–7pm. Every *farmacia* posts a list of the local chemists who are on emergency duty in their window. The following are chemists that are open 24 hours in Florence:

Farmacia Comunale 13, in Florence station; tel: 055-216 761.

Farmacia Molteni, Via Calzaiuoli 7r; tel: 055-215 472.

Farmacia all'Insegna del Moro, Piazza San Giovanni 20r; tel: 055-211 343.

In addition, you can call 800-420 707 to find out which chemists are on the night rota.

First Aid Service *(Pronto Soccorso)* with a doctor is found at airports, railway stations and in all hospitals. See page 277 for numbers to call in an emergency.

I

Internet

Most large hotels offer Wi-Fi , email and fax facilities. There are numerous internet cafés around Florence, and most other cities, including the chain Internet Train, which allows you to connect using its computers or your own laptop. Most main post offices, travel agencies and hotels have fax facilities.

M

Maps

Touring Club Italiano does a good fold-out map of the Tuscany region

showing major and minor roads. The Siena and Florence tourist offices supply reasonable city maps. *Insight Guide Fleximaps* are also available for Florence and Tuscany.

Media

Each large Italian town has its own newspaper. The centre-right *Il Corriere della Sera*, and the centre-left *La Repubblica* also have a national following. *La Nazione* is the paper favoured by most Tuscans for regional matters.

Television is deregulated in Italy. In addition to the state network, rai (which offers three channels), there are about 1,000 channels, of which the main ones are Canale 5, Rete 4, Italia 1 and Telemontecarlo.

There are several useful publications for visitors to Tuscany, including *The Florentine*, a bi-weekly English-language paper focusing on current events and city life, *and Firenze Spettacolo*, a monthly listings magazine in Italian (with some listings also in English), focusing on nightlife, clubs, bars and the live arts in Florence.

Money

In common with the other eurozone countries of the EU, Italy's monetary unit is the euro (€), which is divided into 100 cents. The currency is available in 500, 200, 100, 50, 20, 10 and 5 euro notes, and 2-euro, 1-euro, 50-cent, 20-cent, 10-cent, 5-cent, 2-cent and 1-cent coins.

Italy is a society that prefers cash to credit cards, except for large purchases, or, for instance, hotel bills. In the case of petrol stations, more modest restaurants and smaller shops, it is usual to pay in cash. Check beforehand if there is any doubt. Most shopkeepers and restaurateurs will not change money, so it is best to change a limited amount at the airport when you arrive, especially if it is the weekend, when banks are closed. Try to avoid changing money in hotels, where the commission tends to be higher than in banks.

Cash Machines and Credit Cards

Given the long queues for money-changing in Italy, it is simplest to get cash from cashpoint machines. Most main cards work in Italian machines, with your normal PIN number, though you may sometimes have to look for particular "Bancomats" (cashpoint machines) that take your card.

In cities, many restaurants, hotels, shops and stores will take major credit cards, but in rural areas especially, you may be able to pay only in cash.

Banks

Banks offer the best exchange rates (small exchange booths often charge up to 3 percent commission) and are normally open Mon–Fri 8.30am–1.30pm. Some banks also open in the afternoon, 2.30pm–4.30pm. Outside these hours and at weekends you can use automatic exchange machines to change cash, which helps to avoid bank queues. There is a high concentration of banks in Florence, including foreign banks, to the west of Piazza della Repubblica, around Via de'Tornabuoni.

Florence

Banca d'Italia, Via dell'Oriuolo 37/39.
Banca Toscana, Corso 6.
Cassa di Risparmio di Firenze, Via Bufalini 6.
UniCredit, Via Vecchietti 11.

Siena

Banca Nazionale del Lavoro, Viale Vittorio Veneto 43.
Cassa di Risparmio di Firenze, Piazza Tolomei 11.
Monte dei Paschi di Siena, Via Banchi di Sopra 84.
UniCredit, Via dei Termini 37.

Exchange Offices

Florence
Omega Viaggi, Piazza della Stazione 14, Int. 37 (under the station).

Siena
Viaggi Seti (Piazza del Campo 56).
Forexchange (Via di Città 80-82).

O

Opening Hours

Shops in the main cities open Monday to Friday 8.30am–1pm and 3.30–7.30pm. The majority open on Saturday, and several are open on Sunday, too, especially in high season. Some shops in coastal resorts and tourist centres now stay open all day throughout the summer and have Saturday and Sunday opening. Stores in most cities will close for at least two weeks around the *Ferragosto* holiday on 15 August. This is especially true of smaller cities not on the coastline.

Food shops are closed on Wednesday afternoons in winter

Public Holidays

1 January *Capodanno* (New Year's Day).
6 January *La Befana* (Epiphany)
Easter *Pasqua*.
Easter Monday *Pasquetta*.
25 April *Anniversario della Liberazione* (Liberation Day).
1 May *Festa del Lavoro* (Labour Day).
24 June *San Giovanni* (St John the Baptist) – in Florence only.
15 August *Ferragosto* (Assumption of the Virgin Mary).
1 November *Ognissanti* (All Saints' Day).
8 December *Immacolata Concezione* (Immaculate Conception).
25 December *Natale* (Christmas Day).
26 December *Santo Stefano* (Boxing Day).

and Saturday afternoons in summer. Clothes shops are closed on Monday mornings.

Offices are usually open 8am–1pm and 2–4pm, although many have more extensive opening hours.

On Italian national holidays, all shops and offices are closed.

P

Postal Services

Main post offices in major towns are open all day; otherwise the hours are 8am–1.30pm (12.30pm Saturday). Stamps are sold at post offices and tobacconists *(tabacchi)*.

There is also a courier service for sending important documents worldwide in 24/48 hours. This service is only available at major post offices. In Florence, these are at Via Pellicceria 3 (main post office) and Via Alamanni 14/16 (by the station).

T

Telephones

Public telephones are now virtually nonexistent as Italy has the highest ownership of mobile phones in Europe. Annoyingly, many people, including small companies, only use their mobile phone, thus making calls to them more expensive. To keep costs down, it's worth getting an Italian SIM card while there, or keeping a second mobile for this

purpose. For long-distance calls, the cheapest time to telephone is between 10pm and 8am Monday to Saturday, and all day Sunday.

For directory enquiries, dial 12. For international enquiries, call 176, and to make a reverse charges (collect) call, dial 170.

When dialling Italy from abroad, dial the country code (0039) and the area code **including** the initial zero. In Italy, when calling numbers either inside or outside your area, dialling must always be preceded by the area code including the zero. Key area codes are: Florence (055); Pisa (050) and Siena (0577).

Tipping

Most Italian restaurants levy a *coperto* of around €2 per person – a cover charge for linen, bread and service – and so tipping isn't as common as in other countries. However, in pricier places, a tip of around 10 percent is an appropriate indication of appreciation of good service. Only in the finest hotels, and for lengthy stays, is it customary to tip bellboys, maids and head waiters. You may wish to note that according to Italian law, you should keep the bill with you until you are at least 100 metres (300ft) from the restaurant.

Tourist Board

The Italian State Tourist Board, known as ENIT (Ente Nazionale per il Turismo), provides tourist information. ENIT's headquarters are in Via Marghera 2/6, 00185 Rome (tel: 06-49711; www.enit.it).
In the UK, ENIT, Princes Street 1, London W1B 2AY; tel: (+44) 020-7408 1254.
In the US, ENIT, 686 Park Avenue, New York, NY 10065; tel: 212-245 5618. There are also offices in Chicago, Los Angeles and Toronto, Canada.

The ENIT website for all offices worldwide is: www.enit.it.

Calling Home

To call abroad from Italy, dial 00, followed by:
Australia 61
Canada 1
Ireland 353
New Zealand 64
UK 44
USA 1
Then dial the number, omitting the initial "0" if there is one.

Tourist Offices

The current local tourist office details in each Tuscan province are listed below. If you are unable to contact them, consult www.turismo.intoscana. it, Tuscany's official tourism website, which should list all the new contact details for each province as they emerge in connection with the restructuring of the Tuscan tourism system. This umbrella website also contains useful information about the region, offered in several languages.

In addition to the institutional tourist offices, there are also dynamic tourism consortia that act as tourist offices in many destinations. The best are also listed throughout the book, as here below.

Arezzo Province

Arezzo: Piazza Risorgimento 116, Arezzo; tel: 0575-23952; Piazza della Repubblica 28; tel: 0575-377 678.
Cortona: Via Nazionale 42; tel: 0575-630 352. www.apt.arezzo.it

Florence Province

Florence: Via del Termine 11; tel: 055-315 874; Via Cavour 1r; tel: 055-290 832; Piazza San Giovanni 1; tel: 055-288 496; and Piazza della Stazione 4; tel: 055-212 245. www.firenzeturismo.it
Fiesole: Via Portigiani 3/5; tel: 055-596 1323.
www.comune.fiesole.fi.it

Grosseto Province (including the Maremma)

Grosseto: Viale Monterosa 206; tel: 0564-462 611.
www.turismoinmaremma.it
Maremma park (Parco della Maremma):
Alberese: tel: 0564-407 269; www.naturalmentetoscana.it

Livorno Province (and Etruscan Coast with Elba)

Livorno: Piazza Cavour 6; tel: 0586-204 611.
www.costadeglietruschi.it
Elba: Calata Italia 26, Portoferraio; tel: 0565-915 555.
www.aptelba.it

Lucca Province (Lucca, Garfagnana and Versilia Coast)

Lucca: Piazza Guidiccioni 2; tel: 0583-91991; Piazza Santa Maria 35; tel: 0583-919 931; Vecchia Porta San Donato, Piazzale Verdi; tel: 0583-442 944. www.luccatourist.it
Bagni di Lucca: Via E. Wipple; tel: 0583-804 557.

Italy works on GMT + 1 and switches to DST – daylight saving time, GMT + 2 – at the same time as the rest of Europe.

Versilia (including the Viareggio and Forte dei Marmi coast)

Viareggio: Viale Carducci 10; tel: 0584-962 233
www.aptversilia.it and www.turismo. provincia.lucca.it

Massa-Carrara Province

Marina di Massa: Lungomare Vespucci 24; tel: 0585-240 036.
Marina di Carrara: Via Bassagrande 54; tel: 0585-632 815.
www.aptmassacarrara.it

Pisa Province

Pisa: Via Matteucci; tel: 050-929 777; Piazza Arcivescovado 8; tel: 050-560 464. www.pisa unicaterra.it
Volterra: Piazza dei Priori 20; tel: 0588-87257; www.volterratur.it

Pistoia Province

Pistoia: Piazza del Duomo 1; tel: 0573-21622.
Montecatini Terme: tel: 0572-772 244; www.montecatiniturismo.it
San Marcello Pistoiese: Via Marconi 70; tel: 0573-630 145.
www.pistoia.turismo.toscana.it

Prato Province

Prato: Piazza Santa Maria delle Carceri 15; tel: 0574-24112.
www.pratoturismo.it

Siena Province

Siena: Piazza del Campo 56; tel: 0577-280 551.
www.terresiena.it

Chianciano Terme (and Val d'Orcia area)

Piazza Italia 67; tel: 0578-671 122.

Visas and Passports

Citizens of European Union countries require either a passport or a Visitor's Identification Card to enter Italy. A visa is not required. Holders of passports from most other countries do not require visas for stays of less than three months, except for nationals from Belarus, the Russian Federation or Ukraine, who need to obtain visas

from the Italian Embassy in their own country.

Police Registration

A person may stay in Italy for three months as a tourist, but police registration is required within three days of entering Italy. If staying at a hotel, the management will attend to the formality.

You are legally obliged to carry a form of identification (passport, driving licence, etc.) with you at all times. This rule is often flouted but bear in mind that it would be unwise to call the police or attempt to report a problem (eg theft) unless you are carrying appropriate identification.

Websites

Useful websites are given above and throughout the book. The following is just a selection of the many additional sites on Italy, Florence and Tuscany that are available on the web:
Tuscany Tourist Information: www.turismo.intoscana.it
Tuscany tourist attractions: www.discovertuscany.com
What to see in Tuscany: www.tuscanychic.com
Database on all Italian museums: www.italy-museum.com
Florence: www.firenzemusei.it; www.polomuseale.firenze.it
Best routes in Italy: www.autostrade. it; www.rac.co.uk; www.theaa.com Plan your journey from one Italian destination to another.
Information plus hotels and restaurants: www.firenzeturismo.it
Agriturismi (farm-stays) in Tuscany: www.turismo.intoscana.it; www.agriturismo.com
Events: www.firenzespettacolo.it; www.theflorentine.net

Weights and Measures

The metric system is used for weights and measures.
Multiply by the following:
Centimetres to inches 0.4
Metres to feet 3.3
Metres to yards 1.1
Kilometres to miles 0.6
Kilograms to pounds 2.2
Italians refer to 100 grams (about a quarter of a pound) as *un etto*; 200 grams are therefore *due etti*.
Liquid measurements are in litres. One litre is 1.75 pints.
Temperatures are given in Celsius (Centigrade).

LANGUAGE

UNDERSTANDING THE LANGUAGE

LANGUAGE TIPS

In Tuscany, everyone speaks the Italian language but regional dialects and accents survive. The Tuscan accent features a strongly aspirated "h", much like in Spanish. In major centres, many people speak English, French or German. It is well worth buying a good phrase book or dictionary, but the following will help you to get started. Since this glossary is aimed at non-linguists, we have opted for the simplest options rather than the most elegant Italian.

PRONUNCIATION AND GRAMMAR TIPS

Italian speakers claim that pronunciation is straightforward: you pronounce it as it is written. This is approximately true but there are a couple of important rules for English speakers to bear in mind: c before e or i is pronounced "ch", eg *ciao, mi dispiace, coincidenza*. Ch before i or e is pronounced as "k", eg *la chiesa*. Likewise, sci or sce are pronounced as in "sheep" or "shed". Gn in Italian is rather like the sound in "onion", while gl is softened to resemble the sound in "bullion".

Nouns are either masculine (il, plural i) or feminine (la, plural le). Plurals of nouns are most often formed by changing an o to an i and an a to an e, eg *il panino, i panini; la chiesa, le chiese*.

Words are stressed on the penultimate syllable unless an accent indicates otherwise, generally speaking.

Like many languages, Italian has formal and informal words for "You". In the singular, *Tu* is informal while *Lei* is more polite. For visitors, it is simplest and most respectful to use the formal form unless invited to do otherwise. There is, of course, rather more to the language than that, but you can get a surprisingly long way towards making friends with a few phrases.

BASIC COMMUNICATION

Yes *Sì*
No *No*
Thank you *Grazie*
You're welcome *Prego*
Alright/OK/That is fine *Va bene*
Please *Per favore* or *per cortesia*
Excuse me (to get attention) *Scusi* (singular), *Scusate* (plural)
Excuse me (to get through a crowd) *Permesso*
Excuse me (to attract attention, eg of a waiter) *Senta!*
Excuse me (sorry) *Mi scusi*
Could you help me? (formal) *Potrebbe aiutarmi?*
Certainly *Ma, certo*
Can I help you? (formal) *Posso aiutarLa?*
I need ... *Ho bisogno di ...*
I'm sorry *Mi dispiace*
I don't know *Non lo so*
I don't understand *Non capisco*
Could you speak more slowly, please? *Può parlare piu lentamente, per favore?*
Could you repeat that please? *Può ripetere, per piacere?*
What? *Quale/come?*
When/why/where? *Quando/perchè/dove?*
Where is the lavatory? *Dov'è il bagno?*

GREETINGS

Hello (Good day) *Buon giorno*
Good afternoon/evening *Buona sera*
Good night *Buona notte*
Goodbye *Arrivederci*
Hello/Hi/Goodbye (familiar) *Ciao*
Mr/Mrs/Miss *Signor/Signora/Signorina*
Pleased to meet you (formal) *Piacere di conoscerLa*
Do you speak English? *Parla inglese?*
I am English/American *Sono inglese/americano*
Canadian/Australian *canadese/australiano*
How are you (formal/informal)? *Come sta/come stai?*
Fine thanks *Bene, grazie*

TELEPHONE CALLS

the area code *il prefisso*
May I use your telephone, please? *Posso usare il telefono?*
Hello (on the telephone) *Pronto*
My name's *Mi chiamo/Sono*
Could I speak to...? *Posso parlare con...?*
Can you speak up please? *Può parlare più forte, per favore?*

IN THE HOTEL

Do you have any vacant rooms? *Avete camere libere?*
I have a reservation *Ho fatto una prenotazione*
I'd like... *Vorrei...*
a room with twin beds *una camera a due letti*
a single/double room (with a double bed) *una camera singola/doppia (con letto matrimoniale)*

a room with a bath/shower *una camera con bagno/doccia*
for one night *per una notte*
for two nights *per due notti*
How much is it? *Quanto costa?*
Is breakfast included? *E compresa la prima colazione?*
half/full board *mezza pensione/ pensione completa*
Do you have a room with a balcony/ view of the sea? *C'è una camera con balcone/con una vista del mare?*
Is it a quiet room? *E una stanza tranquilla?*
Can I see the room? *Posso vedere la camera?*
Can I have the bill, please? *Posso avere il conto, per favore?*
Can you call me a taxi, please? *Può chiamarmi un tassì/taxi, per favore?*

EATING OUT

Bar snacks and drinks

I'd like... *Vorrei...*
coffee *un caffè (espresso: small, strong and black)*
un caffellatte (like café au lait in France)
un caffè lungo (weak, served in a tall glass)
un corretto (laced with alcohol, probably brandy or grappa)
tea *un tè*
herbal tea *una tisana*
hot chocolate *una cioccolata calda*
orange/lemon juice *(bottled) un succo d'arancia/di limone*
fizzy/still mineral water *acqua minerale gassata/naturale*
with/without ice *con/senza ghiaccio*
red/white wine *vino rosso/bianco*
beer *una birra*
milk *latte*
a (half) litre *un (mezzo) litro*
ice cream *un gelato*
sandwich *un tramezzino*
roll *un panino*
Cheers *Salute*

In a Restaurant

I'd like to book a table *Vorrei riservare una tavola*
Have you got a table for...? *Avete una tavola per ...?*
I have a reservation *Ho fatto una prenotazione*
lunch/supper *il pranzo/la cena*
I'm a vegetarian *Sono vegetariano/a*
Is there a vegetarian dish? *C'è un piatto vegetariano?*
May we have the menu? *Ci dia la carta?*
wine list *la lista dei vini*
home-made *fatto in casa*

What would you like? *Che cosa prende?*
What would you recommend? *Che cosa ci raccomanda?*
home-made *fatto in casa*
What would you like as a main course/dessert? *Che cosa prende di secondo/di dolce?*
What would you like to drink? *Che cosa desidera da bere?*
a carafe of red/white wine *una caraffa di vino rosso/bianco*
the dish of the day *il piatto del giorno*
cover charge *il coperto/pane e coperto*
The bill, please *Il conto per favore*
Is service included? *Il servizio è incluso?*

Menu Decoder

Antipasti (hors d'oeuvres)

antipasto misto **mixed hors d'œuvres** (including cold cuts, possibly cheeses and roast vegetables)
buffet freddo **cold buffet**
caponata **mixed aubergine, olives and tomatoes**
insalata caprese **tomato and mozzarella salad**
insalata di mare **seafood salad**
insalata mista/verde **mixed/green salad**
melanzane alla parmigiana **fried or baked aubergine** (with parmesan cheese and tomato)
mortadella/salame **salami**
peperonata **grilled peppers** (drenched in olive oil)

Primi (first courses)

Typical first courses include soup, or numerous varieties of pasta in a wide range of sauces.
il brodetto **fish soup**
i crespolini **savoury pancakes**
gli gnocchi **dumplings**
la minestra **soup**
il minestrone **thick vegetable soup**
pasta e fagioli **pasta and bean soup**
il prosciutto (cotto/crudo) **ham** (cooked/cured)
i tartufi **truffles**
la zuppa **soup**

Secondi (main courses)

Typical main courses are fish-, seafood- or meat-based, with accompaniments *(contorni)* like beans, spinach or roast vegetables.

La carne (meat)

allo spiedo **on the spit**
arrosto **roast meat**
al ferro **grilled without oil**
al forno **baked**
al girarrosto **spit-roasted**

Emergencies

Help! *Aiuto!*
Stop! *Fermate!*
I've had an accident *Ho avuto un incidente*
Watch out! *Attenzione!*
Call a doctor *Per favore, chiama un medico*
Call an ambulance *Chiama un'ambulanza*
Call the police *Chiama la Polizia/i Carabinieri*
Call the fire brigade *Chiama i pompieri*
Where is the telephone? *Dov'è il telefono?*
Where is the nearest hospital? *Dov'è l'ospedale più vicino?*
I would like to report a theft *Voglio denunciare un furto*

alla griglia **grilled**
stufato **braised, stewed**
ben cotto **well-done** (steak, etc.)
al puntino **medium** (steak, etc.)
al sangue **rare** (steak, etc.)
l'agnello **lamb**
il bresaolo **dried salted beef**
la bistecca **steak**
il maiale **pork**
il manzo **beef**
l'ossobuco **shin of veal**
il pollo **chicken**
la salsiccia **sausage**
saltimbocca (alla romana) **veal escalopes with ham**
le scaloppine **escalopes**
lo stufato **stew**
il sugo **sauce**

Frutti di mare (seafood)

Beware the word *"surgelati"*, meaning frozen rather than fresh.
affumicato **smoked**
alle brace **charcoal grilled/ barbecued**
alla griglia **grilled**
fritto **fried**
ripieno **stuffed**
al vapore **steamed**
le acciughe **anchovies**
l'aragosta **lobster**
il branzino **sea bass**
i calamari **squid**
i calamaretti **baby squid**
i crostacei **shellfish**
le cozze **mussels**
il fritto misto **mixed fried fish**
i gamberi **prawns**
i gamberetti **shrimps**
il granchio **crab**
il merluzzo **cod**
le ostriche **oysters**
il pesce **fish**
il pesce spada **swordfish**
il polipo **octopus**

il risotto di mare **seafood risotto**
le sarde **sardines**
la sogliola **sole**
le seppie **cuttlefish**
la triglia **red mullet**
la trota **trout**
il tonno **tuna**
le vongole **clams**

I legumi/la verdura (vegetables)

a scelta **of your choice**
i contorni **accompaniments**
ripieno **stuffed**
gli asparagi **asparagus**
la bietola **similar to spinach**
il carciofo **artichoke**
le carote **carrots**
i carciofini **artichoke hearts**
il cavolo **cabbage**
la cicoria **chicory**
la cipolla **onion**
i funghi **mushrooms**
i funghi porcini **ceps best mushrooms**
i fagioli **beans**
i fagiolini **green beans**
le fave **broad beans**
il finocchio **fennel**
l'insalata mista **mixed salad**
l'insalata verde **green salad**
la melanzana **aubergine**
le patate **potatoes**
le patatine fritte **French fries**
i peperoni **peppers**
i piselli **peas**
i pomodori **tomatoes**
le primizie **spring vegetables**
il radicchio **red lettuce**
la rughetta **rocket**
i ravanelli **radishes**
gli spinaci **spinach**
la verdura **green vegetables**
la zucca **pumpkin/squash**
gli zucchini **courgettes**

I dolci (desserts)

al carrello **(desserts) from the trolley**
un semifreddo **semi-frozen dessert (many types)**
la bavarese **mousse**
un gelato **ice cream**
una granita **water ice**
una macedonia di frutta **fruit salad**
il tartufo (nero) **(chocolate) ice cream dessert**
il tiramisù **cold, creamy rum and coffee dessert**
la torta **cake/tart**
lo zabaglione **dessert made with eggs and Marsala wine**
lo zuccotto **ice-cream liqueur**
la zuppa inglese **trifle**

La frutta (fruit)

le albicocche **apricots**
le arance **oranges**
le banane **bananas**
il cocomero **watermelon**

le ciliege **cherries**
i fichi **figs**
le fragole **strawberries**
i frutti di bosco **fruits of the forest**
i lamponi **raspberries**
la mela **apple**
il melone **melon**
la pesca **peach**
la pera **pear**
il pompelmo **grapefruit**
le uve **grapes**

Basic foods

l'aceto **vinegar**
l'aglio **garlic**
il burro **butter**
il formaggio **cheese**
la frittata **omelette**
la grana **Parmesan cheese**
i grissini **bread sticks**
l'olio **oil**
la marmellata **jam**
il pane **bread**
il pane integrale **wholemeal bread**
il parmigiano **Parmesan cheese**
il pepe **pepper**
il riso **rice**
il sale **salt**
le uova **eggs**
lo zucchero **sugar**

SIGHTSEEING

Si può visitare? **Can one visit?**
Suonare il campanello **ring the bell**
aperto/a **open**
chiuso/a **closed**
chiuso per la festa **closed for the festival**
chiuso per ferie **closed for the holidays**
chiuso per restauro **closed for restoration**
Is it possible to see the church? *E possibile visitare la chiesa?*
Where can I find the custodian/ sacristan/key? *Dove posso trovare il custode/il sacristano/la chiave?*

AT THE SHOPS

What time do you open/close? *A che ora apre/chiude?*
Closed for the holidays (typical sign) *Chiuso per ferie*
Pull/push (sign on doors) *Tirare/ spingere*
Entrance/exit *Entrata/uscita*
Can I help you? (formal) *Posso aiutarLa?*
What would you like? *Che cosa desidera?*
I'm just looking *Sto soltanto guardando*
How much does it cost? *Quant'è, per favore?*

Do you take credit cards? *Accettate carte di credito?*
I'd like... *Vorrei...*
this one/that one *questo/quello*
I'd like that one, please *Vorrei quello lì, per cortesia*
Have you got ...? *Avete ...?*
We haven't got (any) *... Non (ne) abbiamo...*
Can I try it on? *Posso provare?*
the size (for clothes) *la taglia*
What size do you take? *Qual'è Sua taglia?*
the size (for shoes) *il numero*
expensive/cheap *caro/economico*
It's too small/big *E troppo piccolo/ grande*
I (don't) **like it** *(Non) mi piace*
I'll take it/I'll leave it *Lo prendo/ Lo lascio*
This is faulty. Can I have a replacement/refund? *C'è un difetto. Me lo potrebbe cambiare/ rimborsare?*
Anything else? *Altro?*
Give me some of those *Mi dia alcuni di quelli lì*
a (half) kilo *un (mezzo) chilo*
100 grams *un etto*
200 grams *due etti*
more/less *più/meno*
with/without *con/senza*
a little *un pocchino*
That's enough *Basta così*

Types of shops

bank *la banca*
bureau de change *il cambio*
chemist's *la farmacia*
food shop *l'alimentari*
leather shop *la pelletteria*
market *il mercato*
news-stand *l'edicola*
post office *l'ufficio postale*
supermarket *il supermercato*
tobacconist *il tabaccaio*
travel agency *l'agenzia di viaggi*

TRAVELLING

Transport

airport *l'aeroporto*
arrivals/departures *arrivi/partenze*
boat *la barca*
bus *l'autobus/il Pullman*
bus station *l'autostazione*
car *la macchina*
ferry *il traghetto*
first/second class *prima/seconda classe*
flight *il volo*
left luggage office *il deposito bagagli*
motorway *l'autostrada*
no smoking *vietato fumare*

TRANSPORT

EATING OUT

ACTIVITIES

A – Z

LANGUAGE

platform *il binario*
railway station *la stazione
(ferroviaria)*
stop *la fermata*

At the station

Can you help me please? *Mi può
aiutare, per favore?*
Where can I buy tickets? *Dove
posso fare i biglietti?*
at the ticket office/at the counter
alla biglietteria/allo sportello
What time does the train leave? *A
che ora parte il treno?*
What time does the train arrive? *A
che ora arriva il treno?*
Can I book a seat? *Posso prenotare
un posto?*
Is this seat free/taken? *E libero/
occupato questo posto?*
I'm afraid this is my seat *E il mio
posto, mi dispiace*
You'll have to pay a supplement
Deve pagare un supplemento
Do I have to change? *Devo
cambiare?*
Where does it stop? *Dove si ferma?*

You need to change in Firenze
Bisogna cambiare a Florence
**Which platform does the train leave
from?** *Da quale binario parte il treno?*
The train leaves from platform one
Il treno parte dal binario uno
**When is the next train/bus/
ferry for Pisa?** *Quando parte il
prossimo treno/Pullman/traghetto
per Pisa?*
How long does the crossing take?
Quanto dura la traversata?
**What time does the bus leave for
Siena?** *Quando parte l'autobus per
Siena?*
Next stop please *La prossima
fermata per favore*
Is this the right stop? *E la fermata
giusta?*
The train is late *Il treno è in ritardo*
Can you tell me where to get off? *Mi
può dire dove devo scendere?*

Directions

right/left *a destra/a sinistra*
first left/second right *la prima a
sinistra/la seconda a destra*

Turn to the right/left *Gira a destra/
sinistra*
Go straight on *Va sempre diritto*
Go straight on until the lights *Va
sempre diritto fino al semaforo*
opposite/next to *di fronte/accanto a*
up/down *su/gìu*
traffic lights *il semaforo*
Where is ...? *Dov'è ...?*
Where are ...? *Dove sono ...?*
How do I get there? *Come si può
andare?* (or: *Come faccio per arrivare
a ...?*)

On the Road

petrol *la benzina*
petrol station/garage *la stazione
servizio*
oil *l'olio*
Fill it up please *Faccia il pieno, per
favore*
lead free/unleaded/diesel *senza
piombo/benzina verde/diesel*
My car won't start *La mia macchina
non s'accende*
My car has broken down *La
macchina è guasta*

FURTHER READING

ART AND HISTORY

The Architecture of the Italian Renaissance, by Peter Murray. Thames & Hudson.
Autobiography, by Benvenuto Cellini. Penguin Classics.
Catherine de' Medici: a Biography by Leonie Frieda. Phoenix
A Concise Encyclopedia of the Italian Renaissance, edited by J.R. Hale. Thames & Hudson.
Etruscan Places, by D.H. Lawrence. Olive Press.
The Florentine Renaissance and *The Flowering of the Renaissance*, by Vincent Cronin. Fontana.
The High Renaissance and *The Late Renaissance and Mannerism*, by Linda Murray. Thames & Hudson.
The Italian Painters of the Renaissance, by Bernard Berenson.
Phaidon Press.
Lives of the Artists, vols. 1 & 2, by Giorgio Vasari. Penguin Classics.
Machiavelli, by Anglo Sydney. Paladin.
The Merchant of Prato, by Iris Origo. Penguin.
Painter's Florence, by Barbara Whelpton Johnson.
The Rise and Fall of the House of Medici, by Christopher Hibbert. Penguin.
Siena: A City and its History, by Judith Hook. Hamish Hamilton.
Silvio Berlusconi: Television, Power and Patrimony, by Paul Ginsborg. Verso Books.

TRAVEL COMPANIONS

A Room with a View, by E.M. Forster. Penguin.
The Italians, by Luigi Barzini. Hamish Hamilton.
Italian Hours, by Henry James.

Send Us Your Thoughts

We do our best to ensure the information in our books is as accurate and up-to-date as possible. The books are updated on a regular basis using local contacts, who painstakingly add, amend and correct as required. However, some details (such as telephone numbers and opening times) are liable to change, and we are ultimately reliant on our readers to put us in the picture.

We welcome your feedback, especially your experience of using the book "on the road". Maybe we recommended a hotel that you liked (or another that you didn't), or you came across a great bar or new attraction we missed.

We will acknowledge all contributions, and we'll offer an Insight Guide to the best letters received.

Please write to us at:
Insight Guides
PO Box 7910
London SE1 1WE
Or email us at:
hello@insightguides.com

Century Hutchinson.
Love and War in the Apennines, by Eric Newby. Picador.
The Love of Italy, by Jonathan Keates. Octopus.
Pictures from Italy, by Charles Dickens. Granville Publishing.
The Stones of Florence, by Mary McCarthy. Penguin.
The Villas of Tuscany, by Harold Acton. Thames & Hudson.
The Birth of Venus, by Sarah Dunant. Random House.
Summer's Lease, by John Mortimer. Penguin.
Death in Springtime, by Magdalen Nabb. Heinemann.
Under the Tuscan Sun and two sequels, by Frances Mayes. Bantam.

OTHER INSIGHT GUIDES

Insight Guides cover nearly 200 destinations, providing information on culture and all the top sights, as well as superb photography and detailed maps. Other Insight Guides to destinations in the region include Italy, Italian Lakes, Sicily and Sardinia.

Italian destinations in Insight's detailed and colourful **City Guides** series include Rome, Florence and Siena, and Venice.

The itinerary-based **Insight Explore Guides**, written by local hosts, come complete with a pull-out map. Titles include Naples and the Amalfi Coast, the Italian Lakes, Venice, Florence, and Rome.

CREDITS

Photo Credits

4Corners Images 234
akg-images 24, 27, 34, 107BL,
106BR, 107BR, 110BL, 111L
Alamy 105BR, 109TR, 133B, 136,
164B
Alinari/Rex Features 112BL
AWL Images 82, 196
Bridgeman Art Library 112/113T
Britta Jaschinski/Apa Publications
5ML, 7BL, 8B, 8T, 19R, 19L, 74R,
74L, 75, 97T, 99, 108BL, 109MR,
109BR, 114, 115, 116, 204T, 204B,
252B, 253, 254, 255, 267, 273,
275
Cathy Muscat 163, 168
Chianti Classico Wine Consortium
194ML
Corbis 10/11, 36, 39, 43, 86,
104BL
ENEL 180, 243B
FLPA 166
Fotolia 58, 120B, 130, 134, 142B,
161, 167, 169, 172T, 172B, 195TR,
269
**Frances Gransden/Apa
Publications** 29, 95T
Gentile da Fabriano 50
Getty Images 23, 40, 41, 42, 45,
47, 66, 69, 95B, 113T, 123, 143,
162, 165, 206/207T, 223, 233
Green Park Resort 259L

**Guglielmo Galvin & George Taylor/
Apa Publications** 25, 142T, 148,
149T
iStock 4BL, 26, 59, 65, 138, 160,
201, 218, 224, 249, 250, 285
Jezza Dennis/Apa Publications
103T, 118
Leonardo 132
Lombardi Siena 31
Mary Evans Picture Library 37
**Mockford & Bonetti/Apa
Publications** 71, 93T, 98B, 98T,
120T, 121, 122, 145, 146, 147,
149B, 164T, 170T, 171, 181T, 191T,
192T, 192B, 208, 210, 212, 214,
215, 220T, 226, 229T, 232T, 236,
237T, 239B, 240T, 240B, 242, 243T,
244, 245, 258
Monte dei Paschi di Siena 200B
Pitti Gallery, Florence 73
Public domain 22, 35, 38, 51, 52,
55, 56, 72, 239T
Robert Harding 4M, 6B
Santa Maria Novella, Florence 53
Scala Archives 5TR, 5BL, 32, 33,
48, 49, 54, 57, 104/105T, 104BR,
105ML, 105BL, 105TC, 106BL,
107TR, 110/111T, 110BR, 111R,
113B
Shutterstock 1, 4MR, 9B, 15T, 15B,
61, 62, 63, 64, 83T, 106/107T,

109BL, 112BR, 117T, 117B, 129B,
131T, 135, 137, 156B, 159, 170B,
173, 177, 183, 189, 193,
194/195T, 200T, 205T, 229B, 231,
232B, 235, 237B, 252T
Sipa Press/Rex Features 44
Steve McDonald/Apa Publications
2/3, 5BR, 5MR, 5TL, 6T, 7BR, 7TR,
9T, 12/13, 14, 16, 17, 18, 20, 21,
28, 67, 70, 76/77, 78/79, 80/81,
83B, 91B, 91T, 93B, 94, 97B,
108BR, 124, 125, 126, 127, 129T,
131B, 133T, 139, 141, 150, 151,
153, 154, 155, 156T, 174, 175,
176T, 176B, 178, 181B, 182T,
182B, 184, 185, 186, 187, 188,
190, 191B, 194MR, 194B, 195BL,
195BR, 197, 199B, 199T, 203,
205B, 206BR, 206BL, 207BR,
207ML, 207TR, 207BL, 209, 213,
216, 217B, 217T, 219, 220B, 221,
222B, 222T, 225, 227, 230, 246,
248, 256, 257, 264, 265, 266, 270,
281
SuperStock 30
The Art Archive 108/109T
Tom Smyth 60R, 60L, 87, 96, 101,
102, 103B, 202
Uffizi Florence/Dagli Orti 46
WestEnd61/Rex Features 5MR, 90

Cover Credits

Front cover: Montepulciano *iStock*
Back cover: Duomo di Firenze *Steve
McDonald/Apa Publications*
Front flap: (from top) San Gimignano
Shutterstock; Palatina Gallery,
Palazzo Pitti *Shutterstock*; Firenze

Santa Maria Novella station *iStock*;
Porto Santo Stefano *Shutterstock*
Back flap: country road *Shutterstock*

Insight Guide Credits

Distribution

UK
Dorling Kindersley Ltd
A Penguin Group company
80 Strand, London, WC2R 0RL
sales@uk.dk.com

United States
Ingram Publisher Services
1 Ingram Boulevard, PO Box 3006,
La Vergne, TN 37086-1986
ips@ingramcontent.com

Australia and New Zealand
Woodslane
10 Apollo St, Warriewood,
NSW 2102, Australia
info@woodslane.com.au

Worldwide
Apa Publications (Singapore) Pte
7030 Ang Mo Kio Avenue 5
08-65 Northstar @ AMK
Singapore 569880
apasin@singnet.com.sg

Printing
CTPS-China

First Edition 1989
Sixth Edition 2015

Every effort has been made to provide accurate information in this publication, but changes are inevitable. The publisher cannot be responsible for any resulting loss, inconvenience or injury. We would appreciate it if readers would call our attention to any errors or outdated information. We also welcome your suggestions; please contact us at: hello@insightguides.com

www.insightguides.com

Editor: Carine Tracanelli
Author: Lisa Gerard-Sharp
Updater: Magdalena Helsztyńska
Head of Production: Rebeka Davies
Update Production: AM Services
Pictures: Tom Smyth
Cartography: original cartography Berndtson & Berndtson, updated by Carte

Contributors

This edition of *Insight Guide Tuscany* builds on the work of previous contributors, notably **Lisa Gerard-Sharp**, an experienced travel writer who is knowledgeable about all things Tuscan. Lisa has contributed to many Insight Guides for Italian destinations, after living in several places in the country.

Other past contributors include **Angela Vannucci**, **Adele Evans**, **Sarah Birke**, **Robert John**, **Christopher Catling**, **Russell Chamberlin**, **Rebecca Ford**.

About Insight Guides

Insight Guides have more than 40 years' experience of publishing high-quality, visual travel guides. We produce 400 full-colour titles, in both print and digital form, covering more than 200 destinations across the globe, in a variety of formats to meet your different needs.

Insight Guides are written by local authors, whose expertise is evident in the extensive historical and cultural background features.

Each destination is carefully researched by regional experts to ensure our guides provide the very latest information. All the reviews in **Insight Guides** are independent; we strive to maintain an impartial view. Our reviews are carefully selected to guide you to the best places to eat, go out and shop, so you can be confident that when we say a place is special, we really mean it.

Legend

City maps

	Freeway/Highway/Motorway
	Divided Highway
	Main Roads
	Minor Roads
	Pedestrian Roads
	Steps
	Footpath
	Railway
	Funicular Railway
	Cable Car
	Tunnel
	City Wall
	Important Building
	Built Up Area
	Other Land
	Transport Hub
	Park
	Pedestrian Area
	Bus Station
	Tourist Information
	Main Post Office
	Cathedral/Church
	Mosque
	Synagogue
	Statue/Monument
	Beach
	Airport

Regional maps

	Freeway/Highway/Motorway (with junction)
	Freeway/Highway/Motorway (under construction)
	Divided Highway
	Main Road
	Secondary Road
	Minor Road
	Track
	Footpath
	International Boundary
	State/Province Boundary
	National Park/Reserve
	Marine Park
	Ferry Route
	Marshland/Swamp
	Glacier / Salt Lake
	Airport/Airfield
	Ancient Site
	Border Control
	Cable Car
	Castle/Castle Ruins
	Cave
	Chateau/Stately Home
	Church/Church Ruins
	Crater
	Lighthouse
	Mountain Peak
	Place of Interest
	Viewpoint

INDEX

Main references are in bold type